XSI
Illuminated
C H A R A C T E R

A comprehensive technical and artistic guide to creating character animation using Softimage | X S I

Anthony Rossano

XSI Illuminated: Character

Copyright © 2002 by Mesmer Inc.

ISBN: 0-9707530-4-7

Library of Congress CCN: 2002108255

Printed in the United States of America

First Printing: July, 2002

Author:
Anthony Rossano

Managing Editor:
Brian Demong

Assistant Technical Editor:
Jason Fortman

Assistant Copy Editor:
Karen Zinker

Artwork Credits:

Leroy model and Sssuperguy sketches/model by Elliot Rosenstein. Icky and Francis sketches/storyboards by Theron Benson. Lorphea model by Jake Kazdal. Along Came a Swinger storyboard by Stephen Peringer. Burn the Floor, Serpent sequence storyboard by Tom Price, Monarch Designs. Angry Pencil and manta ray sketches by Brian Demong. All other artwork by Anthony Rossano unless noted otherwise.

TABLE OF CONTENTS

INTRODUCTION FROM THE EDITOR

Welcome to XSI Illuminated: Character! This book is by far our biggest production to date, and I think you will be hard-pressed to find a more extensive collection of artistic and advanced technical information for character animation, let alone for character animation in XSI!

In case you haven't read the precursor to this book, XSI Illuminated: Foundation, I'd like to review a bit about Mesmer Press' plan, and some of the ideas behind our Illuminated series.

First of all, Illuminated books are written by instructors at Mesmer Animation Labs rather than programmers or demo artists, with comprehension and retention in mind. You'll find this material easy to read and understand, and theoretical and artistic discussion is included with the technical information. The tutorials are not specific recipes; they are flexible exercises that address "How?" and "Why?" instead of simply telling you precisely what to do. The tutorials are also extensively tested for functionality and accuracy, which brings me to my next point...

Many 3D animation books are expensive, include a semi-functional CD, and are printed on a large scale, only once. Unfortunately, computer graphics software is not only written once; it changes very rapidly, resulting in a lot of out-of-date and inaccurate printed material. Our idea is to self-publish smaller books, in small print runs, and have our supplementary material, such as scene files and additional tutorials, available online (at www.mesmer.com/books/) instead of on a set-in-stone CD. That way, the books themselves are inexpensive and easily updated, the supplements can be updated and refined, and new content can be added any time. This also means that your feedback is welcome, and can actually be (and has been) applied!

As the first truly advanced material we've published, the creation of XSI Illuminated: Character was extraordinarily challenging, but also very satisfying. I am confident you will find it to be an effective learning tool. As always, don't hesitate to give us your feedback – let us know what we're doing right, and what we can do better. Good luck, and have fun!

Brian Demong, Managing Editor and Mesmer Publisher

AUTHOR BIO

Anthony Rossano is the Chief Executive Officer of Mesmer, Inc. After receiving his Bachelor of Arts in Psychology from the University of Washington, Rossano went to work for the Microsoft Corporation. In 1988, Anthony Rossano deserted his post at Microsoft to found Mesmer, Inc.

Technically proficient in a wide range of authoring and animation programs, Rossano's expertise lies in Softimage 3D|Extreme, Softimage|XSI, and Alias|Wavefront Maya Composer. Anthony has taught all over the world, and counts among his training clients WildBrain, PDI, LucasArts, Electronic Arts, Microsoft, Monolith, ILM, DreamWorks, Boeing, Lockheed, and Lear.

Anthony is a certified Softimage Instructor, and has been working with XSI throughout its development and beta testing phases. Anthony is the author of Inside Softimage 3D, published by New Riders Publications, XSI Illuminated: Foundation, published by Mesmer Press, the documtation set for Softimage|3D v4.0, and numerous magazine articles and web tutorials.

ACKNOWLEDGEMENTS

ANTHONY SAYS:

I hope you, the readers, get as much out of reading this book as I did from writing it. Producing this book felt like the hardest thing I have ever done, with many scenes, close to 700 images, over 900,000 characters and 150,000 words. It was a lot of work.

My sincere thanks go, as always, to the fine folks at Softimage for developing the tool, for hooking me up with the beta program, and for gracefully dealing with my demands, tantrums, and requests for program fixes. My admiration and respect goes out to my contributors: Theron Benson, Elliot Rosenstein, Jake Kazdal, and to the professionals who took time during my interviews to answer what must have seemed like silly questions: Matt Lind, Bob Bonniol, Ludovick Michaud, and Ed Harriss.

I also owe a debt of gratitude to the Mesmerites who made this book happen, and covered for me while I wrote it. Special thanks go to my Editor and Publisher - Brian Demong, who corrected my spelling and only occasionally tried to modify my ideas. Lastly, for undying loyalty, constant companionship and tireless assistance, thanks to my faithful Apple iBook, Agnes. Oh yeah, and my cat, Musetta.

BRIAN SAYS:

My deepest thanks to Mesmer – Anthony, Karen, Nancy, and the institution itself – the anchor in a tempestuous sea.

CONTACT INFORMATION

Mesmer Inc. provides the content of the book as is, and makes no warranties regarding the accuracy or completeness of the material within it. That having been said, we welcome your feedback. Please tell us how we can make this book better and better!

Questions of a technical nature, for instance those regarding software installation or hardware configuration, will not be answered.

You may email us at: info@mesmer.com

You may write to us at:

> Mesmer Animation Labs
> 1116 NW 54th Street
> Seattle WA 98107

You may call us at: 206.782.8004

Please check out our other wonderful course offerings, onsite classes, and distance learning at http://www.mesmer.com.

DIGITAL CONTENT FOR THIS BOOK

All the scene files, models, and other digital information used in this book may be downloaded free of charge from http://www.mesmer.com/books/xsicharacter.html

You may also use an ftp client to get the material. Direct your ftp software to ftp://ftp.mesmer.com/books/xsicharacter/ then log in as anonymous with your email as the password. Within that directory is a zipped file named xsicharacter.zip for PC based users, and a file named xsicharacter.tar for Irix users.

HELP FOR TEACHERS

We have thoughtfully provided free courseware building materials to make life easier for instructors who choose to use our book in class. If you are an educator, you may download the file XSICharTeacherResource.PDF which contains lesson plans, chapter outlines, sample tests and more useful material. You may obtain this material from the web at http://www.mesmer.com/books/xsicharacter.html or from our ftp site at ftp://ftp.mesmer.com/books/xsicharacter/

Shot # BIG LIGHT CHANGE # 3

Description: RUSHING TIME LAPSE SLOWS TO A STOP SUNSET LIGHT

Credit: Storyboard from Serpent sequence, Burn The Floor, copyright 2001
Monarch Designs LLC (Tom Price, Storyboard Artist)

IN THIS CHAPTER YOU WILL LEARN ABOUT:

- What this book covers, and does not cover
- The importance of pre-production planning
- What goes into a good storyboard
- How to make a quick animatic
- Some things to think about when planning a big character job

HOW TO READ THIS BOOK

This is a book dedicated to an exploration of character animation, using the tool set in Softimage|XSI. It assumes that you are already familiar with XSI, and have been working with that tool for months or years. You should already know your way around the interface. You should already know how to select objects, how to build hierarchies, and how to light and render your scene. You should already have basic modeling skills. If you don't have this level of expertise with Softimage|XSI, you should consider taking an introductory class at an Softimage Authorized Training Center like Mesmer, taking a short course on XSI at your local University or Community College, or reading the introductory level book titled XSI Illuminated: Foundation.

Icky and Francis animatic, (c) 2001 Mesmer Inc., Theron Benson, Storyboard Artist

WHAT THIS BOOK COVERS

This book will cover in great detail the polygonal modeling system and subdivision surfaces. It will cover setting animation keyframes, storing them into action clips, and using them in the Animation Mixer. It will cover animated deformations extensively, and setting shape keys thoroughly. You will learn to build shape trees, and mix between shapes in the Mixer. This book covers lip sync using phonemes and shape animation, Inverse Kinematics systems, and enveloping with weighting.

After all that material, this book launches into the more complex world of the technical director, or TD. The book covers the expressions language, building custom property sets and custom user interfaces (UIs). It delves deeply into complex IK character rigs, and novel facial animation set-ups.

WHAT THIS BOOK DOES NOT COVER

This book does not cover applying materials or textures to skinned and weighted characters, which is a topic for another book entirely. It doesn't cover rendering or lighting, which is covered at a basic level in the XSI Illuminated: Foundation book. It doesn't cover the hair systems, the cloth systems, or the XSI compositor.

SPECIALIZATION

This book was built as a learning tool for all kinds of individuals interested in character animation. However, there are a lot of different roles for people to specialize in, with a topic as broad as character animation. You should pay attention to what you find most interesting as you work through the material in this book. The material you find most interesting will often be the areas where you will show the most skill and talent, and you should always specialize in the areas where your skills are the strongest. Conversely, if you really don't find yourself enjoying the sections on, say, rigging complex IK skeletons, don't worry. Leave that part of the process to someone else, and focus on doing what you enjoy.

STORYBOARDING AND ANIMATIC

There's a great cartoon pinned to Mesmer's back wall where God is looking down on the Earth, speaking to an angel, saying, "Well, first I storyboarded it." This is the truth in 3D animation as well as planet building: any job large enough to be cool is too large to do without planning. The saying "those who fail to plan, plan to fail" is entirely apt, yet too often beginning animators and artists working on projects of their own simply lack the discipline to spend the time necessary to plan out the work to be done. Trying to create an animation more complex than a spinning orb without a storyboard is just plain foolish.

Lack of planning tools makes it hard to know what you are trying to achieve, how far you have yet to go, and when you have arrived at your goal. If you plan to have more than one person working on the project, storyboards are an essential communication tool to keep everyone moving in the right direction, achieving the same results. In large productions, the storyboards are the starting point for large-scale project organization and the breaking up of the tasks for separate teams.

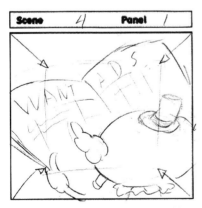

Icky and Francis animatic, (c) 2001 Mesmer Inc., Theron Benson, Storyboard Artist

There are many fine books on storyboarding that describe the conventions; here we'll just enumerate what you need in a storyboard for 3D animation.

Each panel represents one shot, unless the camera is moving. Static camera shots are often very short, between one half-second and two seconds, in modern production. This means a lot of panels in the storyboard. If the camera is moving through one long shot, break up the shot into multiple panels, where features change in the shot or actions happen.

Each panel shows the initial cinematography for the shot: take care to show what you want, posed how you want, framed like you want. Then when you get to actually positioning the camera in the scene much later, you'll have a plan to start from.

Below each panel, detail out the duration of the shot. Use time and frames. If there is action in the shot, time it out. Don't guess, get a stopwatch and time yourself doing the action to get a solid idea.

The artistic quality of the storyboards is secondary to the communication quality and accuracy of the boards; if the characters are drawn as stick figures, that's OK.

When you have completed the storyboarding process, you will have told the story or shown the scene you are working on. The next step is to edit that into a rough animatic to see if the idea is getting across to people, and to refine the idea if necessary. This is simple: scan the storyboards, and edit them together in your favorite editor: iMovie, Premiere, Final Cut Pro, Director, Inferno... whatever you have close at hand. In the edit, hold each panel for exactly as long as directed in the duration of each shot.

Now, play back the digital movie, while recording an audio file with a cheap microphone and your computer's built-in media software, and do the rough voice over and special effects track. Need an explosion? Do it with your voice. Do it all in one take, to save time. If you mess it up, record it over. Do it a few times, then pick the best one, and lay back the sound on top of the rough edit.

Output another movie, this time with sound. That's an animatic: about 2 hours of work.

Now you can look at the animatic, and note weak areas in the action or in the story. Show it to other people, see if they get it or have suggestions to improve it.

A simple character

Icky and Francis animatic, copyright 2001 Mesmer Inc, Theron Benson Storyboard Artist

Make the improvements to the storyboard, re-cut the animatic, and you are ready to proceed with a planning tool that you can show to everyone working on the project.

Making changes at this point in the project is quick and easy: just sketch a new panel, scan it, and recut the animatic. Make as many story changes at this phase as possible, because you won't be able to make them later when the project is underway.

CHARACTER DESIGN

Character design is essentially an art function, but there are a number of technical considerations to keep in mind. Beginning animators most frequently choose characters that have serious technical challenges over simple characters. This causes a great deal of failure, and poor animation. Simple is good in animation, and you shouldn't try to build and animate complex creatures until you have lots of experience creating and animating simple characters.

Examples of complex characters to avoid in your first attempts are: dragons, insects, humanoids, characters with articulated limbs, etc.

Examples of good characters to start with are: desk lamps (well, that's been done…), balls, dots, spheres, cubes, boxes, lumpy blobs, etc.

Once again, failing to design a character before sitting down at the computer to build the character is a recipe for disaster. Without sketches you are flying blind. Make your own sketches, or, if like me you are embarrassed by your drawing skills, have someone else do the illustrations, to your specifications.

PLANNING FOR LARGE PRODUCTIONS

While this book is mainly designed as a reference for individual animators learning and working with characters, a great deal could be said about the organization of teams of people who will all work on a single large project. Because of the nature of modern animation, small one-man jobs are less and less frequent. Working within a structure is much more common. When a team of people is working together to accomplish a goal, many efficiencies can be realized if some traps can be avoided.

Larger teams can specialize. People who are great modelers can build models all day, while great techs can do all the rigging, setup, system administration, and render management. Illustrators can spend all day creating high-quality planning drawings, and character animators can spend all day setting keys and refining timing.

Human dynamics can (and often do) send this happy team right into the toilet, however. Without good communication (this means meetings), the team doesn't all pull in the same direction. If people become complacent and unhelpful, bottlenecks in the team can occur. Personality conflicts can overtake productivity. Simple laziness is a constant threat to the success of the project.

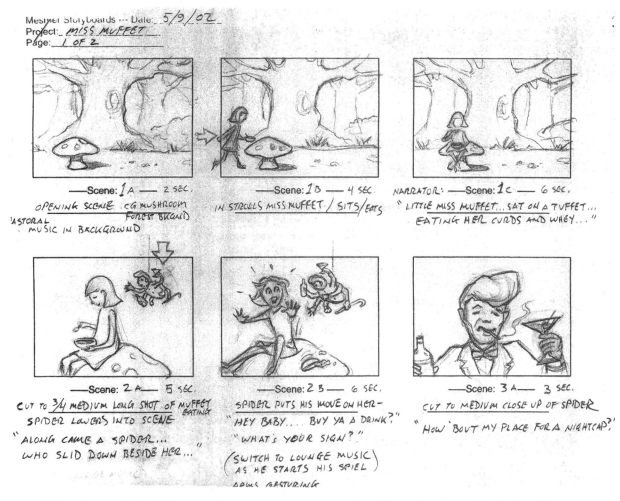

Mesmer Storyboards --- Date: 5/9/02
Project: MISS MUFFET
Page: 1 OF 2

—Scene: 1 A — 2 SEC.
OPENING SCENE CG MUSHROOM
'ASTORAL   FOREST BKGND
' MUSIC IN BACKGROUND

—Scene: 1 B — 4 SEC.
IN STROLLS MISS MUFFET / SITS/EATS

NARRATOR: —Scene: 1 C — 6 SEC.
" LITTLE MISS MUFFET... SAT ON A TUFFET...
EATING HER CURDS AND WHEY..."

—Scene: 2 A— 5 SEC.
                         EATING
CUT TO 3/4 MEDIUM LONG SHOT OF MUFFET
SPIDER LOWERS INTO SCENE
" ALONG CAME A SPIDER...
WHO SLID DOWN BESIDE HER..."

—Scene: 2 B — 6 SEC.
SPIDER PUTS HIS MOVE ON HER—
" HEY BABY.... BUY YA A DRINK?,"
" WHAT'S YOUR SIGN?"
(SWITCH TO LOUNGE MUSIC
AS HE STARTS HIS SPIEL)
ARMS GESTURING

—Scene: 3 A— 3 SEC.
CUT TO MEDIUM CLOSE UP OF SPIDER
" HOW 'BOUT MY PLACE FOR A NIGHTCAP?"

This project included CG, live action, stop motion, and special effects. Storyboard by Stephen Peringer.

THE PIPELINE

The process of getting finished work in the can is called the "pipeline". Shots move through the pipe, passing through different stages, and eventually are completed and put to bed.

The pipeline is not entirely linear: some things can be done concurrently, and sometimes the pipe branches and then comes together again. Each facility has its own pipeline and workflow, so there is no one true pipe.

Here is a sample character animation pipeline:

• Pre-production financing, lunches, and schmoozing

• Scripting and storyboarding

• Animatic and timing

• Scene management – process accounting and control

• Audio recording

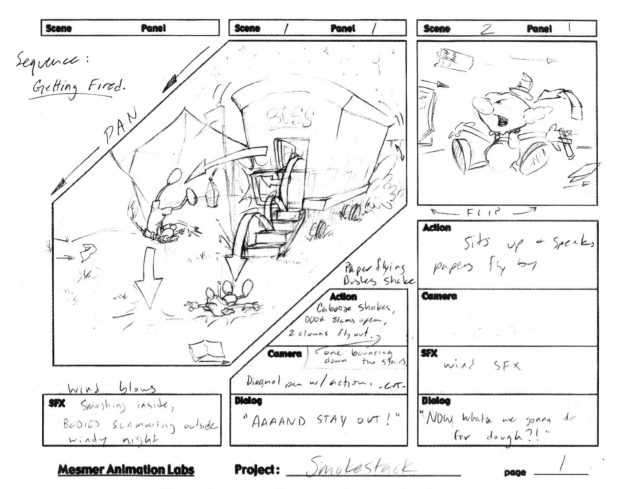

The storyboards were drawn several time to refine the story

- Modeling

- Character TD work

- Sets and set dressing work

- Character animation and lip sync

- Materials and shader development

- Scene-by-scene character dressing

- Lighting plan

- Scene merging: set and character

- Scene-by-scene lighting

- Rendering optimization planning

- Scene-by-scene rendering

- Compositing

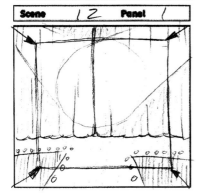

Icky and Francis animatic, (c) 2001 Mesmer Inc., Theron Benson, Storyboard Artist

- Editing

- Film / Video output

- Licensing

- Toy development

- Popcorn sales

- Team vacation / detox management

- Revision of any stage: repeat indefinitely, sending a shot back into the pipe until client signs off or company folds.

PROJECT TRACKING

In a large project with many shots (perhaps several hundred), simply knowing what needs to be done and where each shot is in the pipe overwhelms a paper-based organization system. The solution is to develop a simple custom web-based database application to track each shot, so that the planning staff can assign each shot to a stage in the pipe, then when that stage is complete for that shot, the database is updated and tells the planning staff where to send the shot next. A variation on this is to have the web-database maintain an account for each person on the team, and automatically assign tasks to them in the correct order, by send email notifying the person that a shot is ready for them to take on. As each person completes their stage, they log it in the web-application and the web-app then notifies the next person in the pipe. In this way hundreds of shots can move smoothly through a pipeline with hundreds of people. The final variation is to have each person log the time spent on each aspect of the shots they finish, and then the web-app can reverse-calculate the critical path through the system, and provide daily estimates of completion date and information on bottlenecks to the management staff.

GETTING READY TO START A BIG PROJECT?
Here is a list of considerations to ruminate on before getting started. This is a compendium of issues that have occurred in the completion of large jobs. For each one, imagine what you'll need to do to have an answer for it.

Scalability considerations

How to divide up animation work between many animation teams

How to centrally manage shared Databases and Libraries

How the Technical Director team makes life easy for animators

The building block approach: constant completion and refinement

How to use specialists instead of generalists

Takes more people

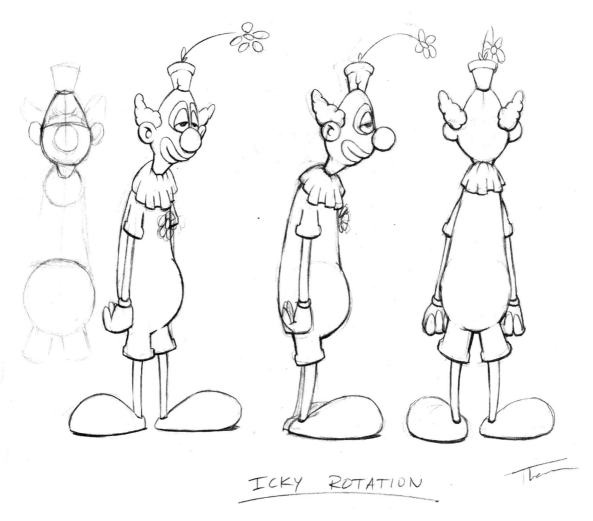

ICKY ROTATION

Icky's poses and Expressions

        Most people are idle in different parts of the cycle

        Better quality because of specialization

How to use standardization

        How to retain character even across different animators?

        Creating pose and action libraries

        Reaping benefits of non-linear animation/mixer

Human Resource considerations

        Team building

        Managing progress

        Identifying Good People and keeping them

        Identifying Bad People and shedding them

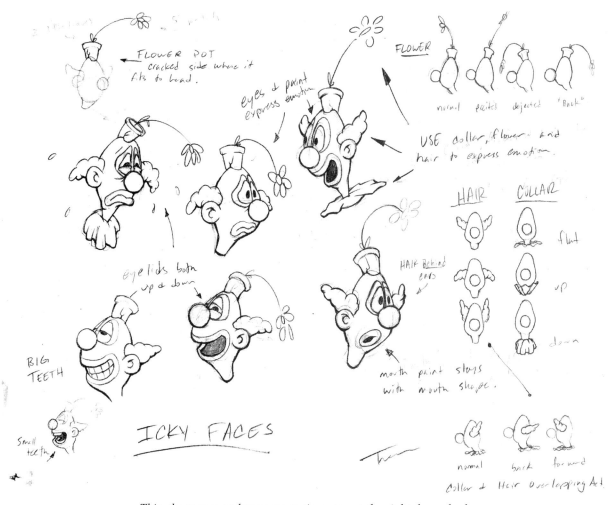

This clown was redrawn many times to get the right dopey look

Division of Labor and the Pipeline

Breaking into teams, and assigning team leads

Team leads to recruit for tasks, by interest and ability

Ideas for making the process faster

Automating Lip Sync with Mocap

Automating Animation with Mocap

What else can be sped up?

Systems Admin considerations

Vendor choice

Server / desktop reliability concerns

OS reliability concerns

Getting enough disk space, wasting disk space

Icky and Francis animatic, copyright 2001 Mesmer Inc, Theron Benson Storyboard Artist

SysAdmin team to create database structure and user accounts

Creating disk structures to facilitate pipeline

Security and control

Email and web time management (reducing wasted time each day)

Render Planning

Distributed rendering and evening rendering

Using scripts to automate creation of motion tests

How much disk space will be needed, and when?

How will work in progress be backed up?

How will completed work be archived?

What's the final delivery mechanism?

CONCLUSION

Now you are ready to dig into the rest of the book, the portion devoted to actually using the software. Remember as you work that it is very natural to want to just spend time with the computer. XSI is seductive in that way. Left to yourself, you would be like those rats in Psychology experiments that just keep pushing the little cocaine dispenser bar, ignoring food and drink until they die. Don't let this happen to you. Spend good solid time before the project planning it out, until you have a complete picture of what will happen, and script, storyboards, and animatic to show other people what you want.

2   NON-LINEAR ANIMATION WITH THE MIXER

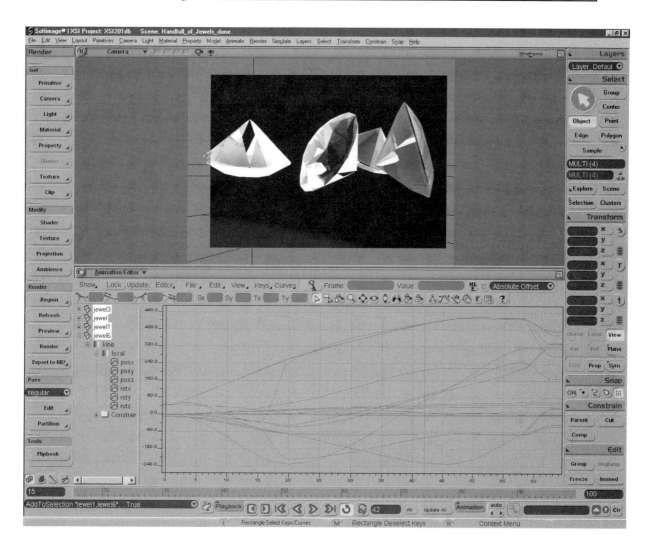

IN THIS CHAPTER YOU WILL LEARN ABOUT:

- How to set and remove keyframes for animation
- How to adjust keyframes with the Animation Editor
- How to modify timing with the Dopesheet
- How to ripple and cycle animation
- Where to find the Mixer in XSI
- All about Mixer Sources and Tracks
- Storing poses
- Storing animation actions
- Sequencing actions in the Mixer
- Adjusting animation clip length and timing
- Setting clip transitions
- Using audio source in the Mixer
- Blending actions in the Mixer

INTRODUCTION

In this chapter we'll dive right in to the nuts and bolts of Animating with XSI, learning how to set basic keys on transformations, how to mark and key other properties, how to set keys in Property Pages, and how to edit new animation in the Animation Curve Editor and Dopesheet.   Then we'll use those new animation skills to build animation clips and discover how to mix and blend animation in the Mixer.

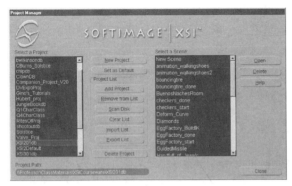

This is the project manager, showing the XSI 201 courseware set as the default project.

XSI was completely designed from the ground up to be a Non-Linear Animation system. This buzzword is more than marketing hype, however. NLA means that in addition to the traditional methods of animating by setting keyframes on individual animatable properties, you can create character animation by mixing together collections of animated keyframes that are represented by simple graphical blocks, representing a collection of any number of keyframes on any number of animated properties on any number of animated objects. Binding up all this complexity into a simple visual element makes it easy to edit, sequence, and mix together different animation sequences just as you would mix together audio or video.

In an audio mixer, for instance, you don't concern yourself with the thousands upon thousands of individual samples that make up the sound file. You just see a rectangle called a clip, which represents that information. You can easily make the clip longer or shorter, move it sooner or later in time, or mix it gradually in and out by clicking and dragging on the simple clips. XSI brings that same concept to 3D animation.

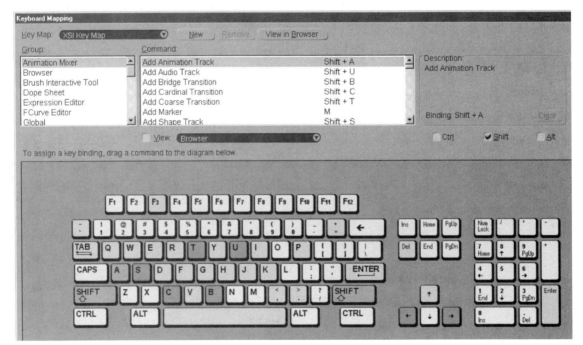

The Keyboard Map dialog is where you can see which hotkeys map to which commands, and change them if you wish.

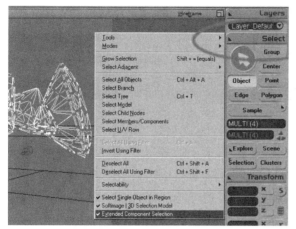

If your Selection settings don't look like this, change them, so you can use the same commands as this book does.

In this chapter we'll briefly examine how to set keyframes and adjust them in the Animation Editor. (This material is covered in more detail in the predecessor to this book, *XSI Illuminated: Foundation*.) Next we'll get right on to setting cycles and creating animation clips that can be mixed together in the Animation Mixer.

In this chapter, and in later chapters, I'll use example scenes to illustrate concepts. You can download the sample files and install them in your user directory on your computer, then load them as they are called for to follow along. Collectively, the sample files and starting points for different exercises are called the XSIcharacter courseware.

You can download the courseware via the web or with an ftp client.

On the web, browse to http://www.mesmer.com/books/xsicharacter.html and click on the xsicharacter.zip link to download the courseware for PCs, or the xsichacter.tar.gz link to download the courseware for Irix or Linux.

With an ftp browser, open the host ftp.mesmer.com, log in as anonymous, with your email address as the password. Then change directory to books/xsicharacter and list the contents.

If you are running the Windows version of XSI, get the xsicharacter.zip file, and unzip it with WinZip.

If you are running the Irix version of XSI, get the xsicharacter.tar.gz file, then gunzip and tar –xf the file.

Run XSI, and using the File➔Project Manager dialog box, add the XSIcharacter project, and make it the default.

SETTING UP XSI

XSI is a very customizable piece of software, which means that you can change the way you interact with it to suit your individual tastes and specific work requirements. While this is great for users, it would certainly make it hard to follow this book if your copy of XSI was set up to behave differently than the author's copy. So, let's take a moment here to make some changes to the user settings, to make sure we are all on the same page.

Open the animation_spring.scn file from the XSIcharacter courseware project.

First, change the keyboard map so that all the key commands active on your computer are the same as those used in this book. Go to File➔Keyboard Mapping, which will pop up a map of the keyboard. In the top-left corner of the dialog, use the Key Map drop menu to choose the SI3D Key Map, and close the dialog.

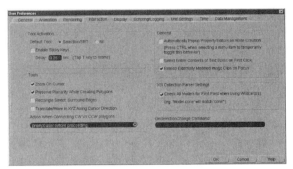

The User Prefs dialog changes how XSI responds to you as you work.

Next, make sure the Selection settings are all as they should be. Go to the Selection menu in the top-right Main Command Area of the interface, and check that the last three options are all checked ON: Select Single Object in Region, Softimage 3D Selection Model, and Extended Component Selection. These settings will provide the fastest and most consistent method of selecting objects and components.

Finally, set up some application preferences. Go to File→User Prefs to open the user preferences dialog.

In the General tab, turn the Tab Style Editor ON. This will simplify long Property Pages, and make them faster.

In the Interaction tab, make these changes: Auto Pop-up Property pages OFF will prevent constant PPG pollution of the interface. Default Selection Tool NIL will make it easier to use the context-sensitive menus. Enable Sticky Keys OFF, so you don't get stuck in sticky modes. Zoom on Cursor ON makes zooming more fun. Display Multiple Transform Axes helps show what's selected. Update all Views During Interaction ON; otherwise, all the views update separately.

In the Unit Settings tab, set Color Space to HSV, which makes it much easier to pick colors and control transparency.

SETTING AND EDITING KEYFRAMES

The most basic building block of animation in XSI is the keyframe. A keyframe is a saved value on a specific property, set at a given time.

The general pattern of setting keyframes is consistent: select the object, change time, change the value, save a key.

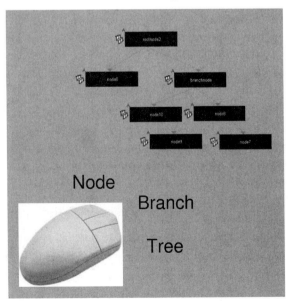

Learning to select nodes, branches, and trees is critical to working quickly in XSI.

 Note: In XSI objects can be animated with expressions, scripts, scripted operators, and constraints in addition to keyframes, so keyframes aren't the only way to animate – just the simplest.

If the object is not in a hierarchy, or if it's at the bottom of a hierarchy (in other words, a child) then you can select it using the Space bar and the Left Mouse Button (LMB), which selects single nodes.

If the object is the parent of other objects, select it with the Spacebar and the Middle Mouse Button (MMB). If you want to set keys on more than one object at once, select all the objects you want keyed by holding down the Shift key and selecting them one at a time with the Space bar, or by holding down Shift and dragging a rectangle around them all with the Space bar held down.

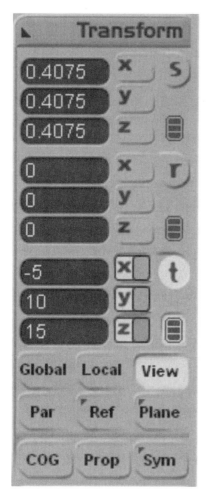

The translate cells are lit up in red, green, and blue to indicate that they are marked.

With the object to be animated selected, decide which property you want to animate. (Since almost all properties in XSI are animatable, you have a lot of choices.) Mark that property.

Drag the time slider to the frame in time where you want the key set. Dragging the time slider sets the Current Frame. You may also directly enter a number in the current frame box to jump directly to a frame if you know exactly where in time you want to be.

Change the value of the property you are interested in animating over time, either by entering a numeric value for the property, dragging the slider in the property page (PPG), or translating, scaling, or rotating the object on-screen.

Finally, save the key, in one of three ways: with the Keyframe button in the timeline, by clicking on the animation divot in a specific property page, or by tapping the K hotkey

That pattern is always the same: Select the object, change time, change the value, save a key.

MARKING PROPERTIES

Of course, before you can set a keyframe on a property, you need to decide which property or properties you want, and somehow communicate your choice to XSI.

The way you tell XSI which properties you will be saving keys on is by first Marking those properties.

Marking the properties tells XSI that when you hit the K button or click on the Keyframe icon in the timeline, you want keys saved on those marked properties.

Because the local transformations are the most frequently animated properties on any object, you can mark them in a special way. Simply activate the transform you are interested in by clicking on it in the Main Command Panel (MCP). Click on the "s" toggle to mark Scale, the "r" toggle to mark Rotation, and the "t" toggle to mark Translation. (You can also use the hotkeys X, C, and V to mark the transforms.) When the transform cells light up in Red, Green, and Blue, you know they're marked.

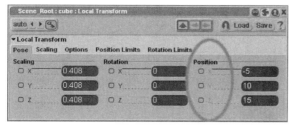

The yellow property name indicates that the property is marked.

To mark any property at all, including the transforms, first locate the PPG for the property you are interested in and display it, most easily done by selecting the object and choosing the PPG in the Selection button of the MCP. Inside of every PPG you can click directly on the name of a property to mark it. The marked property will be highlighted in yellow. You can mark more than one property at a time by holding the CTRL key and clicking on additional properties. You may have any number of properties all marked at the same time, so that when you tap the K hotkey, each of those properties will have a keyframe added at the current frame.

If you need to mark properties in different PPGs or within different tabs of a single PPG, remember to use the CTRL key to extend the selection, or the previously marked properties will be unmarked, and since they were in a different PPG or tab, you won't see them change from yellow to black text.

CHECKING WHAT PROPERTY IS MARKED

If you have marked just one property, look down to the bottom-right corner of the timeline, to the Marked Property box. It will display the name of the property that is currently marked, like "kine.local.pos".

The marked feedback line shows what single property is marked.

Since it can only show one line, there must be a better way to view (and change) multiple marked properties. There is, and it's called the Marked Property List, and is located within the small drop triangle to the right of the Marked Property box. When you click on the drop triangle, an explorer-style window pops up, displaying all the animatable properties on the selected object, flattened out so that you don't have to dig through quite so many folders to find things.

Properties that are marked are listed in yellow highlight.

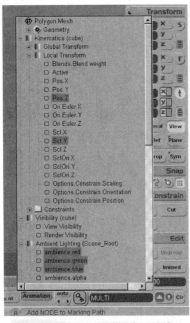

The Marked Property list is the way to mark (and show) many properties at once.

ADDING TO THE MARKED PROPERTY LIST

You can also add items to the list of currently marked properties, by clicking on them directly in the Marked Property List. In this way, if you wanted to set keyframes on the position and rotation of a foot control all at the same time, you could look under the Kinematics, under the Local Transform, mark the Pos.X, Pos.Y, Pos.Z, and the Ori.Euler.X, Y and Z which would then tell XSI that you want keys saved for position and rotation on all X, Y and Z axes each time you tap K or click on the key button.

LOCKING AND CLEARING THE MARKED PROPERTY LIST

Once you've marked a number of properties, it's time to set some keyframes. However, there is a problem. If you marked some properties, then activated a transformation in the MCP (preparing, for instance, to translate a foot), XSI would clear out the markings in the Marked Property List and replace them with the transformation you just activated. Therefore, there needs to be a way to lock the choices you make so they are not changed. If you click on the small keyhole icon next to the Marked Property List, XSI will ignore all further marking attempts until you toggle the lock off by clicking on it again. You can also clear the Marked Property List entirely by clicking the Clr icon.

Click on the keyhole to lock or unlock the marking list, and the Clr button to clear it.

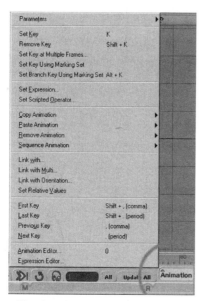

The Animation Menu in the time-line has useful animation tasks.

BEING A PRODUCTIVE KEYFRAMER

In my opinion it is the most sensible, efficient, and effective method of keyframing is to mark one property at a time, lay down keyframes on that property, and then go back, marking another property, and laying down those keyframes on top of the previous ones. In this way you build up animation, like a band laying down tracks. Start first with the simple motion needed to establish the timing and block out the position of the character. This usually means setting keyframes on position. Next, refine the animation by adding in smaller details, rotation, scale, and refining the secondary animation on translation. By working in passes like this you have the benefit of starting simple and building to the more complex. You also have the benefit of seeing the initial animation while you add the later layers of changes.

If you use the Key button either in a PPG or in the Animation toolbar at the bottom of the screen, the first click adds a key at that frame. The button will then change from green to red to let you know that a key was set. If there was already a key there, the next click will remove it, and the icon will change to yellow, indicating that the property is animated, but there is no key at that frame.

THE ANIMATION DIVOT AND THE ANIMATION MENU

You can also add keys in each PPG on just one property at a time without using the marking menu (this is faster for many simple animation tasks, like animating color). In each Property Page there is a small green dot icon next to the name of each property. This is called the Animation Divot, and if you click on it you can set and remove keyframes. It changes color in the same way as the keyframe button, starting out green to show no animation, then red to show a key being set at the current frame, then changing to yellow when a key is removed, to show that the property is still animated even though no key is present at that frame.

A number of important functions are found in the Animation Menu. The Animation Menu is unique, in that it appears once for marked properties in the toolbar at the bottom of the screen and once on each property that can be animated, under the Animation Divot in the context-sensitive menu that drops out when you click the Right Mouse Button.

REMOVING ANIMATION

If you use the Animation Menu at the bottom of the screen, it will apply to whatever is currently marked. If you use the Animation Menu that pops up when you click on an Animation Divot with the Right Mouse Button (RMB), the commands will apply only to the property that the divot belongs to.

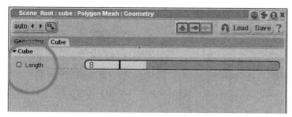

You can set keys by clicking on the Animation Divot with the Left Mouse Button.

If you RMB click over the divot and choose Remove Animation, all the keys on that property will be removed. If you click on the Animation Menu at the bottom of the screen and choose Remove Animation, all the keys on whatever properties are marked will be removed. If you click on the Animation Menu at the bottom of the screen and choose Remove All Animation, all the keys set on any properties of that object will be removed.

OPEN UP THE ANIMATION_SPRING SCENE

In the following sections you'll need a scene to refer to in order to see the effects of the Animation menu. Please open up the animation_spring scene and take a look at the contents. A coil spring is bouncing around. Examine the scene to become familiar with the objects in it.

COPYING AND PASTING ANIMATION

You can easily copy animation keyframes from one object to another with the Animation Menu. As usual, if you use the Animation Menu at the bottom of the screen you need to mark a property first. It's easier to use the Animation Menu located in the Animation Divot inside a property page for this function. In the animation_spring scene there is a coil spring bouncing up and down, squashing as it does so, and you want that animation copied to a Basketball elsewhere in the scene. You could select the spring and locate the Local Transformation property page (perhaps using the Selection button in the MCP).

Copy the vertical bounce of the spring to the soccer ball (or football if you're not an American).

To copy the bouncing up and down, right-click on the Local Translation Y Animation Divot and choose Copy Animation.

Then, select the target Basketball, and in the Animation menu at the bottom of the screen, choose Paste Animation→To All Parameters. Since you had already specifically chosen to copy Local Translation in Y you didn't have to tell XSI what property to replace on the target ball. However, if you wanted to copy the translation in Y of the original ball to the Scale in X of the target ball, you could also select the target ball, open the local transform PPG and right-click on the Scale X Animation Divot and choose Paste Animation, placing the translation in Y data onto the scale in X Animation Curve.

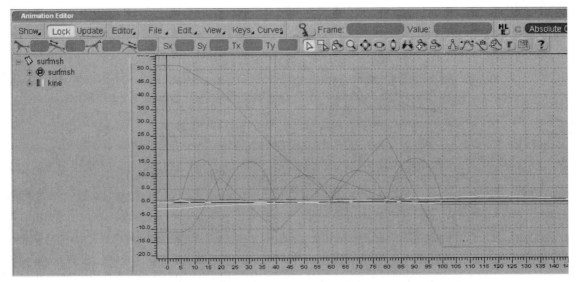

The Animation Editor is one way to fine-tune your animation.

ANIMATION CURVES AND THE ANIMATION EDITOR

Once you have added basic keyframes, you will need to examine them graphically, make changes to the timing and values of the keys, and perhaps add new keys or remove redundant ones. XSI makes this process of fine tuning your keyframe data easy with a program feature called the Animation Editor.

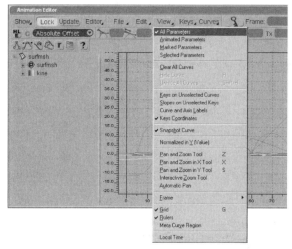

You can choose what you want to see in the Animation Editor.

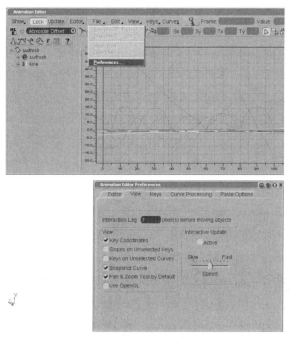

The Animation Editor preferences

SHOWING THE ANIMATION EDITOR

You can display the Animation Editor for a single property or for the currently Marked properties by either right-clicking on a specific Animation Divot and choosing Animation Editor, or by marking some properties in the MCP or Marking List and then choosing Animation Editor from the Animation Menu at the bottom of the screen. In these cases, the Animation Editor will open into one of your view windows and then expand horizontally across the adjoining existing view window, replacing the two views that were there before.

Another useful way of showing the Animation Editor is to pop up the Animation Editor on top of the interface in a floating window, by tapping the 0 hotkey at the top of your keyboard. This floating window can always be collapsed by double-clicking on its title bar.

The Animation Editor is divided into two panes. On the left side, the smaller pane shows a flattened explorer-style list of all the properties that are being viewed in the Animation Editor.

If you see more or less than you want, you can adjust what is listed in the Animation Editor by using the View menu at the top of the Animation Editor.

If you choose the menu item View→Animated Parameters, all the properties that currently have keys will be displayed.

If you choose the View→Marked Parameters menu item, only the marked parameters will be shown in the Animation Editor.

You can click directly in the left pane to select one Animation Curve from all those that are listed there. That Animation curve will then be highlighted in the right side of the Animation Editor so that you can make changes to it.

In the Right pane of the Animation Editor, the actual keys and curves are displayed.

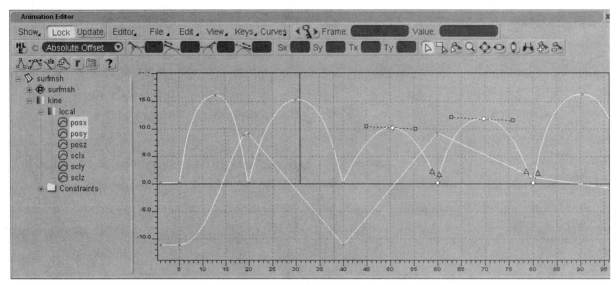

You can select one or more curves, and any number of points, all at once in the Animation Editor.

ANIMATION EDITOR TOOLS AND TIPS

You can move around in the Animation Editor to see different parts of the curves with the same hotkeys used elsewhere in XSI. The Z hotkey and the Left Mouse Button (LMB) will pan, the Z hotkey and the MMB will zoom in on a curve, while the Z hotkey and the RMB will zoom out.

There are a few user preferences you can set to make your life easier. In the File menu at the top of the Animation Editor, choose Prefs to pop up the Animation Editor preferences dialog box. Check the Interactive Update box. Normally, when you change a curve, the object driven by that curve will not change on-screen until you let go of the point. This makes it hard to position objects visually, since you don't get any feedback while moving keys. You can also adjust the slider below, turning it all the way up to Fast, so that the objects update more frequently as you adjust keys. You can also toggle this option on and off at the bottom of the Edit menu.

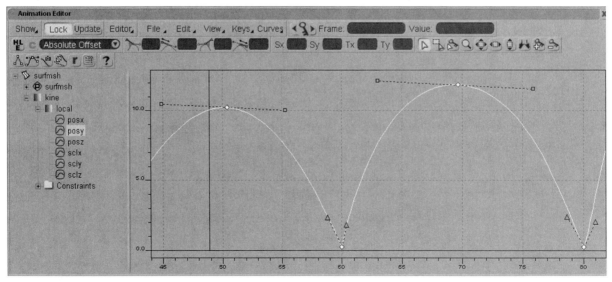

What shows in the value axis changes for each property, but the horizontal axis is always time.

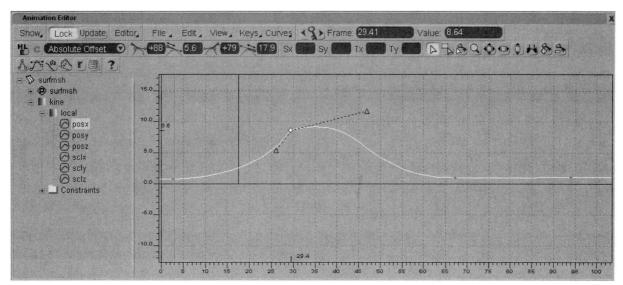

When the curve changes slope, something is speeding up or slowing down.

Also uncheck the box for Pan/Zoom by Default, so that if no tool is active, nothing will happen when you click.

Finally, toggle on the option in the View menu called Curve and Axis Labels. Now each curve will have the property it drives added on top of it for easy reference. While the left side pane shows this information all the time, if you had multiple animation curves selected it would not tell you which was which. Now you'll know.

KEYS IN THE ANIMATION EDITOR

The Animation Editor shows keyframe data as points on a graph called an Animation Curve. Unselected keys are shown as white dots, selected keys are shown as red dots.

The keys represent points on the curve, but the curve exists at all frames in the animation, smoothly changing from one key to another. The line of the Animation Curve represents the value of a property changing over time. The Vertical (Y) axis of the Animation Curve is the Value axis of the chart. The value will be different for different properties. If you are editing a rotation Animation Curve, the value will be in degrees. If you are editing a color, it will be in percent (from 0.0 to 1.0), and if you are editing a translation, it will be in the units of measure you have selected in the User Preferences, such as centimeters, feet, or inches.

The Horizontal axis is always time in frames. You can also work in timecode if you prefer. This preference is set, along with the default frame rate, in the File→User Preferences dialog under the Time tab.

WHAT THE SLOPE OF THE CURVE MEANS

When a line between keys in the Animation Editor is flat at any point, it means that the value is not changing at all during those frames.

When the Animation Curve has a constant slope up and to the right, it means that the value is growing at a steady rate. If the slope is downwards, that means that the value is decreasing.

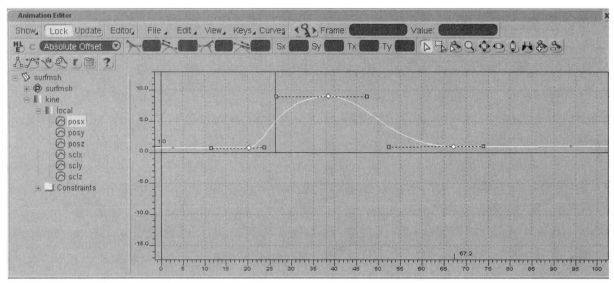

The slope of the curve is the velocity, or rate of change.

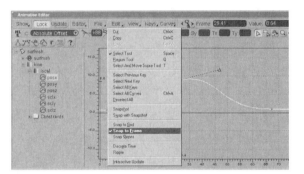

You can enter numbers directly into the value boxes to precisely change a keyframe.

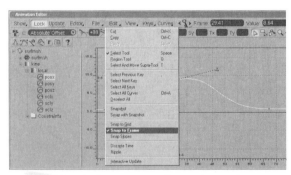

It's a good idea to snap all your keys to exact frames.

When the line curves up and grows steeper, the value is accelerating. When the line curves down, growing flatter, the value is decelerating.

CHANGING ONE KEY VALUE AT A TIME

If you have animated an object, and on further reflection decided that you need to make some changes to the animation, the Animation Editor is the place to be. Using the Animation Editor you can shift keys forward or back in time and change the value of the property at that keyframe, either by dragging keys around or by directly typing in values.

The first step is to select the curve you want to adjust. You can either pick the name of the property in the left pane of the Animation Editor or use the Space bar and click on the curve in the right pane to select it. With the curve selected, the keys will be shown in white. You can hold the M hotkey (for "move") and click directly on a point, holding the Left Mouse Button down and dragging to reposition the key. Dragging the key up and down changes the value, while dragging left and right changes the frame in time at which the key is set.

If you want to precisely change either the value or the time of a key, you can directly enter a numeric value in the Value entry box, or a frame number in the Frame Entry box, both at the top of the Animation Editor.

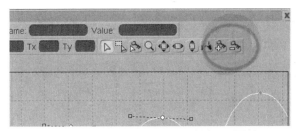

You can add and delete keys in the Animation Editor.

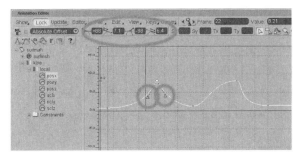

The tangency handles and their precise values

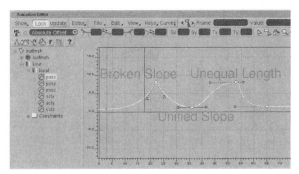

Different combinations of broken tangencies make different motions.

SELECTING MANY KEYS AT ONCE

If you want to change many keys at once, you can in XSI! With one curve selected you can hold down Shift and the Spacebar and click on multiple points to select them. You can also drag a rectangle around a group of keys, again holding the Space bar to select the first group and then Shift and the Space bar to add to the selection. The T hotkey also works in the Animation Editor just as it does elsewhere. Holding T down while dragging a rectangle will select (tag) multiple keys so they can all be adjusted at once.

You can also select multiple curves at once, and create groups of selected keys on multiple curves, using the same method. Once you have multiple keys selected, you can move them all at once (with M), delete them all at once with the Delete key on your keyboard, or change them all to the same value by entering a value directly into the Value box.

LOCKING TO FRAMES

It's always a good idea to make sure that the keys you set fall exactly on frames. That's because when you finally render out your work, XSI will render images at each frame. So, if your spring was bouncing, for example, and struck the floor in between frame 10 and frame 11, it might look OK while you were working on it, but in the render it would never actually contact the floor. It would look like it just stopped a little bit above the floor and hovered there during two frames. XSI has some features to fix this up. If you already have keys that you have edited and they need to be moved to the nearest frame, you can select all the keys (try dragging a rectangle in the Animation Editor to select keys on the selected Animation Curve), then choose the Keys→Move Keys to Nearest Frame menu item and watch as the keys all snap to the nearest whole frame.

If you want to make sure that all the keys stay on frames while you work, choose the Edit→Snap to Frame menu command which will snap them as you move them, similar to a snap-to-grid functionality.

ADDING AND DELETING KEYS

You now know that you can just select keys and hit Delete to delete them. You can also add and delete keys with the Edit Key tool. The Edit key tool is activated by clicking on the small icon in the shape of a key with an arrow pointer below it at the top of the Animation Editor. You can also activate the Edit Key tool with the Keys→Edit Key Tool menu command, or the E hotkey in the Animation Editor.

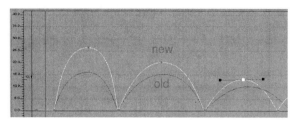

The Swap line shows how the curve was before you messed with it.

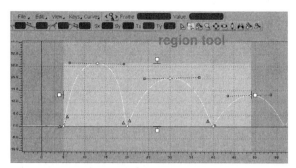

The region tool is a new way to manipulate many keys at once.

When the Edit Key tool is active, you can left-click on it to drag the key around in the Animation Editor, middle-click on a curve to add a new key at the point where your mouse hits the curve, and right-click directly on an existing key to remove it.

When you are done with the Edit Key, tap the Escape key on your keyboard to exit the tool so you don't accidentally add or delete any keys.

CHANGING SLOPE

By default, the Animation Curve gently slopes in and out of keys. This interpolation is called ease-in and ease-out, and gives computer animation its rather fluid look. You can examine how this works by finding a key where the value is changing from a negative direction to a positive one, such as on the local translation in Y (kine.local.pos.y) curve where the spring is bouncing off the street. If you select that key on the curve, you will observe tangency handles stretching right and left. You can now click on these and drag them (with the pointer icon, the E hotkey or the M hotkey) to adjust how the value eases in and out very smoothly.

It is often necessary to disable this, so that an animated property can either stop changing suddenly, or even change direction completely without slowing down first. The bouncing spring is a good example of this, because it needs to accelerate into the street, then as it hits the pavement it needs to suddenly stop and compress, then spring upwards again. The default spline interpolation would make the spring look like it was floating mushily, not springing vigorously. The solution is to change the slope of the curve before and after a keyframe independently. Currently, when you drag one tangent handle, the opposing tangent handle also changes. This won't do. The solution is to "break" the Orientation of the handles' tangency. With one or many keys selected, uncheck the Unified Slope Orientation command from the Keys menu, or better yet, just tap the O hotkey on your keyboard. Now you can adjust the tangency handles independently.

breaks tangents.

To restore tangency handles so that the ease-in and the ease-out are again connected, toggle the Unified Slope Orientation command from the Keys menu, or tap O again.

SWAP AND SNAP

The Animation Editor has a clever form of Undo built in, in addition to the regular undoes available throughout XSI. When the Animation Editor is opened it stores the current shape of each Animation Curve into the Swap buffer. This original shape is shown for each curve as a grey dotted line. As you make changes to an Animation Curve you can see what the shape of the curve used to look like. If you decide at some point that you have been making your animation worse instead of better, you can go back to the original shape, with the Edit➔Swap with Snapshot command, or by clicking on the Swap button at the top of the Animation Editor (next to the Ripple button). When you Swap, your selected Animation Curve returns to the unedited shape, and the edited shape is stored in the Swap buffer, so you can always swap back again if you change your mind once more.

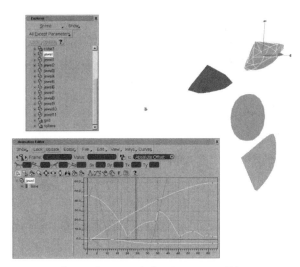

Using the explorer and the Animation Editor, you can quickly switch among animated objects.

Each Curve has its own Swap buffer. If you want to make the current shape of the curve the only one stored in the Swap buffer, choose the Edit→Snapshot command, which snaps the curve shape into the Swap buffer but doesn't replace the current shape of the curve. Now this shape will be the fallback shape in case you change your mind. The curve is automatically snapped when you close the Animation Editor.

THE REGION TOOL

The Animation Editor has a new tool for easily changing any number of keys in any number of curves all at the same time, called the Region tool. With the Region tool you can change the timing of a whole animation, making the action faster or slower, delay it in time to begin at a later frame, and change the values of all the keys at once.

First, select all the Animation Curves you want changed, either by Shift-clicking in the left pane or by dragging a rectangle in the right pane. Then, activate the Region drawing tool, which is an icon at the top of the Animation Editor that looks like a pointer pointing to a square, or use the Edit→Region Tool command, or the Q hotkey.

With the Region drawing tool you can now drag in the Animation Editor (right pane) to select a Region of keys on the selected curves. When you are finished, the region you have defined will be shown in semi-transparent white, with handles on each of the four edges. If you click in the middle of the Region, you can translate all the keys at once, making them happen earlier or later in time or shifting their values up or down.

If you click on the right or left edge Region handles and drag, you are changing the duration of the Region, making the action faster or slower uniformly.

If you Click on the top or bottom edge Region handles and drag you can scale all the values gradually in the direction you drag.

MULTIPLE ITEMS AT ONCE IN THE ANIMATION EDITOR

In general, XSI doesn't care whether you want to work on one object at a time, or a number of different objects. The Animation Editor is no exception, and this fact makes it much easier to adjust animation in complex scenes with many objects in motion at the same time. The easiest way to do this is to use the explorer in conjunction with the Animation Editor. Select all the objects you want to edit in the explorer and pop up the Animation Editor in a floating window with the 0 hotkey.

Now each object and all related curves are shown in the Animation Editor. As you select different objects in the explorer, the Animation Editor updates, showing you those objects and making animation changes.

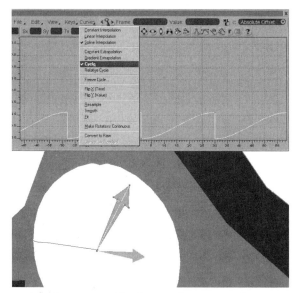

A cycle is a set of keyframes that repeats forever.

CYCLES AND THE ANIMATION EDITOR

Many animation tasks involve repetitive actions. An action that repeats exactly is called a cycle. Examples of cycles in animation would be the swinging of a pendulum, a ball bouncing, or even a character walking along the street. Since it doesn't make sense to have to set the same keys over and over, XSI has features for quickly creating cycles from one set of keys. The big problem with cycles is that if they are always the same they quickly become uninteresting. As an animator, you might use the cycle tools to create the basic animation, then add variation into the cycles to make your work more interesting.

When you select an Animation Curve and choose the Curves→Cycle command, XSI will find all the keys in that curve, and then repeat them exactly, so that exactly after the last key, the first key follows again. The cycle will repeat indefinitely, both before the real keys and after the real keys, limited only by the first and last frame you have set in the timeline. If you extend the last frame, for instance, you get more cycles.

The Curves menu has the options for curve cycles.

If the action is something that should repeat exactly, like a clock pendulum, it is extremely important that the value of the curve is precisely the same at the first frame and the last frame of the cycle. If they are not the same, there will be a visual skip between one and the other, as the object changes instantly from one cycle to the next. This will ruin the effect. In this case it's a good idea to numerically set the beginning and ending keys of the cycle so you know they are the same. For instance, in the example of the pendulum, I would be setting keys on the pendulum rotation in Z, so I would select the first pendulum.kine.local.ori.euler.z (otherwise known as Rot.Z) keyframe and, deciding that I want the pendulum to swing up 45 degrees, would set it by typing 45 in the value text box at the top of the Animation Editor. Then I would select the last key, and also type 45 into the value box, ensuring that the pendulum ends up exactly where it starts, repeating perfectly each time.

CREEPING CYCLES

Another issue to beware of is that you need to be careful of the exact length of your cycles. For instance, in a walk cycle, if you cycled the up and down action of a foot over 20 frames, and the rotation of the foot over 19 frames, the difference wouldn't be very noticeable right away but the error would grow with each cycle, until the rotation of the foot was completely out of sync with the position of the foot. Since the timeline starts on frame 1 by default, it's easy to make this mistake. It's a good idea to change the first frame in the timeline to zero, so it is easier to keep your cycles straight.

RELATIVE CYCLES

The pendulum swings exactly in the same way each time, but many cycles – like walk cycles – are more complex. The translation in Y of the foot (up and down) would be the same each time, but the forward position (translation in Z) of the foot must change each cycle, or the foot would just start over again where it was. To set up a Relative Cycle, select the Animation Curve (or Curves) you want all cycled at the same time and choose the Curves➜Relative Cycle command.

When a value cycles like this, where each cycle starts where the last one left off, it is called a Relative Cycle. If your character is walking up an endless flight of stairs, both the Y and Z translation would require relative cycles. Since the value of each successive key is cumulative in a relative cycle, it is also important to set the value of the starting and ending keys precisely, though they do not need to be the same. Otherwise, creeping error might accumulate and throw off your action later on in the animation.

FREEZING AND REMOVING CYCLES

The cycles in the Animation Editor are special cases of the Animation Curve, because the cycled portions don't actually have any keys of their own. They just automatically repeat the keys that you set manually in the first place. While this means is that if you make a change to the original set of keys it will immediately propagate to all the cycles, it also means that you can't give the cycles any individuality. They must all be exactly the same. Since conformity is dull, you will probably want to freeze the cycles. Freezing the cycles makes actual keys on the curve for each cycle, so you could rough them up a bit in the Animation Editor, changing each cycle to fit your needs.

Use the Curves➜Freeze Cycle command to turn all your automatic cycles into regular keyframes on regular Animation Curves.

Sometimes you just want the cycle to go away entirely, leaving the original keys you set but not changing the rest of the curve. The way to turn off a cycle is to change the interpolation of the curve in question back to Constant Extrapolation, by toggling Constant Extrapolation on in the Curves menu.

TIMING CHANGES WITH THE DOPESHEET

While the Animation Editor is set up to make it easy for you to adjust both the Timing (position in X, along the time axis) and the Value of multiple keys, very often you just need to adjust the timing of the keys without accidentally changing the values of the animation. In traditional character animation this step of adjusting the timing of your actions is the most critical component of good animation, and often takes the most time. Good character animators spend hours poring over each set of keys, making minor adjustments, and checking to see whether the results were enhanced or damaged, then trying again. Only by this process of continual refinement will you get the effect you want. Fortunately, XSI has a tool to make this easier and faster, called the Dopesheet. In the Dopesheet, keys are represented by colored bars in a timeline-like setup.

You can see the Dopesheet in two ways: in the Animation Editor and in the Timeline. While viewing the Dopesheet in the timeline is certainly convenient, it makes it hard to scrub across frames, so we'll use the Animation Editor view.

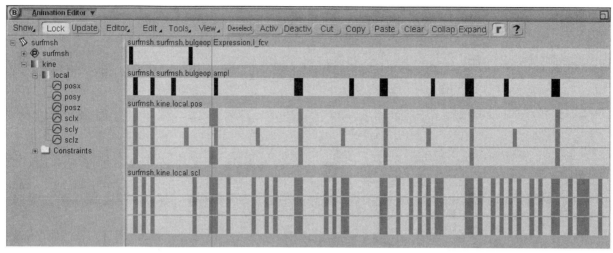

The Dopesheet is a great way to adjust timing.

Select an object that has keyframes already, and pop up the Animation Editor with the 0 hotkey. From the Editor menu, choose Dopesheet.

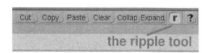

You can drag over frames with the LMB to select them, then use MMB to move the region.

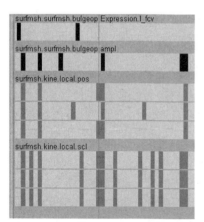

The colored bars show that keys exist for the object on that frame.

DECODING THE DOPESHEET

Time in the Dopesheet is represented as a series of vertical lines that delineate frames. If the frame is empty, there are no keyframes on the object in that frame. If the frame is filled in with a solid color, one or more keys exist at that frame. When the frame is filled in, the color gives you feedback about what kind of keys might be in there.

Purple bars mean that many different keys are on that frame, and that the individual tracks are collapsed. Transformations are color-coded Red, Green, and Blue, while other animated parameters are colored Black.

If you want to adjust all the different keyed properties in a given frame, this view is great, but many times you want to see more precisely what keys you have there, and adjust only the keys on one property. In that case you need to Expand the Dopesheet, to drill down and show more information.

When you click on the Expand button, the single big Dopesheet is replaced by multiple dopesheets, called Tracks. Each animated property has its own track, and all the keys for that property are collected in that track. If that track – say, Translation – has subtracks, you can observe them by clicking in that track and clicking the Expand button again.

To shrink up the tracks and see a less specific view of the Dopesheet, click the Collapse button.

Within each track the keys are represented by filled, colored bars in the frames, just as they were in the overview of the Dopesheet.

When you see a filled bar, you know that the value is keyed right there at that frame, which is often called a "hit" in character animation. The hits show you where in time the character is reaching the extremes of a pose, and changing how long it takes for the character to get from hit to hit is what adjusting the timing is all about.

ADJUSTING TIMING IN THE DOPESHEET

You can only really do two things in the Dopesheet: move keys and cut/copy/paste keys. However, you generally work on Regions of keys, not individual keys. So, if you want to adjust only one key, the region will just be rather small. If you want to adjust all the animation on the entire character, the region will be big.

The general pattern of working in the Dopesheet is as follows: drag to define a region, then adjust the region, which changes the keys inside of it.

Generally, the Left Mouse Button always defines the region in the Dopesheet. The Middle Mouse Button always changes the keys within the region, and the Right Mouse Button always pops up a menu to get to cut, copy, and paste.

One more concept must be understood before you begin actually using the Dopesheet: the concept of Rippling. When you change a set of keys, moving it later in time, it might overlap the keys that come after it. That would really screw up your animation, so XSI has a feature to avoid this, called Ripple. When Rippling is toggled on by activating the R icon in the top menu bar of the Dopesheet, moving keys will pull and push the keys on either side of it, so they stay just as far away as they were before you made the change. In other words, with Ripple on, if you defined a region for the foot of a character taking a step and dragged it to the right, it would push the keys for the next step to the right as well, keeping them a constant period of time ahead of the keys you are changing. If you use Ripple with Copy/Paste, inserting a copied block of keys into a section of frames will also push the later keys ahead in time by however long the copied block is, so they don't overlap.

Let's try it out. Open a scene of your own with animation or use the animation_spring scene file from the courseware for this book. Examine the animation by playing it back. See that the spring is hopping in an even manner. We'll use the Dopesheet to speed up and slow down different hops, and even delay between hops.

(1) Select the Spring Model and Display the Dopesheet in the Animation Editor. Expand the master track to see all the animation tracks you could modify independently in the Dopesheet, by clicking in the track with the colored keys and clicking the Expand button in the toolbar. Fortunately, you don't have to, in fact we want the scale and translation and bulge of the spring to stay bound together (for now). Collapse the tracks back to one big track.

(2) Let's make one hop shorter with Ripple OFF. Toggle the ripple icon off (uncolored) in the Dopesheet.

In the master track, drag with your Left Mouse Button to define a region around one complete hop, from the key where the spring leaves the street to the key where it touches down again. To make this easier, the spring touches down on even multiples of 20 frames: frame 20, 40, 60, 80 and 100. You can also zoom in to see the individual frames in the Dopesheet.

The region will appear in white surrounding these keys. If you need to, click in the middle to drag it left and right, or click on either end to make it bigger or smaller until it fits correctly around just the frames you want. At the top of the region, the start and end frames are listed in white.

Next, carefully click and drag with the Middle Mouse Button on the right edge of the region. It will turn red while you change it to show that you are editing the keys within it. Make the region about half as long as it was, which means that this hop will be faster than the others. Try it out by playing back the animation.

(3) Let's delay that hop with Ripple OFF. This short hop starts right after the previous hop. Let's imagine that we want the short hop to occur later in time. With your Middle Mouse Button (remember, MMB edits the keys under the region), click in the middle of the region and drag to the right a short distance. Play back, and observe the difference.

(4) A short hop with Ripple ON

In the previous steps, we ended up with some slow parts before and after the hop. We don't want that. Toggle the Ripple icon ON.

Define a different region with the LMB around a later hop (or Undo your previous changes and use the same region), and scale it down again with the MMB, shortening the hop. When you release the mouse, see that the later keys are automatically moved left to close up the gap!

Define another region around a different hop and make it longer. See that it pushes the next hop along after it so the keys don't overlap. Cool, huh?

(5) The spring is about out of hops, yet we want it to keep bouncing up and down when it is done. To do this we'll need to copy just the Y translation keys for a single hop and paste them, along with the scale keys and the Bulge deformation keys.

Expand out the master track to locate the Y translation track (surfmsh.kine.local.posy) and drag a region around one complete hop, say from frame 80 to 100. Copy the keys in those frames by clicking in the region with the RMB and choosing Copy. Now pan later in the Dopesheet and click to define a one-frame region right on the last keyframe of the last hop in the Y translation track. Right-click again and choose paste to add in new keys. Repeat as many times as you wish. You may repeat the process with the Scale and Bulge tracks.

The Dopesheet is a critical tool for adjusting how long each animated action takes. Explore it and become comfortable using it to modify the timing of your animations so that the speed of your work looks good.

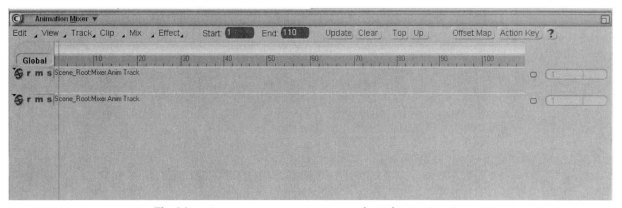

The Mixer is a new way to sequence and combine animation.

ALL ABOUT THE MIXER

So far we've seen keyframes set one after another on Animation Curves, and we've seen that the Dopesheet can shift keys around on Animation Curves, but we haven't seen anything that really lives up to the concept of Non-Linear Animation. That means that it is time for the Mixer. The Mixer is the big gun in the XSI animation arsenal. All forms of animation, keys, expressions, constraints, and scripts come together in the Mixer. In the mixer we can sequence animation clips one after the other, adding transitions between them, and we can layer animation clips one over the other, fading back and forth between them. We can sync up complex actions like walking and running, and change the timing of any number of objects with a simple click and drag interface that will be familiar to anyone who has used a non-linear editor for audio or video. First of all, I'll lay the groundwork with an understanding of what the Mixer is, where Mixers are stored in XSI, and how the Mixer user interface is organized.

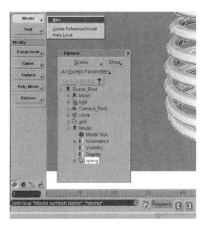

When you turn an object into a Model, it gets a special icon in the explorer.

MIXERS LIVE IN MODELS

The highest level of any hierarchy is called a Model. By default, the top of a scene will be a single model with the same name as the scene, but you can create as many Models as you wish within a given scene. A Model binds up hierarchies, related constraints, lights, cameras, and everything else into one easy-to-use package. Mixers happen to be stored at the Model level in the explorer. What that means is that by default you will have one mixer for each scene, but you are welcome to create more Models within your scene, each capable of having its own Mixer. As a practical matter, you'll want to have one Mixer for each character you work with in a scene, to make it easy to work on a single character without being confused by the animation of the other characters. In this way a Model breaks up the animation in to more easily managed mixers.

MODELS HAVE A SPECIAL ICON

You can always create a Model at any time by selecting a hierarchy of objects or a collection of unrelated objects and clicking on the Model→New menu option.

Open up the explorer to examine your scene. The top of the scene is the Model, and has a special icon that looks like a human figure in the middle of a jumping-jack, with his arms and legs stretched out.

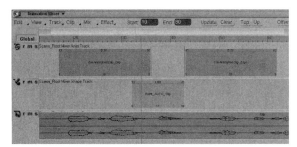

The Mixer has its own timeline.

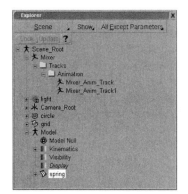

Mixers are only created in the explorer when needed.

In the explorer window make sure that the Show➔Mixers menu option is toggled on so that when you create a mixer it will show up in the explorer window.

Mixers are only created when they are needed, so no Mixer is present yet in your scene. Let's make one. Get a primitive sphere and then change one of your views to the Animation Mixer option.

Two of your views will now be given over to the Mixer, and a new Mixer icon will have appeared in the explorer. There may not be any tracks in the Mixer yet, however.

ADDING TRACKS TO THE MIXER

Locate the Update button in the top of the Mixer window and click on it to refresh the Mixer window with the tracks associated with that Mixer. By default, XSI creates two Animation Tracks, colored minty green. Animation tracks store keyframe data on all the animatable properties except Shapes, which have their own tracks. You may have as many Animation tracks as you wish, so let's add another. Position your mouse over one of the green Animation Tracks and click the RMB to pop up the context-sensitive menu for the track.

Note: The RMB pops up a different menu depending where your mouse cursor was when you clicked. The context-sensitive menu will always show additional commands and options that apply only to the type of object or interface element your mouse was over. Right-clicking over things is an excellent way to find out what you can do with something you are looking at onscreen.

In the popup menu, choose the Add Track➔Animation option, and see that another green track is added into the Mixer.

Let's add a Shape track. Later on in Chapter 4 we'll work with Shape Animation in the Mixer, but for now it's enough to see that Shape tracks also live in the Mixer. Use the RMB context-sensitive menu over the minty green open area and choose the Add Track➔Shape option. A new Shape track, colored a frosty blue, pops into existence.

Add an Audio track the same way, just to see what it looks like. Audio tracks can store audio files like QuickTime movie audio, .aiff, and .wav files. With an audio track you can use the Mixer to sync up actions to sounds, do lip sync, and other timing work.

You may remove any track by clicking with the RMB over that track and choosing Delete Track.

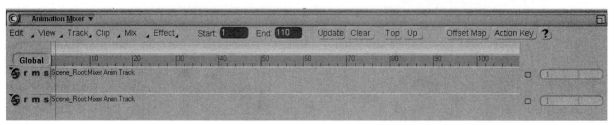

At the top of the Mixer you'll find menus and buttons for common tasks.

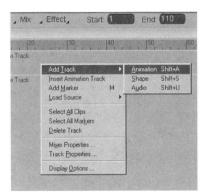

Right-click over a track to see this menu.

There can be three types of tracks in the Mixer: Animation, Shape, and Audio.

WHAT TIME IS IT?

The Mixer has its own timeline at the top of the window, represented by the white bar under the menus. This timeline shows only a subset of the range of frames you have set in the timeline. You can adjust the range that the Mixer shows by entering a start frame and an end frame for just the Mixer region.

In addition to the start and end frame, the white bar can refine your view even further. The idea is that if you had a long animation you could use this sub-timeline to zoom in tight on just a small portion of the animation that extends throughout the whole timeline. Try it out by clicking carefully on the left or right edge of the Mixer Timber and making it smaller. Shortening the Mixer Timber has the effect of zooming in on your animation. You can also slide the Mixer Timber left and right to pan through the animation.

With that brief tour of the Mixer UI behind us, let's see the Mixer at work.

STORING POSE ACTIONS

The Mixer can do two things: sequence animation segments, and blend animation segments. Sequencing these animation "clips" is a form of editing, laying out different clips in time to build up from smaller chunks to a longer animation segment.

Blending animation is a form of layering, where individual simpler animation clips are added on top of each other to create more complex and different animation.

First, however, you need to have animation clips to sequence or blend. The process of creating these clips is called storing, and the clips themselves are called actions.

An action is defined as one or more sources of animation on one or more object. For instance, an action could contain the Scale animation of your bouncing spring, which would be a single animated property on a single object. A single action could also contain all the animation on the spring: the Scale, the Translation, and the Bulge deformation.

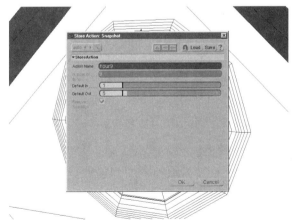

Here you assign a name to the action, and a default duration.

An action could also contain animation on more than one object at a time. For instance, all the animation for a human figure running could be bound up into a single action, even though there are many different objects changing shape, size, rotation, and translation in a running human. Actions can also store the effects of scripted operators, expressions, and constraints on objects.

Actions are stored in the Mixer, in a folder called Sources, but that folder won't be present until you actually have some actions created.

XSI makes three distinct types of animation actions: Current Pose Actions, Animation Curve Actions, and All Sources Actions.

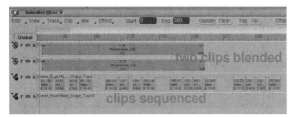

Placing actions one after another is Sequencing, overlapping them on different tracks is Blending.

— store a pose

— store keyframes

— store everything

Different kinds of actions allow you to store just what you need.

When you store a Current Pose Action you will be storing the current pose of the object at the current frame, without any animation at all. When you store an Animation Curve Action (abbreviated Fcurve for function curve, the old name for Animation Curve) you will store all the keys on an object, at all frames in time. When you store an All Sources Action, you will store all the keys as well as all constraint, script, and expression animation on the object. This last type of action is rare.

Within each of these major categories, you can choose to store just the Scale, Rotation and Translation (the transforms), whatever properties you have Marked in the Marking List only, or you can choose to let XSI figure out what you want based on what seems to have been animated.

So, put another way, you will mainly choose between Pose and Animated Actions, and within each you can choose what properties to include.

STORE CURRENT VALUES

Switch to the Animation Module (F4 on your keyboard if you are using the SI3D keymap), and look down the Menu cells on the left-hand side until you find the Action area, and the Store Menu Cell. If you click on the Store Menu cell you'll see that the drop menu is divided into three parts. The first division in the menu is the Current Pose area.

The first option, Store→Transformations – Current Values will create an action for the selected object that contains the current values for Scale, Rotation and Translation. You do not have to set any keyframes to use this option.

The second option, Store→Marked Parameters – Current Values will create an action that contains the current values of whatever properties you choose to mark. In this way you can create more specific actions; for instance, storing only Rotation but not Scale, which is very useful when animating. You can also mark more properties than just the transformations. You might choose to mark the color, the scale, and the geometry properties of a Sphere all at the same time to store a more complex action.

As a practical matter, storing the marked parameters gets more difficult as you select more items with different properties. It's easiest when you are just marking one parameter on one or two objects at a time.

Note: Although the data within an action identifies both the object and the Animation Curves, any action can be used with any object by re-mapping the Object identified by the action. This means that one action for, say, a character kicking, can be easily re-used on different characters.

SEQUENCING IN THE MIXER

Armed with a simple understanding of storing poses, we can try out the most basic function of the Mixer, Sequencing animations.

The Store Menu has all the commands to store actions.

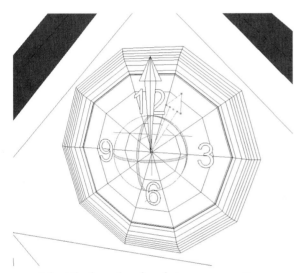

Select the hour hand and store some actions.

Here's the plan: we'll take a model of a Cuckoo Clock, and set some actions on the Hour hand and the Minute hand so we can animate the clock in the Mixer. The end result will be a clock with the minute hand spinning wildly while the hour hand clicks from 9:00 to 10:00 to 11:00 and finally to 12:00. (For extra credit you could animate all the parts of the clock flying open at 12:00.)

CUCKOO CLOCK, PHASE 1

Step 1: Open the Mixer.cuckoo scene from the courseware for this book or just build a clock face yourself.

Step 2: Select the hour hand on the clock face, and rotate it around the local Z-axis until it points at 9:00.

Step 3: With the hour hand selected, choose Action→Store→Transformations – Current Values. This tells XSI to store the current scale, rotation and translation of the hand.

A small dialog will pop up, asking you to name the action. Call it "Hour9". The In and Out frames of the action are not very important, because we can make the action longer or shorter at any time. By default, Current Pose Actions get a duration of 5 frames, which is fine for this. Click the "OK" button to store the action. Look in the explorer to see that a Sources folder has been created under the Mixer, and within that a folder called Animation, and that the action Hour9 is there inside of that folder.

Step 4: Rotate the hour hand to 10:00, and this time make sure that just the Rotation cells are active in the MCP. The marking list should now read "kine.local.ori.euler", which means "Kinematics.Local Transformations.Orientation.Euler Math system."

This time, store the action with the Action→Store→Marked Parameters – Current Values menu cell, which will store just the rotation, which is what you want, instead of storing all the transformation as stored in the previous step. Name this action "Hour10".

Note: Unfortunately, XSI won't save just the Z rotation in an action, even if Z is the only Rotation axis marked in the MCP. However, if you need just one axis stored, you can always mark just one axis manually in the parameter marking list.

Repeat this process for hours 11:00 and 12:00, so that you now have four stored Current Pose Actions in the Mixer→Animation→Sources in the explorer.

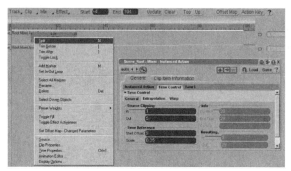

Each clip has a length, or duration.

LOADING ACTIONS INTO THE MIXER

Now that you have four stored actions, they can be loaded into the Mixer and sequenced. You want to view the Mixer that is attached to the Cuckoo clock model, so select the clock as a tree (Space bar and the RMB) and open the Mixer into the lower-left view window, where it will extend across the two bottom views, all the way across the screen. Click the Update button to make sure you are viewing the right Mixer. (That was redundant, but we are building good habits that will serve you well in more complex situations.)

In the top minty green Animation track, right-click to display the context-sensitive menu and choose the option Load Source. You will see the stored actions that are available to that mixer cascaded out. When you select an action (say, "Hour9") then the drop menu collapses and that action is added as an Action Clip to the Mixer.

THE DURATION OF A CLIP

The Action Clip is represented by a darker green rectangle. The length of the rectangle is the duration of the clip. You can extend or shorten any clip by clicking in the middle of either edge and dragging left or right. When you are over the clip, the cursor changes to become a double-headed arrow, helping you to remember that you can extend the clip in either direction.

Making the clip wider makes it take more frames, and therefore become longer. If the clip is an animation action, then the animation will play more slowly. Shortening an animation clip makes the animation faster.

You can set the duration of the clip manually by entering exact values as well, by bringing up the context-sensitive menu for that clip (RMB over the clip) and choosing the Time Properties menu option, or hitting the CTRL-T hotkey combo. Simply enter a number in the Source Clipping in and out entry boxes to set the duration precisely.

You can also trim a clip graphically in the Mixer. Just drag the red current frame indicator in the Mixer over the clip to the place where you want it trimmed. If you are trimming off the beginning of the clip, right-click over the clip and choose Trim Before, while if you are pruning the end of the clip choose the Trim After option.

FEEDBACK ON DURATION

It's nice to know if a clip in the Mixer has been molested, and is shorter or longer than it was originally, either because it has been scaled or because it has been trimmed. Each clip has numbers in the middle at the top and at the bottom. The Bottom number represents the exact duration of the clip in frames, while the top number is the speed of the clip now relative to the original speed, as a percentage. So, if the top number reads 0.5, you know that the clip runs at 50% of the original speed. The lower the number, the slower the clip. A number higher than 1 indicates that the clip is playing faster than it was originally stored.

You can also position the clip in time by simply clicking in the middle of the clip and dragging it left or right in the Mixer track.

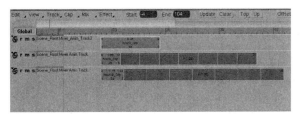

Bounce means the clip plays back and forth; Cycle means it repeats over and over.

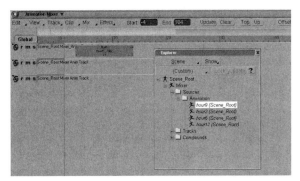

You can drag and drop actions from the explorer to the Mixer.

BOUNCE AND CYCLE

What do you want XSI to do after the end (or before the beginning) of an action is called Extrapolation. You can have XSI hold the first or last frame for any length, or you can have the action Bounced or Cycled.

Action clips are really easy to cycle. If you point your mouse at the bottom-right or bottom-left corner of a clip and click, then drag out from the clip, one or more cycles will be created, depending how far you drag away from the clip. In a clip cycle, as soon as the clip is over it immediately plays again, jumping precisely to the values of the first frame in the cycle and playing over again exactly.

If the first and last frames of an action are precisely the same, the cycle will be smooth and flawless. However, if they aren't quite perfect, a visual pop will give away the cycle. One solution is to use Bounce instead of Cycle. If you click and drag from the upper corners, XSI will create a Bounce, which is like a cycle except that it plays once through forwards, then plays backwards, then forwards again, oscillating like a pendulum.

To get rid of your bounces or cycles, just click again on the lower or upper corner, and drag back towards the clip to eliminate the extrapolation. To examine the Extrapolation parameters manually – for instance, to set the hold on a first or last frame – right-click over a clip and choose the Time Control menu option to inspect the Extrapolation property page.

DRAG AND DROP ACTIONS

You can also add actions to a track by opening the explorer window, and dragging them from the Mixer→Sources→Animation folder into the Mixer track where you want them.

You may also copy existing clips in the Mixer by holding the CTRL key and dragging them with the Left Mouse Button. A new clip will be pulled out of the original and deposited wherever you let go of the mouse, even in another track than the original.

CUCKOO CLOCK, PHASE 2

Step 1: Continue to build your Cuckoo clock animation, by dropping in all four positions for the hour hand in one track of the mixer.

Step 2: Make each clip 22 frames long, and space the clips evenly so they extend from frame 1 to frame 100, with about 5 frames of empty space between each of them.

Step 3: Play back your animation. See that when the current frame is over a clip, the information stored in that clip is used to drive the hand of the clock. Whenever only one clip is present in the timeline, that clip drives the animated object at the current frame.

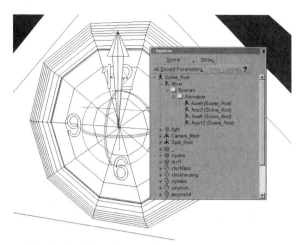

Add all the hour clips to the first animation track in the Mixer.

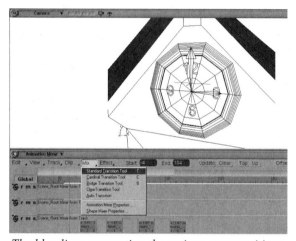

The blue lines connecting the actions are transitions.

However, the hand snaps instantly from one pose to the next when the current frame is over a new clip, which is a little more abrupt than we want. What we need is a smooth transition from one clip to another.

THE TRANSITION TOOL

The Mixer has a simple method of smoothly interpolating from the end of one clip to the beginning of another, called a Standard Transition. The Standard Transition tool makes a smooth interpolation between the property values at the end of the first clip and the property values at the beginning of the second clip. The standard Transition tool is located in the Mixer under the Mix menu, and can also be activated temporarily with the T hotkey, which is much easier.

To create a transition between clips, choose the Menu command Mix➔Standard Transition and click first on the leftmost clip (the first one) and then click on the clip to the right (the second one). A purple bar will appear, connecting the tops of the two clips.

If you don't need to create any more transitions right away, immediately click the RMB to end the transition tool before you accidentally add transitions you don't intend. The better way is to hold the T hotkey, then click on the first clip, then the second, then let go of the T hotkey.

If you right-click over the transition, you can see the context-sensitive menu for the transition. If you choose Animation Editor from that pop up menu, you will see the shape of the Standard Transition, moving smoothly from one clip to another. You may certainly edit this by adding keys with the I hotkey, or adjusting the ends with the M hotkey.

CUCKOO CLOCK, PHASE 3

Step 1: Add Standard Transitions between the four clips for the hour hand

Step 2: Examine the difference by scrubbing the current frame indicator in the timeline. See that the hour hand holds its position during the clip, then gradually eases into the next position.

You can use the Menu, or the T hot key, to add transitions.

Step 3: The motion of the hour hand is lifeless and uninteresting. It would be cool if it snapped into its next position, then wobbled a bit after it hits there. Right-click over the first transition and adjust the Animation Curve to smoothly slope up to the right without easing out much. Then add 5 keys with the I hotkey after it reaches the top, waving up and down in a wave pattern, so that the hand overshoots a bit, then swings back and forth just a little bit before settling in to the next position. Change the other transitions, too.

STORING ANIMATION ACTIONS

You now know how to store simple poses and work with them in the Mixer. In fact, Animation Curve Actions work exactly the same way, with just a few additional capabilities.

When you have an object with keyframes set on it over time, like the minute hand of the Cuckoo clock, you may bind up all those keys into an Animation Curve Action.

If you choose Action➜Store: Transformations – Fcurves, all the keys on the Scale, Rotation, and Translation will be bound into an Action. If you don't actually have animation on all three properties that would be a bad idea, because you might later want to blend in another action for those properties, and although it would work, having blank animation in one Action would make your work more complicated.

If you choose the menu command Action➜Store➜Marked Parameters – Fcurves then only those properties that you have marked will be stored in the action.

The menu command Action➜Store➜Animated Parameters – Fcurves will search all currently selected objects for properties that have keys on them, and store them all.

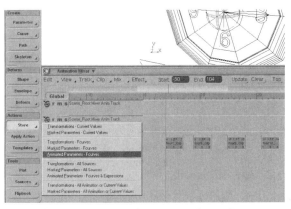

Remember to store just what you need – nothing extra.

By default, after keyframe animation is stored in an action, the keys are stripped off the objects. This is a feature that is intended to make it easy for you to move on to setting up the next action you want, without having to manually remove all the animation. Since you just stored the Animation, you can always get it back in the Mixer, so it makes sense to get rid of it from the Animation Editor.

Also by default, when you store an animation, the dialog box that pops up has the first and last frame set correctly to the duration of all the animation keys on the object. You can change this, to create an action that is either longer or shorter than the keys present, for instance if you want the object to remain motionless for a few frames as a part of the action.

In practice, creating actions with Store➜Animated Properties – Fcurves is the easiest and best way to store almost any action, whether it is a static pose or an animated action. All you have to do is set keys on the objects and properties that you want XSI to bind up into an action, select all those objects, and choose the Actions➜Store➜Animated Properties – Fcurves. No marking is required, and XSI automatically searches out and stores all the animated properties on the objects for you. Even when I am setting poses, I use this method, by setting only one key and changing the length of the action created to be 5 or ten frames long.

CUCKOO CLOCK, PHASE 4

Step 1: Now, for the minute hand. Since we have three hours (9:00 to 12:00) we need 180 minutes, or three revolutions around the clock face. Since the minute hand will be moving, we'll need to store an Animation Curve Action, not the more basic Current Pose Action as we did earlier.

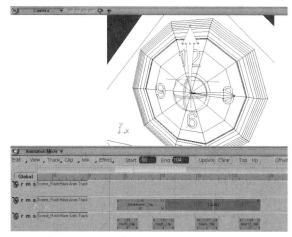

Now the minute hand animation is mixed with the hour hand poses.

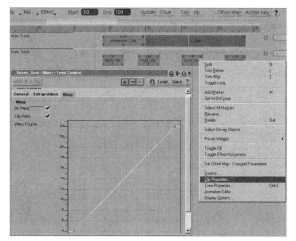

The TimeWarp property page

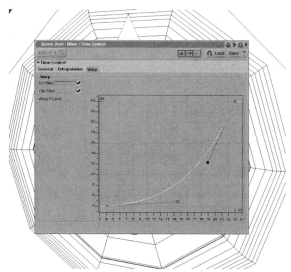

The curve of the TimeWarp shows the action going faster and faster.

Set a key on the minute hand Rotation in Z pointing straight up at 12:00 at frame 1. Change the current frame to frame 100. Rotate the minute hand in Z only, clockwise, three times around till it points back at 12:00. The Rotation in Z should now read -1080 degrees. Save another Rotation key.

Step 2: Store the rotation Animation Curve in an action. With the Minute hand selected to tell XSI that this is the object you want the action on, and the rotation cells active in the MCP to indicate that you have Rotation marked, choose the Action→Store→Marked Parameters – Fcurves. In the dialog that pops up, call this action "Minute3revs". See that it is stored in the same place as the poses: in the explorer window, in the Mixer→Sources→Animation folder.

Step 3: Add it to the Mixer, in the second track. You may drag and drop the action from the explorer, or right-click on a track and choose Load Source from the context-sensitive menu. Adjust the position and length of the clip to match the hour hand actions.

Step 4: Play back the animation and season it to your taste by adjusting the clips in the Animation Mixer.

TIMEWARP AND ACTIONS

Action clips can clearly have their own timing, since we can make them faster and slower. What isn't so obvious is that clip time is extremely plastic, and can change over the life of a clip. If you RMB over the Minute3revs clip and choose Time Properties, you can click through the PPG to the Warp tab, and toggle on Do Warp to make the TimeWarp Active. The small chart in the TimeWarp tab is actually a full Animation Editor in a small window, so the usual hotkeys for adding, deleting and moving keys are all available. If the curve was a straight line stretching from bottom-left to top-right, that would indicate that time was progressing as you would expect: linearly from start to finish. However, we are now in charge of time and can bend it to our will. If the slope of the curve changes and now curves down to the right, time will start running backwards. If the slope flattens out, time will come to a standstill, just like "bullet-time". However, the keys are locked now, and the curve has linear slope interpolation. Change this by tagging both start and end points, then using the RMB to unlock the points in X and Y with the Key→Lock in X or Y menu command. Finally, untag the points, select just the curve, and use the RMB to change the curve interpolation with Curve→Spline Interpolation.

CUCKOO CLOCK, PHASE 5

Step 1: View the Minute3revs clip's TimeWarp PPG as above, and toggle it on if you have not already done so. We want the minute hand to gradually accelerate, faster and faster as the hours click by, then finally come to an abrupt stop as the clock hits 12:00.

Adjust the slope of the first and last keys in the TimeWarp curve editor so that the curve starts flatter, and gradually slopes up and up, until it hits the last key with no ease out at all.

Step 2: View your work, and make any adjustments necessary. Save your work.

AUDIO TRACKS IN THE MIXER

The next kind of track available in the Mixer is the audio track. Audio tracks are designed to help you synchronize animation to pre-existing audio files. For instance, you might record the sound effect track of a character bumbling around in a glass shop, then animate the actions of the character so the timing matches the crashes of the glass. Or, you might record a voice track for a character and use the audio track to hear what the character is saying so you can adjust the timing of the lip sync to match perfectly.

In the Mixer, right-click in the empty area of any existing track and choose the option Add Track→Audio. A new salmon-colored track appears below the current tracks. You can bring audio into the track either by dragging and dropping an audio file from a browser window, or choosing Load Source from the RMB context menu. XSI can use .wav files, .aiff files, or the audio track from a QuickTime or an AVI movie. Make sure that you save your audio files with the correct file extension so that XSI knows what kind of file you are giving it.

When you have imported a valid audio file, XSI will show you a new clip in the audio track, and will show a curve in the clip that represents the waveform of the audio contained in the clip. You can then use the shape of the curve to visualize what is happening in the audio clip even without hearing it, and easily line up actions to start and stop with features in the audio clip. If you don't see a curve representing the waveform, you have a problem with your audio file. Check that it plays correctly somewhere else and that it has the correct file extension, and try it again. If you still don't see the waveform, try using a different file.

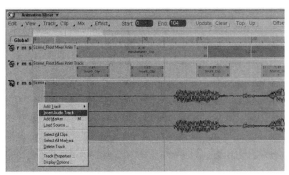

The salmon-colored track is an audio track.

To hear the audio track, click the Play button in the timeline. If you don't hear anything, try toggling on and off the Audio button in the timeline (it looks like a pair of headphones). You can also set XSI to play the audio when you scrub the time slider back and forth, which is the most useful way to use the audio track. To turn this behavior on, go to the File→User Prefs dialog, and in the General tab, make sure that "Play Audio When Scrubbing" is turned on.

If none of this works, you might have a problem with the sound setup on your PC (which is common, since PCs all support sound in different ways, and there is little standardization).

All four actions are being mixed, in various degrees, to determine the final result.

BLENDING DIFFERENT ACTIONS

So far we've worked with simple actions, each on one object and one set of properties. That's not necessary, because one action can bind up all the animation on as many different objects and as many different properties as you wish.

To store more complex actions, simply select more than one object at a time. Then, mark all the properties you want saved in the Marking List, and store the action in the normal way.

In the case of a complex hierarchy of human character controls, you could Shift-Select all the controls at once and then save an action on translation and rotation.

The process of saving more complex actions is no different from saving simple action, but they can be used in different ways in the Mixer.

THE BLEND SLIDER IN THE MIXER

Each track in the Mixer has a slider on the right edge, with an associated green animation divot right next to it. This slider controls how much influence the track has over the final result. If the Slider is at zero, that track will not have any effect on the objects driven by the clips in that track. If the slider is all the way up at 1, the clips will have the maximum possible effect over the objects that they drive.

Since there are multiple tracks, each with a Blend slider, it is also the case that one object can be driven by more than one clip at the same time. For instance, the position of a foot could be driven by both a "walk" clip and a "run" clip. In this case, the blend slider will change how much of each clip is expressed in the final animation. The animation divot next to the blend slider indicates that the blend can also be animated, changing over time to create cross-dissolves among clips. For instance, the walk slider could be animated down exactly as the run blend slider was animated up, causing the foot to transition from a walk to a run.

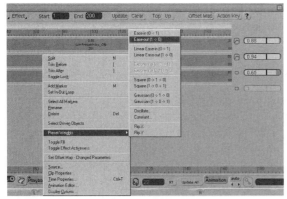

There are many preset weight curves, or you can make your own.

WEIGHT CURVES

The blend slider and the animation divot next to it actually create Animation Curves called Weight curves. When a weight curve is all the way up, that means that its clip is fully considered, or weighted, in the result at that frame. When the weight curve is all the way down that means that its clip isn't influencing the result at all at that point in time. Basically, the weight curve is like a volume knob that turns the effect of that clip up and down, from 100% to 0%, that can change all the way through the animation. By default, the weight curves show on top of the clips. You can turn them on or off yourself with the View→Weight Curves menu item.

There are some handy pre-built weight curves that can save you the time and energy of setting keys on the blend slider yourself. If you right-click over a clip to pull up its context-sensitive menu, you can slide your mouse over the Preset Weights menu item and see a list of all the possibilities. The Gaussian 0-1-0 curve is great for bringing in an action smoothly, then fading it out.

The Oscillate option brings up a dialog where you can choose how frequently a clip fades in and out. Try the others to see what they do as well.

ADDITIVE VERSUS AVERAGE WEIGHTS

In the section above on Weight Curves, I said that the blend slider and the weight curves made from the sliders determine to what degree each clip is considered in the final result, but I didn't say exactly how they would be considered, or what the result would be. That's because there are two different ways of blending clips that are each useful in different situations: Average and Additive.

By default, the Mixer uses the Average method. That means that if you create two action clips for a toy car, one placing the toy car 10 units in positive X, and the other at 2 units in positive X, then you put both clips in the mixer and turned the blend sliders up to 100%, the toy car would go to the average location between the two clips, or 6 units in Positive X ((10 + 2) / 2 = 6). However, there are many cases where you don't want the action in one clip to reduce the effect of another clip. In that case you would want them both at 100%, which would be the Additive method. If you set the Mixer Properties to use the Additive method and did the same experiment, the toy car would go to 12 units in positive X, or the location of one clip plus the location of the other.

The Average method tends to make actions less potent, since each layered action reduces the effect of the others in the mix. However, it is the appropriate method for blending joint rotations (most of the time). The Additive method would be a bad choice for blending IK actions, but it's the way to go for blending Shape animations. If you understand the difference, you can always choose the correct method for each occasion.

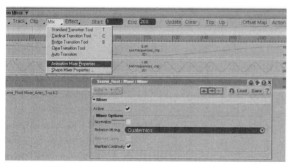

Here, Normalize means to average all the clips to arrive at the result.

To set the Mixer to use the Average method, right-click on a track and choose the Mixer Properties menu item, or use the Mix→Animation Mixer command from the menus at the top of the mixer, and make sure that the Normalize check box is checked on. (Normalize means limit the total to 100% in programmer-speak.)

To set the Mixer to Add each action on top of the others, make sure the Normalize button is unchecked.

THE SUBWOOFER: AT A GLANCE

The completed Subwoofer scene

TOPICS COVERED

In this tutorial, we'll create animation actions, find them in the Mixer, then load them into Animation Tracks and mix them with the Blend Weights sliders to mix up a complex animation.

You'll learn how to:

- Store Poses
- Store Animation Clips
- Load Clips into the Mixer
- Blend and Mix Clips

MATERIALS REQUIRED

This tutorial uses the Mixer.speaker scene from the courseware that accompanies this book. That courseware may be downloaded from www.mesmer.com/books/xsicharacter.html if you do not already have the courseware loaded on your computer.

TUTORIAL: THE SUBWOOFER

To examine what is possible, we'll work with some action clips for a big Speaker sub-woofer cone and an associated volume knob and volume indicator. If you open the Mixer.speaker scene, you will find the models, without animation on them. The actions have already been stored and are waiting in the Mixer Sources. The Subwoofer has three actions. The first action, named "LowFrequencies", causes the woofer to move in and out slowly, and change color to the red range at maximum extension. Simultaneously, the indicator needle moves, because it has also been animated at the same time, and both objects were selected when the action was stored. The "Midfrequencies" action contains the woofer moving faster but not as far, and changing to green at maximum extension. The "HighFrequencies" action moves the woofer fastest and least far, and changes the cone to a light blue color.

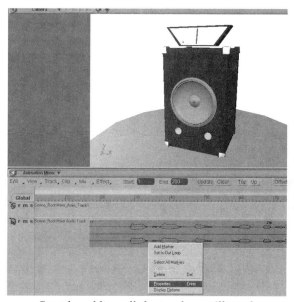

Start by adding all the tracks you'll need.

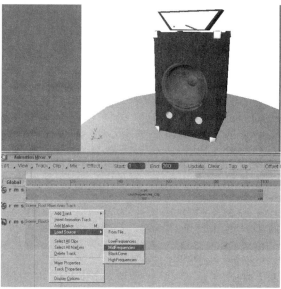

Add in the actions, either with the RMB context menu, or drag and drop from the explorer.

STEP 1: SET UP THE TRACKS

Select the body of the subwoofer, change a view to the Mixer, and hit Update if you don't see two minty green animation tracks. In the Mixer, create one more animation track by right-clicking over one of the empty animation tracks and choosing Add Track→Animation to make a total of three animation tracks, one for each frequency range on the subwoofer.

Also add one audio track, and import the audio file called "beats.aif" by right-clicking over the audio track, and choosing Load Source. Get the "beats.aif" file from the Audio folder of your courseware scene.

STEP 2 BRING IN THE LOW FREQUENCIES

Right-click over the top animation track, choose Load Source, and choose the LowFrequencies action to drop it into the mixer. Slide it left or right and adjust its length to extend completely from frame 1 to frame 100, clicking on the middle of the edge of the clip to stretch it out. Make sure the Blend slider is up to 100. Play back the animation to see the speaker cone move, the needle dance, and the cone change color as it's driven by the LowFrequencies action.

The low frequencies are the slower movements of the cone, and represent the bass portion of the audio file.

STEP 3: BRING IN THE MID FREQUENCIES

Right-click over the second track and bring in the MidFrequencies action, which has the action for the needle and the cone from the mid range of the audio track. Make sure the Blend slider for this track is up to 100%, and play it back to see it blended (averaged) with the low frequencies.

Now you're a Mix Engineer.

STEP 4: BRING IN THE HIGH FREQUENCIES

You guessed it: bring in, adjust, and blend the HighFrequencies action clip up to 100% to see it averaged in against the other ranges.

STEP 5: CHANGE THE MIXER BLEND METHOD

Right now, each frequency range is averaged in with the others, so the low range is brought down by the high range, and the mid range is made less effective by the other two. If real life were like this, the music would sound terrible. In real life each range is just added on top of the other, so that each component is at 100% all the time. Right-click over an animation track and choose the Mixer Properties option, and turn OFF Normalize to make the Mixer add the tracks together instead of averaging them. Play back the animation and see that the woofer cone moves more dramatically, and the colors are brighter.

STEP 6: THE MIX ENGINEER

You now can operate the Mixer like an audio mixing board. By sliding the blend sliders up and down you can bring each range in more or fade it out to affect the woofer less.

You can even set keys at certain frames to automatically change the mix over time. Set the playback to repeat, then play your scene and dynamically adjust the mix to your liking.

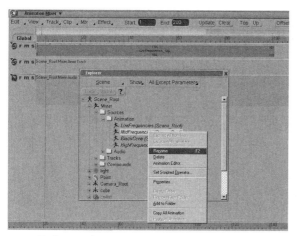

Delete and rename actions in the explorer.

DELETING AND RENAMING ACTIONS

Actions are stored in the Mixer folder, which is located under the Model node in the explorer view. The easiest way to see the Mixer node is to tap the 8 key to pop up a floating explorer window showing the scene, then select the Model node there (it will have an icon of a human form with arms and legs outstretched), and then tap the E key to change the scope of the explorer to Selection Scope, showing only that selected item and its properties.

If you expand the Mixer node, you'll see a folder for Sources and under that, one for Tracks, and another for Compounds. All the saved animation actions will be listed under Sources in the Animation subfolder. If you select one and right-click on it you can see the context-sensitive menu displaying what you can do to that action, including renaming it, and inspecting its properties. The Properties option will pop up a PPG that shows what animation curves on what objects are stored in that action, which is often interesting.

To delete a selected action, just tap the delete key on your keyboard.

MUTE, SOLO AND SIZE TRACKS

When editing actions, it is often useful to see only one track playing in the Mixer, or to just turn some tracks off to isolate other tracks. In the left margin of the Mixer are small circular icons with the letters "m", "s" and "r".

The "m" stands for Mute, which will take that track out of consideration in the scene until it is toggled back off.

The "s" stands for Solo, which is the opposite of mute, and means that all other tracks will be muted, and only that one track will play in the animation.

The "r" stands for ripple, which means that when you insert or move action clips, all other clips already in that mixer track will be moved later in time to make room for the new clip. This is not often as good an idea in animation as it is in video and audio editing, so it's best left off.

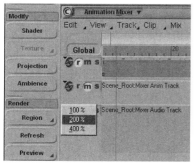

Mute and Solo help you fine-tune one track at a time.

Each track can also be made larger or smaller by clicking on the small drop-triangle icon at the top of the left margin.

CONCLUSION

In this chapter you took a whirlwind tour of ALL the major animation editing features in XSI. You went from setting keyframes with the k hotkey to fine-tuning them in the Animation Editor, then moved on to perfecting their timing with the Dopesheet. Next you learned to store your keyframe animation in easy to use containers called action clips, and then you learned how to blend and sequence actions in the Animation Mixer.

With this foundation, the world of Animation in XSI is opened to you, and all the rest is just practice and technique.

QUIZ

1. THE K HOTKEY ALWAYS SETS KEYS ON ALL THE TRANSFORMS AT ONCE.

    a. True

    b. False

2. HOW MANY ANIMATABLE PROPERTIES ARE THERE IN XSI?

    a. 1272 props

    b. 534 props

    c. Unknown and unlimited

3. THE ANIMATION CURVE SHOWS WHAT ALONG THE HORIZONTAL AXIS?

    a. Value

    b. Color

    c. Time

4. WHAT DO SWAP AND SNAP DO?

    a. Match one object to another

    b. Undo changes in the animation editor

    c. Flip animation curves horizontally or vertically

5. WHAT DOES THE REGION EDITOR DO?

    a. Moves whole animation curves in time

    b. Edits any number of points on one animation curve

    c. Edits a selection of keys within one time period on any number of animation curves

6. CAN YOU HAVE KEYS IN BETWEEN FRAMES?

    a. Yes

    b. No

    c. I don't know

7. CAN YOU SET THE VALUE OF MORE THAN ONE KEY AT A TIME?

    a. Yes

    b. No

    c. I don't know

8. WHICH CAN YOU CHANGE IN THE DOPESHEET?

    a. The value of a key

    b. The time of a key

    c. Both value and time

9. IN THE DOPESHEET YOU INSERT A REGION OF COPIED KEYS, AND ALL THE LATER KEYS SHIFT TO THE RIGHT AUTOMATICALLY. THE RIPPLE FUNCTION IS:

    a. On

    b. Off

    c. In auto-mode

10. WHAT S THE DEFAULT DURATION OF A STORED POSE CLIP?

    a. 10 frames

    b. 20 frames

    c. 5 frames

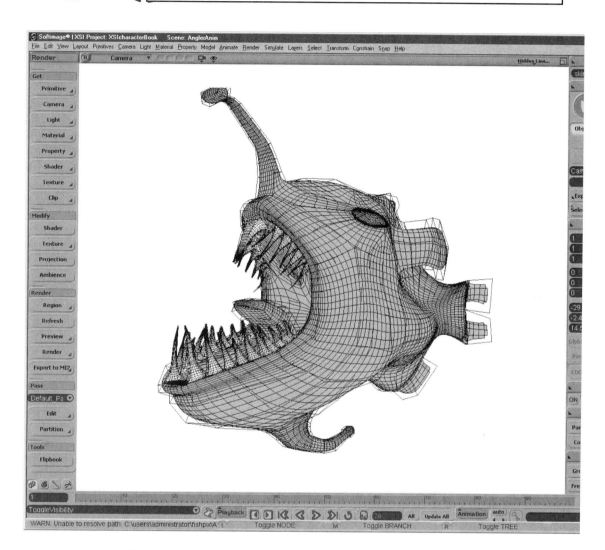

IN THIS CHAPTER YOU WILL LEARN ABOUT:

- How to choose whether to work on polygons or NURBS
- All about Polygon terminology
- How to use the Polygon building tools
- How to create Objects starting with a polygon primitive
- The process of sculpting and gradual refinement
- What Subdivision Surfaces are, and how they work in XSI
- Sub-D Surface technique

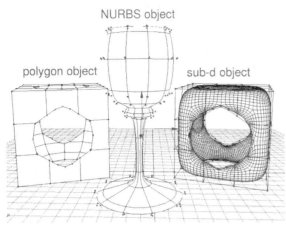

polygon object

NURBS object

sub-d object

*A NURBS object, a Polygon object, and a
Subdivision object*

INTRODUCTION

XSI uses two main surface types for building objects: NURBS and Polygons. Each has distinct advantages and disadvantages, and so each one is better for some tasks than for others. NURBS are mathematically defined curving surfaces that are infinitely smooth, while polygonal surfaces are made up of many straight line segments. This means that it is easier to make (and edit) a really smooth NURBS surface than a really smooth polygonal surface. However, NURBS are always rectangular patches, and are very hard to connect together into more complex shapes. Using polygon modeling tools and techniques, an artist can easily make shapes of whatever topology he wishes (not just rectangular). Separate Polygon objects are easy to merge together into one object, and won't show seams. And, best of all, new Subdivision Surface tools can turn Polygon mesh objects into very smooth surfaces, just like NURBS.

Even though XSI has some fantastic tools for easing the pain of NURBS modeling, like Surface Assemble and the Continuity manager, building characters is just plain easier with polygons, and so it's the technique we'll use for character modeling throughout this book.

POLYGON MODELING HISTORY AND USES

Way back in the early days of CAD, a schism developed in software makers. Initial systems built for design of cars and planes and other mechanical devices tended to represent surfaces as either Solids or Surfaces. In a Solid modeler, a shape like a rollerblade wheel is a solid form, with material inside and a surface boundary that is mathematically perfectly smooth. Engineering software like Catia and Pro-Engineer use this method. In a Surface modeler, objects have no density; no material inside their shapes. Objects are just infinitely thin shells surrounding nothingness. Those shells tended to be built of many small line segments, connecting the dots to form a surface Mesh. The Solids-based software became more appropriate for manufacturing, where the surfaces had to be precise and manufacturable, while surface modelers evolved towards games and entertainment, where objects just have to look good. Now virtually all entertainment modeling and animation systems, like XSI, are surface modelers. In surface meshes, the simplest way to connect the dots was with straight lines. An object created from a series of dots connected by straight lines is called a polygon mesh.

POLYGONS IN GAME ENGINES

One of the big advantages of polygons is that they are simple to display on-screen. All a computer has to do is transpose the straight lines onto a view plane, fill in the shape either with a solid color, a shade, or a texture map, and move on to the next polygon. As a result, where computers need to draw to the screen rapidly, polygons have been used most often. How many times each second the game can draw the screen is largely dependent on how many polygons are in the scene. As a result, early 3D game systems had very limited polygon "budgets", and were able to display only 2,000 to 5,000 polygons per frame while drawing 30 frames per second.

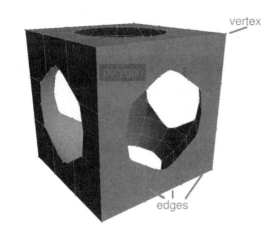

A polygon is a shape defined by straight edges.

All NURBS objects are broken down to triangles at render time.

More modern game machines have increased in power to the extent that they can easily draw more polygons per frame than there are pixels on the screen, resulting in near-perfect resolution, very crisp images, and few visible polygon artifacts. Certainly, the next step will be to use the ever-increasing computational power to draw more complex curved surfaces, but for now games still rely heavily on polygonal modeling.

POLYGONS IN THE RENDERER

Even when surfaces are represented as NURBS or other smooth patches, they must still be broken down into polygons to be drawn to the screen for the shaded and textured display. What's more, the rendering engine in XSI (called mental ray) must break down each curved surface into many smaller polygons before the rendering can commence. This process of breaking a curved surface up into polygons (usually triangles) is called tessellation. If few polygons are created to represent the curved surface, the object will appear chunky onscreen. When more polygons are used to represent the NURBS object, the final render gets smoother. Generally, if polygon lines are less than 5 pixels long onscreen, you can't perceive them as straight lines.

POLYGONS IN SUBDIVISION SURFACE MODELING

Subdivision Surface modeling is an extremely exciting innovation creating a new workflow that rewards artists by functioning in a more human way. Subdivision surfaces work by taking a polygonal cage as a starting point and progressively refining it, rounding corners, and smoothing edges, to produce a smooth, organic surface from a hard, chunky polygonal shape. The thing to remember is that you as the artist do all your sculpting with the polygonal cage. As a result, polygonal modeling has never been more vital, and XSI has fantastic tools for sculpting with polygons.

SCANNED MODELS AND POINT CLOUDS

Sometimes it makes sense to use a data collection device of some kind to capture the shape of an object you need in 3D, rather than modeling it by hand in the computer.

Desktop-sized stylus scanners are designed to let you touch points directly on a small model and capture that location as a point in space. After you pick points all over the object you have a representation of its surface, generally saved directly as a polygonal mesh, often in the .dxf format.

3D scanners can be used with objects as large as a human, and often use a rotating head with a laser to sample points on the object surface. This method generates a lot of data points.

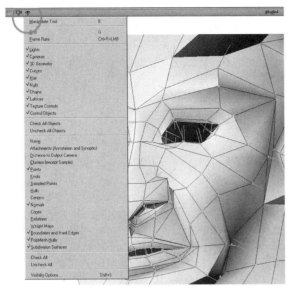

Adjust the options in the View menu to show boundaries, points, and normals.

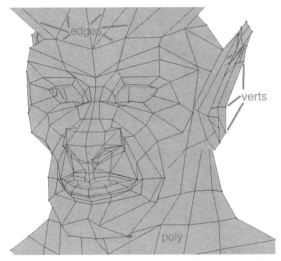

Poly meshes are made up of vertices, edges, and polygons.

POLYGON TERMINOLOGY

Polygons are simple, but there is some terminology to learn first, before we begin exploring the polygon tools in XSI. First, let's change the feedback that XSI gives us so that we can see the parts of the polygon being talked about.

In the Camera view, go to the Show menu, which is located under the eye-shaped icon at the center of the View title bar, and make sure that Points, Normals, and Boundaries are checked on, so they will show up in the Camera view.

Now get a Primitive→Polygon Mesh→Sphere and examine it in the Camera view.

Each polygonal mesh is made up of many smaller individual polygons. A polygon is a geometric shape with at least three sides. Three-sided polygons are called triangles, four-sided polygons are called quads, and polygons with more than four sides are called n-sided polygons. A polygon can generally have as many as 255 sides, but it's a much better idea to keep them simple. A complex polygon with many sides can always be broken up into more polygons each with fewer sides.

EDGES

The side of a polygon is called an edge. When an edge of one polygon abuts the neighboring polygon, we say that the edge is shared, or closed. When the edge is on the outside of the shape, or abutting a hole, we say that the edge is open.

VERTEX, VERTICES

The points in space that connect the edges are called vertices. A single point is called a vertex. Vertices are located in Cartesian space with values for the X-, Y-, and Z-axis, so we might say that a vertex is at –3,5,8, which would mean that it is 3 units in the negative direction in X, 5 units up in Y, and 8 units forward in Z, relative to the global center.

NORMALS

Each polygonal mesh, being an infinitely thin shell of a surface, has an inside and an outside. Since the render can render just the inside, just the outside, or both, it's important to know which way the surface is facing.

If you built an object that was inside-out (and this happens a lot) then it might not shade or render correctly. The best way to check the direction of the surface is to examine the Normals. Normals are the thin blue lines radiating from each vertex like spiky blue hair. Normals extend in the outside direction of the surface. Technically, they are perpendicular to the surface, but sometimes we just call that "normal to the surface". If the normals are pointing inside your object, it's inside-out and needs to be inverted.

Try using the Modify→Surface→Inverse Normals command on a sphere to see what that would look like.

It is very important that all the polygons in a mesh have normals facing the same direction. Imagine that if some of the polygons faced out in your sphere and some faced in, it would be really hard to figure out how to render it correctly. If you were developing the model for use in a real-time renderer, it would show strange holes and artifacts in the object that would look bad. As a result, you should pay attention to the Normal direction as you build polygon objects. Generally, XSI tries to not let you create such mixed polygon surfaces, but should you accidentally create one, you can select just one polygon (covered next) and invert just that selected polygon with Modify→Poly Mesh→Invert Polygons.

So, to repeat the terminology: polygonal meshes are made up of polygons, and polygons are made up of vertices and edges. Polygons, vertices, and edges are called components. You will work with each type of component using that component mode from the filter selection at the top-right of the Main Command Panel (MCP).

THE POLYGON COMPONENTS FILTER

Each component type (polygon, edge, and vertex) can be selected so that you can work with it. You can select just one at a time or groups of components. You cannot, however, select some edges and vertices at the same time; it's one component type at a time. This one-at-a-time selection method is called a Filter. With the Polygon selection filter active you can only select polygons, with the Edge filter on you just select Edges, and so on.

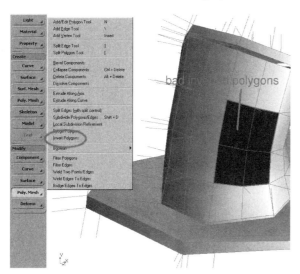

The Selection Filter is located in the MCP near the top. Since point (vertex), edge, and polygon are so common, buttons for just those filters appear automatically in the MCP whenever you have a polygon object selected. They do not show when you have a NURBS object selected.

When you click on the Point button, you can select points using the standard selection tools, by holding the Space bar and clicking on vertices or dragging a rectangle around them. Similarly, if you click the Edge button at the top-left of the MCP, you can select groups of Edges. The Polygon button filters the selection tool so that it only works on Polygons.

Good normals all face the same direction: out.

You can choose which components to select with the filter in the MCP.

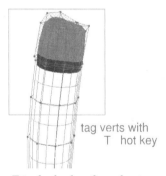

tag verts with
T hot key

T is the hotkey for selecting and unselecting vertices.

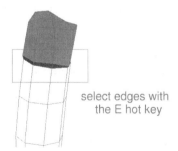

select edges with
the E hot key

E and I are hotkeys for selecting edges.

SETTING SELECTION PREFERENCES

There are two selection methods in XSI: the standard Windows method, which uses Shift and CTRL to extend selections, and the Softimage 3D Selection model. Since the Windows method is a bad joke, we'll refer only to the Softimage 3D Selection model in this book. Please make sure that your copy of XSI is set to use the Softimage 3D selection model by opening the Selection menu at the top-right of the MCP and making sure that all three menu items are checked on: Softimage 3D Selection Model, Extended Component Selection, and Select Single Object in Region.

While you are at it, check the File→User Preferences→Interaction tab and make certain that Sticky Keys is OFF.

Note: You need a good three-button mouse for polygon modeling, because you need to use one finger per button. The kind with a wheel in the middle just won't do, because your middle finger doesn't stay there easily. If you have a wheel mouse, get a regular three-button mouse and see how you like it.

SELECTING COMPONENTS

While there are buttons in the MCP which activate the component filters, using them would be very slow. You would have to take your eyes off the object you are working on, move the mouse cursor up to the MCP, make a change, then go back to the object, hold the Space bar and make the selection. Since you'll be doing this thousands of times each day as you sculpt, that method just won't do. The faster way is to use the hotkeys for component selection.

SELECTING VERTICES

If you hold down the T key with your left hand you can select, deselect, and toggle vertices with the three mouse buttons, respectively. With the T hotkey down, drag a rectangle selection around some of the vertices on your sphere. Note that the vertices become tagged in red (hotkey T for Tagged). Also note that the Point filter is automatically enabled when you hold the T key, and stays on until you tap the Space bar to re-enter the object selection mode.

If you want to add to the group of selected points, just hold T again and drag a rectangle around those points using the Left Mouse Button, and they will be added to the others already tagged in red. If some points became selected that you didn't want, drag a rectangle around those with the Middle Mouse Button and note that they are removed from the tagged group. Try dragging a rectangle around the whole sphere with the Right Mouse Button, and see that the tagged group is inverted: those that were not tagged now are, and those that were tagged are no longer. This convention – where the Left Mouse Button adds to the group, the Middle removes, and the Right toggles – is called the Extended Component Selection model, and works for all components.

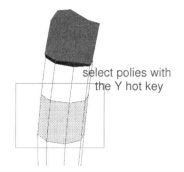

select polies with
the Y hot key

*Y and U are hotkeys for selecting
and deselecting polygons.*

SELECTING EDGES

If you hold down the E key with your left hand (hotkey E for Edge) you can select, deselect, and toggle edges with the three mouse buttons. The Left Mouse Button adds edges to the selection, the Middle deselects edges, and the Right toggles edges. Selected edges show in red, deselected edges show in amber. Drawing a selection rectangle will select all edges that are within the rectangle or touch the rectangle, on both sides of the object. The hot hey I will also select edges by raycast, as your cursor rolls over them.

SELECTING POLYGONS

Polygons are special – they have two different component selection hotkeys. The Y hotkey selects polygons in the same way that you select edges and vertices, by dragging a rectangle that selects all the polygons that are entirely within the selection rectangle.

The selected polygons will show in translucent red. The problem is that while you are working in shaded view, you might be selecting polygons on the back of the object without knowing it, and messing up your model. To solve this problem, the U hotkey was pressed into service. When you hold the U key, you can click over the middle of a polygon, and only the polygon facing out of the model towards you will be selected. This is called Raycasting, and it is very useful. You can also hold U while dragging a stroke across the model to paint in a selection. As usual, the extended component selection model means that the Left Mouse Button adds to the selection, the Middle removes polygons from the selection, and the Right Mouse Button toggles polygons.

USING THE HOTKEYS

Remember that the hotkeys are crucial to fast, efficient workflow. Practice with them until they are second nature. Hotkey E works on edges, T selects vertices, Y selects polygons by rectangle, and U selects polygons by raycasting.

For the truly adventurous, each of these can also be modified with the other selection tools, freeform and lasso, though this requires the manual gymnastics waggishly called "Finger Olympics".

TRANSFORMING EDGES, VERTICES, AND POLYGONS

Once you have a component or a group of components selected, you can sculpt the shape of the polygon object by transforming them. Polygons, vertices, and edges can be scaled, rotated, and translated to change the shape of the object.

You may also move individual vertices by holding the M (for Move points) hotkey, click-and-holding with your mouse at an individual vertex, and dragging to translate it.

When you have a component or group of components selected and you plan to transform them, the big question is always, "Transform them relative to what?"

To clarify that: polygons, vertices and edges can be moved relative either to the view, the global object, or the local axis of the selected components.

You can change the way that the components are transformed by clicking on the mode buttons in the MCP, right below the Transform cells: Global, Local, and View.

Generally, the most useful method when working with components is the local mode. When you translate a single component in the local mode, that component moves relative to its local axis. When translating a polygon, for instance, local Y is always normal to the surface (out from the surface) no matter how the polygon is facing in global space.

When you have more than one component selected in a contiguous block (that means that they are touching), then there is only one local axis for all the touching components together. That axis is the average of all the individual axes. Keep in mind that when the components are not touching, each has its own axis.

You can choose to see just one axis or many axes in this case in the File/User Prefs dialog, in the Interaction Tab, by toggling on the Show Multiple Transformation Axes check box.

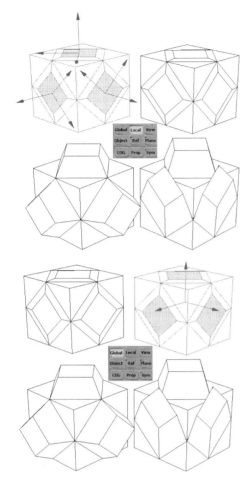

The local mode transforms polygons, edges, and vertices relative to their own centers.

In global transformation mode, the selected components move relative to the global axis, which is always oriented the same. If you want to move some polygons exactly up in Y, use global mode.

In the view mode, the selected components will move relative to whatever view window your mouse is in when you click and drag the Left Mouse Button. This is hard to control, so use it carefully, and then generally in the 3d perspective view.

Now try out transforming the components:

1. Try selecting every other polygon in a ring around the equator of your sphere (use U to raycast polygons), and in local mode carefully translate them in each axis to see the effect.

2. Try selecting all the edges around the middle of the sphere with the E hotkey, and scale them uniformly. See the effect that shortening them will have on the circumference of the sphere.

3. Try selecting a group of vertices near the top of the sphere with T, then extend that selection to include the similar points around the bottom again with T and the Right Mouse Button. Translate, scale, and rotate these vertices to see the effect.

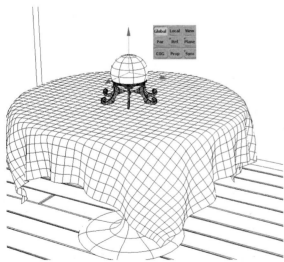

Global translation is good for precision, while view mode is good for organic modeling.

DRAWING POLYGONS FROM SCRATCH AND ALIGNING EDGES

	Selected	Total
Objects	0	--
Triangles	188	--
Polygons	1	82

Local transformation is very useful, because each poly goes in a different direction.

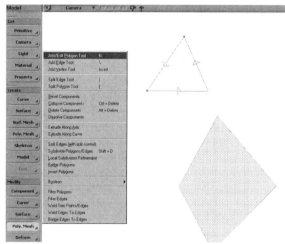

Use Add/Edit Polygon to start from scratch, or to patch holes in a poly mesh.

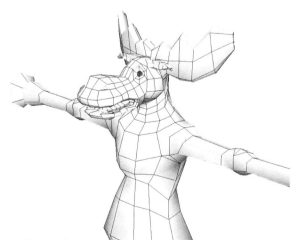

This model came from Maya, with some bad edges shown as Boundaries.

You may also draw polygons one at a time by plotting points in space for the vertices, either starting from scratch or by sharing an edge with an existing polygon.

The important thing to understand when manually drawing polygons is that the polygons you draw must be kept facing the same direction as those around them. In other words, you want the normals of the new polygons you are drawing to match the direction of the normals all around them. If you drew one polygon with normals facing the wrong way, that might show up as a hole, or create problems later in modeling.

The direction that you draw the vertices of the polygon (either clockwise or counter-clockwise) determines which direction the normals will face. XSI will also warn you when you create a bad polygon by highlighting the edge between the good and bad polygons in green, as long as you have turned on Show Boundaries in the Show menu at the top of the view window you are using.

To draw a polygon from scratch, choose the Add/Edit Polygon tool from the Polygon Mesh menu in the Model Module, and click with the Left Mouse Button to drop the first vertex in space wherever your mouse cursor is pointing. Move your cursor and click again to drop the next vertex. A line will connect the two, showing where the edge will be, with an arrow showing the correct direction of the polygon. Click a third time to drop the next vertex, and complete the most basic polygon, a triangle. You may continue to click if you wish to create a polygon with more edges. If you click with the Middle Mouse Button you will start a new polygon.

The Add Polygon tool wants to connect the new polygon you are drawing to the existing polygons that you have drawn already whenever possible. If you click on a vertex of the selected polygon while in the Add Polygon tool, that vertex will be used and shared, and any edges that can be drawn in will also be added and shared. This intelligence ensures that your polygon geometry is as accurate as possible, that it shares vertices and edges whenever possible, and that the normals all point in a consistent direction.

When you are done with that tool, tap the Escape key on your keyboard to escape the tool and stop dropping vertices. Try to use the hotkey for Add Polygon, which is N, instead of the menu command.

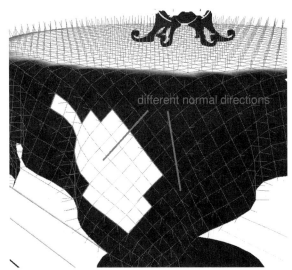

It's a sad day when neighboring polygons turn against each other.

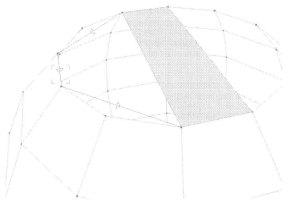

It's easiest to click on edges to add a new polygon to an existing mesh.

Invert Surface turns the whole object inside-out, while Invert Polygons flips just the selected polygons.

Often you have an existing polygon mesh, and want to add some new polygons onto it. Reasons for this task include patching holes, and adding detail. In these cases it's important to add the new polygons in so that they share the vertices and edges at their borders. Sharing the vertices and edges ensures that there will be no seam visible, and requires less memory to store since there are fewer vertices and edges.

To create a new polygon that shares one or more edge with an existing polygon, first select the existing polygon object and choose the Add/Edit Polygon tool, or just hold the N hotkey. Now XSI is in the Add Polygon mode, and is waiting for you to tell it where to add in the new polygon.

Note: you can only add a new polygon to an open edge. You cannot build a new polygon using an edge that is already shared.

Click with the Left Mouse Button on the first open edge you wish to share, then on the second edge you wish to share. If you pick on the vertices of the mesh instead of the edges, XSI cannot ensure that you are building the new polygon in the right direction, and so the normals may be reversed. When you pick the second vertex, if it's a bad choice XSI will prompt you to make a new choice. For this reason it's a better idea to use the edges than the vertices when adding polygons to an object.

CONFORMING NORMALS

Sometimes, despite your best efforts you create – or are given – a model with weird normal orientations.

If all the normals of an object seem to be facing inside, you can turn the object inside-out with the Modify→Surface→Inverse Normals command. If only a single polygon is inverted, you can select that polygon (use U for polygon raycast) and choose the command Modify→Poly Mesh→Invert Polygons.

When you receive models from other people, make it a habit to turn on Boundaries and check the model for green edges that would indicate bad edge orientation, and fix the model up by conforming the Normals before you try to work with it.

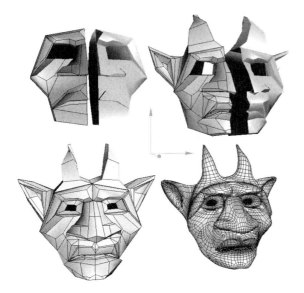

The gargoyle started out as a cube.

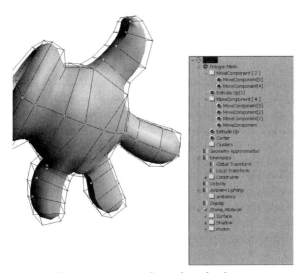

This Operator stack needs to be frozen.

SERIOUS POLY MODELING

Usually, the most productive manner of polygon modeling is to start with a primitive object, and then refine that shape gradually to get the shape that you want. When you use this method, there is no right or wrong command to use at any given time, no set sequence of steps that must be followed, and no clear point at which you are done. You just look at what you have, imagine how you could make it better, and gradually refine the model. By turning it in the Camera view, you examine the form of the model, and make decisions about how you could move polygons around, where you could add more edges to increase detail, and where you could translate vertices to make a more perfect shape.

You may choose a primitive object that is similar in some way to the shape of the object you are modeling. Most people start with either a cube (easiest), a cylinder, or a sphere.

As you create more detail on the object by adding edges and duplicating polygons, the model takes on the shape you want.

Since this is a process of refinement, it makes sense to approach the task with more of an artistic, sculptural approach than the technical engineering approach required of NURBS modeling.

Start with a drawing or picture of the object you want to end up with, preferably in front, side and top views. Then consider the volume of the object, and the proportions. Don't worry at all about the details of the surface, just modify the polygonal primitive to match the volume of the object. As you add more detail, pay attention to the proportions of the model first and foremost.

THE OPERATOR STACK, IMMEDIATE MODE, AND FREEZE

When you execute a command on the polygon primitive object, it becomes an operator in the operator stack. Each and every move – each added vertex, each added edge, and each transformation of a component – is logged. In many ways, the model is actually still a primitive, and XSI rebuilds it constantly, repeating each command you have ever made. Since you'll make hundreds or thousands of changes to the model while sculpting it into a new shape, this method is overkill, and will slow down your productivity. There are two options to resolve this problem.

The Freeze button compacts the Operator stack just once when you click it.

Immediate mode is a toggle. When on, operators are frozen constantly.

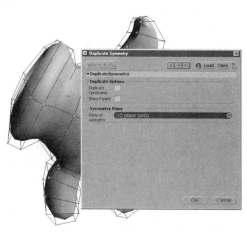

If the command requires input, you'll have to click OK to go on.

FREEZE

When you use the Freeze Operator Stack command from the Edit menu in the MCP, or click the Freeze button near the bottom of the MCP (which does the same thing), all the changes that have been preserved in order in the operator stack will be combined and cooked down into the final shape of the mesh, then discarded. After a Freeze operator stack command you will be left with a simple polygon mesh in the same shape it was before, but with no operators. While you cannot now edit those operators, you could always Undo (CTRL-Z) to restore the operator stack.

IMMEDIATE MODE

It is sometimes a hassle to first create a big operator stack then freeze it to remove the stack, so the Immediate mode was invented. When the Immediate mode is toggled on with the Immed button at the bottom of the MCP, operations are frozen as soon as they are completed, so that no giant operator stack is created. This does not mean that Undo won't work – it still remembers the last 20 things you've done so you can recover from mistakes.

If the operator is something that never requires you to see a Property Editor, like moving a point with the M hotkey, the operation will just be done and frozen without any further intervention on your part. If the operator requires a Property Editor to take input, like the CTRL-D Extrude command, the Property Editor will open as a modal dialog box with OK and Cancel buttons. You can make changes and when you click OK: the command will execute and the operation will be frozen.

Immediate mode is the most convenient way to work when polygon modeling.

POLYGON DUPLICATE MEANS EXTRUDE

When polygon modeling, you are essentially creating new polygons exactly where you want them, and shaping them how you want them to be shaped. The first way to do that is to extrude selected polygons. In XSI, you can execute the Extrude Along Axis command from the Polygon Mesh menu or you can use the hotkey for Duplicate, CTRL-D. When you select one or more polygons and duplicate (extrude) them, new polygons are created all the around the initial polygon, connecting the edges of the selected polygon to the edges that are left behind. You may then scale the selected polygon to make it smaller, leaving a border of new polygons, or translate it to change the shape of the object. Whether you use Extrude along Axis or CTRL-D, an Extrude property is added to the object. If you select the object with the Space bar, and use the Selection explorer in the MCP to display the Extrude Property page, you may set the extrusion length and many other parameters. It is often faster to just adjust the selected and extruded polygon using the regular transforms in the MCP.

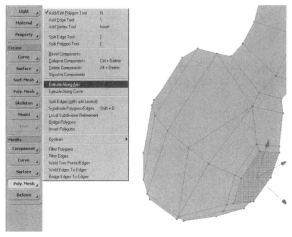

Extruding a polygon creates a skirt of new polygons around it.

Try selecting every other polygon around the circumference of a polygonal sphere, and extruding the polygons with the CTRL-D hotkey. The Polygon Extrude command does create an operator by default, so if you have Immediate mode on, or have Auto-Popup of Property Editors toggled on in the User→Preferences, you will see a Property Editor with a variety of options for different extrusion options. Generally the default values are what you want, so close the PE or click OK to dismiss the dialog.

Check your transformation mode and make sure that it is on Local. Scale the polygons, which are still selected, uniformly in X and Z (height and width in local mode) by clicking on the scale transform cells, and holding your Left and Right Mouse Buttons. Make them just a bit smaller, so there is a border.

Now try translating the selected polygons inside the sphere a little bit, creating recessed windows. Practice on your own with Extrude/Duplicate polygons.

EXTRUDE ALONG CURVE

You may also extrude selected polygons along a curve, creating strange modeling effects. In the front view, draw a simple curve with four points using the Create→Curve→Draw CV NURBS Curve command. On a new polygon mesh sphere, select some polygons that do not touch each other. Use the Polygon Mesh→Extrude Along Curve menu command to start the tool, then pick the curve you drew to complete the command. Select the resulting mesh as an object (change the filter to Object or just use the Space bar) and then Get the PE (Property Editor) for the Extrude Op command from the Selection button in the MCP, and interactively adjust the Subdivisions and the transforms to see the result.

Freeze the object when you are done, to remove the Extrude operator from the stack and finalize your modeling decisions.

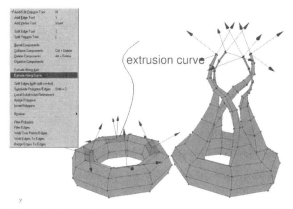

Extrude Along Curve is a great way to animate tentacles.

DUPLICATING A VERTEX

You can also duplicate a Vertex by tagging it and using the CTRL-D hotkey. This interesting new feature will create a series of edges around the vertex, so that if you pulled it from the surface it would form a pyramid.

DUPLICATING AN EDGE

You may duplicate an Edge by selecting it with the E hotkey (select edges by rectangle) and then using the CTRL-D (Duplicate) hotkey. When an edge is duplicated it creates a new set of edges connecting it to the neighboring edges, then moves the original edge a short distance out from the object along the normal direction. This also creates new polygons, so extruding an edge is also a good way to add detail to an object.

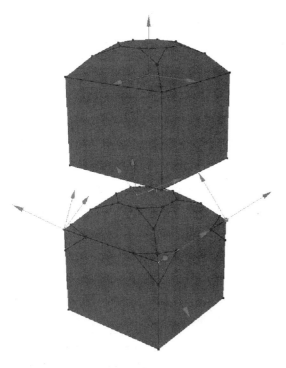

Duplicating a vertex creates new vertices around it.

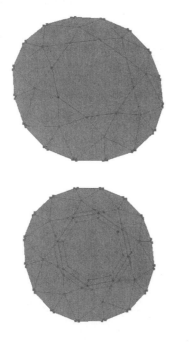

Duplicating an edge creates new edges around the original.

ADD EDGE

Many times a fantastic way to add more detail is to split one polygon into two. XSI has a fantastic tool for dividing polygons exactly how you want them, called Add Edge. Using Add Edge, you can either create just a new edge stretching from two existing vertices on the same polygon, or you can add a new vertex along the edge of a polygon and connect it to an existing vertex, or create another new vertex to join it to with a new edge. The tool provides excellent feedback as you work, and will not let you create bad edges.

To use Add Edge, first select the polygon object, then click on the Polygon Mesh➔Add Edge command and move your mouse over the mesh. Note that as you move over vertices and edges they are highlighted in Red to indicate which you are about to split. Click to approve a starting vertex or edge, and then move your mouse to the opposite vertex of the same polygon, and click to select it. A new edge will be created connecting the two vertices. The tool cannot connect vertices that are not part of the same polygon. Tap the Escape key on your keyboard to complete the tool so you can start over fresh.

Try it again, but this time start with an edge, and rather than clicking, click and hold your Left Mouse Button to keep the command active, and slide the point back and forth along the edge by dragging the mouse left and right. When you have the spot you want, let off the mouse button. Wave your mouse over another edge of the same polygon (add edge cannot work across multiple polygons in one shot) and click again to split the polygon in two. Note that this time new vertices were also created, in addition to the edge.

You can use the Add Edge tool to chain together edges, each one starting where the last left off. On your sphere, start in the middle of an edge, and click in the middle of the next edge over. Then, immediately click with the Left Mouse Button again on the next edge along the sphere to continue the edge, and keep going around the sphere. When done, you can click the Right Mouse Button to stay in the tool but choose a new starting position for a new edge. You can stay in the tool as long as you have edges to create, then tap the Escape key on your keyboard to quit the tool.

SPLIT EDGE AND SPLIT POLYGON

When you split an edge, you are really adding a new vertex along that edge. To do this, hold the] (right bracket) key, which is the hotkey for Modify→Split Edge Tool, and then point your mouse at an edge in your polygonal mesh. The edge under your mouse will be highlighted, and when you click with your Left Mouse Button (and hold it) a new vertex will appear. You can then slide that vertex along the edge to find the point where you want to place it. Often while modeling you need to keep the vertices you add exactly even and accurate. You can use the midpoint snapping key, CTRL, to find the exact midpoint of the edge, or you can click with the Middle Mouse Button to add vertices to other parallel edges.

When you split a polygon, you are creating a series of new edges and new vertices, all coming together at a point on the surface of the polygon you have selected. The Split Polygon tool, hotkey [(left bracket), breaks one polygon into several new polygons in this manner. Try this out: Choose Modify→Poly Mesh→Split Polygon Tool, and aim your mouse over polygons in a polygon mesh. The polygons under your mouse will highlight, and when you click with the Left Mouse Button you add new edges in a cross pattern, perpendicular to the edges of the polygon. The Middle Mouse Button adds new edges from the vertices into the middle of the polygon. The Right Mouse Button adds new edges from the midpoint of each edge on the polygon, to some non-perpendicular point inside the polygon.

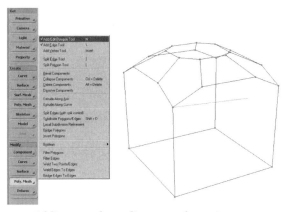

Adding an edge splits one polygon into two.

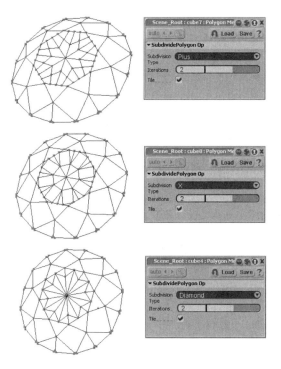

The PPG for the SubdividePolygon OP can divide the polygon in different patterns.

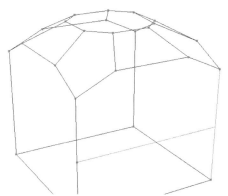

Use the hotkey \ to add edges, and modify it with CTRL to split evenly.

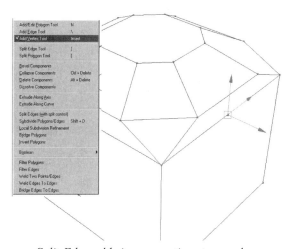

Split Edge adds in new vertices to an edge.

The completed, rendered Manta Ray

EXERCISE: MANTA RAY

Modeling with polygons is a fundamentally different process from most other forms of computer modeling. It's more like traditional art, in that there is no right or wrong way to do it, and you are free to continue working on the model until you like the results. You will usually want to start with the general and work to the particular. Another way of saying that is to start working out the shape of the broad form, then gradually refine it as you go, until you decide you are done. You will be most effective if you leave the smallest features for last. Since there are no absolutely right or wrong steps, we'll need a different format for the modeling exercises presented here.

Instead of giving you specific tools to use in discreet steps, this chapter will present a series of modeling exercises showing you the progression of the model, along with suggestions about how to approach building it. The exact steps used will be up to you.

Step 1: Sketch or research what a Manta looks like. Get an idea in your mind about what you want it to look like. In this case, the manta has a rounded bulge in the center of the body, sloping down to smooth, thin wings that are roughly triangular, but with square tips.

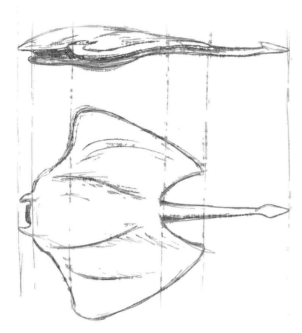

A quick sketch of the Manta

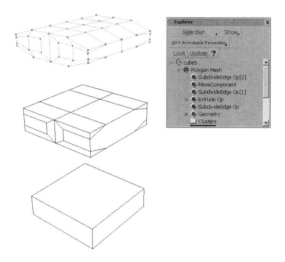

Start with a rotated, flattened poly cube.

Step 2: Decide how to start. It's often easiest to start with a primitive shape, and this is no exception. A flattened polygon Sphere isn't too far off the shape of a Manta. Get a polygon sphere, and rotate it so the poles are flat along the Z-axis. The poles will be front and back along the Manta. Flatten the Sphere, then experiment to find out how many subdivisions in the U and V you'll need. You'll want to create enough detail in the sphere to start with to make your job easy. Too many rows will mean that you have more to do, but too few rows will mean that you have to add edges to get enough detail to rough out the shape.

Step 3: Freeze the sphere to simplify the operator stack, and turn on Immediate mode, so your every change is not logged as a new operator. Now in the overhead view, tag points to sculpt the sphere in to the rough shape of the manta.

Step 4: Now look at the sphere edge-on (front and side views). Tag the points on the wings and scale them to be flatter. You don't have to do this all in one move. Make different tagging groups as needed. Try to imagine a bulge in the middle of the manta running down the axis of the creature.

Step 5: Add some detail for the tail. You can select the polygons in the middle of the back of the manta, and pull them a bit in local Y, which will be out away from the body. Duplicate them (extrude them) with CTRL-D and translate them some more, and make them smaller. Repeat this until you have pulled out a tail.

Step 6: Add some horns to the front of the manta, again selecting polygons, extruding them, and transforming them.

Step 7: Add a mouth. Select the polygons around the pole in the front of the manta, and delete them to make an opening. Scale the opening to be a flat scoop. Add edges in the middle of the mouth for the lip contour. Pull the outside of the lip out from the body, and the inside of the lip in towards the body.

Step 7: Look at your work all over and just keep making changes. Every once in a while save your model with a different revision number in the name so you can see your progress later. Add contours to the creature with new edges, and add protuberances by duplicating polygons. Sculpt the shape by moving vertices. When you like the results or run out of time, you are done!

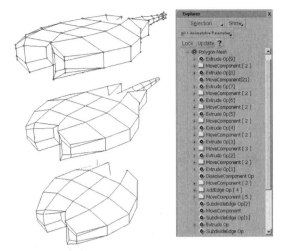

The horns and tail are now added

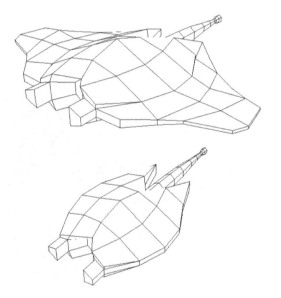

The basic wing shape

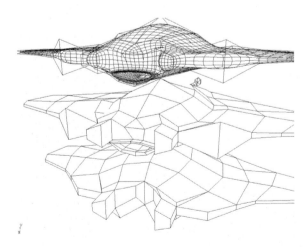

Here's the Manta mouth.

DELETING POLYGONS, VERTICES, AND EDGES

Just as you can add more polygons, vertices, and edges, you can also delete them. When you select a polygon or group of polygons with the hotkey U, you can delete the polygons with the Delete key on your keyboard, or the Edit→Delete Selected menu command from the MCP, leaving holes in the model. This tool is great for creating windows, doors, and other openings in polygonal models.

However, if you select either a vertex or an edge and use the Delete button or the Edit→Delete command, that component is removed, and XSI tries to patch the space by creating a bigger polygon surrounding it. This method of removing polygons is called Dissolving.

COLLAPSING POLYGONS, EDGES, AND VERTICES

When you collapse a component, something entirely different happens. Collapsing a polygon or an edge generally means to shrink that component down to a single point in space, and then replace it with a vertex. This keeps your surface whole and unbroken, which is generally a good thing.

However, when you select a Vertex and use the Poly Mesh→Collapse Component tool, it removes that vertex and all the edges that were connecting it, then creates a new polygon to patch the hole.

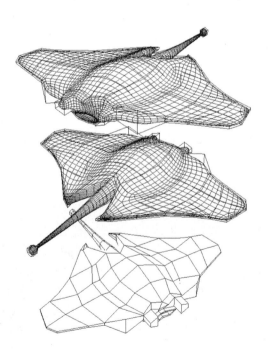

This is the completed rough shape

DISSOLVING EDGES, VERTICES AND POLYGONS

Dissolving a component is like deleting a component, but then the resulting hole is filled in with a new polygon so that the surface is still complete and unbroken.

EXERCISE: MODELING DIAMONDS

Diamonds and other jewels are a great study for polygon modeling, because they are in fact made up of perfectly flat facets just like polygon models are. The tough part about making jewels, however, is not adding detail, as it is in regular modeling. In jewels, your job is to start with a cube and actually remove slabs of the cube, slicing off bits and pieces to form the facets of the jewel.

Step 1: Mine your basic material. OK – it's a lot easier than it is in real life. Just get a primitive cube. Make it a little shorter in Y. By default, XSI tries to make all poly objects look smooth by shading flat surfaces differently across their surface. We don't want that, so we need to tell XSI to shade each facet so it looks flat. In the Geometry Approximation PPG for the cube, look in the Polygon Mesh tab, and change the Discontinuity Angle to 1, meaning that when facets meet at angles of more than 1 degree, XSI will leave a discontinuity (edge) there.

Diamonds rendered with caustics and global illumination

Step 2: The jewel needs to have facets on the top, and on the bottom. So, we'll need a line around the equator. Select all the edges around the middle (the vertical edges) and use Shift-D to split them in half. Because they are all parallel, XSI will connect the new vertices with an edge all the way around. Move that up to be closer to the top of the jewel, so the top facets are smaller.

Step 3: Slice off the top facets. You can select the top corner vertices, and use the Bevel command to slice them clean off, creating new edges. Enter Object mode, and look at the Bevel operator on the cube. Adjust the Bevel Ratio to your liking.

There will still be a vertical edge below the bevel, connecting to the midpoint of the jewel. We don't want this. One by one, select these edges and collapse them.

Step 4: Make the bottom pointy. Select the bottom polygon, and use Collapse from the context menu or the Poly Mesh menu so the jewel is now conical.

Add new edges from the midpoints of the facets down to the bottom to make eight facets around the bottom. When you add an edge with the \ hotkey, also hold CTRL to make sure the vertex goes in the exact middle of the edge.

Step 5: Make sub-facets on top. Sometimes you have to manually add edges where you want a facet, then delete the point rising up from the middle.

Step 6: Keep refining, adding edges to break up the big facets into smaller facets. When you have points sticking up out of facets, delete them to slice off the facet clean. Keep going until you like the results. Maybe do it again a few times, varying the pattern to get different cuts of jewels.

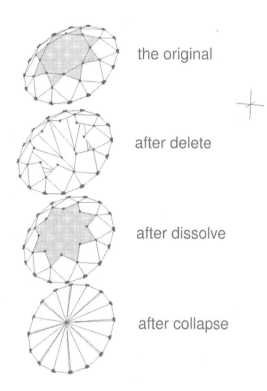

the original

after delete

after dissolve

after collapse

Delete, Dissolve, and Collapse all do different things.

KEEPING MODELS SYMMETRICAL

Often you'll find yourself modeling something that is symmetrical across a plane, like a human being. In a human face, for instance, the eye on the right side of the nose is pretty much the same as the eye on the left side of the nose. It seems like redundant work to have to model both eyes. In fact, you don't have to. It's easy to model on one half of a model and let XSI create the other half for you. Then, as a final step, you can merge the resulting meshes together into one object, when you want to test the model, or when you are actually done with it.

The process of automatically mirroring your work is as follows:

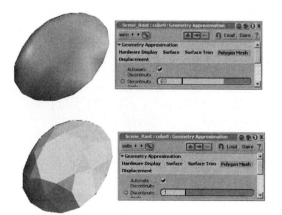

Discontinuity creates hard edges between polygons.

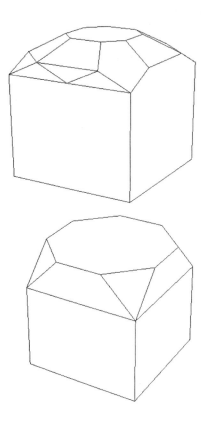

Start with a primitive cube, and add some edges.

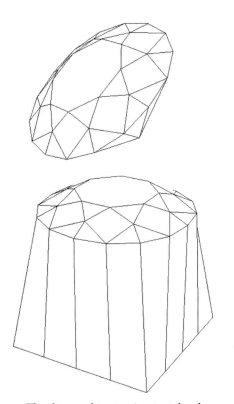

The diamond is starting to take shape.

Step 1: Although you can certainly mirror the object in any plane, we'll assume that your object is facing forward in the front view, and will therefore need to be symmetrical around the YZ plane. We'll then cut off half of the object, leaving a seam aligned in that plane.

Start with a primitive object or other shape that has vertices running down the middle, along the center of the global axis in Y. Select all the polygons on the left side of the center in the front view, by holding the Y hotkey (select polygon by rectangle) and drawing a selection rectangle around that half of the object. Be sure to get all the polygons on one side of the axis.

Step 2: Delete those selected polygons with the Delete key on your keyboard. In some cases you won't have a line of vertices perfectly located flat in the YZ plane, for instance if you started with a model that is slightly skewed, or were using proportional modeling, or just weren't very careful. In this case, you should move all the vertices of the seam to lie exactly in the YZ plane, so that later when you make the other half of the object, it connects perfectly without a gap or any overlapping points. It is a big help here to turn on Show Boundaries if you have not already (Show is the eyeball menu).

To move errant vertices to the exact YZ plane, tag those vertices on the boundary and then scale them all to 0 in X by typing the value 0 into the Scale X entry cell in the MCP.

Freeze the model to make XSI's job easier. This will keep crashing down to a minimum.

Step 3: Make an instance of your model. An instance is like a copy, only it dynamically remains the same as the original, even as you make changes to the original shape, adding and deleting polygons. In the MCP, choose the Edit→Duplicate/Instantiate→Instantiate Single command. A new object has been created, lying exactly on top of the original.

Step 4: Turn the instance inside-out to form the other half. With the instance selected (still) and in Object mode, scale the instance by -1 in X. This will turn it inside-out, mirrored on the YZ plane.

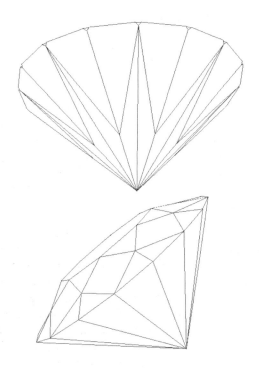

Manually define more triangular planes and chop off the extra vertex in the middle.

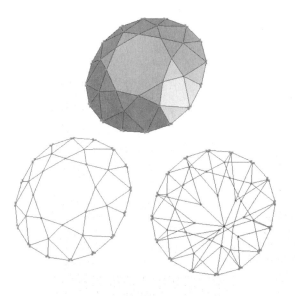

The finished gems

Step 5: Select the original again (on the right side of the front view), and turn on immediate mode in the MCP. This means that XSI won't keep an operator stack while you edit it (you can still Undo). Without the dynamic operator stack, XSI will be faster, more responsive, and a lot more stable. Try making some changes to your original model now, moving points, adding edges, etc., and see that the instance remains an exact copy of the original as it changes, no matter what you do. Be careful not to move any of the center seam vertices off the YZ plane, which would create a gap or overlap in the final model.

Step 6: After you have modeled to your heart's content, it's time to make one single model from the two halves. Turn the Immediate mode OFF in the MCP. Select both halves, and choose the Polygon Mesh➞Merge command. A new object will be created, out of both halves. Translate it up in vertical Y above the two halves. Since Immediate mode is off, you can still model on the original half, see it mirrored in the instance, and the final full model will update. This operator stack magic and relational model hierarchy will slow down XSI and make it unstable after a while, so although it certainly is cool, it's not a good idea to work dynamically with instances, new objects, and operator stacks.

MERGE AND BLEND POLYGON MESHES

You will frequently build models in parts and need to assemble them. Although creating a parent-child hierarchy is often good enough, many times in polygonal modeling you want to take two parts that are separate objects and combine them into one object with no seams. You can do this with the Merge and Blend commands.

The merge command takes two objects and looks for vertices and edges that are in the same place in space. This works best when the objects being merged each have an open edge to merge. When it finds vertices and edges on the two models that seem to be overlapping, it makes a new model with all the polygons of each, but shares the overlapping vertices and edges so that they form an unbroken mesh. The important thing is that the vertices must be right on top of each other. The easiest way to make this happen is to tag the points on the open edge of one object, and use the Snap to Point feature of XSI to move the points on the open edge of the second surface to the position of those on the first surface. Blend does the same thing as the Merge Command, but can connect points that don't lie in exactly the same point in space.

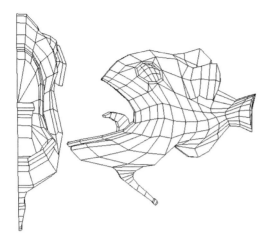

You'll often make just one half of a model.

A simple example is joining a leg and a torso:

Step 1: Open the MergePoints scene. Move the torso and leg into position, with their open edges as close as possible.

Step 2: Check the Snapping options, and make sure that Snap to Point is turned on, so you can easily pop one point onto another. Enable Snap by toggling the ON button in the Snap area of the MCP, and also toggling the Point button on and the Grid button off. If the Snap to Grid option is on, your vertex will snap all over the place, not just where you want it to go.

Step 3: Maximize the Camera view, and get a good angle on the area of interest. Use the M hotkey to move points. They should snap to points on the opposite surface. Remember that you can continue to move a point until you release the mouse button. If it goes to the wrong place, use Undo (CTRL-Z). Continue until the two open edges overlap exactly. It's OK to move more than one vertex to one on the opposite mesh (that's part of what is so great about polygons).

Step 4: Select one mesh, and run the Merge command from the Create→Poly Mesh menu. Pick the other surface to complete the command. A new object will be created, but you'll have to hide the others (or move them) to see it. In the Explorer or schematic, hide the old parts and examine the new one.

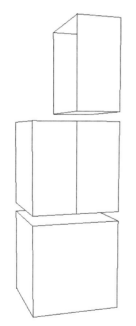

After you add edges right down the center, delete one half.

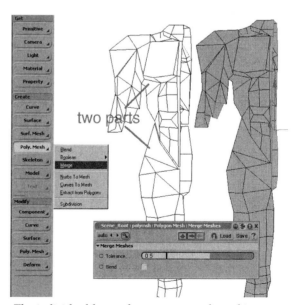

The individual leg and torso are now bound into one poly mesh.

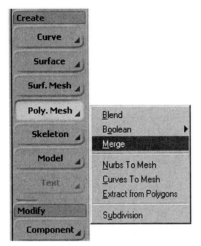

Merge takes two objects and makes one, sharing the vertices and edges that are common.

BOOLEANS AND POLYGONS

Very often the best strategy for making a complex shape is to build it up out of simpler shapes. The Boolean tool is an exercise of that strategy, with a twist. You see, the Boolean tool allows you to combine shapes in three different ways. Taking two simple shapes, you can add them together to make one shape that encompasses the whole of both together, you can subtract one from the other so that the second shape takes a bite out of the first, and you can make a single shape out of the space where the two shapes overlap.

These three options are described as a Union, a Difference, and an Intersection.

To understand the Boolean more completely, let's discuss it more precisely.

The Boolean tool always takes two shapes to start with, Shape A and Shape B. Each of those two shapes can be thought of as a volume in space. That volume is the area inside the surface of the object. (If the object is inside-out, or an unclosed shape, that can cause problems for the Boolean tool.)

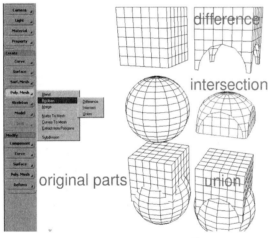

The three Booleans: Union, Difference, and Intersection

When you combine the volume of Shape A and Shape B into a single volume, that is called a Union.

When you subtract the second volume (B) from the first (A) that is called a Difference.

When you find only the volume that is common to both shapes – the volume that they share because they overlap – that is called an Intersection.

To use the Boolean tool, select the first shape, Shape A, and execute the command Create→Poly Mesh→Boolean→Difference. To complete the command, pick on Shape B.

The Boolean tool is an operator, so a new object will be created and it will have a Boolean Generator operator in its operator stack that you can edit. It will also be dynamically related to the original objects (until such time as you Freeze the operator stack) so you can continue to adjust the placement or shape of the original shapes to see the resulting shape of the Boolean.

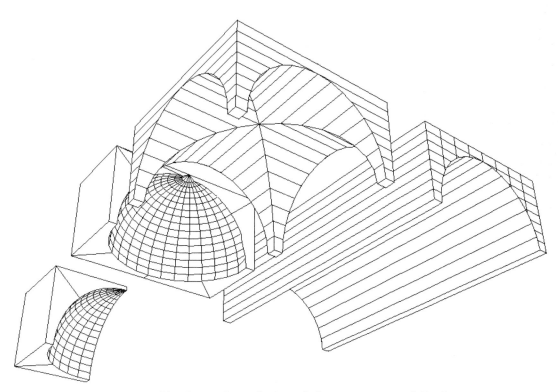

A variety of hard-to-make architectural shapes are easy with Booleans.

EXERCISE: ARCHITECTURAL ELEMENTS

Some shapes that would be completely impossible to sculpt manually are trivial to create using booleans. Many interior architectural elements are just such shapes. A dome, for instance, has an interior hemispherical shape and an exterior hemisphere of a different shape, connected together at the bottom and top edges, made so that the surface is thicker at the base and thinner at the top. A barrel vault is just a cube with a cylindrical shape cut out. Combinations of more complex shapes can be made by combining simpler elements.

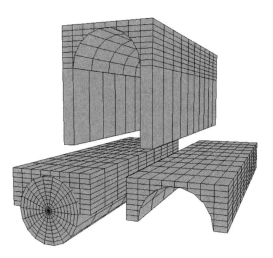

In this exercise, look at the shapes provided, and figure out how to make them by combining simple primitive polygonal shapes into boolean objects.

EXAMPLE 1: THE BARREL VAULT
Hints: Adjust the U and V subdivision of the starting primitive objects to determine the resolution of the resulting object.

Remember, one shape minus the other is a boolean difference.

EXAMPLE 2: A VAULT AND WALLS IS A HALLWAY
Hint: It's a good idea to freeze the booleans after they are made to speed up the interaction.

A simple barrel vault

Select the first object, choose a Boolean, and pick the other object.

EXAMPLE 3: WHEN VAULTS COME TOGETHER

Hint: Try combining the pieces with all the booleans to see what you end up with.

EXAMPLE 4: DOMES, HALF DOMES, QUARTER DOMES

You get the idea!

POLYGON BRIDGE

The polygon bridge tool is a simple effect that takes two unconnected polygons from the same polygon mesh object and connects them by adding new polygons from the edge of each to the corresponding edge on the other. This tool can easily connect extruded polygons to create handles or closed shapes. However, if the two polygons selected for bridging are not facing towards one another, the effect may not produce any useful results. Similarly, if the two polygons are facing each other, but the body of the object is in the way between them, the resulting polygon mesh may self-intersect.

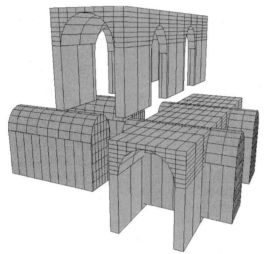

Walls and a vault

To use the command, select two polygons using the polygon select by raycast hotkey (U) or perhaps the select polygon by rectangle hotkey (Y), and then choose the Modify→Poly Mesh→Bridge Polygons menu command. This tool is an operator, so a persistent Bridge Op operator is added to the object, although it cannot be edited.

FROM NURBS TO POLYGONS

Both polygonal surfaces and NURBS have unique advantages and downsides. The key is to use the right tool for the right job, and sometimes that means swapping from NURBS to polygons and vice versa. XSI has some wonderful tools to do just that.

GOING FROM NURBS TO POLYGONS

Getting from NURBS to polygons is easy, since all NURBS are eventually broken down (tessellated) into a polygon mesh anyway. XSI has a neat operator called NURBS to Mesh that will tessellate for you, while giving you control over the level of detail in the resulting polygon mesh. This level of detail is even animatable (until you freeze the operator stack). Simply select a NURBS model and choose the NURBS to Mesh command in the Create→Poly Mesh→ menu. A new object is created, with an operator in its operator stack. If you open that operator into a Property Editor, you can adjust the Step in U and Step in V sliders to gain more or less detail in the resulting mesh.

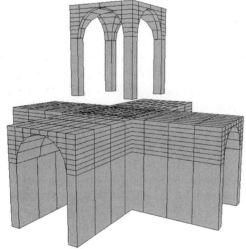

Intersecting vaults – try different Booleans to see results.

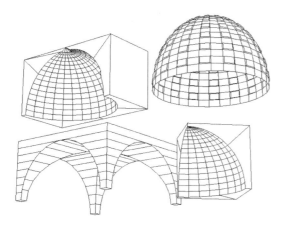

Combine several Booleans to chop up the domes.

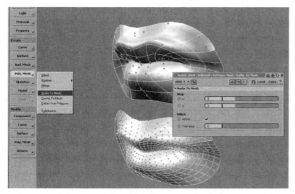

A poly object can easily be made from any NURBS object.

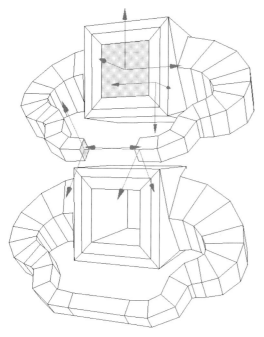

The Bridge operator connects polygons.

POLYGON REDUCTION TOOLS IN SOFTIMAGE | 3D 4.x

While the detail you get from the NURBS to Mesh tool in XSI is regular and depends entirely on the detail built into the original NURBS model, Softimage 3D | Extreme 4.x has other polygon reduction tools that will reduce detail in models non-uniformly, preserving edges and areas where the surface changes, while getting rid of more detail in the smooth low contrast areas of the model. These tools, Effect→GC_Polygon Reduction and Effects→Polygon Reduction, are more appropriate for really low polygon level of detail work. XSI has simple tools – called Filter Polygon and Filter Edge, located in the Modify→Poly Mesh menu in the Model module – that perform simple polygonal reduction.

After you select a polygon object and apply a Filter Polygon operator to it, open the Filter Polygon Op PPG to see how to reduce the detail. By toggling filter Tyoe, you may choose to reduce polygons based on either the angles between polygons, or the size of polygons. If you chose Incidence angle, you can enter an angle, in degrees, below. If you put in 15 degrees, for instance, all polygons meeting a neighboring polygon at an angle of under 15 degrees would be replaced with just one flat poly where previously there were two.

If you choose to filter by area, you enter a number representing the size of the smallest polygon you want to have in your mesh. All polygons will less area than that will be removed from the mesh.

SUBDIVISION SURFACES

One of the most exciting developments to come along in computer graphics recently is the emergence of a new modeling method usually called Subdivision Surface modeling. Often shortened to Sub-D modeling, Subdivision Surfaces are a new way to think about surface geometry. The Sub-D technology was developed to make character modeling a more creative and less frustrating exercise. Before we dive into the subdivision surface operator and modeling techniques, let's get a little background so we understand how Sub-D helps us.

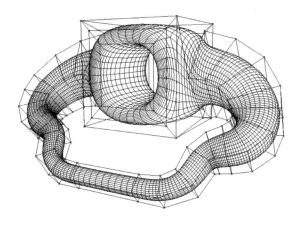

A Subdivision Surface is an implicit surface defined by a polygonal cage called a hull.

In XSI, surfaces can be made either of NURBS patches or of polygons stitched together. The NURBS are mathematically perfect, completely smooth and easy to texture, but they have one main shortcoming: they are always rectangular. As a result, when modeling a character out of NURBS patches, a modeler has to 'quilt' together a whole bunch of smaller NURBS into one big NURBS surface mesh. Aligning the edges of the patches can be quite a chore, keeping them together isn't always easy, and making changes once you have completed assembly is awfully hard. What's worse, the big advantage of NURBS – easy texturing – goes away when you have a lot of smaller NURBS quilted together into a big surface mesh.

On the other hand, polygons can be made in any shape and topology. This means that one polygon object can be edited to take on any shape you can imagine. However, it is still made from straight line segments connecting vertices in space, so the object will tend not to be as smooth as is required for a character outside of low-polygon gaming.

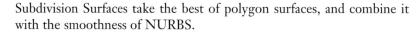

Subdivision Surfaces take the best of polygon surfaces, and combine it with the smoothness of NURBS.

Sub-D is really nothing more than a good smoothing algorithm for polygonal characters. As the modeler, that means that you can use all the polygon tools you already know, combined with standard low polygon gaming techniques, and throw in the Sub-D smoothing to dynamically create smooth, organic, lifelike characters.

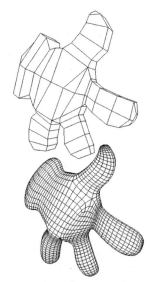

The blocky poly model becomes a smooth Subdivision Surface.

What's the hitch? Well, just one. Since Subdivision surfaces are really just more complex, smoothed polygonal surfaces, adding textures that follow the contours of the character is no easier than before, and possibly harder because the model has so much more smooth detail. To be precise, Sub-D surfaces do not have any inherent texture space, no start and no end, and since they are not required to be rectangular in topology, there is no easy way to map rectangular surface textures onto them.

THE SUBDIVISION OPERATOR

In XSI, Sub-D can be used either as a geometry operator that creates a new Sub-D object, or a simple Geometry Approximation property.

If you choose to use the Create➔Poly Mesh➔Subdivision operator, you will be creating a new object based on an original poly shape. This method has more overhead for XSI to keep track of, and so tends to be slower. However, if you choose this method, you can open the Mesh Subdivide operator in a Property Editor and choose between two different algorithms for smoothing the polygons: Doo-Sabin and Catmull Clark. The Doo-Sabin method more closely approximates the original shape of the polygonal cage, but the Catmull Clark method works in some situations where the Doo-Sabin method fails and creates bad geometry.

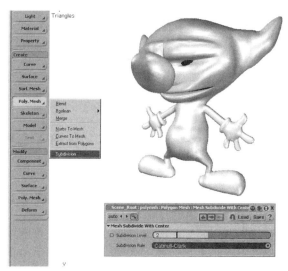

Use the Subdivision command, then inspect the operator on the resulting object.

The Geometry Approximation method is recommended.

THE GEOMETRY APPROXIMATION METHOD

Mesmer recommends the alternate Geometry Approximation method. Since every polygon object in XSI has this Geometry Approximation property, every poly object can use Subdivision Smoothing.

To turn Subdivision Surface smoothing on for any polygon object, select the object and find the Geometry Approximation property editor in the Selection menu of the MCP. Each object in XSI has a link to the default Geometry Approximation property page. When you ask to see the Geometry Approximation PE for a single object, XSI asks you if you want to create a local copy of the page. Say yes, which will make this property page separate from the global default. If the object is a NURBS, the Geometry Approximation property page controls the tessellation smoothness with the Parametric Surface Step. If the object is a Polygon, the Polygon Mesh Subdivision level determines how smooth the surface is.

If you turn the Subdivision level from 0 to 1 you will see that the surface becomes more complex and smooth. Increasing the Mesh Subdivision will result in a smoother mesh that is slower to deal with. Since the Geometry Approximation property is always available, you can change the level of smoothing whenever you want. It makes good sense to set it low while working, then turn it up to examine your work and for the final render.

WORKING WITH SUB-D SURFACES

When you model with Sub-D you use all the regular polygon tools to modify the regular polygonal shape of the object. That shape is then smoothed. Each edge is cut in half several times to generate a finer mesh, and special care is taken at intersections of many polygons to create good geometry. As you turn a polygon object into a Sub-D surface, the Sub-D surface seems to shrink, staying inside the polygonal 'cage'. This is useful. The general technique of Sub-D modeling is to view the Sub-D surface while working directly on the polygonal cage that surrounds it, adding edges, extruding polygons and moving vertices. The Sub-D surface underneath automatically updates to reflect the changes you make in the cage, also called a poly mesh "hull".

In the Show menu for each viewport (the small eye icon) you can chose to toggle on and off either the Poly Mesh Hull or the Subdivision Surfaces. In general, you will want to leave them both on while modeling, but you can mix and match.

Try this: in the camera view, turn the Hulls off and the Subdivision Surfaces on. In the other views, turn the Hulls on and the Subdivision Surfaces off. In this way you can see the smoothed object unobstructed in the camera viewport, while working on the Hulls in the orthographic (Side, Top, Front) windows.

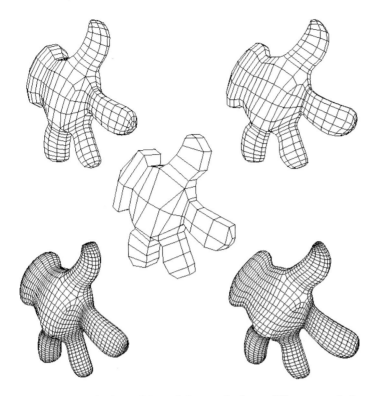

The Catmull-Clarke and Doo-Sabin methods, at different resolutions

LOCAL SUBDIVISION

The Subdivision Surface operator and the Geometry approximation settings are really just subdividing all the polygons according to special rules intended to make good surfaces. You can direct the subdivision manually, creating detail in the shape, by manually adding edges with the Modify→Poly Mesh→Add Edge tool. When you add an edge manually to the mesh, the smoothing algorithm will smooth that edge further. Adding two edges close together will result in more of a crease, while adding edges farther apart will result in smoother transitions between planes in the final shape.

Try this out on a polygon cube: turn on Sub-D in the Geometry Approximation property page under the Polygon Mesh tab, and turn the Mesh Subdivision level up to 3. With the Polygon Mesh→Add Edge (hotkey \) tool, add an edge in the middle of one face, and add another edge on another face very close to the corner. You should see a gradual transition where you added the edge in the middle of the face, and a more distinct crease where you added the edge close to the corner.

In XSI you can also select one or more polygons on a mesh and ask XSI to perform a local subdivision. A local subdivision chops up the selected polygons in the manner of a Subdivision Surface, effectively smoothing the area you selected, while leaving the rest of the polygon mesh exactly as it was. The incredible, earth-shattering importance of this fact is that you can now have different levels of detail in a single polygon mesh object quite easily, something that was not really possible in NURBS modeling.

The area with finer detail has a local subdivision applied.

Try this out on a polygon cube: turn on Sub-D in the Geometry Approximation property page under the Polygon Mesh tab, turn the Subdivision up to 3, then select one face of the cube with the U (raycast) hotkey. Choose the Local Subdivision Refinement command from the Modify→Poly Mesh→ menu and observe the results. Now you have more detail on one side of the polygon than the others. You can tag and transform the new vertices of the polygonal cube to see the results in the smooth surface.

Note: Extruding an edge or vertex is another good way to create more local detail. Try this on the cube: select one corner vertex with the T hotkey, and choose the Extrude Along Axis command from the Modify→Poly Mesh menu.

See that the vertex was moved out from the surface, and new vertices and edges were added to increase the detail there.

EXERCISE: ANGLER FISH

The Angler fish is a fearsome deep-sea creature with tiny vestigial eyes and a mouth full of wicked teeth. It hangs a lure growing from an odd protuberance extending from its top lip. When other creatures investigate the attractive lure, they of course are devoured in a savage frenzy of gnashing teeth, rending flesh, and snapping bone. This fish is an excellent candidate for modeling with Subdivision surfaces, since it has a simple shape with fleshy, lumpy contours.

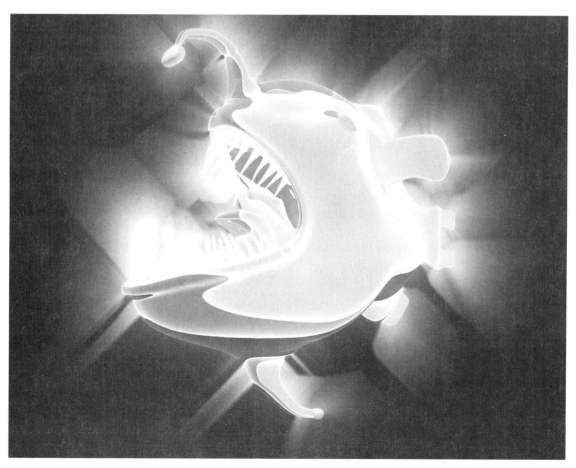

The Angler rendered with glows

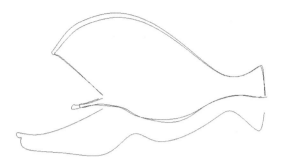

Rough out the shape with lofted splines.

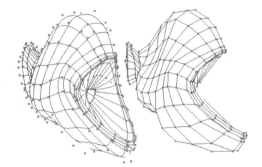

Half a polygonal fish shape

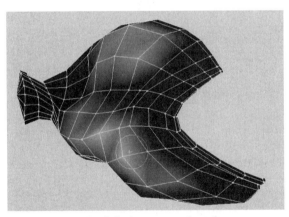

Sculpt the fish shape to make it lumpy.

Add some fins by extruding edges.

Step 1: Make the general shape. Instead of using a primitive here, draw NURBS splines for the top and bottom of the fish. Then, duplicate the top spline twice and rotate those duplicates 45 degrees off the top curve in either direction. You can adjust their shape if you wish. Repeat with the bottom curve. Skin the curves together with the Loft command. Adjust the subdivision to get a fairly even and regular number of U and V parameters.

Snip the resulting NURBS mesh with Modify→Surface→Snip at the top ridge along the spine of the fish and again at the bottom along the belly to get just half a fish. If you are stuck in the snip because the snip operator is removing the half you want to keep, open the operator and check the box to keep the other half.

Step 2. Turn it into a Poly model with the NURBS to Polygon operator. Hide the other parts. Freeze the new poly object and enter immediate mode. Show boundaries on the model so you can see the open center line. This line must lie exactly in the YZ plane to mirror correctly, so select all the vertices on the boundary and scale them to 0 in X, which will make sure that they all lie exactly in the center plane.

Step 3: Mirror the one side, using an instance so that the mirrored side updates as you model on the original side. (Remember: scale by -1 in X to make the mirror.) Try turning up the Geometry Approximation and examining your handiwork, then set it back down and continue work.

Step 4: Now for the fun part, sculpting the fish. Get the Push tool with Property→Paint Push Tool, adjust the brush weight for easy sculpting (low opacity and high softness) in the Brush PPG (Property→Brush Properties or CTRL-W) and adjust the shape of the fish, giving it a big bulging jaw, a small belly, and a flat tail. You can also sculpt the shape by tagging points and scaling the tagged groups.

When done, put the boundary (middle) points back on the XZ plane, as the Push Tool may have moved them around a bit if you weren't careful. If the middle points don't lie exactly on the mid-plane, you won't be able to connect the two halves cleanly when you are done.

Step 5: Add fins at the top and bottom by selecting edges on the boundary and duplicating them CTRL-D, and translating them in Y.

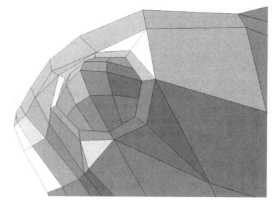

Angler eyes: make a round bulge.

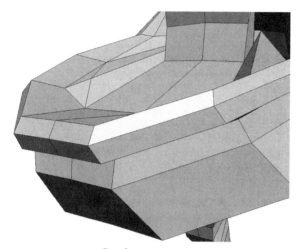

Big lips are scary.

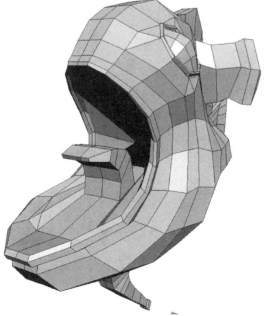

You'll need some flat spots in the mouth to extrude teeth and tongue.

Add little fins in the middle of the fish by selecting polygons and extruding them, translating them and scaling them a few times.

Step 6: Add the Eye. Make new edges in a diamond shape inside one of the square polygons, and then split those edges to make 8 points. Arrange them in a circle, and make another line of edges surrounding them. Select the inside polygons between the inner and outer lid, and extrude them out a bit away from the fish. Select the poly in the middle of the eye and split it with Shift-D. Select the new middle vertex and translate it out away from the fish a bit to bulge the eye. Try turning up the Geometry Approximation and examining your progress, then set it back down and continue work.

Step 7: Work on the mouth. The mouth is round now, but inside it needs a flat bottom and top. Remove some excess edges and translate the points at the back of the mouth to make a flat floor to the mouth. Add a series of connected edges around the bottom of the gums. In the middle of the mouth, extrude one polygon out, rotating it and translating it each time you extrude it more, to form the curving tongue.

Step 8: The lips and gums. To be truly fearsome, the fish needs big lips. To make big lips we need three contour lines around the mouth: one inside (the gums), one outside, blending into the jaw, and one in the middle, translated way out to make a bulge between the gums and jawline. Add this middle edge and pull it way out to bulge the lip. Examine your work as you go with the Geometry Approximation PPG by turning up the Mesh Subdivision Level in the Polygon Mesh Tab.

Step 9: Teeth. Teeth need a square base to emerge from. Inside the gumline, make a series of square polygons that are perpendicular to the direction you want the teeth to emerge from. Do this by adding edges and moving points to make the inner gum composed of small squares. Next, select every other square and extrude it, scaling it down a little as you go. Make the teeth uneven, and crooked, extruding them each four or five times, scaling them down to needle points. You can vary the length of the teeth for additional effect. Go back and do the teeth buds that you skipped in the first round.

Step 10: Make the lure. This is easy: again, just select a polygon, extrude it (CTRL-D), and move it out, scaling and rotating as you go.

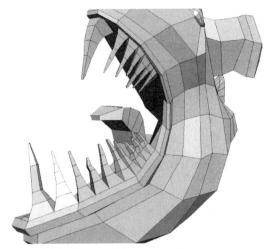

Make the teeth jagged and uneven.

The lure attracts fish food.

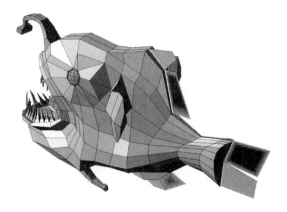

Both halves, merged together

Step 11: Fix the middle boundary. Whenever you changed points or polys on the middle boundary (like when you built the tongue or the lure) you changes the middle seam. We need this seam to be open. Hide the instance temporarily, and examine the boundary of the fish. If there are closed polygons along the boundary, select them and delete them, so that the green boundary indication makes a perfect seam around the fish. You might have to move the boundary points into the center YZ plane again with scale to 0 in X.

Step 12: Unhide the instance, select both halves, and merge them.

Now you have one fish! Smooth that fish, and look to see where you can improve it. This is the art part – just continue messing with the original half and examining the resulting fish, until you like what you get.

Remember, it is traditional for artists to throw out a lot of their work, do it over, and keep only what is good. Fortunately for us, we don't have to pay for paint and canvas, or sculpting materials. Take advantage of this fact, and re-do your work. It's always better the second time (and the third, and fourth...).

SETTING HARDER EDGES AND BOUNDARIES

One advantage that NURBS have is the ability to weight a point or an isoline to create a crease or hard edge in the middle of an otherwise smooth surface. Subdivision Surfaces can do this, too. You can mark any edge or combination of edges as either entirely hard or just partially weighted harder than the neighboring edges. When you do this, the smoothing algorithms will take your wishes into consideration, and leave more edge detail.

This means that you can have both smooth organic surfaces and sharp edges in a single polygon model. To Mark an edge as entirely hard, select the edge (or group of edges) with the E hotkey, then choose the Modify→Component→Mark Hard Edge/Vertex command. That edge will now be sharp in the subdivided model. Try this on your cube: select one corner that has not yet been divided and mark it as Hard with the Mark Hard Edge/Vertex command. Look at that area of the Sub-D surface in the shaded camera view, and compare it to the edge you manually creased by adding a parallel edge.

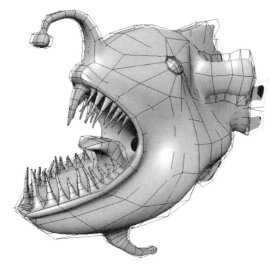

The final fish, with the Subdivision level turned up

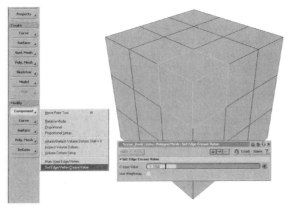

Marking an edge as hard creates a crease in the Subdivision Surface.

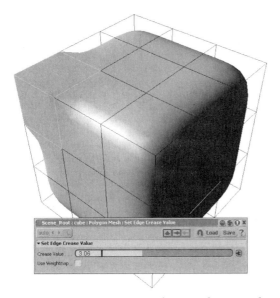

The hard edge remains creased, even after smoothing.

You can also define edges as partially hard or soft. Select the edges in question, choose the Modify→Component→Set Edge/Vertex Crease Value command. Select the subdivision surface as an object and pull up the SetEdgeCreaseValue property page. (If you are working in Immediate mode, which you should be while doing polygon modeling, this won't work because the effect is immediately frozen before you can make the change. Turn Immediate mode OFF while adjusting edge creases.)

Carefully adjust the EdgeCreaseValue slider while looking at the smoothed surface in the shaded view to observe the results.

CONCLUSION

The polygon toolset in XSI is fantastic, and brings both a new level of sophistication and a standardized ease of use to both beginning and sophisticated polygon modelers. XSI's ability to work with vertices, edges, and polygons all in the same way certainly makes life much easier and more productive. The wealth of tools for adding, splitting, adjusting, transforming, and subdividing those edges, vertices, and polygons are second to none, while the complete integration between polygons and Subdivision Surfaces opens new doors for the XSI user. Taken together, the XSI polygon tools and Sub-D tools make organic character modeling easier than ever.

QUIZ

1. THE SUBDIVISION SURFACE TOOLS WORK ON NURBS
   a. True
   b. False

2. WHICH IS NOT A PART OF A POLYGON?
   a. Edge
   b. Control Point
   c. Vertex

3. WHICH DO YOU FIND ON A POLYGON?
   a. Boundary
   b. Knot Curve
   c. Normal

4. IN XSI POLYGON MODELING, WHAT CAN YOU EXTRUDE?
   a. NURBS curves
   b. Normals
   c. Edges, Vertices, and Polygons

5. WHAT IS THE HOTKEY FOR SELECT POLYGON BY RAYCAST?
   a. R
   b. P
   c. U

6. WHICH ONE OF THE OPTIONS BELOW DOES NOT MAP TO A MOUSE BUTTON WHEN YOU HAVE THE E HOTKEY HELD DOWN (IN THE SOFTIMAGE 3D SELECTION MODEL, EXTENDED COMPONENT SELECTION)?
   a. LMB: Add to Selection
   b. MMB: Start Over
   c. RMB: Toggle Selection

7. THE OPERATOR STACK ALWAYS STORES EVERY CHANGE YOU MAKE TO A POLYGON OBJECT.
   a. True
   b. False
   c. False if Immediate mode is on

8. HOW DO YOU FLATTEN THE OPERATOR STACK TO SIMPLIFY MODELS?
   a. Immediate mode
   b. Freeze
   c. Delete the operators

9. SUBDIVISION SURFACES:
   a. Rule
   b. Suck
   c. What's Sub-D?

10. WHICH IS NOT A BOOLEAN MODELING OPTION?
   a. Intersection
   b. Condition
   c. Difference

4 SHAPE SHIFTING

IN THIS CHAPTER YOU WILL LEARN ABOUT:

[a] How XSI Deforms Objects with Operators
[a] How How Operators are stored on Clusters
[a] How to Paint Deformations with Weight Maps and the GAP
[a] How Lattices and Cages work to mold objects easily
[a] How Spline and Surface Deformations work
[a] How QuickStretch adds cartoon physics to models
[a] How XSI Stores Shapes
[a] How XSI freely morphs object shapes
[a] Shape animation terminology and technique
[a] Additive versus Average Shape Animation
[a] Using Libraries of Shapes
[a] Facial Shape Animation

The Deform menu can be found in either the Model or Animate modules.

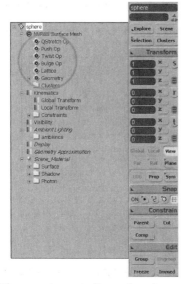

The gear icons indicate that these deformations are persistent operators.

INTRODUCTION

The history of computer graphics is filled with examples of rigid models moving through space. That's because moving a model from point A to point B in three dimensions is fairly easy. As a result, CG has featured a lot of space ships, tanks, race cars, and metal war machines. Even the characters in Pixar's amazing CG series, Toy Story, were for the most part, rigid.

However, in real life things bend, wave, bulge, flex, and change shape constantly. In addition to real life, most classical cartoon animation relies on conventions of characters changing shape radically in response to their environment, to react to movement, or just as a dramatic device.

To create realistic (or surrealistic) human emotional impact and believable lip sync we really need our characters to be completely plastic and easily deformable, with simple controls that an animator can love.

Fortunately, XSI has a wide range of tools for the range of animation behaviors you will need to create. Deformations can be added to models to create very simple effects, while with Shape animation the only limit will be your creativity and skill.

DEFORMATIONS IN XSI

When we talk about Deformations in XSI we are really talking about changing the form of an object over time. Since the form of the object (or hierarchy of objects) is determined by the control vertices (in a NURBS object) or by the vertex location (in a polygon), then what you really need to do is change the location of those vertices over time, and the form will change as well.

When a deformation operator is used, rather simple controls on that operator will change the location of the control vertices on part or all of the object at once. Shape animation works differently: you'll need to manually specify exactly what happens to each vertex in an object, and manually blend between different shapes in the Mixer. Deformation operators are much easier to use, but Shape animation is infinitely powerful. The key is figuring out which method is most appropriate for each occasion you have to make an object change shape.

The Deformation operators are added by selecting an object or a cluster and making a selection from the Deform→Deform menu stack in the Animation module, or the Modify→Deform menu in the Model module. Before you try it out, read on a bit longer to find out more about how deformations are applied to objects.

DEFORMATIONS ARE STORED ON CLUSTERS

Both Shape animation and Deformation operators have this in common: they work on clusters, not the entire mesh object all at once. This is a huge advantage over previous methods, which often operated on entire objects all at once. Since you can define clusters yourself, you can apply a deformation to just one specific part of the character at a time. For instance, you could create a cluster for the belly area of a character and apply a bulge deformation to just that area to make the belly swell and bounce. You might choose to create a cluster on the ears of a character and apply a QuickStretch deformation operator to that ear cluster so that the ears bend and bounce as the character walks. Each character can have as many clusters as you need, and the clusters can overlap. Since they can overlap, each vertex can be affected by more than one deformation.

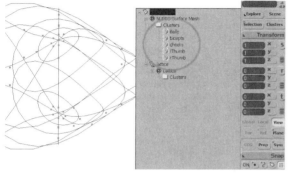

Deformations are operators, which means that they are persistent effects, and they have Property Editors located in the operator stack for the object itself. Although you generally want to select a cluster before adding a deformation, the deformation PPG itself is located at the object level, not the cluster level. While this makes them easier to find in the Selection eexplorer in the MCP, it often means that if you have a cluster selected and therefore are in cluster filter mode, you'll have to tap the Space bar to reenter object mode before you can see the deformation operators in the Selection explorer.

Clusters are saved groups of points or polygons.

If you do not create a cluster and deliberately apply your deformation to that cluster, XSI will create a cluster for all the points in the whole object and apply the deformation to that global cluster. However, if you have a cluster selected (and you are therefore in cluster filter mode), then when you add a deformation it will be applied only to those vertices that are a member of that active cluster.

MAKING CLUSTERS ON YOUR CHARACTER

Clusters are really groups of selected vertices, saved for later use. In this way you can define areas of your character, save those areas, and use them again. You can use clusters to apply local materials to a surface of an object, to apply deformations and WeightMaps, to manually deform the surface with transformations on the cluster, and to constrain to and from other objects. Clusters are extremely versatile.

To make a cluster on your character, follow these steps:

First, select the objects, and pop up a floating explorer window with the 8 key on your keyboard. With your mouse over the explorer, tap the E key (or change the scope of the explorer to "Selection" with the menu at the top left of the Explorer window).

Now the explorer shows just the selected object. In the explorer, open up the hierarchy to show the cluster folder. In a Polygon object, the Cluster folder is located under the Polygon Mesh operator (under the Geometry operator, if the object has never been frozen), while in a NURBS object it is located under the Surface Mesh operator.

Clusters are collected under an object's mesh, in a Cluster folder.

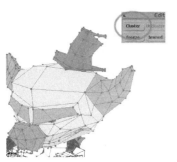

The Cluster button turns tagged points into a cluster.

Lock the explorer now, so that the contents won't change when you make a different selection. Now you will have this explorer locked down to show you the clusters you are about to create.

Hold down the T key and select all those vertices you want included in the new cluster. It's a good idea to do this in wireframe view mode, and rotate the object when you are done to check that no extra unexpected vertices were accidentally tagged.

When you have vertices tagged, you are in point mode, and when you are in point mode, the button at the bottom of the MCP that normally reads "Group" now reads "Cluster". Click this Cluster button to create a new cluster on the selected object that will contain all the vertices you have selected.

You will see the new cluster appear in the Explorer window that you have locked to show the cluster list. It's a good idea to change the name of the cluster so you know what it is later on. You can immediately tap the Enter key to pop up the general PPG for the cluster and change the name there, or you can right-click over the new cluster in the Explorer window and choose the Rename command from the context-sensitive menu that pops up. This menu also allows you to delete unwanted cluster definitions (which will not harm the model itself).

You can make as many clusters as you wish, and vertices may be members of more than one cluster at a time.

WEIGHTMAPS MODIFY DEFORMATIONS

Being able to localize the effect of a deformation to just the vertices on an object that you want affected is a great feature, but XSI doesn't stop there. In fact, you can change how strongly the deformation affects each vertex in that cluster, so that the deformation doesn't have to be applied to all those vertices in the cluster evenly. In other words, you can modify the strength of a deformation, with another XSI feature called a weight map.

The WeightMap modulates the effect of the deformation.

A weight map is a way of storing a decimal value on each vertex of the mesh that can be hooked up to the deformation to determine how strongly the deformation works on that vertex. Since the weight map is stored on vertices, the resolution of the weight map changes with the detail of your model, which is very good. Weight values are interpolated smoothly across the surface between vertices.

Weight maps can be added in default patterns – for instance, falling off from a center point gradually – but they are most useful when you paint them on the model manually, using the Paint tool.

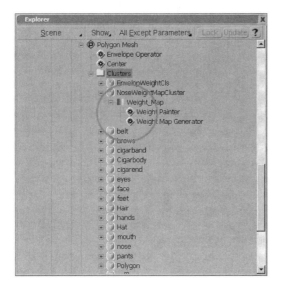

Weight maps and their properties are stored on clusters.

Weight maps can be viewed as a gradation of color in the Constant or Shaded views. First change the camera view to be either constant or shaded, then in the Show menu (eyeball icon) toggle on WeightMaps to indicate to XSI that you wish to see the weight map on the selected object. A blank weight map, or an object without a weight map, will appear in black.

Note: Vertex colors are a similar concept, containing values that are stored on each vertex. Vertex colors can also be used to modify shaders in the Render Tree. Weight maps can be used in the RenderTree as well, with the special MapLookup nodes, hidden under Nodes→Texture→More… in the Render Tree.

Weight maps are also stored on clusters. If you do not manually choose a cluster before adding a weight map, a new cluster will be created that covers the entire object, and a weight map will be applied to that global cluster. Generally, this is not a good idea, since the whole point of a weight map is to modify a specific deformation on a specific cluster.

The Cluster explorer in the MCP shows all of an object's clusters.

Weight maps are properties, and so they are created and added from the Property menu in either the Model or Animation module.

Note: Once a weight map exists, you can find it in the Cluster folder, under the WeightMapCls node for WeightMaps on the whole object, and under the individual cluster nodes if they are applied on clusters.

First, select the cluster you want the weight map stored on, perhaps by first selecting the object and then using the Cluster selection menu in the middle of the MCP. Next, choose Property→WeightMap to add the weight map. Next, bring up the WeightMap operator by looking in the Selection explorer in the MCP and clicking on the operator icon for the weight map, which looks like a black-to-white gradient.

The default WeightMap definition dialog will be shown. You can make some important changes here, in the WeightMap Generator tab. The range of values that the weight map contains are set with the Weight Value Range Minimum and Maximum sliders. It's a good idea to set the Minimum to –1 and the Maximum to +1, so that the weight map can remove from the deformation as well as add to it.

If you set the default Base Weight value to 0, then the weight map will dampen the deformation completely until you paint in some value. While this is often useful, it means that nothing will happen right away when you add a deformation. It might be a good idea to set the default Base Weight to 0.5 or so just so you see something happen.

You can adjust the default values of the weight map.

You can also play with the default patterns by choosing from the options listed in the WeightMap Type. Usually the Constant type is preferable, but in some cases you might choose Radial XYZ to get a smooth falloff to the edge of the weight map.

CONNECTING WEIGHTMAPS TO OTHER OPERATORS

In cases where an operator like a deformation can be used with a weight map, some certain properties of that operator will have a small plug icon located at the right end of the property slider. This indicates that the property can be hooked up to a weight map. When a property is plugged into a weight map, you can no longer directly change the value of the property, and instead it gets its value from the weight map itself. This means that previously the property applied at the same value all across the object, but now the value of the property can change at each and every vertex. Click on the plug with the Right Mouse Button, then choose Connect to see a list of the weight map available on that object and cluster, and choose one by clicking directly on the name of the weight map, and then clicking anywhere back in the operator PPG to close the list of available weight maps. The Plug will change color to red, indicating that it is plugged in to a weight map.

Property sliders with a plug can be connected to a weight map.

To unhook or choose a different weight map, right-click on the plug icon and choose a command from the pop up menu there. To view the Weight Properties for the connected map, click with the Left Mouse Button on the plug.

Once you have clusters where you want them, and weight maps on those clusters, you are ready to add the deformations. When you have the groundwork laid properly like this, XSI will automatically hook everything up for you, applying the deformation to just the cluster you want, and then attaching the weight map to the deformation as well.

The order in which you add deformations, shape animation, and IK enveloping to a model matters. Each of these forms of moving vertices around on a model are done in the order that they were added. This order can be partially seen in the operator stack. I suggest the following order as a place to start:

First, add Shape Animation (covered later in the chapter)

Next add Deformations

Finally, bind your Skin (Envelope) to your IK skeleton.

BULGE AND TWIST DEFORMATIONS

Bulge and Twist are excellent and simple tools in the arsenal of the character animator. Bulge simply moves vertices out from the center of the deformation, with a built-in gradual falloff so that the effect falls off over a definable range.

You can change whether the bulge pushes points in all axes evenly, or just in X, Y or Z.

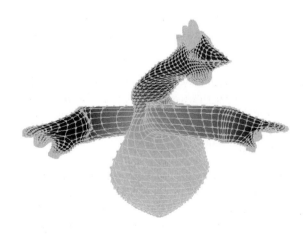

A Twist deformation easily mangles the chicken.

You can drag a slider to change how much the object is bulged, and the object can even be bulged negatively, causing it to shrink. The Bulge operator can be added to a single model or a hierarchy of objects. You can adjust the center of the Bulge operator relative to the center of the object, or relative to a bounding box that the operator uses to surround the objects affected by the operator.

Note: Deformations are not currently applied relative to the center of the Cluster, but instead relative to the center of the object. This causes problems sometimes, and I hope that in later versions of XSI the deformations will be applied relative to the cluster they are on.

Bulge could be used to swell part of a snake after it has eaten someone, or make a character's thumb throb after being struck with a hammer.

Twist can be applied to a single object or a hierarchy, and moves the vertices of the object in such a way that it twists up around a user-definable axis. To examine the effects and uses of these two deformations, let's practice on the eggExtraction scene. In this scene from the Egg Factory animation, a hand robot is taking extra measures to help a hen lay a particularly large egg. The hands grip the chicken around the neck, and then the lower hand rotates as it moves down through the chicken, to squeeze and twist the unfortunate hen until an egg is produced. The hands are already animated, but the hen is not changing shape, so the animation is unconvincing. Your role will be to add Bulge and Twist operators to the hapless bird.

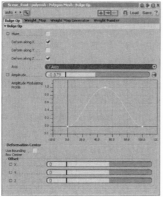

A bulge is an easy way to animate the egg in the chicken.

STEP 1: TWIST THE BIRD

Select the Bird as a tree (Space bar and the Right Mouse Button) so that the whole bird hierarchy is selected. In the model module, choose Deform➜Twist to add a twist operator to the top of the chicken hierarchy. In the MCP, click on the Select button and then on the Twist operator icon to examine the Twist PPG. We want the chicken twisted around the Y-axis, so set the Axis drop menu to Y.

Try out the Angle slider to see the effect of the deformation.

You can adjust the center of the twist to lie exactly between the robot hands by adjusting the Y offset slider.

STEP 2: BULGE THE BIRD

As the bird is wrung out, the giant egg inside should seem to be moving down from top to bottom. A bulge would be a good way to do this, because you can animate the center of the bulge moving down as the bird twists.

Add a Bulge operator to the chicken in Branch mode. Pop open the Bulge PPG, and locate the Offset Y slider. Try changing that slider to see the results, then set two keys on it so that the center of the bulge moves down towards the feet of the chicken as the chicken twists.

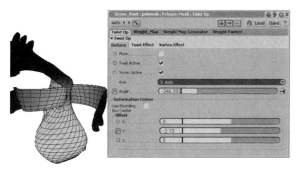

Add a Twist deformer, and animate the Angle and Center Y position.

SPLINE DEFORMATION AND CONSTRAIN CLUSTER TO OBJECT

Spline deformations make smooth, gradual deformations along a curve that you create.

There are two general cases to use a curve deformation: when you want an object to move along the curving path, like a snake or a worm travelling along, and when you have a complex model that you want to wave around in a fluid manner.

You can apply a curve deformation to a single object or to a hierarchy of objects all at the same time.

What a curve deformation really does is take the object to be deformed, and reposition the control points of the object to now be relative to the curve you chose as the deformer. The points are re-mapped into the space of the curve: the Y values of the points are re-mapped to the U direction (along the curve), the X values of the points are re-mapped to be normal to the curve (perpendicular to the U direction) and the Z values of the points are remapped to the Binormal values of the curve (perpendicular to both the U and the normal direction of the curve.) This means that now as the curve bends, the points that are located in space based on that curve will also bend in the exact same way.

The Sea Creature is deformed by the curve.

The more complex object can then be animated in a simple way, by moving points on the curve.

The thing to remember when setting up curve deformation is that whatever axis of the object was facing in local Y will now face forward along the curve. Therefore, if you have modeled a dart that will travel along a curve, twisting and turning to reach a dart board, you had better model the dart in such a way that the needle of the dart faces forward along the Y axis. If you have modeled the object some other way, turn the object so that it faces up in global Y, and then Freeze the rotation of the object with the Transform➔Freeze Rotation command.

Here are the steps you'll need to use to create a working Curve deformation.

Step 1: Draw the Curve you will use as the new backbone of your object. If you want to use the Curve deformation to make something travel along a flexible path, bending to follow the shape of the curve as it goes (unlike a Path constraint, in which the object stays rigid while it travels down the path), draw a long curve in the top window.

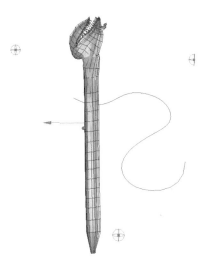

Whatever you want to end up facing along the curve must start facing up in Y.

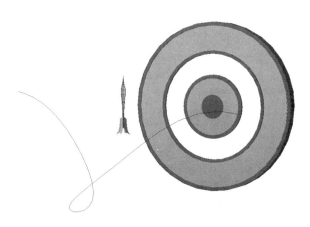

The curve is the path the dart will travel.

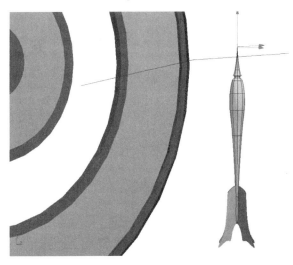

The tip of the dart is Y up, and the local center is frozen to the global center.

Note: If you want to deform the object with a curve in place, so that the object remains where it is but you can move points on the curve to make it wriggle, dance, etc, draw a short curve of five or so points in the front view, starting at the bottom of the window and plotting points up wards along the Y axis.

Step 2: Prepare your model properly. Since the deformation really re-maps the location of points from XYZ space into the space of the curve, the current position and orientation of the object is very important. First, rotate the object so that whatever axis you want aligned along the curve is aiming up along the global Y-axis. In other words, if your model is a snake or a fish, rotate it so that the mouth is facing straight up in Y.

Next, position it at the global origin, in the middle of the scene where the X-, Y- and Z-axes intersect. With the object selected, freeze the operator stack with the Freeze button at the bottom of the MCP, and also freeze the transformations of the object with the Transform➔Freeze All Transforms command also in the MCP. Now your model is a simple mesh, ready to be deformed.

Step 3: Apply the deformation. If what you want to put on the curve is more than one object in a hierarchy, select the hierarchy as a branch (Middle Mouse Button and Space bar); otherwise, select the object as a single object. Choose the command Deform➔Deformation by Curve and then pick the curve to complete the command.

The menu command Deform by Curve

Your object should now have snapped in space to the origin of the curve. If you didn't have the object at the global origin when you froze it, your object may be offset from the curve.

Step 4: Modify the Curve Deform Properties. With the object still selected, open the Curve Deform PPG. You can now adjust the transformation of the object, in the Curve Space with the PPG. The regular transformations in the MCP will not do what you want here, so ignore them.

If your object is not exactly aligned along the Curve, enter the Constraint Tab, and try toggling on Constrain to Deformer.

Click back on the Curve Deform tab. You can scale the object here, to make it bigger or smaller if the object became distorted when it is attached to the curve. Changing the Scaling Along Curve slider will extend the object to occupy more of the curves U space. Scaling the object normal or binormal to the curve will make the object fatter around the curve.

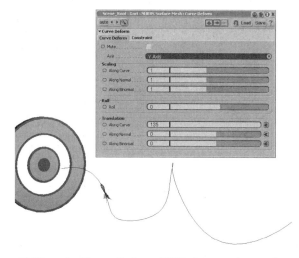

Editing the Curve Deform PPG changes the results.

You can also translate it along the curve, setting keyframes to animate progress along the curve over time. If the slider for the translation along the curve does not go high enough to place the object at the end of the curve, you may type in a higher number directly into the text entry box in the PPG. You can also rotate the object with the Roll slider so that it spins along the axis of the curve, to control the bank of the object as it travels along the curve.

Step 5: Modify the curve. Now select the curve, and use the M hot key to modify the points on the curve. See that if you change the part of the curve that the object is over, you can dynamically animate the deformation of the object. This is a common technique for quick animated deformations of hair-spray cans, scissors, gas pumps, credit cards, and a lot of other things you see dancing on TV.

EXERCISE: SEA CREATURES SWIMMING WITH SPLINE DEFORMATION

In this exercise we'll quickly create a simple animation of the fearsome Angler fish traveling along a curve. However, instead of using a path constraint, which would make the fish rigid, you'll use a Curve Deformation so that the fish wriggles fantastically as it travels.

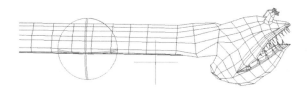

This eel is mis-aligned.

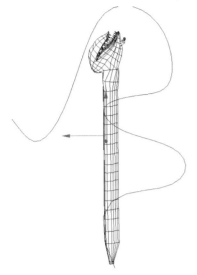

The Eel is Y –up, and there is a curve.

Step 1: Inspect the scene. Open the Cmonster.CurveDef scene and take a look at it. The fish is sitting in space, deliberately misaligned for the deformation. We'll have to fix that. Rotate the fish so that the mouth is facing exactly up in Global Y. Translate the fish to the global center. Freeze the Transformations with Transform➔Freeze All Transformations. Scale should now read 1,1,1, Translation should read 0,0,0, and Rotation should also be 0,0,0. If the transforms are not all reset as above, something went wrong, so select the fish and do it again. If you rotate the fish numerically, don't rotate it to perfect increments of 90 degrees – instead use 89.99 degrees to avoid a nasty bug in the Freeze Transformations command. Finally, freeze the operator stack with the Freeze button in the bottom of the MCP.

Step 2: Draw a path for the fish. In the top view, plot a NURBS curve with between 12 and 15 points. Make a few good twists and turns. In the front view, tag and translate a few points so the path is not completely flat in the XZ plane.

Step 3: Select the fish, choose the Deform➔Curve Deformation command, and pick the path. The fish will hop to the start of the path, but may be lying on its side. With the fish selected, open the Curve Deform PPG, and look for the Roll slider. Adjust it to your liking. (If the eel isn't on the curve, try checking the Constrain to Deformer toggle.)

Step 4: Set some keys to make the fish swim. At frame 1, click on the green animation divot next to the slider marked Translation Along Curve. At frame 100, find the right number for the end of the curve by typing in high numbers, like 100 or 150, into that slider. When you find the right number for the end of the curve, save another key. Play back your animation and examine the results!

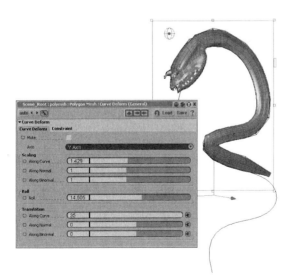

The eel now travels along the curve, courtesy of the Curve Deformation.

DEFORMATION BY SPINE: QUETZAL NECK

Splines are also a good way to animate complex skeletal elements, like tails and long necks, that need to move fluidly. Here we have a long-necked Quetzalcoatlas. While the wings and body already have some IK in them, we need some clever way of animating the neck that will be flexible (no pun intended) and, more importantly, easy.

The game plan is to draw a simple five-point curve right in the neck and head. We'll create a cluster for all the points in the head and neck of the Quetzal, and deform it to the curve with a close relative of the Curve Deformation, named the Deformation by Spine.

Step 1: Examine the scene. Open the Quetzal_Curvedef scene, and take a look at the bird. The body and wings have IK that is constrained to some control boxes.

In the right view, draw a five-point curve, starting at the base of the neck and progressing up the neck to the base of the jaws. In the top view, make sure the curve is centered inside the quetzal neck.

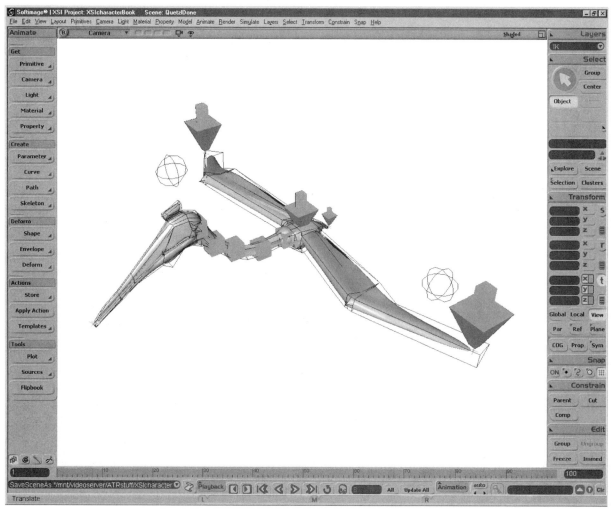

A complete Deform by Spine

Step 2: One control box sits at the base of the neck. You'll want to attach the neck spline to that as a child so that the neck goes with the rest of the body when the Quetzal is eventually animated. Locate the shoulder control box and make it the parent of the curve.

Step 3: Add in the Deformation by Spine. Tag all the points in the neck and head of the Quetzal, and make them into a cluster, so you can apply the curve deformation just to that part of the bird, and not mess with the body and wings. Name the new cluster 'Neck' in the explorer.

Select the new 'Neck' cluster and choose the Deformation→Deform by Spine command. Pick the Curve. Open the PPG for the Spine Deformation by selecting the whole object (tap the Space bar) and looking in the Selection explorer in the MCP for the Deform by Spine Operator PPG. The way Spine Deformation works is that each point is weighted with a weight map to move with the control points on the curve selected. You can change the falloff, or how far away on the mesh each point on the curve will have influence. Try moving some points on the curve with the M key to see the effect.

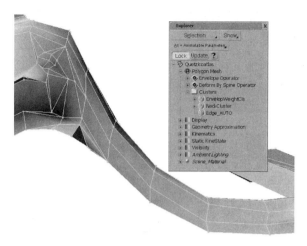

Just the neck of the Quetzal is now a cluster.

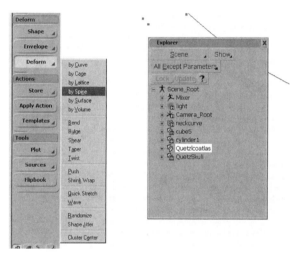

The Deform by Spine command links a cluster to a curve.

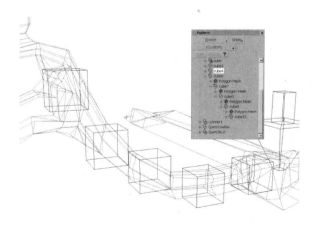

These boxes will control the curve.

To examine the weight map that controls this deformation, select the deformed object, and in the Selection Explorer, open up the Clusters folder and click on the icon of the DeformBySpineWeightCls cluster to see the Spine WeightMap Operator.

Look at the Amplitude tab, and adjust the falloff curve. Change it slightly to see the changing effect of overlapping the areas of influence. Smooth Gaussian curves usually give the best results. In the Radius tab, the Radius slider changes how far away, in Softimage units, the effect extends around the curve.

DEFORMATION➔CLUSTER CENTER

In both the cases of Deformation by Spine and Deformation by Curve, the purpose is to simplify the process of animating a complex shape, by instead linking it to a simple curve and animating the curve itself. However, any way you cut it, Shape animation is more complicated than just saving translation keyframes. It would make a lot of sense if we could just save keys on the translation of the points somehow. Well, we can't actually save translation keys on individual control points, but what we can do is connect these control points to regular objects, and then save translation keys on those objects, which will therefore drive the control points that are attached to them.

The key to this is the Cluster Center Deformation. This used to be called "Deform Cluster to Object" in the old Softimage 3D application. You just make each control point (or group of points) on the curve into a cluster. Then, you select that cluster and constrain it to an object with the Deformation➔Cluster Center Command.

You can try this out on the Quetzal neck that you made above, if you wish.

Step 1: Build the control objects. Get a primitive implicit cube, name it 'neckcontrol1' and scale it down to fit around the neck, but be easy to select. Since it is an implicit object, it has no surface, and therefore will not render. We'll use it to translate the points on the curve. We need one per control point on the curve. Duplicate the control box for each point on your curve, and distribute the boxes along the neck, over each point.

Step 4: Make the neck curve clusters. We need to constrain each point on the curve to one of the boxes, and to do that we need to make each point into a cluster. To make this easy, select the curve, open the explorer in a floating window with the 8 hotkey, tap E in the explorer to inspect just the curve, open up the cluster folder (now empty) and lock the explorer so it doesn't change. Now select the first point on the curve with T, and make it a cluster with the cluster button at the base of the MCP. Name it 'NeckCluster1' by RMB clicking in the Explorer over the new cluster. Select the next point, and repeat the process. Make all the points on your curve into clusters.

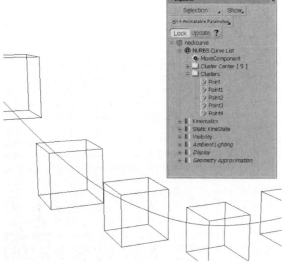

The Cluster folder shows all the clusters made on the curve.

Step 5: Constrain the clusters to the controls. Start with the cluster at the base of the neck. Select it by clicking on it in the explorer, and constrain it to the first box, by selecting the Deform➔Cluster Center command, and then picking the first control box 'NeckCluster1'. The cluster will now be permanently placed relative to that box. Select the next cluster up the neck, and constrain it to the next box, with the same Deform➔Cluster Center command. Repeat for all the clusters. Now you can change the shape of the curve by just moving the boxes around. This is important, because it means you'll be able to animate the shape of the neck by saving simple translation keys on the boxes, rather than the more complex Shape animation covered later in this chapter. Make all the boxes the child of the first one so that the bird stays together later if you move the whole hierarchy.

LATTICE DEFORMATION

The Curve deformation is a winner because it is so easy. Instead of manipulating a much more complex object, point by point, you can just move points on a simple curve to change the shape of the complex object. Lattices work in a similar manner, except with more control over the results. A lattice is a box of points that surrounds your object. You can then move the points on the lattice to change the shape of the object within the lattice. Since you get to determine how many points go into the lattice you use, you can choose to trade between lower detail lattices that are easier to animate, and higher detail lattices with more local control over the shape of the object within.

A Cluster center locks a cluster to another object.

Lattices are an easy way to squash and stretch.

Lattices are easy to think about as being a distortion of space. When the lattice is in the original shape (a cube) then the space within it is not distorted. When the shape of the lattice is changed, usually by tagging and transforming points on the lattice, then the space within the lattice is distorted, and whatever objects were within the lattice will also be distorted. You can have one lattice on one object, you can have one lattice on a hierarchy of objects, and you can have a hierarchy of lattices, so the effect is quite flexible. You can join the lattice and the object it distorts in a hierarchy (either parent-child or child-parent), so the lattice travels with it, or you can choose to move the lattice and the object independently. If the Lattice and the Objects deformed are independent, then you can move the object through the lattice, creating some very interesting effects, like pouring a car into a glass bottle.

The lattice is itself just a primitive object. You can create one with the Get→Primitive→Lattice command in the Model module. If you have an object selected when you choose the command, the lattice will be positioned and scaled to match the shape of the selected object, and the selected object will be hooked to the lattice deformation.

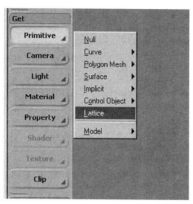

You can get a Lattice with or without another object selected.

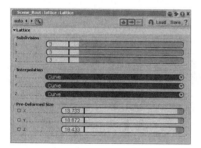

The Lattice PPG

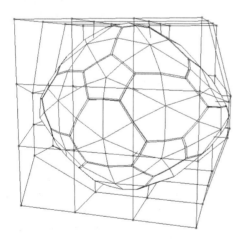

A simple lattice is a cube of sample points.

If you don't have an object selected, the lattice will be created at the global origin. Select the lattice, and inspect its properties by opening the Lattice PPG in the transient Selection explorer in the MCP.

The lattice is a big grid of control points, and you can determine how many points lie in each axis of the Lattice with the Subdivision sliders in the PPG. Simple is good, so begin by changing the sliders to 4 in Y, and 1 in X and Z.

If you had an object selected when you made the lattice, that object is already connected to the lattice deformation, and you can now begin to change the lattice to see the results. You can also make the lattice separately, and connect it manually to one or more objects, which is more flexible.

First, make a free-standing lattice. With nothing selected, choose the Get→Primitive→Lattice command, and scale and translate the lattice as you require. Select the object you want deformed, and choose the Deform→Lattice command, then pick the lattice to complete the command. In this way you can arbitrarily connect any number of objects to any number of lattices. If you have a hierarchy that you want deformed, just select the hierarchy as a branch or a tree (Middle or Right Mouse Buttons) when you apply the lattice, and it will deform everything within the hierarchy.

 Note: You can explore Lattices more fully in the LeroyWagon Exercise, later this chapter.

DEFORMATION BY CAGE

Deformation by Cage is a very cool variation on the effect of a Lattice deformation. While a Lattice is fundamentally a cubic array of data points that deform whatever is within it, a Cage can be of any shape. In fact, you can model the Cage you want to use as a deformation using all the modeling tools, because a cage can be any polygon or NURBS object. The benefit of a cage is that the deformation can be sculpted to a shape that more closely matches the shape being deformed. For instance, if you needed a big toe to throb, without the toes around it changing, that would be hard to accomplish with a lattice around the whole foot. With a cage, you could build a low-res polygonal mesh in exactly the shape of the part of the foot than needs to be deformed, and since the points would make more sense it would be easier to control.

To make a Cage deformation work, you'll need two objects, the model and the cage object. With the model to be deformed selected, choose the Deform→by Cage command from either the Model Module or the Animate Module. Then pick on the cage object, or objects, and right click to complete the command.

To see the effect, move some points on the cage object to see a similar effect on the object within it.

EXERCISE: SMALL SEA MONSTER EATS LARGER ONE

A Cage deformation controls the fish.

In this example a small, unassuming little fish will surprise the heck out of a bigger toothier cousin by expanding dramatically at a crucial moment. We'll use a lattice to control just how the little fishie changes shape.

Step 1: Load the Survival.scn scene which has the fearsome, tooth-ridden angler fish approaching the little gulper. Play it back to get an idea of the action. At frame 120 the big angler comes to a stop right over the smaller gulper.

Step 2: Make a cage. A good cage fits around the object to be deformed, but has a lower density of points. For this gulper, a sphere might fit nicely around the head. Get a polygon sphere and scale and rotate it to fit around the head and jaws of the gulper. Freeze the scale and rotation of the new sphere cage. Now select the gulper, and choose Deform➜by Cage from the Model module, and then pick the cage sphere you made.

Now when you modify the points on the simpler sphere, the gulper also changes.

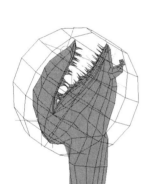

A good Cage fits around the object to be deformed.

Step 3: You will be animating the shape of the cage in the Animate module, with the Shape➜Save Shape command (which will be explained later in this chapter). For now, it's enough to know that it saves the shape of the cage. With the cage selected, move the timeslider to frame 1 and choose the Shape➜Save Shape command to save the initial shape of the cage. At frame 69, just before the action starts, save the shape again, so that the cage stays put until you are ready for it.

Step 4: As the angler approaches, the little gulper anticipates by opening its mouth and drawing back a bit. Change the timeslider to frame 100, and simulate this by selecting the points on the front half of the cage with T and scaling them back in X, causing the fish to get shorter. Also scale the points up in Y and Z just slightly, causing the fish to swell a bit. Next, tag just those control points near the corners of the fish mouth and pull them back towards the tail a little bit. Save another shape on the cage with Shape➜Save Shape Key .

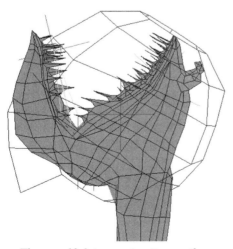

The angelfish is opening its mouth.

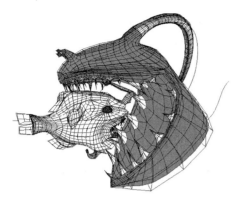

I love seafood...

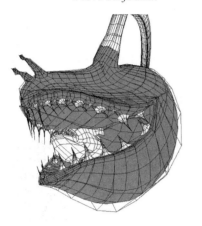

As soon as the angler is within the jaw, scale it down.

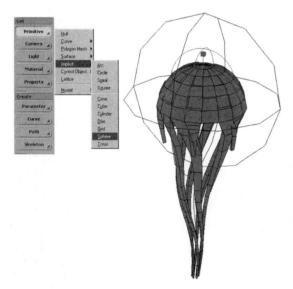

Deform by Volume uses an Implicit Sphere.

Step 5: Now all hell breaks loose for the angler. A half second later, at frame 115, the little gulper will suddenly grow like crazy, lunging forward, with a mouth that dislocates and hinges downwards to swallow the whole angler fish. Change the current frame to frame 115, and tag all the points on the lattice. Scale them all up, gradually deselecting points at the back of the fish as you go, so the tail is slightly smaller than the head, which will make the gulper fish more dramatic.

Deselect all the points, and select just the points around the lower jaw. Translate and rotate those points to open the jaw wide. Do the same for the top jaw. Also bulge the stomach region out a bit, to the bottom and to the sides.

Save another shape on the cage.

Select the unfortunate angler fish, which we'll scale down a bit in the next step, and save a keyframe for the scale of the fish.

Step 7: At frame 130, tag and move the points of the cage around the jaw to close them again, and bulge out the stomach further to the sides and bottom. Save a shape for the cage. Finally, select the angler fish and scale it down enough to fit within the gulper, carefully considering it from all sides to make sure none of it protrudes through the gulper.

Now save your scene and play back your handiwork. Render a capture in the camera view to see what it would look like in real time.

DEFORMATION BY VOLUME

Deformation by Volume looks at the source object, and requires that some of the CVs or vertices on the source object be within a bounding volume defined by an Implicit Sphere. When the Implicit sphere moves, scales, or rotates, the deformed points also transform. The interesting virtue of a Deformation by Volume is that the influence of that Implicit sphere, called the Falloff, gradually falls off from the center of the volume to the outside edge. You can adjust the profile of this falloff, and even animate where along the radius of the volume the falloff starts. This effect is great for animating a before and after type deformed pose, with a very smooth transition from the deformed vertices to the undeformed vertices. To see the Deformation by Volume in effect, get a primitive grid, and increase the number of U and V points to 14. Then get an Implicit Sphere (nothing else works) and scale and position it in the middle of the grid.

Select the grid, then choose the Deform➔Deformation by Volume command, and pick the implicit sphere. Right-click to end the command. Open the Proportional Volume Operator on the grid, and lock it in place. Then move the implicit sphere to see the results. Try adjusting the Power and Damping sliders in the Volume operator PPG to see the effect, and remember that Implicit objects don't render.

SHRINKWRAP DEFORMATION

In the example above, where a smaller creature grew suddenly to engulf a bigger one, it would certainly be funnier if the large, vicious angler fish could be seen reacting to this sudden change in his fortunes by thrashing around a little in the belly of the innocent angel fish. A Shrinkwrap deformation would help us pull this off. A Shrinkwrap deformation takes an object (or a cluster of points on an object) and shrinks the points on the surface of the object towards an inner reference object that you provide. When the points of the outer object hit the inner object, they stop. You can also adjust how close to the inner object those points get in the PPG for the Shrinkwrap deformation.

If either the inner or outer object is animated, the Shrinkwrap effect will of course change the shape of the outer object to respond to that.

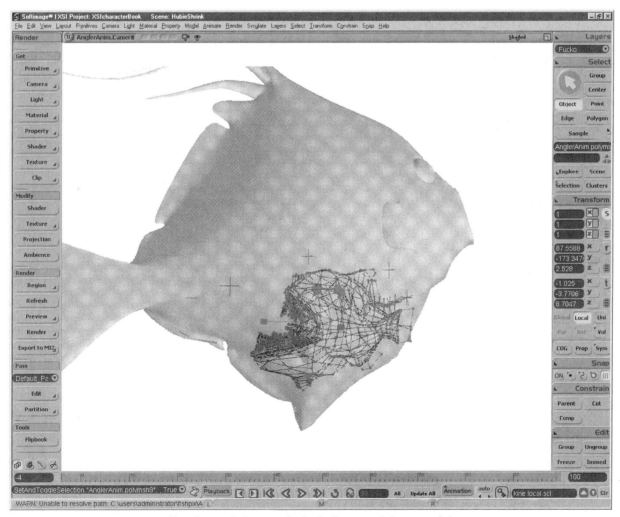

Shrinkwrap helps you fit the belly around the inner fish.

EXERCISE: SMALLER MONSTER WRAPS AROUND LARGER ONE

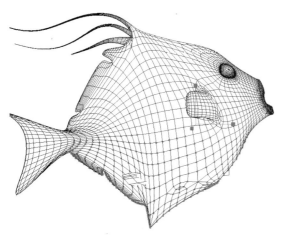

Tag the belly, make a cluster

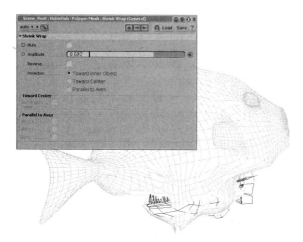

The cluster shrinks inwards. Adjust the Amplitude.

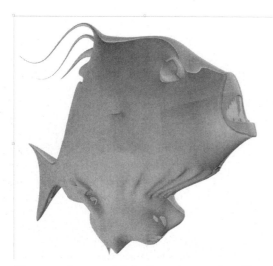

The smoother angel fish, digesting comfortably.

Here's the game plan: we'll define a cluster of points on the belly of the angel fish and apply a Shrinkwrap deformation to them. We will use the Angler fish as the inner object. We'll adjust the Deformation PPG a bit, and make the Angler fish non-renderable so it won't show up in the render even if part of it happens to stick out of the belly while it thrashes around.

Then we'll animate it moving a bit.

Step 1: Get your cage deformation scene, or open the Cmonster_Shrinkwrap.scn scene file if you want to work on a clean version.

Tag all the points around the belly of the angel fish, all around the sides and approaching the tail, and define them as a cluster. Name the cluster Belly.

Step 2: With the cluster selected (you can always select the object, then use the Clusters button in the middle of the MCP to select the cluster again if it has become uns-elected) choose the Deform➜ShrinkWrap command, and pick the Angler fish to complete the command.

Step 3: Open the ShrinkWrap deformation PPG for the angel fish, and adjust the sliders in the PPG as follows: Make sure the Projection is toward the center, and adjust the amplitude to see the effect of the Shrinkwrap. This can be animated to make one fish contract around the other.

Step 4: Select the angler fish and open the Visibility property page. Toggle off the Render Visibility check box so that it won't show up in the render. Since it won't show in the final render, don't work about it if parts seem to stick out of the angel fish in the shaded view.

Step 5: Move the angler fish around a bit. Select the angler fish and save some transformation keys for him moving back and forth, turning around, and in general desperately but unsuccessfully trying to get out of the belly of the angel fish.

Step 6: Select the angel fish, and in the Geometry Approximation PPG, under the Polygon Mesh tab, turn up the Mesh Subdivision Level to 2. A short cut for increasing the smoothing on any polygon is to tap the Plus key (+) on your keyboard. The Minus key (-) will reduce the smoothing level. In the Camera view, drag out a render region with the Q hotkey and then in the Camera menu for that view window (camera icon at top) start a capture. Choose to make the files of type .pic, make the range of frames to capture start at 1 and end at 150. Make the size 400*300.

Examine your work!

QUICKSTRETCH DEFORMATION

Softimage|XSI has a few different operators that simulate physical effects, but the easiest (and fastest) to use is the QuickStretch operator.

When you add the QuickStretch operator to an object, QuickStretch examines the motion of the object between the previous and next frames to generate values for the object's velocity, acceleration, rotational velocity, and rotational acceleration.

These acceleration and velocity values can then be used to displace each control points in the object geometry mesh from the center of mass of the object, according to parameters that you set up in the QuickStretch PPG. Why would you want to displace the points on an object mesh?

QuickStretch adds physics to your animation.

The Deform→QuickStretch Menu

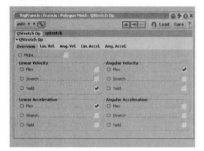

The Overview of QuickStretch Modes

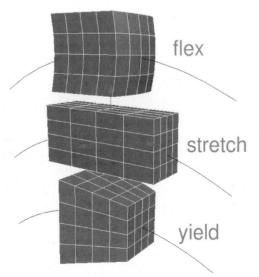

flex

stretch

yield

The three main tyoes of Quickstretch

Well, for example, in cartoon animation, the faster a character is moving, the more the character stretches out from the leading part of his body (usually the legs of belly). Or, when a rubber tire bounces down stairs, it should deform when it strikes each step, squashing down as it absorbs kinetic energy, and stretching up as it releases that energy and rebounds off the stairs. When a cartoon racer peels out, his tires balloon out due to the effect of centripetal force on the elastic rubber, and when a cartoon character is flung into a wall, he flattens out on impact. You can add these soft-body effects to your scenes automatically by adding the QuickStretch deformation operator to the objects in your scene.

Note: You can actually look at the acceleration and velocity values in the Kine.Global PPG, and use them in your own expressions and scripts.

You may also plot the Kine.Global acceleration and velocity values to generate function curves that may be edited and used later to fine-tune the effect you need. The commands to plot them are located in the Animate module, in the Plot menu cell.

The net effect is that QuickStretch lets you deform your objects to suggest the forces working on them. As objects accelerate, you can stretch them backwards to suggest conservation of momentum. When objects are moving quickly at a constant rate of speed, they can become more teardrop shaped as if deformed by air friction. As objects spin, they can stretch and wobble as if pulled apart by centripetal force.

There are three ways in which an object with QuickStretch can deform, and each works better in some cases than others. Objects can Flex, Stretch, and Yield. And each Flex, Stretch, and Yield can be paired with Acceleration, Velocity, Rotational Acceleration, and Rotational Velocity.

Flex is good for adding motion effects to objects that will be traveling quickly. When an object flexes, it appears to experience wind resistance, and the faster it moves, the more it flexes. Flex is best paired with Velocity in the Quick Stretch Setup Dialog.

Stretch is good for adding generic cartoon squash-and-stretch effects, in which characters seem to elongate and stretch when they start moving, and then compact and flatten when they come to a stop. Stretch is best paired with Acceleration in the Quick Stretch Setup Dialog.

Yield causes objects to bulge in ways that simulate the internal mass of the object shifting due to acceleration, like a bowling ball shifting around in a character's fat belly. Yield works well with both Velocity and Acceleration.

The grid of check boxes in the Quick Stretch PPG helps you quickly pair the accelerations and velocities with Flex, Stretch, or Yield, while the drop box in the middle of the dialog allows you to pick one acceleration or velocity at a time and precisely adjust the degree of Stretch, Flex, or Yield.

QuickStretch is best added to a finished animation, as the last step before the render, to add in a very slight variability to the motion of the characters. However, since it uses the movement of the entire object to determine the vectors for velocity and acceleration, it won't work well on just parts of an object. For instance, if your character shakes his head, QuickStretch won't make his ears wobble, because the ears are part of the body and the body didn't move. The softbody dynamic system would be the way to go to make the ears wiggle.

EXAMPLE: THE FLYING EGG

Open up the Egg_Quickstretch scene from the courseware project. In this scene, the egg is moving through the factory to reach the egg packing department, traveling through some rather violent machines. Although an egg is in reality quite rigid, we could add QuickStretch to the egg to suggest just how forcefully the egg is being moved through the machines.

The completed egg animation

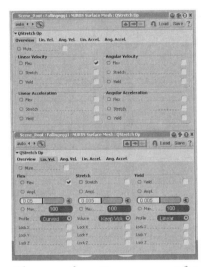

These are the settings you want for the QuickStretch.

Play back the animation in the Camera view now, before QuickStretch to get a feel for the animation.

Step 1: Add the QuickStretch. QuickStretch is pretty easy: just select the egg and choose the Deform→QuickStretch command to add the QuickStretch operator to the egg.

Step 2: Use the Selection explorer in the MCP to find and open the Qstretch Op PPG.

We want the egg to deform mainly due to changes in direction. In other words, when it suddenly changes location we want it to flex as if it can barely hold up under the strain. Either or both of Yield and Stretch would work for us here. Also, we said we want the egg to mainly change shape when it rapidly changes direction. This means that we want to use the Acceleration of the egg to determine how much Yield and Flex to apply.

Step 3: Try the effects one at a time. Turn off the Yield, Flex, and Stretch boxes in the first tab (Overview) of the PPG. Then, turn on just the Flex check box that is in the Linear Acceleration area of the overview. Play the animation to see the effect. Click on the Lin. Accel. Tab, then try adjusting the Flex Amplitude, Profile, and Max amount to change how strongly QuickStretch affects the egg. You can also lock the deformation so that it will not mash the egg in specific axes.

Step 4: Turn off all the Flex effects in the Overview tab, and try out the Linear Velocity effects. In the Lin. Vel. tab, toggle on Flex, Stretch and Yield and again experiment with the values to see if you like the effect.

That's it! Just noodle with the values to get the amount of effect you want: enough deformation so it's obvious that the egg is flexing, but not so much that you can't believe the egg wouldn't shatter.

THE PUSH TOOL

The Push tool is really just a simplification of the workflow in using the push deformation with a weight map. You can manually achieve the same result by selecting an object, adding a weight map to it, then adding a Push deformation to the object and connecting the amplitude of the Push Op to the weight map. However, all that was complicated enough that the Softimage engineers decided to make us a one-button solution.

When you have an object selected and choose the Property→Paint Push Tool command in the Model module or the Animate Module that object gets a weight map, WeightMaps are made visible in the view port under your mouse, a Push Op is added, and the Weight Painter tool – the Generic Attribute Painter (GAP) – is activated.

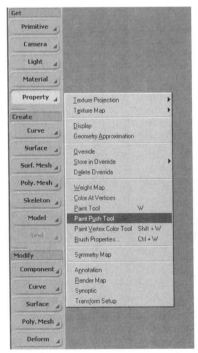

The Push Tool menu command

Set a low opacity, and high softness.

The GAP is represented by a small circle, centered on the mouse cursor, that floats over the object and indicates the direction of the surface. When you click and drag with the Left Mouse Button, you add weight to the map at that part of the object, causing it to bump out towards you. When you click and drag with the Right Mouse Button, you take away value from the weight map, which indents the surface away from the Paint tool. When you click and drag with the Middle Mouse Button you can change the size of the circular GAP, so you can work more or less precisely.

It is also very often convenient to adjust the GAP brush settings. Imagine that the GAP is an airbrush, and you want to make a larger number of gentle strokes with that airbrush to layer on paint gradually, so you don't make too large of a change to your object.

Bring up the Brush Properties PPG from the Property menu, or by pressing Ctrl-W.

The opacity slider sets how much virtual 'paint' the GAP spits out. Set it low, like 30%. The Softness slider changes how solid the edges of the airbrush pattern are. You want them to be very soft, to slide away very gradually from the center of the stroke to the edge of the stroke, so set the softness value quite low, like 10%.

The Weight Paint Mode drop box tells you what the GAP will do: Normal mode adds and removes paint from the weight map, Set Weight changes the area under the brush to be exactly the value set by the opacity slider. The coolest (and most useful) brush type is the smoothing brush, which you get when you set the Weight Paint mode to Smooth Weight. You can also invoke this brush temporarily while painting regular weight by holding the Alt key (in addition to the W key which shows the paint brush). The Smoothing brush blends adjacent areas of the weight map to make a smoother transition on the model. Smoothing is often the answer to problems of weird weighting.

The Shape Menu

The Push Tool is a valuable modeling tool. You can use it to quickly refine simple shapes, or to add in detail that would be impossible to model in. For example, use the Push tool to paint in wrinkles on clothing, or to paint fatty jowls into a character face. You could also use the Push tool to edit a model into different shapes for shape animation. In the case of the angel fish, if you chose to deform it with Shape Animation instead of with a Cage or Lattice, you could make the different shapes of the fish by painting on the fish belly with the Push tool to distend it into a giant sac.

ALL ABOUT SHAPE ANIMATION

Throughout the first half of this chapter we set up simpler deformations. Many of them could be animated by just adjusting sliders in the Property Page for the deformation, but others – like the Deformation by Curve, the Lattice, and the Deformation by spline – really just replaced the original high-res object with one that was simpler to modify and save keys on, but still needs to be animated with Shape animation.

Shape animation is the process of creating and storing different shapes for the objects in your scene, and then animating between them. First, a little background.

The shape of any object is determined by the control points or vertices that make up its geometry mesh. Obviously, if we move those points around, we'll change the shape of the object. Since the control point is really the lowest level component of the object, we can change the shape however we want by moving the points around, so we have a great deal of flexibility.

One object, changing shape

In fact, shapes are actually stored on clusters, just like all the other deformations in XSI. When you modify a few points on a model and then save that shape, XSI figures out which points are changing, and makes a cluster for just those points. Then the location of each point is stored as a vector relative to the local center of the whole object.

If you had two different shapes for the same object, you would have two different sets of locations for each point on the object (or, at least, for each point that you changed on the object, since those points would be saved in a cluster).

Then, if you asked XSI to interpolate from one shape to the other over time, the points would migrate over time from one location to the other, causing the shape of the object to change as well. This process, called Shape Animation in XSI, is sometimes called Morphing or Blending in other programs. However, Morphing and Blending both imply that you must change from just one shape to one other shape, which is untrue in XSI. In XSI you are welcome to transition between shapes, add shapes together, sequence shapes, and generally mix as many different shapes on as many different clusters together as you wish.

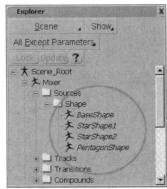

SHAPE TRACKS IN THE MIXER

Each shape has two components; the shape source, and the shape instance.

The Shape source is the actual information about the position of the control points in the cluster. This information is dynamic, as we'll see later, meaning that the shape source always points back to an origin shape, which can in some cases be modified later (we'll go into this in detail later in the chapter). The Shape source can be found, after you make it, in the Mixer of the model that the object with the shape animation is a child of.

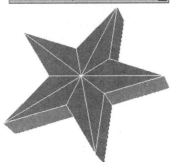

Shapes can be found in the Explorer, under the Mixer.

Under the Mixer, shape sources are located in the Sources➔Shape folder. It's a good idea to have an explorer open to the Mixer, and the Shape folder cascaded open, so you can see the shapes as you make them. It's also a good idea to re-name them as you make them by RMB clicking on the new Shape Source to pop up the context-sensitive menu, and choosing the Rename command.

The other component is the Shape Instance. A Shape Instance is the actual clip that you will see in the Mixer when you begin to animate. Shape Instances are stored in the Mixer→Tracks→Shape→Mixer_Shape_Track→Clip list folder. You create Shape instances by bringing a shape into the Mixer, either by right-clicking in a blue shape track and choosing Load Source or by dragging and dropping a Shape from the Explorer to the Animation Mixer.

You can drag and drop a single Shape Source into the Animation Mixer many times, creating many Shape Instances (Shape Clips) that all refer to the one saved Shape source.

You create Shapes for an object with the commands in the Shape menu in the Animation Module. There are really two steps to using a shape, which are Storing the Shape, and Instancing the Shape, but some of the commands in the Shape menu do both for you at the same time.

easy but not as good ←

The first command, Save Shape Key, will make a Shape Source from the selected object, and then instance that shape source into a brand new shape track in the Animation Mixer, at the current frame. This is the quick-and-dirty, all-in-one approach, but is probably not appropriate for more considered use.

better option ←
＊ offers more control

The second command, Store Shape Key, does less, but is more useful. Store Shape Key looks at the selected object, creates a cluster containing the control points that have changed position, and then saves that Shape Source into the Explorer, in the Mixer→Sources→Shape folder. It will be up to you to get it out and place it where you want it.

BEST OPTION →

The third command, Select Shape Key, is the most useful for facial animation and lip sync. Where the previous commands required you to change mold and sculpt one object into different shapes, saving Shape Sources as you went, the Select Shape Key makes new Shape Sources for you based on any number of different objects. To explain, consider that you want to make a shape animation of the Seven Dwarves. Using Select Shape Key, you would copy your dwarf model eight times: one master dwarf and seven different dwarf shapes. Then you would model the different faces into each of the seven dwarves, to use as a Shape Library. Each drawn shape must have the same number of vertices or control points arranged in the same manner.

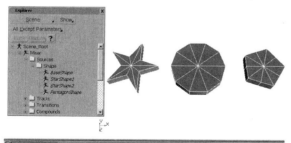

Then, you would select the master dwarf, and run the Select Shape Key command, which would prompt you to select the other objects to be used as shapes. You can then select all seven different dwarves at once, and right-click to end the command. Seven new Shape Sources would be created in the Mixer→Sources→Shape folder, all named after the different dwarf models so they are easy to organize and use.

You would then drop these Shape Sources in the Mixer as you wish.

Shape clips in their natural environment: the Mixer

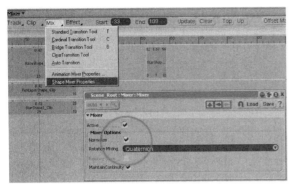

The control for Normalize toggles between Average and Additive mixing.

SHAPE INTERPOLATION VS. SHAPE WEIGHTS

Before using the Shape Mixer, you also need to understand the different Shape Mixer Modes, listed at the Bottom of the Deform➔Shape menu: Instance Only Mode and Mixed Weight Mode.

Instance only mode assumes that you will only ever be transitioning from one shape to one other shape. In other words, you will be moving from Grumpy to Sleepy to Bashful in the example above. You will never combine any features of more than two dwarves at any one time. When you use this mode in the Mixer, you'll be dropping in clips one after the next, and then connecting them with transitions. Basically this is like sequencing audio or video, one chunk following the next, perhaps with a short transition to smooth out the space between.

When you use Mixed Weight mode, however, the power of the Shape Mixer is unleashed. In Mixed Weight Mode, you can have as many shape tracks as you want, each with a different Shape Source in it, and they can all be considered all at the same time to generate the result. In the dwarf example, you could make a dwarf that combines elements of Grumpy, Sleepy, Bashful, and also mix in lip sync and facial expressions on the result. This is much more powerful, and it's the type we'll focus on in this book.

ADDITIVE VS. AVERAGE SHAPE ANIMATION (NORMALIZE)

When using the Mixed Weight mode, you also need to understand the difference between adding shapes together and averaging between shapes. Imagine, for instance, that you have two face models, one with its eyes bugged way out, and the other with eyes in a normal shape, but the mouth hanging wide open. If you want to get a face with both eyes bugged out and mouth hanging open, you could drop instances of each Shape into a Shape track on the Mixer, and blend them both together. But, by default, the total final shape will be the average of each base shape, so the eyes will be in the average shape of the two, which is only halfway bugged out, and the mouth will only be half way open, since one shape has the mouth open and the other has it completely closed. This is Average, or Normalized, Shape Animation. What we want, however, is each shape added to the other, so that all the points that make up the eyes can be moved completely to the 100% bugged-out position, and the mouth vertices can be mixed up 100%, all the way to completely open. To make this happen, use the Mix➔Shape Mixer Properties menu command to see the Shape Mixer properties, and toggle OFF the Normalize option box. Now the shapes can be added together in the Mixer to create more dramatic poses, and more potentially different options.

SAVE KEY SHAPE

Let's examine the simplest form of Shape animation, by saving individual Shapes for a lattice that deforms a Clown Wagon, and using mixing those shapes to create an animation.

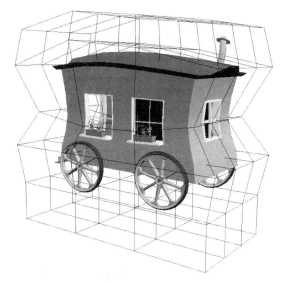

Lattices deform everything inside them.

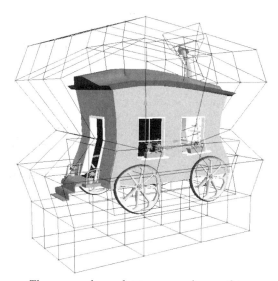

The wagon has a lattice around everything.

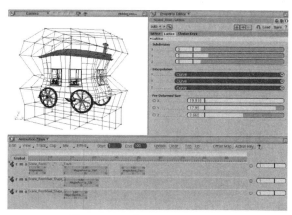

The wagon, lattice, and Mixer

Open the Lattice_Clownwagon scene from your courseware project. In it, a Circus Wagon has a Hierarchy of lattices applied to it – one set of lattices on the wheels, one lattice on the stove pipe, and a big lattice over the whole wagon. Lattices can be used in hierarchies like this; each lattice just goes on top of the others, adding its deformation to the results of the others. Inside the wagon, two clowns are beating each other savagely. We need the wagon to hop, rock, squash, bulge, and shake as if some serious violence is occurring inside.

STEP 1: CHECK YOUR SETTINGS.

We want to start simple, so make sure that the Shape menu is set to use Cardinal Transition Mode, which means that when you save shapes they will be added to the Mixer automatically, with a nice transition between them. Also check the Mix➜Shape Mixer Properties menu and make sure that Normalize is toggled on, because we want these shapes averaged together, not added on top of one another.

Now select the Wagon and change your bottom left view pane to the Animation Mixer, hit the Update button to show the wagon animation tracks. When you save a shape in the next step, a new Shape Track will be created automatically. You'll get one new Shape track for each object that you animate with Shapes.

STEP 2: SAVE A BASE SHAPE

You'll want to save a basic shape for the Wheel Lattice so that you can always bring it back to a starting position if you want to. Select the Wheel lattice – which surrounds all four wagon wheels – and choose Shape➜Save Shape Key from the Animation module. This will add a new Shape track to your Mixer, and drop in a compound clip that contains the first shape, the base shape. You can double-click to open the compound to see the individual shapes. Open the Explorer with 8, open Mixer➜Sources➜Shape, locate that first source, (probably called Point_Auto_Clip), right click and choose the rename option, then change the name to "BaseWheels" so you can find it easily later.

STEP 3: SAVE SOME MORE SHAPE KEYS.

A few frames later in time, tag and move the points on the lattice to make the wheels squash down towards the ground. A few frames after that, stretch the wheels up, and save a key. Keep moving forward in time, bending, squashing and stretching the wheels with the Wheel Lattice, and saving Shape Keys, until you reach frame 60.

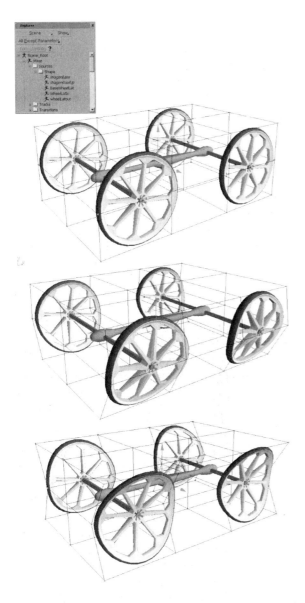

The Wheels bend in and out.

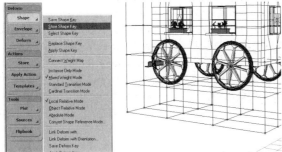

Save a Base Shape so you can return to the original shape.

STEP 4: ANIMATE THE STOVE PIPE.

The stove pipe needs to contract and stretch out rhythmically. As it compresses, it should get fatter, and as it stretches, it should get thinner, to conserve its mass. Save some Shape Keys on the lattice around the stovepipe to make this happen. You'll automatically get a new Shape track and a new Shape compound just for this lattice.

STEP 5: ANIMATE THE WHOLE WAGON.

Inside the wagon, the clowns are bashing each other, so we want to see the whole wagon leap and shimmy with the force of the blows. We also want to see the walls bulge out when a clown is slammed into them, and the whole wagon can bulge out in the middle of the walls during particularly vicious blows.

Select the big lattice surrounding the whole wagon. This is a branch lattice, applied to everything inside of it, including the other lattices. Save a starting base shape for it, and then 8 frames later, tag some points in the middle of the side of the lattice that deforms the outer wall of the wagon, and pull, scale and rotate them to make the wall bulge way out in a roughly clown-shaped way. Save a shape key. Drag the time slider back to frame 1 to restore the lattice to the base shape, then right-click and drag to frame 15, which will change time without updating the shape of the lattice. Save another key to restore the wagon to the original shape. Now tag points in the middle of all four outer walls and pull them out to bulge the walls, and scale down the top of the lattice to make the wagon shrink down, again conserving mass and volume. Save a shape key. Proceed like this until you are satisfied, watching the shape tracks grow in the Mixer.

When you play back your animation, see that all the lattices work in concert, mixing to form a more complex animation. Shape animated lattices are an easy, effective way to get a good Chuck Jones-style rubbery animation look.

Extra credit: apply a motion blur to the Wagon hierarchy before rendering it, from the Properties menu in the Render Module. Make sure to check on the Deformation Blur option in both the Motion Blur PPG and the Render Options Motion Blur tab, or the changing shape won't count as motion to blur. Rendering like this takes a lot more time and CPU power, but the extra smoothness of the animation is worth it for professional character animation.

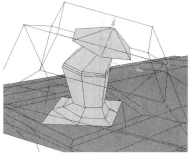

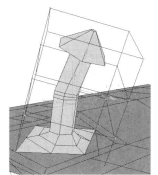

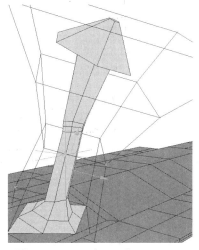

The stove pipe has a lattice, too.

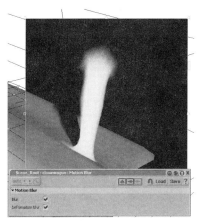

Add Motion Blur for better looking deformations.

STORE KEY SHAPE

Store Shape Key works very much like Save Shape Key, with the difference that it does not automatically insert the saved shape directly into a Shape container in the Mixer. Instead, it simply stores the Shape in a Shape Clip, in the Mixer→Sources→Shape folder. This means that you can then rename the clips as you make them, and then drag and drop them into the Mixer as you wish to, in whatever order you need to. As a practical matter, this is a much more flexible method of saving shapes. If you had used Store Shape Key with the lattices in the previous section, you could saved fewer shapes, and then dropped them into a Shape track you created, in different orders to make different sequences of deformations on the Clown Wagon. Store Shape Key is also useful when you are blending and mixing shapes, not just sequencing them as you were in the previous example. In general you will use Save Shape Key when you are modifying just one object to make the intermediary shapes.

It's helpful to have some idea of how the Shapes are stored, and what they mean to the computer. When you store a shape, each vertex or control point in the object is initially stored as a vector offset from some known point. These vectors describe the direction and distance of each point in the object. When you modify some points and again store a shape, XSI looks to see which points on the object have changed, and where the vertices or control points have moved to, also as a vector from the original position. That set of information describing which points changed, and where they moved to, is called a Shape Instance.

However, there are several options for deciding how to store the vector locations of the points. You can choose to store the changes relative to a global center in the scene, relative to the local center of the object, or relative to the surrounding group of vertices in the model. If you chose to use the Global Center by checking the Absolute Mode in the Shape menu, it might work for something like the lattice animation in the Clown Wagon scene, where the lattices are fixed in space, but it wouldn't work for a shape animation on a character skin, where the skin is constantly changing location in the scene, as well as shape. The next option, Object Relative Mode, stores the shape relative to the whole object which is better, but still if two deformations were stacked up on top of each other, you might get unexpected results. This is commonly the case when using Shape animation with IK or other deformations. The best option, Local Relative Mode, stores the moved shapes relative to the points surrounding all those that changed (technically called the local reference frame), which is kind of hard to grasp as a concept. The advantage is that shape animation can then be chained on top of other deformations, like IK envelopes, and it will all still work. Make sure that your Shape menu has the Local Relative Mode option toggled on for this next example.

EXERCISE: SHAPE ANIMATION FOR MUSCULATURE

Your goal here is to sculpt a simple arm musculature to set Shapes on it that correspond with different arm positions. For instance, if the arm is down at the character's side, the muscles will be relaxed and stretched out. As the arm curls, the biceps will contract, bulge, and move up the upper arm. The shoulder will change shape and gain definition.

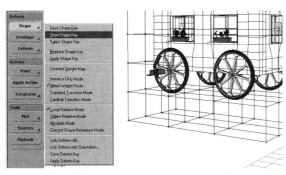

Save a Base Shape so you can return to the original shape.

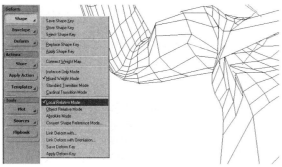

Shapes combine with other Deformations using the relative modes.

STEP 1: OPEN THE STRONG_ARM SCENE

The Strong_Arm scene in your courseware contains a simple low polygon arm and torso, with an IK rig in it. You can select the Effector (the null at the end of the IK) and translate it to move and bend the arm. Practice that so you will know how to put the arm in different poses.

STEP 2: OPEN THE MIXER

Show the Mixer, add a shape track, and also pop up the explorer in a floating window with 8, then open up the Mixer node to see what's in there. Open up the Mixer➔Sources➔Shape folder as well.

STEP 3: STORE A BASE SHAPE

It's always a good idea to save a base shape for whatever you are planning to Shape Animate, so you can get back to the original shape after you mess with the points. To do this, select the arm skin, and choose the command Shape➔Store Shape Key in the Animation module. This will add a new Shape clip in the Sources folder in the Explorer view of your Mixer that you have open in a floating window.

Click on it with the RMB and rename it BaseShape.

Note that the Store Key Shape command didn't actually add it to the Shape track in the Mixer.

STEP 4: STORE A STRETCHED POSE

Select the Effector, and stretch out the arm as if it was reaching for something. Now using M to move points, or T to tag and transform points, change the shape of the skin to a thinner, stretched shape, with the biceps thinner and flatter, and the shoulder smooth. Store a shape, and rename it StretchedShape. This shape is not actually connected in any way to the stretched out pose of the IK, you just used the IK to put the arm in a position where you could visualize how the muscles would be shaped

STEP 5: STORE A CONTRACTED POSE

Now select the IK Effector and pose the arm in a contracted position, with the arm clenching to contract the biceps and flex the shoulder. Use M to modify the shape of the arm, building a bigger biceps and creating some muscle definition in the shoulder. Store the shape, and rename it Flexed.

The completed arm with deformations

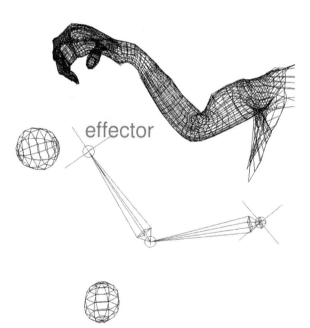

The effector moves the arm.

STEP 6: SEQUENCE IN THE MIXER

In the Mixer, drag and drop the named Shape Clips into the Shape track in whatever order you wish, including repeating clips several times. Add a transition between them by holding the T hot key and clicking in series from one clip to the other. Play back your work.

At this point, the bulging is not linked to the pose of the IK. Later in this book we'll use the pose of the IK to automatically drive the Shape Animation.

SELECT KEY SHAPE

There is a third method for using Shape animation in XSI, and it is the most powerful and useful of the three ways. Using Select Key Shape, you can create a library of Shape clips that all reference different objects in your scene. All those instances can be mixed together on one base shape, using the Mixer. This method has several advantages: you can individually sculpt each of the objects that will become your final shapes, you can see them all together at the same time while you are working, and any changes you make later on to the original shape objects will be automatically carried all the way through all your animation, even if you've already moved along to the Mixer stage.

The short version of the workflow is simple: model your base object, then make duplicates of it. Modify those duplicates as you wish to, then with the original one selected, choose the Shape→Select Key Shape command, and then pick with your Left Mouse Button on the new modified versions, one at a time. When you've picked on them all, click with the Right Mouse Button to complete the command.

This tells XSI to look at the objects that you picked, find those vertices or control points that have changed from the original selected object, and make new shape clips to represent them. These new shape clips are stored in the usual place, under the Mixer→Sources→Shape folder in the Explorer, and given names based on the names of the modified objects you picked, so it's a good idea to name everything before you execute the Shape→Select Key Shape command.

Once your shape clips have been created, you can use them in a shape track in the Mixer in the usual ways, sequencing them with transitions, but you can also use them in a new way, with Additive Shape animation (which means toggling Normalize OFF in the Shape Mixer properties).

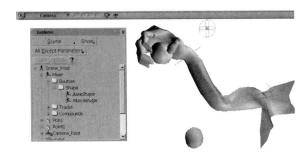

Show the Mixer, the arm, and the Explorer.

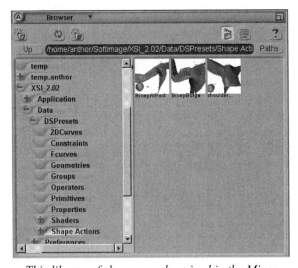

This library of shapes can be mixed in the Mixer.

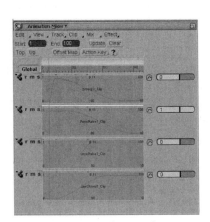

Now you can see the weight curves in the Mixer.

If you have four shapes, like the faces below, you can create one shape track for each shape clip, then drop each clip onto its own track at frame one, and drag the right middle of the clip to extend it all the way to the end of your animation. Now you can blend between the shapes any way you wish by dragging the Shape Weight sliders at the right edge of each track. When your timeslider in the Mixer is over a shape clip, you can adjust that Weight slider to mix the influence of that clip into the base model that was originally selected when you used the Select Key Shape command. By setting keyframes on the green animation divot next to the slider, you can animate the shape changing over time.

Make sure View➜Weight Curves is toggled on so you can see a feedback curve describing the current Weight of each shape clip in the Mixer.

EXERCISE: PRACTICE WITH SHAPE MIXING

In this simple exercise, you'll look at a base Leroy head with four facial expressions: two eyebrow raises, a mouth open, and a mouth closed. You'll make some Shape clips using Select Key Shape, and then mix them together in the Mixer to create some simple animation.

STEP 1: OPEN THE LEROYFACE.SCN

In the lower-left view window, change the view type to show the Mixer, which will extend across the bottom.

Make sure View➜Weight Curves is toggled ON.

Make sure Normalize is toggled OFF in the Shape Mixer Properties PPG, so that the Leroy expressions can be really extreme, not limited to an average of all of them.

In your Camera view, examine the five heads. The bottom head will be the base shape that you animate – the shape clips will drive this object. The four heads above will be the source material you pick to add the shape clips that do the driving of the base shape.

STEP 2: MAKE THE SHAPE CLIPS

Open a floating explorer view with 8 and look in the Mixer to see that there are no shape sources yet.

Now select the Base Shape, the lower head. Since it's selected, the Shapes you add will drive this head, the Base Shape. Choose the Shape➜Select Key Shape command from the Animation Module, and pick with just the Left Mouse Button on each of the four upper heads in order from left to right. When you have picked them all, right-click to end the command.

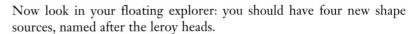

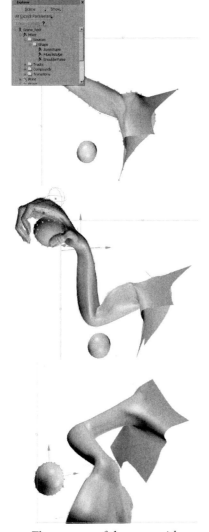

Three poses of the arm, with shapes for the muscles

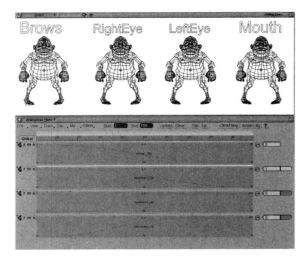

Each of the four face shapes has its own shape Mixer track.

Now look in your floating explorer: you should have four new shape sources, named after the leroy heads.

STEP 3: ADD SHAPES TO THE MIXER

Make four blue Shape tracks in the Mixer. (The green Animation tracks won't work for this.) Drop one shape clip into each track, either drag-and-dropping from the explorer or using the RMB context menu.

Make each clip as long as the entire Mixer, starting at frame 1, so they are all the same length, stacked above each other.

STEP 4: MIX MASTER

Start with all the Weight sliders down to zero. Then, drag one up to see the change on the bottom head in the Camera view. Try each slider one at a time, then try mixing them on top of each other. Finally, set some keys on the Weight for each Shape track by clicking on the green animation divot next to the slider. Play back to see the results.

SHAPE ANIMATION FOR EXPRESSIONS AND LIP SYNC

Facial expressions, mouth movements, and lip positions really do lend themselves to Shape Animation in XSI, and since the Select Key Shape method is the most flexible, it's also the most useful for facial character animation.

Using Shape animation, we can create different models to represent the different actions of the muscles in the face, and the different shapes of the mouth formed by phonemes during speech, and then mix all these different shapes in any way we wish. Then, we'll have a relatively few shapes that can be combined in an endless variety of ways.

USING PROPORTIONAL MODELING

Proportional modeling is a huge help in setting up facial shapes. Normally, if you tag or move a point on an object, like the corner of the mouth on the Leroy model, only that point moves, leaving the neighboring points behind. It's almost impossible to move all the points in exactly the same way, so the more you mess with the points while animating, the more messy and ugly your model tends to become. Proportional modeling introduces the concept that when you move a point with the M hot key, or tag and translate a point or group of points, those points in the surrounding area will also move, in a smooth, fluid manner that gradually blends into the unmoved points elsewhere on the model.

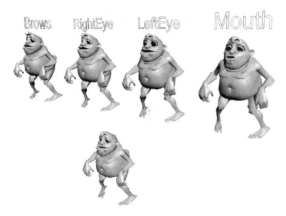

One base head, four to use as shape sources. Leroy model by Elliot Rosenstein.

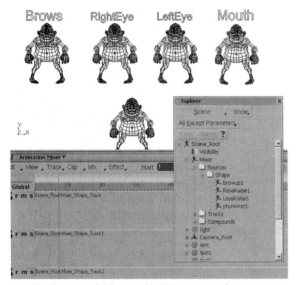

The Sources folder in the Mixer now shows new shapes.

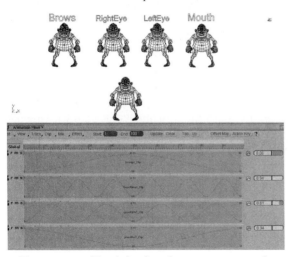

Now you can blend the four face sources onto the result head.

PROPORTIONAL SETUP

You can determine how far away the Proportional modeling effect extends from the points that you move, which controls how much the model distorts when you change something. You can also control the manner in which the effect blends, which is called the falloff. Modeling facial shapes with Proportional effect is like pulling on a rubber mask. The distance of the falloff determines how stretchy the mask is when you pull on it.

To use Proportional modeling, just toggle on the Modify➔Component➔Proportional toggle. Open up the Proportional Setup PPG with the Component➔Proportional Setup command.

You'll have to change the Distance Limit for each different model that you use Proportional modeling on, since each model is likely to be a different size. Look at your model, and count the number of grid squares across the object, and figure out what portion of that you want to be rubbery when you move a point. You can always try it out, Undo, and then go back and change the Distance Limit. You'll also see a graphical representation of the Distance Limit when you invoke Proportional Modeling. Try that out by turning on Proportional Modeling the other way, with the Prop button in the bottom of the transform panel in the MCP, then select a model and hold the M key to modify a point. A circle will appear around your mouse cursor, showing the range of the Proportional Falloff on that model.

If your object is a Surface Mesh, you can also express the falloff distance in terms of the number of U and V parameters that you want to be rubbery around the points you move, by checking on the Use U/V Limits option. This will do nothing to a polygon mesh object, since polygon vertices don't have Us and Vs. You can now specify how far away in terms of U and V the effects of your modeling will ripple through the NURBS mesh.

Open the LeroyHead.scn file from your courseware, turn on Proportional Modeling, and experiment with the M hot key, tagging and transforming points, and adjusting the falloff distance limit.

HIERARCHIES OF SHAPE ANIMATION

Since shape clips contain instances or pointers to the vertices or CVs in the original model, when you change the original model that a shape clip was based on, the contents of the shape clip itself also change.

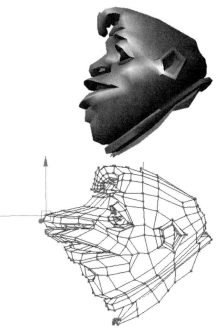

A face before and after proportional modeling.

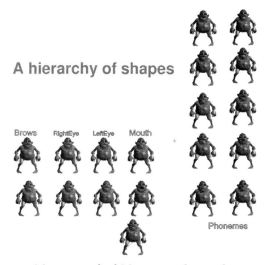

A hierarchy of shapes

Mixers can feed Mixers in a hierarchy.

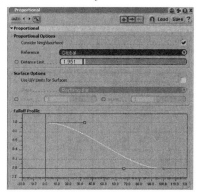

The Proportional Modeling setup PPG

The shape clips are dynamically linked back to the original objects you used to make them – at any time you can go back to modify the originals and the changes will be reflected properly. If you delete the original shape objects, then the shapes remain, but you won't be able to modify them.

The real magic here is that shape source models can themselves have shape animation on them, creating the possibility that you could have shape animation on shape animation on shape animation... the mind boggles at the possibilities. For instance, imagine that you have a character, with shape animation for facial expressions and for lip sync, so the character can talk. On top of that, you could create shapes for emotional state – anger, sadness, fear – based on the musculature in the face that contracts during these emotions. Then you could go back and change the emotional state of the character after you've done the basic expressions and lip sync, giving each scene in your animation a different emotional flavor. Then, imagine that you make three more shapes for your character: a normal shape, a fat shape, and an emaciated shape. Now you can blend these shapes in to change the character's facial fattiness, on top of emotion, on top of expression, on top of lip sync. It's crazy.

As a practical matter, each new Shape should be its own Model, because each model can have its own Mixer. This way, you'll end up with a hierarchy of Mixers, each containing shape sliders controlling the blend of objects in that Model, and contributing to the Models above them in the hierarchy. While you could accomplish the same effect with only one Mixer, you would soon have far more Shape tracks than you could keep track of, and animating would become very difficult. In the extended Exercise below the exact workflow for accomplishing this will be detailed.

A SHAPE TREE FOR FACIAL ANIMATION: AT A GLANCE

TOPICS COVERED

This tutorial covers adding complex facial animation with a hierarchy of shape models, blended together in the Mixer, and finally controlled with expressions driven by a custom property panel.

You'll learn how to:

- Add shapes to a base model head
- Organize a hierarchy of Emotions, Expressions, and Phonemes
- Blend these different shapes in the Mixer
- Animate the shapes changing over time

MATERIALS REQUIRED

This tutorial uses the LeroyShapeTree scene from the courseware.

TUTORIAL: A SHAPE TREE FOR FACIAL ANIMATION

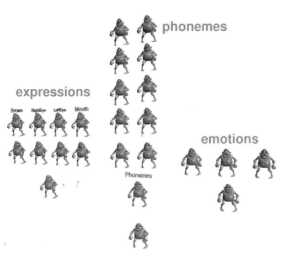

All these heads contribute to Leroy's emotions.

A character's face is really the most important part of character animation. Modern computer animation has not often done a good job here, and as a result, the characters tend to look dull and lifeless, or waxen. In many ways, the more accurately the character is modeled, the more dead the resulting animation will look. Compare your favorite CG character to the range of expression exhibited by Bugs Bunny, for instance, to see that the CG industry has much to learn from the traditional animation styles. CG animation has also been focused (unnecessarily, in my opinion) on precise control over mouth shapes determined by phonemes, or the sounds we make with our lips, mouths, and tongues. Since CG characters don't actually make sounds, this seems a bit silly, and results in characters that enunciate well, but don't change their facial expression, kind of like Kevin Costner.

Your characters can overcome this dead look only by expressing emotion through changes in the shape of the face, in the muscles around the mouth, the eyes, and the brows, in addition to enunciating.

Our Leroy will have quite a hierarchy of shapes driving it. We'll start out with a base shape, as Leroy was modeled. Then we'll build a hierarchy of shape clips to drive the final Leroy shape.

STEP 1: LOAD THE LEROYSHAPETREE.SCN SCENE FROM THE COURSEWARE

The LeroyShapeTree scene has one base head, named BaseHead, and above it, an emotionally disturbed head, named Emotions, which has shapes for rage, happiness, and fear, a head for Expressions, and a head for Phonemes. Take a look at all the heads, select them and check out their names, and become familiar with the organization of the tree of heads.

The first level of heads

STEP 2: MAKE THE BASE HEAD MODEL

You want to have a series of Mixers, one for each of the main head shapes, so you can isolate what goes on in that head, and don't have to look at all the possible shapes in one huge Mixer. Let's start with the BaseHead. Select it, and choose Model→New from the Model module to turn it into a Model. In the explorer, see that this is so, and name the new Model "BaseHeadModel".

Save a Base Shape for the BaseHead, so you can always mix back to the default beginning point if you need to. With the BaseHead Selected, choose the Shape→Store Shape Key, and in the explorer, locate the Mixer→Sources→Shape folder, and rename the new shape clip to be "BaseHeadShape" so you'll know what it is later.

The EmotionHead mixer

Now you'll add the five heads above the BaseHead as Shapes, so that everything you do will filter down to the BaseHead. With the BaseHead polygon mesh (not the Model) selected, choose the Shape→Select Shape Key command, and pick on the EmotionHead, the ExpressionHead, and the PhonemeHead. Right-click to end the command. Now the BaseHead has its own Mixer.

Open the Mixer for the BaseHead by selecting it, showing a Mixer window, and hitting the Update button. Add four Shape tracks, and in the first one, drop in the BaseHeadShape, and make it 100 frames long.

Now drop in the other three shapes – Emotion, Expression, and Phonemes – each into its own Shape Track.

Change the shape mixing method to Additive, by turning off Normalize in Mix→Shape Mixer Properties, so you can add the effect of each shape on top of the others, without diluting the results.

STEP 3: MAKE THE EMOTION HEAD MODEL, AND ADD THE SHAPES; RAGE, HAPPINESS, FEAR

Select the Emotion Head, and make it into a model, as in the previous step. Name it "EmotionHeadModel".

Now, select just the EmotionHead mesh, and run the Shape→Select Key Shape command. Pick on the three heads stacked above the Emotion head, from top to bottom, representing Rage, Happiness, and Fear. Right-click to end the command. With the EmotionHead selected, open a Mixer window. This Mixer will belong to just the EmotionHead.

Open the Mixer, and create three Shape tracks. In the top track, add the shape clip Rage, and make it 100 frames long. In the next track, add Happiness, and make it 100 frames long, right below the Rage clip. In the third track, add Fear, and make it the same length as the others. Rage, Happiness, and Fear represent the continuum of muscular contraction in the facial muscles. In Rage, the corners of the mouth are constricted into a grimace, the brows are knotted, and the muscles under the cheeks are tight. In the Happiness pose, those muscles have all relaxed to a dopey state. Then in the Fear pose, they constrict again, in a different manner from fear. Since you want these shapes to be blended to one another, no two should be up at 100% at any one time. This is Average mixing, so you should leave the Normalize flag on. Experiment, starting with Happiness all the way up, then blend happiness down as you increase fear, or decrease Happiness and increase Rage. Always mix back to Happiness when done. Note that the BaseHead also changes when you do this.

STEP 4: EXPRESSION HEAD SHAPES; MOUTH SHAPE HEADS, EYES SHAPE HEADS, BROW SHAPE HEADS

Now you'll carry out the same plan for the Expressions.

What you need to do is create a new Model for the ExpressionHead, as above, and then add Shape Clips, with Select Shape Key, for the Mouth Shapes, Eye Shapes, and Brow Shape heads, just as you did in the two previous steps.

When done, examine the Mixer you made for the ExpressionHead, and drop in the Shape clips you made. This Mixer should have Normalize Off for best results, so the shapes are added on top of one another.

ALL ABOUT PHONEMES AND MOUTH SHAPES

The noises you make in English can be broken down to 24 distinct phonemes. A phoneme is a sound, not a letter, and sometimes is less than a letter or more than a letter. While different languages have slightly different phonetic structures, some with more and some with fewer mouth sounds, phonemes are closer to a universal description of speech than languages are. The noises we make with our mouths are different because we use our lips, our mouth shape, our teeth, and our tongues to modify the noise made with our vocal cords. This is all very complex, but fortunately, as animators, you don't need to understand all of it. That's because our characters don't have vocal cords, so they aren't actually going to make any noise. The actual noise will be made by voice actors. You generally just have to make it seem like the characters could be making those noises. Depending on the style of your animation, that may require very little more than flapping the mouth open and closed, or it might require carefully perfecting the exact lip shapes of an actual human so that your work matches perfectly.

STEP 5: CHOOSE THE PHONEMES

We'll take a middle approach in this exercise, creating only those phonemes that result in different mouth shapes, using teeth and tongue. Note: This is the author's abridged, inaccurate, hack of the phonemes. Many have done a better, more complete job. This is just the minimum you need.

THE PHONEMES WE NEED

> (B,P,M,) – Lips lightly closed
> (R,L) – Lips slightly open, tongue on roof of mouth
> (V,F) – Lips open slightly, lower lip touching teeth
> (Th) – Lips open a third of the way, tongue on front teeth, corners of mouth contracted
> (Da,Ta,Sa,Ja,Ya,Ch) – Lips open halfway, lips loose, tongue in middle of mouth
> (Ih) – Lips one third open, lips slightly curled down, tongue down
> (Ee, Ye, Gee) – Lips one-third open, lips pulled back to corners, no teeth, no tongue
> (Aa) – Lips all the way open, no teeth, tongue on floor of mouth
> (Oo) – Mouth pursed to O shape, no teeth, no tongue

I've reduced the number of Phonemes we'll use to nine, and you could reduce it further, based on the accuracy you need.

STEP 6: PHONETIC MOUTH SHAPES

Select the PhonemeHead, and use Shape→Select Key Shape to add in the 9 phonetic shape clips. In the Mixer, you can drop the 9 clips. Remember, phonemes are mutually exclusive, which means that you can't have two phonemes going at the same time. You can only blend from one to the next, so you could use these in a sequenced fashion, or you can blend them as you've done above, making sure that as one is weighted up, all the others are weighted down. Since no more than two shapes should be in the process of being blended together at any one time, you should use Average shape animation, so leave the Normalize toggled on for this Shape Mixer.

STEP 7: SAVING KEYS IN THE MIXERS

You now have a hierarchy of Mixers:

One Mixer on the BaseHead, with tracks for the EmotionHead, the ExpressionHead, and the PhonemeHead. These should all be on their own tracks, all blended up 100%, and this Mixer should be Additive, to add the components of each together.

One Mixer on the Emotion head, blending Rage, Happiness, and Fear.

One Mixer on the Expression head, blending shapes for the brows, the eyes, and the mouth.

One Mixer on the Phoneme head, for adding in lip sync.

Because this is a whole lot of information, and a ton of tracks in the Mixer, you'll want to animate in layers, synchronizing to a planning document like a timing sheet or a video animatic.

Start with the Emotion head. Open up the Emotion Mixer, and looking at the BaseHead (the one you'll actually render) move through the animation, choose an emotional state for the character. If the emotional state doesn't change within the shot that you are working on, you won't even need to set keyframes. Just adjust the Weight sliders to get the emotion you want.

Move on to the Expression Mixer, and when your character reacts to something else, either another character's actions or something in the dialog, save keys for the change in the facial expressions. If the character is surprised, look in the EyeBrow Mixer, and blend up the shape with the raised eyebrows, look in the mouth Mixer to blend up the shape with the open mouth, and look in the eye Mixer to blend up the shape with both eyes wide. In this manner, you can combine the effects of the eyes, mouth, and brows independently, setting keys on the green animation divot at different frames to overlap the muscles in the face, combining to make a very wide range of facial expressions. In the next section we'll look at a custom control panel to simplify this process.

Finally, after all the other animation has been roughed in and edited, you would add in the dialogue in an Audio track in the Mixer, and adjust the Phonemes, setting keys to match the sounds in the dialogue to the phonemes in the Phoneme Mixer.

This setup process is long and complicated, but you are working on the front end of the process to make it easier to animate large volumes of material later on. In a professional setting, the tasks of defining the shapes, setting up the Mixers, and getting the whole character ready for the animators would be performed by a Technical Director.

STEP 8: USING EXPRESSIONS TO SIMPLIFY SHAPE MIXING

One significant problem with blending shapes is that to do everything you want to do, you create a great many shapes, and each of these has a track in one of many Mixers that needs to be animated. If you have too many Mixers, each with too many tracks and too many shapes, animating will become confusing, and unproductive, not to mention un-fun. Another problem is that many of the shapes you define are exclusive to each other, meaning they can't (or aren't supposed to, more specifically) occur at the same time. For instance, it will never make sense to mix the mouth open shape with the mouth closed shape. You really need to come up with a logical way to make sure this doesn't happen, and also to simplify the process of animating the character.

The solution is to build a custom control system that aggregates the multitude of small controls into a much smaller number of very high-level controls, using custom sliders that control the Weight sliders in the Mixer.

For instance, you could create one slider that has three positions. When it is in the middle position, the mouth is slack. When it is at the low end (the left end) the mouth would be wide open, and when it's at the right, high end of the scale the mouth will be pursed shut tight. This slider would make sure that contradicting shapes are never blended together, would group three Weight sliders into one, and would mean you don't ever have to actually open up the mouth Mixer while animating.

Let's decide on some standard ideas. Whenever possible, we'll build shapes, Mixers, and sliders that mimic the muscle groups in the human face. Whenever possible those muscle groups will have three positions: contracted, slack, and extended. Then, you can build sliders that mix in such a way that as slider smoothly brings up each shape in turn, gradually transitioning between the neighboring shapes, but never actually mixing all three together, and never mixing the contracted with the extended pose.

To do that, you'll have to understand Custom Controls, covered later in this book in Chapter 7, and Expressions, covered in Chapter 10. For now you can see the expressions set on the Mouth Weight sliders, to give you an idea of how it's coded, and you can see the final result.

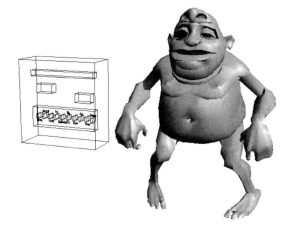

This custom control drives all those head shapes in the Mixers. Leroy model by Elliot Rosenstein.

Open the file LeroyShapeDone.scn from the courseware.

Select the only Leroy there. Open his Mixer to see all the tracks necessary (in this case flattened out of the hierarchy for speed and efficiency). The blends on the tracks are driven by expressions that reference the 3D controller. The shape references have been frozen and the original shape models deleted to simplify the scene.

As you can see, the sky is the limit for what you can do with mixing hierarchies of shapes. The dynamic interconnections between the original shape models and the ultimate shape target create a completely unlimited shape animation system. You can combine hierarchies of shape mixers in an unlimited number of ways to create complex characters with emotion, phases, ages, or anything else you can think of.

ORDER OF OPERATORS

The order of operators is important to understand when setting up your final work. Your character will have Inverse Kinematics enveloping, perhaps some other local bulge or other deformations, and Shape animation. All these things work by displacing the vertices or control points on the object, so you can imagine that the order in which they are added is quite important. For instance, if you built your shape animation first, then installed the IK, the character might not operate correctly.

Until XSI has an easy to use interface for re-ordering which operators deform your mesh first and next, it's a good idea to follow this order:

> First, add Shape Animation
> Next add Deformations
> Finally, bind the Skin (Envelope) to the IK skeleton.

To re-order operators on your characters, just view the model in the Explorer window, open the polyMesh or NURBS Surface Mesh folder to view the operator stack, click on the lower operator and drag it above the upper operator in the explorer list, then let go. Now the order of the operators has been switched! Different operator order can have a significant impact on performace. If your model is moving really slowly, try switching the order of the Envelope operator and the other Shape and Deform operators.

CONCLUSION

Animation in XSI isn't just about moving, rotating and scaling objects. Each and every object can bend, twist, wriggle, slink, flatten, or bulge using simple deformer operators. QuickStretch is a simple way to add a physics-based, soft-body look to your animation. And when you need the ultimate level of control, you can actually sculpt the different shape poses for your objects, and then use shape animation to sequence, mix, and blend any manner or shape change on your objects.

QUIZ

1. **THE BULGE DEFORMER IS:**
    a. A weight map
    b. An envelope
    c. An operator

2. **WHICH AXIS WILL BE ALIGNED ALONG THE CURVE IN A CURVE DEFORM?**
    a. X
    b. Y
    c. Z

3. **YOU CAN T USE A CURVE DEFORM TO MOVE OBJECTS THROUGH SPACE.**
    a. True
    b. False

4. **DEFORMATIONS ARE APPLIED ON:**
    a. Clusters
    b. Weight maps
    c. Operators

5. **WHICH MOUSE BUTTON ADJUSTS THE RADIUS OF THE PAINT TOOL?**
    a. Left
    b. Middle
    c. Right

6. **YOU CAN USE A WEIGHT MAP ON:**
    a. Push Operators
    b. All operators
    c. Any property with a weight plug

7. **DOES A LATTICE NEED TO HAVE THE SAME NUMBER OF STEPS IN X, Y AND Z?**
    a. Yes
    b. No

8. **WHAT SHAPE IS A CAGE DEFORMER?**
    a. Cubic
    b. Spherical
    c. Any shape

9. **HOW MANY SHAPES CAN YOU STORE FOR AN OBJECT?**
    a. 99
    b. unlimited or unknown
    c. 999

10. **TO MAKE SHAPES ADDITIVE, NORMALIZE SHOULD BE:**
    a. On
    b. Off

5 INVERSE KINEMATICS

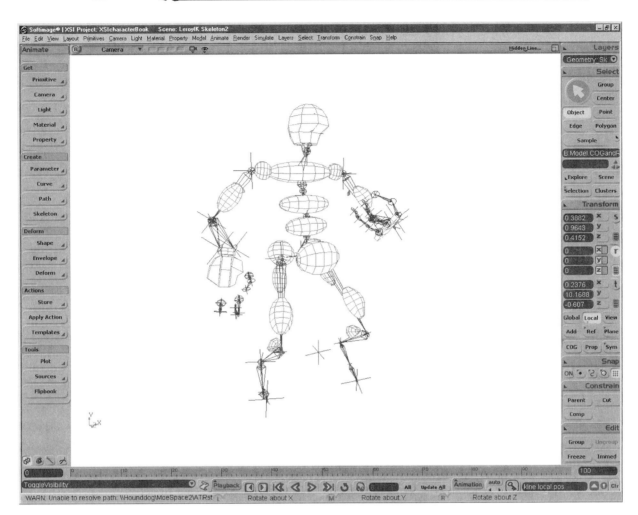

IN THIS CHAPTER YOU WILL LEARN ABOUT:

- Inverse Kinematics (IK) Concepts and Terminology
- When to use IK and when to use Forward Kinematics (FK)
- How to draw and use 2D and 3D IK chains
- How to animate your IK chains
- How to blend FK and IK animation
- How to control the Resolution Plane with Constraints
- How to change Bone Length and set Rotation Limits
- How to use Joint Roll and Joint Friction.
- Rigid Attachment of geometry to IK chains
- How to parent many chains together for complex skeletons

INTRODUCTION

Inverse Kinematics (IK) is probably the most popular topic in 3D animation today. Softimage 3D was one of the first 3D animation programs to implement a production IK package, and now Softimage XSI has one of the most complex and flexible models in the animation business. The Softimage IK system is a large part of why Softimage XSI is considered the greatest character animation tool in the world.

IK bones are just deformers.

Forward Kinematics means rotat-ing each joint.

Despite the fact that IK is a very complicated way to animate, takes lots of setup time, and that it is just plain tough to understand, everybody wants to do it. But what is it? In this chapter we'll answer that question and lead you through practical examples starting simply and working up to complex IK systems.

INVERSE KINEMATIC CONCEPTS

At the most basic level, IK is just a deformer, like the simpler Bulge, Bend, Taper, Twist, and Lattice Deformers. You will use Inverse Kinematics systems to bend and twist your character's skin. What's different is the way that the IK works, to create deformations of the skin that seem to mimic the way that skin or another similar membrane stretches over your own skeleton and musculature, bending at the joints, twisting around the spine, and bulging over the paunchy parts.

Each IK Bone influences the skin around it, so that where the bone goes (and scales and rotates) so does the skin. That part of the concept is easy but IK has another component: the joint.

FORWARD KINEMATICS VS. INVERSE KINEMATICS

To understand Inverse Kinematics, first consider Forward Kinematic systems. If you make an arm by building the upper arm, attach a child forearm object to it, then a palm to the forearm, then a first finger joint to the palm, and then each other finger joint to the previous, you are constructing a Forward Kinematic system. If the local center of each child object is located at the joint position between the child and the parent object, as you rotate the parent all the children move as well. By a painstaking process of saving rotational keyframes for each joint in the bone structure, you can animate the arm moving while opening and closing the fingers.

Back in the day, all motion was performed this way, with a hierarchy of transformations on each object. The major problem with this approach was that, although accurate, it was a very slow way to generate animation. Each and every joint was keyframed at each and every transition frame, and when changes were necessary, each and every joint was re-keyframed. Forward Kinematics lacks the ease, speed, and flexibility of Inverse Kinematics as an animation system. On the other hand, since the animator gets to key the rotation of each and every joint whenever he or she wishes to do so, it is possible to create fluid motions and gestures that are simply impossible to get any other way.

Inverse Kinematics is the simple theory that if you build an articulated model, such as an arm, you should be able to move the arm by simply pulling on the finger, not just by rotating the shoulder joint, the elbow joint, the wrist, and then each joint in the finger. Since the arm is anchored at the shoulder, the software should understand the relationship between each bone in the system and how they are connected by joints that can rotate. When you translate the end of the bone structure (the finger), each joint in order from the finger to the wrist to the elbow to the shoulder should flex and rotate to allow the arm to move. That is, after all, the way it seems to work in real life.

(Actually, in real life if you grab your friend's arm and pull it, that is Inverse Kinematics. If you wave your own arm, that's Forward Kinematics, because you have muscles that rotate each joint independently, while your brain calculates how much of each is required to get the finger where it needs to go. It's just that your brain is so darn good at calculating these joint rotations in real time, you don't need to consciously think about it.)

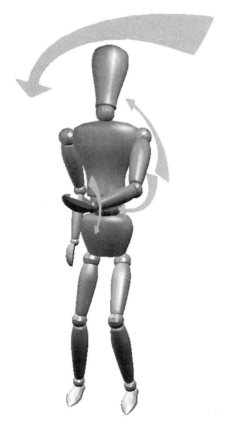

The arcs show the fluid motion possible with FK.

In an Inverse Kinematic system, you need to save a keyframe for only the position of the end of each joint structure at different points in time. The IK system then has to look at where the top of the chain is (the shoulder), and where you wanted the end of the chain, then figure out the rotation of each joint in that bone structure to get the end (the finger) where you want it, when you want it.

WHAT'S A SOLVER?

The solver is the code that actually makes the IK work correctly. The IK solver is easy to use in XSI. Instead of pulling on someone's finger, you select the effector of an IK chain, which is the null at the end of the chain, and then translate it to activate the IK solver. The solver then figures out the joint rotations to make everything happen the way you want. When changes are necessary, only the effector at the end of the bone structure needs to be re-keyframed or edited in the Animation Editor, not each and every joint rotation in the whole chain.

The root of the IK can move, and the effector of the IK can move, and either way the solver will figure out how to rotate the joints appropriately.

What's more, in the XSI IK system, a number of smaller bone structures can be connected together to form a more complex skeletal structure. Each bone structure can move relative to the other bones.

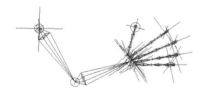

This is an IK arm.

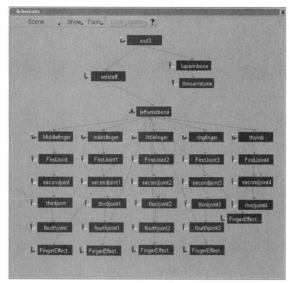

A hand is an example of a hierarchy of IK.

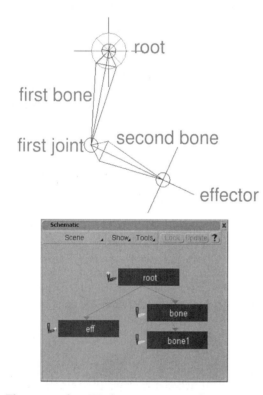

The parts of an IK chain: root, joint, bone, effector

IK isn't all smiles and roses. Unlike Forward Kinematics systems, in which each joint rotation is specified explicitly, the rotation in IK systems is implied by the position of the ends of the bone structure. This means that there could be more than one way to get the bone structure to its end position (called an IK solution). When there is more than one IK solution, the bone structure may behave erratically. The capability to precisely control the behaviors of the bone structures, and the skins over them, is the first part of what makes using IK so tough. Controlling the way that skin is deformed by complex IK (called Enveloping) is the rest of the problem.

MORE IK TERMINOLOGY

In XSI, all the Inverse Kinematics controls, along with the other controls necessary for applying skins to your characters (Enveloping), are located in the Animate Module. Select the Animate Module at the top of the screen, or press the F2 button to go there.

In XSI, each entire bone structure is called an IK chain. In the arm analogy, the arm itself is a chain, while each finger is a separate chain.

On a single chain, the top of the hierarchy is called the root of the chain. The root is a null object that anchors the chain in space. After the root comes a bone. The bone has length, and a radius to make it easy to select. Then, at the end of the bone, comes the joint, shaped like a small circle or sphere. Then, usually, more bones and more joints. An IK chain can have any number of bone and joint pairs.

Finally, at the end of the last joint is the effector, the most important part of the chain. The effector is a null object that acts as the handle for the IK chain. When you select the effector and translate it, the IK solver rotates each joint in the chain to try to get the effector just where you want it. If you try to translate the effector far away from the chain, the chain just rotates to its maximum length and points towards the direction you are trying to move it. IK chains are not elastic.

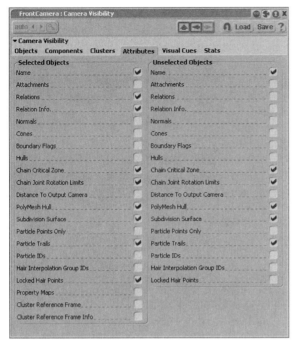

The Visibility Options→Attributes options can be different in each view.

The IK tools are in the Skeleton menu.

The Draw 2D Chain command in the Skeleton menu.

THE CONES OF DOOM

When you create an IK chain, there are some special feedback options you can turn on in each viewport to give you additional useful information. Under the Show (eyeball) menu, in the Visibility Options at the bottom of the list, look for the Attributes tab and turn on the Chain Critical Zone, Chain Joint Rotation Limits, and Name options, in the Selected Objects column. Seeing the name superimposed on the parts of the chain will be helpful as you learn what each element looks like, and turning on Critical Zones shows information you'll need to avoid flipping. When the effector is translated into the area of the critical zone, unexpected flipping may occur as the IK chain changes orientation rapidly, and the solver finds multiple solutions to the rotations. It's a good idea to keep your effector away from the critical zones.

EXERCISE: DRAWING YOUR FIRST CHAIN

It's time to put all this theory into practice and forge an IK chain.

STEP 1: ENTER THE ANIMATE MODULE

Click the Animate Module at the top-left of the screen, or press the F2 key on your keyboard. The Animate Module is where all the commands that control Inverse Kinematic systems are located.

STEP 2: DRAW THE CHAIN

Choose the command Skeleton→Draw 2D Chain. Click with your Left Mouse Button in the Right window to drop the root. Then, move your mouse and click and hold the Left Mouse Button to place the first combination of a bone and a joint. While your mouse button is down, you can drag the end of the joint to a favored position. Click again to place a second joint, a third, and so on until you have all the joints you need. To end the command, click the Right Mouse Button or tap the Escape key on your keyboard. You can complete this chain while keeping the Chain tool active by clicking the Middle Mouse Button, so you can immediately draw another chain without having to go to the menu cells again.

STEP 3: MOVE THE CHAIN

Convert one of your View windows (the lower-right one is traditional) to the Schematic view, and examine the schematic representation of the IK chain. Observe the root at the top, with a series of bones underneath it as children. Because each bone is the child of the bone (or root) above it, each bone inherits the transformations of that bone or root. However, the exception to this is the effector, which not a child of the first bone, as you might expect, but a child of the root. This means that the motion of the effector, if you keyframe it directly, will be stored relative to the root. If you animated the effector, then picked up the whole chain and moved it to somewhere else, the effector would still move correctly relative to the top of the chain, which is most often what you want.

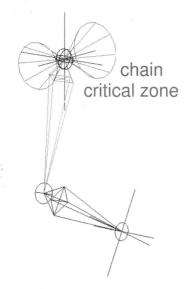

chain
critical zone

The Chain Critical Zones are also called Cones of Doom.

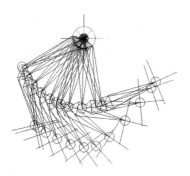

The effector drives the chain.

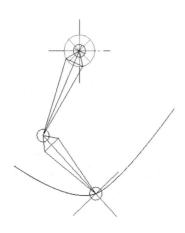

You can keyframe the effector's translation in space.

Select the effector, either in the Right view or in the Schematic view. Activate all the Translate menu cells, and check to make sure you are in View mode, the easiest method of translating things around. Drag in the window you drew the chain in to move the effector, which causes the joints to rotate to keep the effector moving where you want it!

STEP 4: ANIMATE THE CHAIN

At frame 1, place the effector somewhere in space, and save a keyframe for the local translation of the effector. At frame 10, move the effector and save another keyframe. Set a few more keys at later points in time. Play the animation to see the IK system interpolate the joint rotations to get the effector where it needs to go.

That's it! Creating and animating a basic IK chain is that easy! Of course, it becomes more complicated and difficult from here.

SELECTING IK BITS

It's important to be able to identify and select the different parts of an IK chain, because each part has a different property page, and therefore has some different capabilities. Let's practice selecting the different parts of the IK chain you just drew.

The root is the null at the top of the chain. If you select it as a node with the Space bar and the Left Mouse Button, then translate the root, it drives the top of the chain. Most often you will select it as a branch, with the Space bar and the Right Mouse Button, so that the entire chain becomes selected and you can move the root and the rest of the IK around to wherever you need it.

The bone is the next part. Bones are the longer elements that are thicker at the top and thinner at the bottom. You can select a bone with the Space bar and the Left Mouse Button. Try it out!

The Joint comes next. Joints are represented as small circles or spheres at the large end of bones. The Joint is really the top of the bone, so the bone below the joint rotates when the joint rotates. Carefully select a joint by holding the Space bar and either dragging a rectangle that intersects the circular joint shape or just clicking right on it.

Last comes the effector, which is technically a child of the root (although it can be cut from the root and still function correctly).

The effector drives the bottom of the chain, just like the root drives the top of the chain. The effector is the business end of the IK chain, though when you become an advanced IK user you will want to control both the root and the effector of the chain separately.

TYPES OF CHAINS

XSI offers two major categories of IK chains: 2D chains and 3D chains. The difference revolves around the kinds of joints found in the chain. Each type of joint is appropriate in different circumstances, and a given IK chain can also mix and match different joint types.

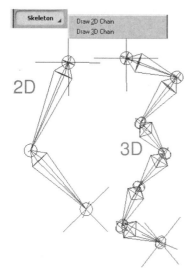

XSI has two kinds of chain behavior.

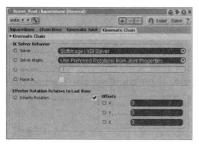

The property options for the whole chain are on the first joint.

The properties of the bone are in the Chain Bone property page.

Before I explain all the differences, you should know that each bone and joint in an IK chain has its own property page describing how it will behave, and offering different options for controlling it. To see these, select the top bone of your chain, and in the MCP, use the Select button to find the Chain Bone PPG and open it up.

The faster way to view all the PPGs for a given bone and the associated joint above it is to select the bone, then hit the Enter key on your keyboard to pop up a larger PPG with all the properties available. Take a look at the options; I'll explain them as we go.

The first bone in a chain is a special case: it has the PPGs that control options relevant to the entire chain. These special properties are located in the Kinematic Chain PPG, and only the first bone has one of these PPGs. This means that often when you want to change an important option, you'll select the first bone, the one closest to the root, and open up all its Property Pages with the Enter key on the keyboard. Try this now.

2D CHAINS

A 2D joint operates like a hinge. In a 2D IK chain, all joints except the first joint rotate in a 2D plane, meaning that they rotate on only one axis. In a 2D chain you can absolutely count on this fact: the joints rotates around the local Z-axis. When you draw a chain, the joints are created with the X and Y local axes in the plane you were moving the mouse in, and the Z-axis extending perpendicular to the drawing plane. The second and subsequent joints in a 2D chain, therefore, rotate around their Z-axes. This means that which View you choose to draw the chain in will determine what direction the joints will bend in.

Knowing which axis a 2D chain rotates around is vital when you try to animate and constrain the chain. Repeat to yourself right now: "It's always the Z-axis. It's always the Z-axis. It's always the Z-axis"… at least on 2D chains after the first joint.

The position that you draw the chain in, therefore, has a great deal to do with how it functions. The chain also has an inside and an outside for each hinge joint, which will determine which way the hinge will bend when you move the effector. The inside of the joint is the side where the joint segments form an acute angle (less than 180 degrees), while the outside is the side where the joint segments connect at an obtuse angle (more than 180 degrees). Look at your own leg to find the inside and outside of your knee. The IK joint behaves as if it doesn't like to rotate past the full extension, the 180 degree rotation where the upper and lower joint are aligned. On your own body, the preferred angle keeps your knee bent in the right direction, and going past 180 would break your knee. (Ouch!) The moral of this story is that it's a great idea to draw your chains in the View window that is in a plane with the movement you want from the chain, and to draw the chain with a slight bend to indicate which side of the hinge is inside and which is outside. Imagine that you will build a character with a slightly loose pose, as if he is standing with arms and legs slightly bent. The angle that you draw the chain in is called the Preferred Rotation Angle.

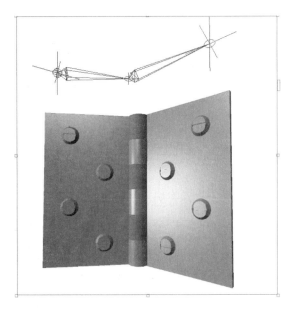

A 2D chain has hinge joints.

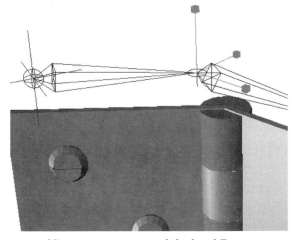

2D Joint rotates around Z

2D joints rotate around the local Z-axis.

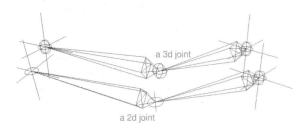

The 2D Joint has a flat icon, 3D has a spherical icon.

You can see the preferred angle you have for any bone by selecting that bone and looking in the Kinematic Joint PPG, in the General Tab. If at any time before you actually key any parts of the IK you want to get the IK back to the way you drew it, you can always select each bone and choose the Skeleton→Reset Bone to Preferred Rotation command.

If you have the option to display the Chain Critical Zones on, 2D joints will have a perfect circle icon, to show you that they are flat, 2D hinge joints.

Note: The IK system doesn't like to hyperextend hinge joints when you move the effector, but if you forget to draw the chain facing in the right direction, you can rotate the joint in the Z-axis manually with the Rotate menu cells until the joint bends in the right direction, and then resume using the effector to move the chain.

3D CHAINS

3D chains are built so that each joint can rotate completely in all three axes. These joints are much harder to control than the 2D hinge joints, but some types of bone structures, such as spines and tails, have joints that rotate in all directions. 3D chains can be used for these occasions when you want the IK chain to have a full range of motion. 3D chains still have a preferred angle, however, so it's still a good idea to draw them with a slight bend at each joint. If you are showing the chain critical zone (and you should) the 3D joints will be drawn with a wireframe sphere icon, to show you that they are 3D ball joints.

XSI complicates this simple picture just a bit, however, with a couple special cases. The top joint in a 2D chain, which is the base of the first bone right under the root, is always a 3D joint, which is to say that it can rotate around any axis freely.

You may think of this first joint in a 2D chain as a ball joint. The reason that the first joint is always a ball joint is that most creatures start each articulated skeletal segment with a ball joint, and then move on to 2D hinge joints for each subsequent joint. Think about it: your arm starts with a ball joint (the shoulder) and then has a hinge (the elbow). The same goes for your legs (hip to knee). Your fingers each work the same way, connected to the palm with a ball joint (a 3D knuckle) and then a series of hinges (2D knuckles).

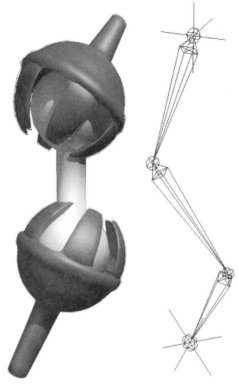

A 3D chain is built of ball joints.

The rotation of the effector at the end of the chain is another special case and is very important to understand, because the effector is often used as a parent for other objects in the skeleton. By default, the effector is rotated by the last joint in the chain, so the effector always has the same orientation as the last joint. In some cases, that is not desirable, so the effector rotation can be toggled on and off at will with the Inherits Rotation toggle in the Kinematic Chain PPG, which belongs to the first bone in the chain. So see this option, select the first bone and open the Kinematic Chain PPG from the Selection explorer.

Toggle off the effector Rotation Relative to Last Bone check box, and drag the effector to see that now it doesn't rotate to match the joint above it. When effector Rotation is off, you can rotate and keyframe the effector according to the global axes, not the local axes of the joint above it. You would turn effector Rotation off, for instance, to keep a character's feet parallel to the floor, no matter what the character's shin is doing.

You can convert chains between the 2D and 3D chain types easily by selecting a joint (the circular or round part of the bone) and opening the Kinematic Joint PPG. Look for the option labeled Chain or Subchain Behavior and change it from Default to 3D to make a 2D joint into a 3D one.

Skeleton	Draw 2D Chain
	Draw 3D Chain
Deform	
Shape	Chain Up Vector
	Chain Preferred Axis
Envelope	Add Bone to Chain
Deform	Break Chain at Bone
	Set Minimum Rotation Limit
Actions	Set Maximum Rotation Limit
Store	Reset Bone to Preferred Rotation
Apply Action	Create Chain from Curve
	Create Rig from Guide
Templates	Key All Bone Rotations
Tools	Duplicate Symmetry
Plot	Store Skeleton Pose
Sources	Apply Skeleton Pose
Flipbook	

Reset Bone snaps it back to the original angle.

Because they come complete with one ball joint and a number of hinges, 2D chains are the most useful for performing the majority of animations, particularly animations of humans.

THE RESOLUTION PLANE

In a 2D chain, the hinge joints enable the segments to rotate in a 2D plane, but the ball joint at the top of the chain controls what exactly that 2D plane of rotation is. For accurate animation, you must be able to specify the 2D plane in which the 2D chain's hinges rotate. This 2D plane is called the resolution plane of the chain, because it is in the space of this plane that the IK system resolves the rotations of the joints necessary to get the effector where you want it.

To get the real idea, stand up and perform this exercise. First, make a fist and extend it in front of your face and then flex your biceps like you are lifting weights, doing a biceps curl. As your arm bends, it forms an angle at the elbow. That bend occurs in a 2D plane extending in front of your face. When doing a biceps curl, that plane (your arm's resolution plane) remains static. Unless you change the resolution plane, all you (or your character) can do is biceps curls.

Now pretend that you are playing tennis, and swing your racket underhand as if returning a lobbed tennis ball lazily floating over the net. Do that a few times, examining how your elbow is bending.

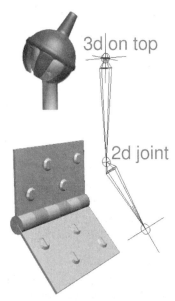

A 2D chain starts with a ball joint, then the others are hinges.

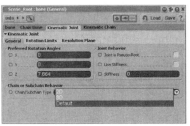

You can actually choose 2D or 3D behavior for each joint.

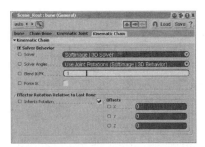

The effector can rotate automatically, or not.

Your elbow joint is bending the same as it was, but the motion is obviously much more complex. That's because the resolution plane of the elbow doesn't remain static during your tennis return; it animates as your shoulder changes the angle between your arm and your body. If you couldn't control the resolution plane of your own arm you would move very stiffly, bending only at the waist to get your arm in position to bend. That's what badly-animated IK characters look like: stiff. If you stop to examine the motion of your own arm as you make routine motions, you'll find that you change the resolution plane of your elbow constantly. Your characters should as well.

The resolution plane of a 2D chain is always perpendicular to the Z-axis, because that's the one axis that the hinge rotates in. You can control the resolution plane of your chain by rotating the top (ball) joint in Y and X. Fortunately, there is a pair of easier ways to animate the resolution plane: you can constrain the axes of the first joint with a Preferred Axis constraint or an automatic Up Vector. This means that you can control either Y or X (but not both at the same time) with the any other object in your scene (typically a null or an implicit object, since these won't render). Each of these constraints gives you an object that controls the resolution plane, so you can set simple translation keys to animate the motion of the plane.

PREFERRED AXIS CONSTRAINT

The Preferred Axis of rotation in a 2D IK chain is, by default, the Z-axis. The second and subsequent joints in the chain then rotate like a hinge to change positions in the plane perpendicular to the Z-axis, the XY plane. If you visualize the hinge of the joints, the hinge pin on which they rotate is pointed directly in the local Z-axis.

An easy way to change the orientation of this hinge (in reality, it is the Preferred Axis) is to constrain it to an implicit sphere floating in space so that the Z-axis always is pointing towards that sphere, which won't render, and will be easy for you to see and select while animating. This is called the Preferred Axis constraint. On your own arm, imagine a hinge in your elbow pointing directly to the side of your body. If you welded a bar to the hinge and then welded a ball at the end of the bar, the ball would be the Preferred Axis null. When you grab the ball and pull it to a different position, it changes the orientation of the hinge in your elbow and the resolution plane of your entire arm changes. Therefore, you could control which direction that the bend in an IK chain is going to point if you could control the Preferred Axis.

You can manually add a Preferred Axis constraint to any chain by getting any object (Implicit spheres are traditional) and positioning it to the side of the chain in the local Z-axis of the first joint (more or less is fine). Then, select the first joint in the chain, right under the root, choose the Skeleton➔Chain Preferred Axis command, and pick the implicit object you made as the constraint. Now select that constraint object and translate it around to see the effect on the resolution plane of the chain. These changes are necessary for controlling the direction that knees and elbows point, for instance.

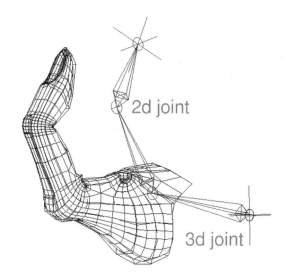

Most human chains start with a ball joint, then some hinges.

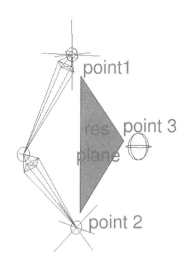

The resolution plane for one IK chain

The one problem with using a Preferred Axis constraint is that since the constraining object will be in the positive Z direction from the top bone in the chain, if you have two similar chains, like arms or legs, both constraining objects will be on the same side of the body. Though this works just fine, it bothers the natural symmetrical tendencies that we humans have, and confuses the organization of the character.

UP VECTOR CONSTRAINTS

The Up Vector constraint is another way of controlling the resolution plane of each chain in your IK system. The Up Vector precisely constrains the Y-axis of the first joint to point at a null object that is the constraint object. The location of the effector determines the X-axis of the resolution plane.

Therefore, between the two objects (the null and the effector) you can control the Y- and X-axes, and the Z-axis must always be perpendicular to that plane. In that slightly roundabout way, you control the resolution plane of the chain. When I began working with IK systems, I found the Preferred Axis constraint simpler to visualize and use than the Up Vector constraint, but in some ways the Up Vector constraint is more useful in IK systems with symmetry, like bipedal humans.

Unlike the Preferred Axis constraint, the Up Vector constraint is usually placed above the first joint in the Y-axis. Visualize a rod strapped onto your biceps, protruding above your head with a ball at the end of it. As you move the ball at the end of the rod, your arm is forced to rotate around the shoulder in a predictable way, changing the resolution plane of your elbow.

To add an Up Vector constraint to an existing chain, create an implicit sphere object and translate it above the root of the chain. Then select the first joint, choose the command Skeleton→Chain Up Vector, and pick the implicit sphere object to complete the command. Translate the sphere to see the effect on the chain.

The Up Vector constraint and the Preferred Axis constraint accomplish the same task, so it's not possible to have both added automatically, although you can add both manually.

If you want to know what's actually controlling the resolution plane of a given chain, select the first bone in the chain and open the Kinematic Joint PPG, and look in the Resolution Plane tab for the drop box named Resolution Plane. If you assign both a Preferred Axis constraint and an Up Vector constraint, you can switch between them here, since only one can be active at a time. Choosing which type of constraint will control the resolution plane can actually be animated, or linked with an expression to another parameter.

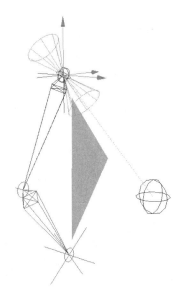

The Preferred Axis is the Z direction of the first joint.

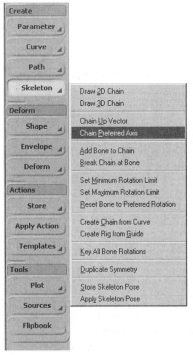

You add a Preferred Axis with the Skeleton→Preferred Axis command.

CHANGING THE IK SOLVER TYPE

There are several IK solvers in XSI, each with its own capabilities. It's important to choose the right one each time you build an IK chain, because some IK features don't work with the simpler solvers. To see the options, Select the first bone of an IK chain and open the Kinematic Chain PPG (tapping the Enter key is fastest). Look down to the Solver drop box, and look at the two options. The Softimage|3D solver is included for compatibility reasons, but the one to use in all cases for this book is the Softimage|XSI Solver. The XSI solver takes the base solver developed for Soft|3D and extends it, with options for joint roll, pseudo roots, joint stiffness and multiple constraints. If you build an IK chain and don't use the XSI solver, this new stuff won't work correctly. Make absolutely sure that each chain is using the new XSI solver.

Note: In XSI versions 1.0, 1.5 and 2.0 the default solver was set to the Soft|3D solver, so make sure you change it for each chain you build. It seems to be bug-free now.

BONE LENGTH AND SHADOW RADIUS

Imagine that you built a wonderful IK hierarchy for a specific figure, which worked great, and you want to re-use it for another character that has different proportions. For instance, you've built the IK for a dwarf and now you want to use it in an elf. Each has the same number of bones and joints, but the dwarf has shorter, thicker bones with a stumpy build, while the Elf has long, thin bones and a graceful figure. To make your rig match each one you'll need to control the length and size of each bone. If you simply scale a bone using the transformation cells, when you eventually attach your skin to that IK, the skin will be scaled in the same way you scaled the bone, which would be bad because it means that your skin model will be all twisted or stretched or shrunk in various places, depending on what you did to the bones in that area. Don't scale the bones. Instead, you can use a special property of bones, called Bone Length.

Select a bone, and open the Chain Bone PPG, then look for the Bone Length slider, and use it to adjust the length of the bone. This can make each part of the IK longer or shorter without propagating any deformation to the skin when you eventually bind the skin to that bone.

If the bone is too thin, which would make it hard to see in the character, or so thick that it overlaps the other bones, you can control the circumference by toggling OFF the Display Real Transform toggle and turning on the Display Shadow Radius Toggle, then adjusting this new circumference indicator with the Shadow Radius slider. The diameter of the bone won't affect the results at all, but it's helpful to be able to change it for characters that are either really small or really big. Make the shadow radius a size that's easy to see on screen when viewing the whole character.

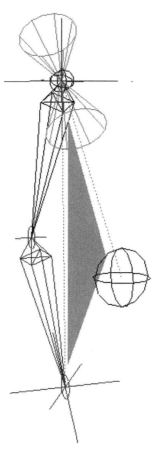

The Up Vector also shows the resolution plane, by defining a third point in the plane.

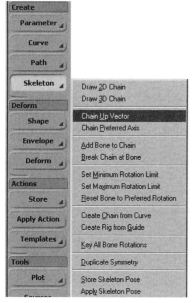

Add an Up Vector to the first joint with Skeleton→Chain Up Vector.

SETTING JOINT ROTATION LIMITS

Unlike real skeletons, IK chains are perfectly limber. They can put their legs behind their ears with no problem, or break an elbow and spin the arm freely around and around. Besides being disturbing to watch, this spaghetti joint capability makes IK challenging to animate convincingly.

One solution to this problem is to set some rules for each joint, determining where and how much it can rotate. For instance, the hip joint should be able to revolve freely with about 30 degrees of freedom, but the knee should bend only one way, and then only about 120 degrees, otherwise your character could plant his own foot in his butt.

In XSI, you may establish these rules for each joint by setting rotation limits on each axis of each joint. This is accomplished by selecting a joint and then choosing the Skeleton→Set Minimum (or Maximum) Rotation Limit command in the Animate Module, or by directly entering values in the Rotation Limits tab of the Kinematic Joint PPG.

If you do plan to set joint rotation limits, be sure to first go to the Show (eyeball)→Visibility Options menu in the Camera view and in the Attributes tab, make sure that Chain Joint Rotation Limits is toggled on. Now you'll see a graphical representation of the rotation limits on the selected joints.

Once an IK chain rotates a joint to the limit you set, that joint just won't rotate any further. If other joints still rotate in a way that gets the effector closer to the goal, they continue to rotate until they hit their limits and stop. Each joint can have a minimum and a maximum rotation limit for each axis, so you can set a range of motion. The problem with setting joint rotation limits is that when a joint hits the limit, it may stop suddenly (which might look funny) or even worse, it might pop suddenly to a different angle.

To see this in action, make sure the Chain Joint Rotation Limits feedback is toggled on, then select the top joint of a chain and open the Kinematic Joint PPG, and look in the Rotation Limits tab. Toggle Rotation Limits Active (ON). Now slide the Minimum Angles X slider to about 100 and the Max Angles X slider to about 90 degrees. The Red semi-circle around the joint indicates the region that the joint won't rotate. Try out the Z min and max sliders as well, adjusting them to create a blue semi-circle above the joint, in the area where it should never go. Now grab the effector, and translate it around, to see that the IK joint you adjusted won't rotate into the circular areas you set up. Also note that the joint may pop suddenly from one position to another as you force it above the limited area.

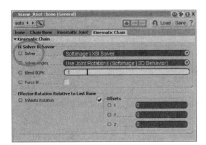

You can choose different chain behaviors here.

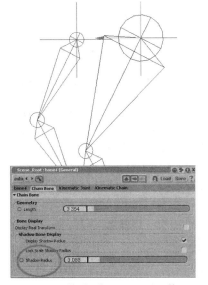

Don't scale the bones manually – use the Bone Length slider.

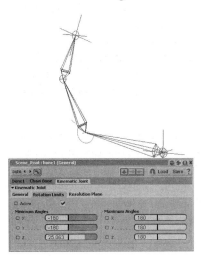

You can set joint limits manually in the Joint PPGs.

Note: I never use joint rotation limits, and instead just carefully control and animate the IK. If this seems like a cop out, consider how traditional animators deal with this problem. Since the pencil is capable of drawing the arms and legs of a character wherever they need to go, the animator just takes care not to draw the leg in the middle of the character's head, unless that's called for in the script. Having the equivalent of joint rotation limits would mean the animator couldn't draw the leg in the middle of the character's head even if the script did call for it.

USING JOINT ROLL

In a 3D chain, which is the type that is most useful for things like spines and necks, you'll also need to be able to control the rotation of each joint around its lengthwise axis, the X-axis. For instance, while the aforementioned Preferred Axis and Up Vector constraints control the plane of the first joint in the chain, if you had a character like a dinosaur with a long neck, and you wanted the character to turn it's head to look over its left shoulder, you would need to gradually roll each IK joint in the neck to make the motion look right. You might also use the joint roll in a human character, for the spinal column, so that when the shoulders rotate relative to the hips, each vertebrae in the spine gradually rolls a bit to make the chest area twist correctly.

It's not a good idea to manually rotate the joint in the X-axis, because the job of the IK solver is to determine that rotation (though you could, but technically you'd be blending FK and IK if you did). So you'll need a different way to control the roll of each joint (that isn't already controlled with a constraint). That way is the Roll property of each Kinematic Joint.

To see it in action, draw a three-bone chain, select the middle joint, open the Kinematic Joint PPG, and in the Resolution Plane tab drag on the Roll slider to see the bone that belongs to the selected joint and all subsequent bones below it in the chain rotate. We'll use this more in the chapter covering advanced human IK setup.

Note: Currently, the roll requires each joint to have an Up Vector or Preferred Axis constraint in order to work. You can make just one constraining object, and then add an Up Vector constraint on all the joints in the chain, picking the same reference object. Then control the different roll (for instance in a spinal column) with the roll property.

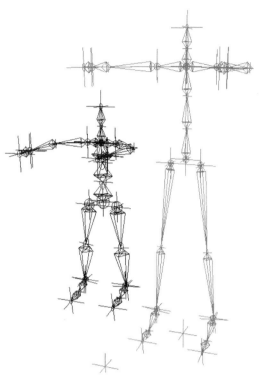

The same chain, but with different bone lengths and radii

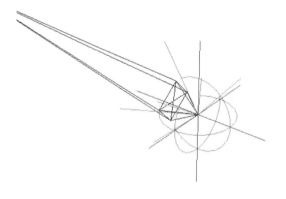

With feedback, rotation limits look like this.

JOINT FRICTION

If you build a chain with two or more bones and joints in it, then drag the effector of the chain to activate the IK and stretch it out, each one of the joints will rotate as the IK solver figures out how to position the chain bones to get the effector where you want it to go. The important thing to note is that you won't have any direct control over which joint rotates first, or in what proportion the joints will rotate to get where they need to go. The Solver will just pick the angles, spreading the rotation of the joints amongst all the joints in the chain more or less evenly. Often, this is not so good for character animation, because it means that a finger, say, will unroll very evenly, while we might want it to seem to unroll first from the base of the finger, then rotating the middle knuckle, and lastly the fingertip. Rolling joints out like that is more aesthetically pleasing for exaggerated motions, and makes it easier to create the arcs of motion that are a hallmark of Disney-style animation.

The best way to get this effect is to directly keyframe the joint rotations (covered in the next topic), but XSI has another option that will add some of what you might want automatically. This is the concept of Joint friction, or stiffness. If there are two joints (in a three-bone chain, for instance) and the top joint is stiffer than the bottom joint, then when the chain unrolls, the IK solver will rotate the bottom joint more than the top one, until the bottom joint reaches its maximum rotation. Draw an IK chain with three or more bones so you can try it out. In the Kinematic Chain PPG (on the first bone) make sure that your chain is using the XSI solver, or your chain will look like it has a drug problem when you try to move the effector, twitching and flapping around.

Step 1: The Joint stiffness is set in the Kinematic Joint PPG. Select a joint, open that PPG, toggle on the Use Stiffness option to enable joint stiffness, and then enter a value for the relative stiffness of that joint, from 0 to 1, where 0 is completely without joint friction, and 1 is as stiff as possible, relative to the other joints.

Step 2: Repeat with the other joints, setting whatever values you wish.

Step 3: Since you often want to set the stiffness of all the joints in a long chain, like a tail, there is a slick way to do this. Select the first joint, and open the Joint PPG, with the PPG in the default re-cycle mode, so that as you select more joints they all get added to the current PPG.

It's easier to set Rotation Limits here.

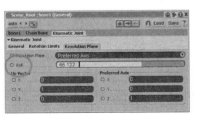

Joint roll is the way to control IK twist.

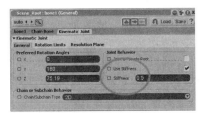

You can change the friction of each joint relative to the others in the chain.

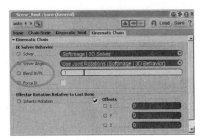

The Kinematic Chain PPG has a simple slider to blend IK and FK.

Step 4: Select all the rest of the joints in the chain in order, from the top of the chain to the bottom, using the Shift key to add each to the current selection. Now the open PPG is in Multi mode, and whatever changes you make will apply to all the joints that are selected, which is a real time-saver.

Step 5: Toggle on the Joint Stiffness property, and then click in the Stiffness text entry box to drop the cursor, erase whatever number is there, and type: "L(0.05,0.95)" without the quotes. Hit the Enter key on your keyboard when you are done.

This tells XSI to look at all the selected joints, and assign each one a value starting with 0.05 for the first joint and ending with 0.95 for the last joint. It's up to XSI to figure out how many are in between the first and the last, and to give each a smoothly increasing number.

XSI even has some neat feedback for joint friction: if your View→Visibility Options→Attributes→Chain Rotation Limits property is toggled on for the view you are using to look at your IK, you'll now see a dot filled in the middle of each joint, smaller when the stiffness is low, and bigger when it is high.

Select the effector of the chain and translate it to see how the joint stiffness works.

FORWARD KINEMATICS WITH IK CHAINS

The purpose of setting the Joint Stiffness is to attempt to control which joint rotates first, and by how much, but in many cases, it's smarter just to hand-key the rotations of each joint manually, so that you can perfectly control how the chain unrolls. If you set rotation keyframes on the joints of an IK chain, you are using Forward Kinematic animation. If you set translation keys on the root and the effector of an IK chain, you are using Inverse Kinematics.

It's important to remember that if you set both rotation keys on the joints and translation keys on the effector, the IK will take precedence and override the FK (by default), so your rotation keys won't do anything. However, setting rotation keys on joints is a very common way of animating the arms and hands of characters, so there are a few ways to do it in XSI.

The first method is to simply select first joint at the top of the chain, drag the current frame indicator to the desired time, rotate the joint, and set a keyframe for all the rotations X, Y, and Z in the usual manner. Then drag the timeslider to the next point in time where a keyframe is needed, and rotate the top joint a bit, then select and rotate the next joint a bit. Save an X, Y, and Z rotation keyframe for the top joint, and if the chain is a 2D chain, mark just rotz in the marking parameter list and save just that rotz key for the second and all subsequent joints. In a 2D chain, only the first joint can rotate in all 3 axes, all the rest of the joints rotate only around Z, so setting keys on just Z makes it easier to edit and change timing later.

Key All Bone Rotations will put keys on each joint in the chain.

The menu command Break Bone adds a Psuedo Root for you.

The second method is easier, but generates more keyframes and is therefore messier to work with later.

On a fresh, un-animated chain, move the timeslider to the first frame, and then pose the chain, using whatever combination of translating the effector and manually rotating the joints that you want.

Select the whole chain as a branch, and set a rotation key on each and every bone all at once with the Skeleton➜Key All Bone Rotations command in the Animate Module.

Move to the next frame you need, re-pose the chain with effector translation and joint rotation, and set a bunch of keys again on all bones with the Skeleton➜ Key All Bone Rotations command. Repeat as necessary.

This method is fast, but it generates keys for each joint whether or not you wanted that joint to be keyed at that frame, so it's not as good as the first method.

FK/IK BLENDING

XSI is all about layering and blending animation together, and the skeleton chain system is no exception. You can always create FK joint rotation animation, store it as an action clip, then create IK effector translation animation, store that as an action clip, then mix them together as you wish in the Mixer. There is an easier way to do that, which is the FK/IK blending slider, which is in the IK Solver Behavior area of the Kinematic Chain PPG. By default, it's set to give 100% preference to the IK animation, but you can adjust the slider to blend in any proportion you want. To see this in action, follow these steps.

Step 1: Build a four-bone IK chain, curled up.

Step 2: Set up some FK animation. At frame 1, key all the joint rotations (either manually, or with the Skeleton➜Key All Bone rotations command). At frame 20, rotate the joints to unroll the chain 1/3 of the way, and re-key all the joint rotations. At frame 40, unroll the chain 2/3 of the way, leaving the last joint alone. Re-key the joint rotations. At frame 60, repeat the process, opening the chain all the way, keying that as well.

Step 3: Set up some IK animation. Back at frame 1, select the effector, and key the translation. At frame 60, drag it to some other place, and set another keyframe on the effector translation.

Step 4: Test the animation. When you scrub the current frame indicator in the timeline, you'll see that the IK animation prevails, and the chain goes straight from where it is at frame 1 to where you put the effector at frame 60.

Step 5: Blend the FK and IK. Select the first bone and tap Enter to open the Kinematic Chain PPG. While the animation is playing back in loop mode, change the Blend FK/IK slider. See that the rotation keys are now blended in with the IK effector translation keys!

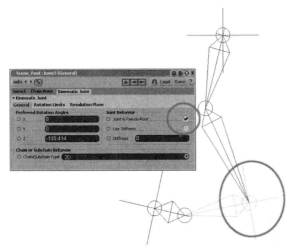

This chain has a Psuedo root, which works like an extra effector.

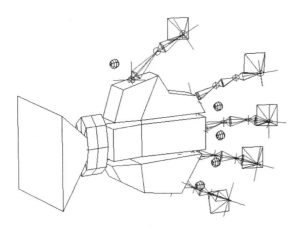

The finger bone's connected to the hand bone.

Step 6: Animate the Blending of the FK and IK. Turn off the looping playback, and at frame 1, set the blending slider to 0 so that it favors the FK 100%. Click on the green animation divot next to that slider to set a key there. Now at frame 60, drag the slider to 1 so that it favors the FK 100%. Set another key on the green animation divot. Now the actual blending will animate, even as the IK and FK on the chain animates. Play back to see the results.

FK and IK blending is really an amazing feature, because it means that you can use whichever method is most appropriate for the motion of the character that you need to create, without having to build two separate rigs (like in other animation programs) and with complete flexibility to change your mind at any time. It's an extremely productive workflow method to use IK first, roughing in the larger motions and gestures of your character, then when the timing is more or less correct, go back and set FK rotation keys on the joints to get that extra little bit of fluidity that you need to make your characters come to life.

Pseudo Roots

Up until now, all our chains have had one root at the top of the chain, and one effector at the bottom of the chain. The job of the solver was to figure out how to rotate the joints to stretch the bones out between the top root and the bottom effector. However, we can throw a monkey wrench into that plan by adding Pseudo roots to chains. A Pseudo root is actually more like an effector. Adding a Pseudo root to a joint turns that joint into an effector that can be animated by selecting the joint and translating it, just like the root and the effector can be translated. Keys can be set on the Pseudo root, so that now you can control the top, the bottom, and the pseudo root of the chain.

Pseudo roots really act as if two smaller chains have been parented together, so they don't really add anything in terms of functionality, but they simplify the setup of a character in areas like the leg.

You could draw one chain that starts at the hip and ends at the toe, then make the joint in the heel a Pseudo root so that you can control the chain correctly.

To make a joint into a Pseudo root, select the joint and open the Joint PPG. Toggle on the Pseudo root box. You'll see that a null-like icon has been added to the joint to show you that it is a Pseudo root.

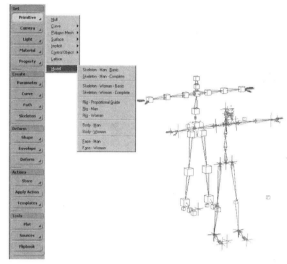

Here are a number of pre-made IK hierarchies built by Michael Isner.

You may also create a Pseudo root by breaking a chain. To do it this way (which is equivalent), draw the chain, then choose the joint that you want to be able to control manually with translations. Finally, choose the Skeleton→Break Chain at Bone command, which simply toggles on the Pseudo Root property for that bone. Now you can translate that bone and set keyframes on it.

Be careful with Pseudo roots: there are several things to be aware of. First, they only function correctly if the chain solver is the XSI Solver. Second, to use the Pseudo root you actually select the joint itself and translate it, not the cross-shaped null icon, which is confusing since you do select the cross-shaped null icon when using the root or the effector. Pseudo roots are also prone to odd flipping behavior when controlled with Preferred Axis or Up Vector constraints. If you encounter problems with Pseudo roots, just use two simpler chains instead of one more complex one, as discussed in the next section!

PARENTING IK CHAINS TOGETHER

So far we have dealt only with single IK chains, the simplest case, but except for worms, snakes, and other creatures that slither on their bellies, a single IK chain isn't good enough. People, for instance, have the head bone connected to the neck bone, the neck bone connected to the back bone, the back bone connected to the leg bone, the leg bone connected to the foot bone, and the foot bone connected to the toe bone.

You can use Duplicate Symmetry to cut your workload in half.

IK chains can be parented together to form complex hierarchies of IK motion. A chain root, joint, or effector can become the parent of another entire chain or several chains in the usual manner, with the Parent button in the MCP. If you make the effector the parent of another IK chain, the root of the child chain will be transformed by the effector, moving and rotating in space to stay attached to the effector. Then that second child chain can become the parent of a third IK chain, and so on, indefinitely.

Each bone in a chain can also be the parent of another chain, and as the effector rotates the joints and bones, the bones drive the translation of their children appropriately. Try it out by building a millipede with one 20-joint IK chain as the spine and a bunch of simple, one segment IK chains as the legs.

In XSI, since the effector of each chain is attached by default to the root above it, you can make functional (though simple) human characters this way.

Look at the Get→Primitive→Model menu to see some pre-made Skeleton hierarchies.

Storing the base pose means you can always return to it.

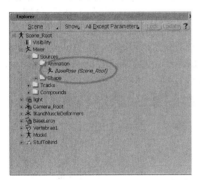

The Base Pose ends up stored in the Mixer, in the Sources folder.

SKELETON SYMMETRY

Very often when you are building an IK system, you'll be building something symmetrical. A human being is a good example of this: the right arm is a mirror image of the left arm. It seems like a shame to have to build both arms, one at a time.

There is an option to duplicate IK chains with mirror symmetry, however, it must be used carefully, since there are ways to use it improperly. If you select an entire IK chain, like a leg, then choose Skeleton→Duplicate Symmetry, a dialog will pop up asking you to choose the plane of symmetry you want the duplicate made with. Imagine a mirror flat along two axes, so that it would reflect a mirror image of your chain. Which would those two axes be? It depends on how you drew your chain, and in which view you drew it in. If you drew your leg in the Right view, with the knees bent facing in positive Z, the mirror plane would be the YZ plane. Look at your chain and imagine what the mirror plane would be, then pick the correct option in the Plane of Symmetry drop box, and hit the OK button. A new IK chain will be created.

Now for the requirements. If you have a constraint controlling the resolution plane, it must be an Up Vector constraint, since Preferred Axis constraints are not symmetrical in nature. That constraint must also be a child of the root, or it won't be copied by the Symmetry command.

GET BACK

It's often the case that you want to get back to where you once were (to paraphrase the Beatles). For instance, after you've built an IK hierarchy, with some chains parented as children of others, you'll want to try it out, but you also need to be able to get the whole assembly back into the original shape, generally called the bind pose, before you go about enveloping it. For that reason it's a great idea to store an action for the base pose, so that you can always use it in the Mixer to restore your IK hierarchy back to the original bind pose. While you could just select all the bones, mark the scale, rotation, translation, bone length, and preferred rotation angles, and store a current transformation Action, there is an easier way. If your IK is all in one hierarchy, you can select it as a tree (or select the root as a branch) so that all the IK is selected, then use the Skeleton→Store Skeleton Pose command.

Store Skeleton Pose will find everything in the hierarchy and store all the important properties into a new Action Clip called basepose_clip. If you display the explorer with the hotkey 8, and open the Mixer→Sources→Animation folder, you'll see the clip there. When you need it you can drag it back onto an empty animation track in the mixer, and your IK will regain its original shape. Remember that you can always mute a track in the mixer so it won't affect your work, then un-mute it again when you want your IK to go back to the base pose.

rigid envelope   flexible envelope

Rigid vs. Flexible enveloping

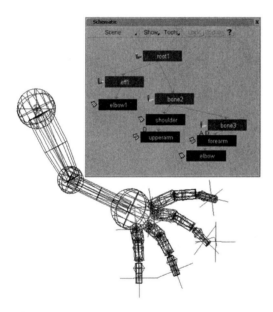

The geometry is parented directly to the bones.

METHODS OF ATTACHING GEOMETRY TO IK

So far, we've built IK chains and moved them around, but we haven't attached any geometry to them. IK chains can do two things to the models you attach to them. They can transform them in space just like a normal parent/child hierarchy, or deform them by moving vertices and control points on the skin.

When an IK chain transforms an object without deforming it, the object stays rigid. This method is best for mechanical objects and other non-organic models. The joints in the IK chain need something to cover them in a rigid model to hide the fact that there is nothing at the joint. That's why the ubiquitous robot and mechton models frequently seen stomping through bad animation invariably have shoulder pads and knee guards.

When an IK chain deforms a model, much more complex and accurate animations can be created. The IK chain can bend the model where the joint is to simulate the crease in the skin caused by bending, or the IK chain can bulge the model to indicate changes in the musculature beneath the surface of the skin. When using IK to deform a model, you can add one piece of skin over the entire IK system to avoid unsightly seams and missing joint geometry. The rotations of each joint in the IK can even be linked to separate shape deformations to make the skin change shape as if the bones were pulling muscles under the skin. We'll tackle these sorts of flexible envelopes in the next chapter.

RIGID ENVELOPING

The simplest way to attach geometry to an IK system is to directly parent the pieces onto the IK chains, connecting each element of the model to the IK joint that controls it. This method transforms the geometry but does not deform it, making parenting most appropriate for very simple mechanical characters and objects.

The process is simple: create the IK system you want and then make some geometry (either polygonal or NURBS) for each joint. Position each segment of the model directly over the joint that will drive it, and rotate it appropriately to face in the same direction as the joint. Next make the geometry a child of the joint that lies under it. After all the models are connected to the IK hierarchy, you can translate the effectors of the chains to see the geometry objects translated and rotated by the chain.

EGG FACTORY IK SETUP: AT A GLANCE

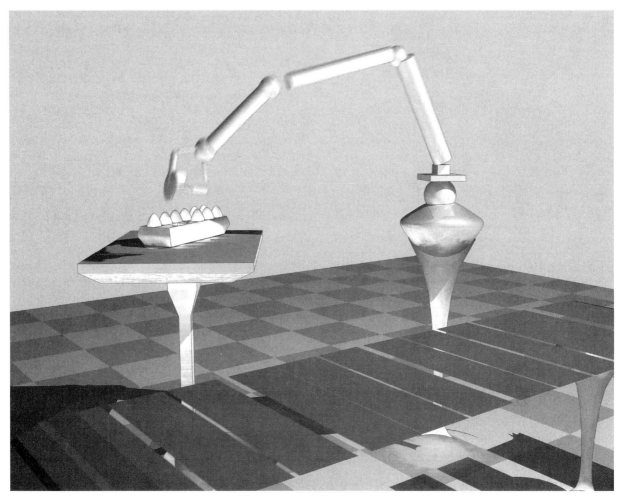

The completed Egg Factory

TOPICS COVERED

In this tutorial you'll be building the simple IK to control a robot arm. The robot arm will also have IK pincers at the end of the arm to grasp eggs coming out of the egg shoot, so it can move them to the Egg packing crate. You'll draw IK chains, adjust the length, modify the stiffness of the joints, parent smaller IK chains to the main arm, add a Preferred Axis constraint to control the rotation of the arm, and finally attach simple primitives to the IK with rigid enveloping.

You'll learn how to:

- Build IK chains
- Modify Bones and Joints
- Animate the IK effector
- Add Constraints to control the resolution plane
- Attach geometry to the chains

MATERIALS REQUIRED

The EggFactoryIK scene from the courseware project.

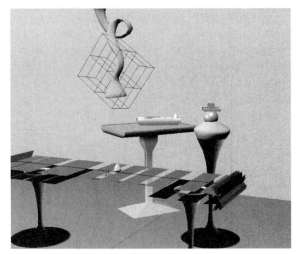

Examine the starting scene.

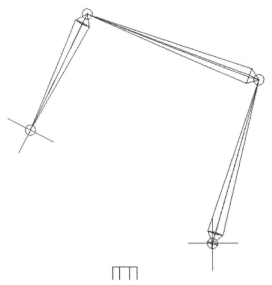

Draw a three-bone arm, then make the effector bigger.

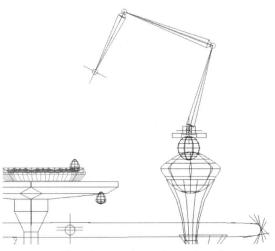

Now the arm is on the pedestal.

TUTORIAL: EGG FACTORY IK SETUP

The Egg Factory is an automated environment where chickens are managed by robots, which take the eggs, measure them, sort them, and eventually pack them. You'll be working in the basement of the Egg Factory, in the packing department. You'll need to build an Egg Packing Robot arm, using Inverse Kinematics.

STEP 1: EXAMINE THE SCENE

Open the EggFactoryIK.scn scene from the courseware that accompanies this tutorial. Orbit around the scene and play back in the timeline to see the eggs dropping out of the chute to the conveyor belt and then magically appearing in the egg crate. Your Robot needs to be able to reach from the conveyor belt where the eggs disappear to the packing crate where the eggs appear. Locate the pedestal sitting on the floor between the conveyor and the egg crate. Your IK arm will attach to this.

STEP 2: DRAW THE MAIN ARM

In the Right view, draw a three segment IK chain, using the Skeleton➔Draw 2D Chain command from the Animate Module. Start clicking at the base of the arm, near the pedestal, then click again to draw the first bone segment, again for the middle bone segment, and once more for the last bone segment. Right-click to end the command, and a new effector will be added to the chain. Now do yourself a favor and select the effector, and scale it up using the regular Scale cells in the MCP.

Now it will be easier to grab when you want to animate it. You could even change its color in the color palette layout (the small palette icon in the view switcher at the bottom of the left-hand menu stacks). You should now have a three-bone chain arching from the pedestal over towards the Egg Crate. Examine it in the Camera view. It's not really on the pedestal, is it?

STEP 3: ADD THE PINCERS

The arm has no fingers to grab an egg. Before you move the arm at all, add these fingers by drawing two simple IK chains, each with two joints, using the Skeleton➔2D Chain command. Draw them starting from a little bit away from the effector of the arm chain so the arm chain will be easy to grab when you want to animate it.

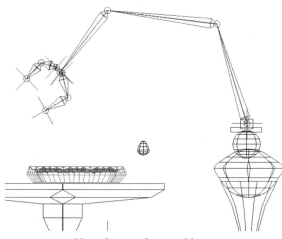

Now the arm has grabbers.

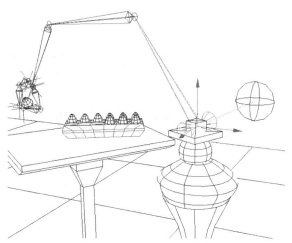

Now you have a Preferred Axis to control the swing of the arm.

The Pincers need to be attached somehow, so that when the arm moves, they move with it. The easiest (and best) way is to make the arm's effector the parent of the other smaller IK chains you drew for the pincers. Select the arm effector and use the Parent button in the MCP to make it the parent of the two pincer IK chains by clicking on the roots of those smaller chains.

STEP 4: PLACE THE ARM ON THE PEDESTAL

The quickest way to get the arm right on the pedestal is to constrain the root of the IK to the ball on the pedestal. Select the whole IK arm as a branch, by selecting the root with the Space bar and the Middle Mouse Button, then in the MCP, choose the Constrain→Position command and pick on the ball at the top of the Pedestal. The arm should snap to the ball on top of the pedestal.

STEP 5: CONTROL THE SWING OF THE ARM

The IK solver will handle the extension of the robot arm, but how will you control the swing of the arm so it can reach from one side to the conveyor, and then to the other, reaching the egg crate? You'll need a Preferred Axis constraint on the first joint of the IK arm, or you'll run into big problems when you animate.

Start by getting a Primitive Implicit Sphere, and scaling it down to be big enough to select easily but small enough to not be obtrusive. Position it in the top view to the side of the robot arm nearest the egg crate. The Z-axis of the first joint will point at this object, so if you put it too far away from the direction that the Z-axis of the first joint is currently pointing, the arm will suddenly rotate, which is OK, but might confuse you.

To add the constraint, select the first joint (the one next to the root, nearest to the ball on the pedestal) and choose the Skeleton→Chain Preferred Axis command.

Finally, pick on the implicit sphere you made. Now try it out: in the top view, select the sphere and move it around, to see how it makes the arm swing around. Practice making the arm swing from the conveyor to the egg crate.

STEP 6: ADJUST THE BONE LENGTH

When you drew the arm, you couldn't really see how it would reach from side to side, therefore your arm might be too short or too long.

You can test this by using the constraint to swing the arm over to the egg crate, and then selecting the effector of the main chain as a branch and translating it to reach down to the egg crate. Be certain to select the effector as a branch, because it's now the parent of the other pincer IK chains. If you don't select the effector as a branch, the pincers will get left behind in space, which would suck.

You can now adjust the bone length of each segment to your liking. Select the first bone, and tap the Enter key on your keyboard to pop up the Bone PPG, and adjust the Length slider however you see fit. Repeat for the other bones, testing the reach of the arm to both sides to make sure it's all good.

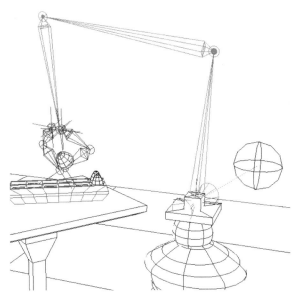

Now you can see the stiffness and the constraint.

STEP 7: ADJUST THE JOINT FRICTION

Right now, the IK solver just rotates each joint the same amount when you move the effector of the arm. But we want the arm to act differently. We want the IK to be looser at the root and stiffer as it approaches the effector. This way the arm will rotate first at the lower joint, then a bit more at the middle joint, and finally at the last joint.

If your Chain is not using the XSI Solver, this won't work. Select the first bone, pop up the Bone PPG, and under the Kinematic Chain tab, make sure that the XSI Solver is selected.

Select the first Joint, pop up the Kinematic Joint PPG, toggle on the stiffness, and make the Stiffness value 0.2 for the bottom joint. Repeat for the other joints, making the middle joint 0.5, and the last joint 0.8.

Now select the effector and translate it to see the difference in the behavior.

STEP 8: TURN ON SOME FEEDBACK

XSI can show you some useful info while you work. In your Camera view, go to the Show (eyeball)➔Visibility Options menu and under the Attributes tab, turn on Chain Critical Zone and Rotation Limits. Now you'll see the name of the selected item, and you'll see the IK feedback icons, showing you a line to the Preferred Axis constraint, the cones of doom, and the joint friction indicator.

STEP 9: TOGGLE OFF EFFECTOR ROTATION

Right now, the effector of the main arm rotates when you translate it, so that it stays perfectly oriented with the last bone of the chain. This is usually a good thing, but in the case of a robot, you'll want to rotate it yourself, and it will look more mechanical and less organic if it stays oriented the same way while the arm swings around.

This is a simple change: select the first bone, and pop open its PPG with the Enter key on your keyboard. Toggle off Effector Inherits Rotation and then translate the effector around (in branch selection mode) to see how that works.

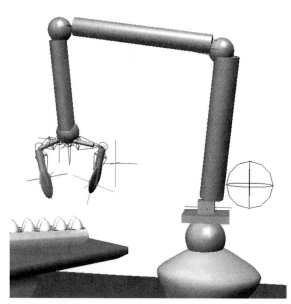

Since IK doesn't render, you need to add some geometry.

STEP 10: ADD SOME GEOMETRY

Your robot arm works great now, but it won't render. You need to attach some geometry to each bone and joint! Get a primitive Cylinder, and scale and rotate it to match the angle and size of the first bone. In the top and right views, place it right on top of the first bone. Now make it a child of that first joint. The slick method here is to select the geometry, then click on the Parent button in the MCP. Now because you want the Cylinder to be a child of the bone, you will click on the bone with the Middle Mouse Button, which hooks up a parent to a child backwards. Look in the status bar to see a reminder of this. Click the RMB or tap the ESC key to end the Parent mode before you accidentally parent something else. Check to see that when you drag the main arm effector, the cylinder also moves, since it is attached as a child of the first bone. Make more cylinders, and spheres to cover the joints, and repeat the process, placing each one where you need it on the IK chain and attaching it as a child of the nearest bone.

STEP 11: TRY IT OUT

You are done! Try it out, setting some translation keys on the main arm effector, and the implicit sphere that controls the rotation of the arm. Also try keyframing the rotation of the main arm effector, and the position of the effectors in the pincers.

That's it! You've built a fully functional IK system, with a hierarchy of IK, controlled with a constraint, and you've modified the bone length and joint friction. These are the building blocks of the IK system, and from here on out, you'll just be combining them with other things you've learned to build even cooler IK systems.

CONCLUSION

Inverse Kinematics is just a simpler way of controlling the rotation of linked joints. It's not the only way, and you've learned in this chapter that sometimes it's better to just manually rotate and key a whole bunch of individual joints and bones. Fortunately, you also learned how to mix and match IK and FK, using them when each is most effective, and even blending them when necessary. You learned that controlling the resolution plane is really the most important part of working with IK, and you learned that the XSI solver adds some important new features like joint friction and pseudo roots.

QUIZ

1. WHEN YOU SAVE KEYS FOR FK, YOU ARE SAVING:
   a. Translation keys
   b. Rotation keys
   c. Scale keys

2. YOU NEED TWO SEPARATE IK RIGS TO BLEND FK AND IK AND XSI.
   a. True
   b. False

3. THE SOLVER FIGURES OUT:
   a. Effector translations
   b. Root locations
   c. Joint rotations

4. IN A 2D CHAIN, THE PREFERRED AXIS IS ALWAYS:
   a. Y
   b. Z
   c. X

5. MOVING WHICH ITEM ACTIVATES THE SOLVER?
   a. The root
   b. The effector
   c. Both root and solver

6. WHICH SOLVER HAS MORE FEATURES?
   a. The SI3D Solver
   b. The XSI Solver

7. A 3D CHAIN WOULD BE APPROPRIATE FOR:
   a. A car door
   b. A bull whip
   c. A clock pendulum

8. A 2D CHAIN WOULD WORK BEST FOR:
   a. A finger
   b. string
   c. rope

9. BY DEFAULT, THE EFFECTOR IS A CHILD OF:
   a. The last bone
   b. The last joint
   c. The root

10. IF YOU CUT THE EFFECTOR LOOSE, IT MUST BE MADE A CHILD OF WHAT FOR IT TO WORK?
    a. The last bone
    b. Anything
    c. Everything

MATT LIND

ANIMATOR / TECHNICAL DIRECTOR

SOFTIMAGE CERTIFIED INSTRUCTOR: SOFTIMAGE│3D, SOFTIMAGE│XSI

SPEYE_21@HOTMAIL.COM

Anthony Rossano: Tell us what you do.

Matt Lind: I don't have an official title as I wear a lot of hats. Appropriate descriptions would be character animator, technical director, 3D instructor, and perhaps project trouble shooter. I figure out how to get the important day-to-day stuff done efficiently, such as moving file data around, making characters more quickly, and creating tools for tasks performed repeatedly in whatever software happens to be used at the time. What really turned me on to 3D was a film noir, cartoon project I worked on back in college. It involved a little thief character who performs actions to music, much like Disney's "Peter and the Wolf", but in sync to Duke Ellington instead of classical music. In doing this project, I discovered that I needed to do it in 3D to get the most out of the idea. 2D just didn't have the full potential. Being able to sculpt the characters in light and shadow, providing depth - that was really important.

ATR: People seem enthralled by 3D animation more than 2D. What is it about 3D images that is so much more appealing than 2D images?

ML: I think people connect with 3D more because no matter where they are or what they do on this planet, everything is 3D - even if they are looking at pictures. People like to feel that connection even to something as outrageous as a cartoon. Also, in this particular day and time it is something new they haven't seen alot of.

"Speye" (c) 1997 Matt Lind

"Squeak" (c) 1997 Matt Lind

ATR: Do you think that like 2D animation in the 1970s, 3D animation could get overblown, and people might get sick of 3D characters?

ML: I think that's true of almost anything, whether it be fashion, politics, sports, etc. There's usually a sharp increase in popularity until people reach of point of saturation, then it consolidates for a while. After a little time it comes back to a certain level of popularity and stays there.

ATR: How far out in the future is that for 3D animation?

ML: It's still on the upswing, because the people who make the content are able to do new things they couldn't do even five years ago. But now they can do it more quickly and at lower cost.

Manufacturing is a good example as prototypes traditionally had to be created and photographed on a stage which can take anywhere from a few weeks to a few months. Besides being slow, it's also expensive. If designs change, then the process must be performed all over again. Today, the turnaround can be significantly less using data from a CAD/CAM system to render out images as if they were real, playing with color and lighting, then sending them on to print. When revisions are made to the original designs, it's often just a few minor tweaks to update the rendered images.

ATR: Do you think 3D is growing into industrial applications?

ML: Not many companies are using 3D that way now outside of automotive design. Quite a few still use the photographic process, but that is changing as we speak.

ATR: At what point after school did you decide that you wanted 3D to become a career?

ML: I was in college training to be a cel animator and realized the 2D market was shrinking even though films such as "Who Framed Roger Rabbit" and "Beauty and the Beast" had been very popular just a few years earlier. Entertainment was already moving to 3D even if just in limited capacity. At the time that's where the consumer interest was, as well as my head. I got involved in 3D to expand my creativity in the cel animation world rather than recreate reality.

ATR: If you trained as a cel animator, and are both a technical and artistic person, do you script better than you draw, or draw better than script?

ML: I think I do both fairly well, but if I had to choose, I'd say I draw better than I script. Drawing is something I have been doing most of my life, but ironically, it's not something I enjoy doing. I don't like drawing still lifes - it bores me to tears. I feel I'm good with a pencil and have a lot to show for it, but it's not something I enjoy doing outside of solidifying ideas. As for scripting, growing up I was always good at math and science and for a while in high school I considered physics as a career since it always interested me. But in late high school I had a falling out with my teacher, and focussed on humanities from there on. In college I realized that with animation I could do both: I could be technical and creative at the same time. I didn't have to give up one for the other.

"Squeak" (c) 1997 Matt Lind

"Speye" (c)1997 Matt Lind

ATR: How often do you find other people that you are working with who are both technical and creative?

ML: Not very. I'd say less than 5% of people. There are people who are very good at technical things, but sometimes get so tied in the details that they lose sight of the big picture. On the other side, there are people who are very creative and very good with animating characters, color theory, design, and composition, but when it comes to figuring out why the software isn't working, or to figuring out how to make the software work for them to accelerate their creative abilities, they don't know where to begin. To do both well, one needs great discipline, patience, and attention to detail. Competitive people usually do well as they have that extra motivation to perform their best.

ATR: Do you think working with 3D apps is getting easier or harder?

ML: I think doing the basics is getting easier, but to push the envelope, it gets not necessarily harder, but more complex. Regardless of whether it's home-grown software or something purchased off the shelf, the standards are all growing vastly, making packages much more complex - much deeper. One almost needs to make a decision whether to be a generalist knowing every software a little bit to get the project done, or a specialist that knows one or two softwares really well. I've always been in the camp of learning one tool really, really well. Just like a pencil - using various leads and shading techniques doesn't make you a better artist, but it does facilitate the realization of ideas as there is a wider palette of options to draw from.

ATR: How often is the limitation the tool and how often is the limitation the user?

ML: I think it depends on what you are trying to accomplish. If you are trying to work with something that is well-established, like fireworks or flying logos, then the limitations will most likely be within the artist. There are a lot of tools available to do those types of things. On the other hand, if you are doing something that has not been pursued very much, such as making 3D characters look like 2D, then the limitations are probably on the tools as that's not something that is pushed much in the industry, though it is now starting to get some attention.

ATR: Do you see yourself using 3D tools to the grave?

ML: I go with whatever interests me at the time. I may not necessarily use 3D to create films, games, or TV ads all the time. At some point I may hang that portion of my life up and refocus on education, planning, or using it to do something that I become interested in at a later point in life - perhaps as a design tool for a mini-golf course I want to put in my back yard. I see 3D becoming more a part of everyone's lives. Common every-day things like household appliances, how they interact with laundry, to make the bed, to clean the floors, to wash the dishes... you'll see more 3D interfaces. Even going to the market and getting groceries could become a 3D experience. There could be a 3D holographic representation of the store where you can put your finger and pick your groceries. The interface could be flexible enough to display your picked items in full 3D with stats such as weight and freshness for full inspection before you commit to purchase. When you make a final decision, someone (or something) goes down that aisle and gets the items for you. A virtual produce selection.

ATR: Certainly a lot to think about, Matt! Thanks!

6 | SKINS; ENVELOPING AND WEIGHTING

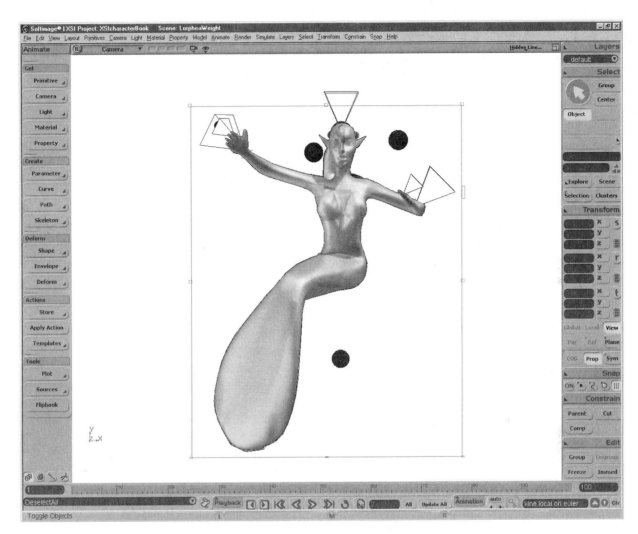

IN THIS CHAPTER YOU WILL LEARN ABOUT:

- How IK really deforms a skin (called Enveloping)
- How to Assign Envelopes to IK Bones
- All about assignment depth
- How to use anything as an Envelope Deformer
- How to manually edit Envelope Weighting
- How to Paint Envelope Weights with the Weight Paint panel
- How to Smooth Envelope Weights for better results

INTRODUCTION

Without the capability to animate seamless models and wrap hierarchies of geometry around IK skeletons, a modern animation system would be pretty limited. Fortunately, XSI offers a powerful method of assigning geometry to IK chains that allows the user to animate just about anything with an IK chain, while retaining complete control over how the skin models bend and move as they are transformed and deformed by the IK system.

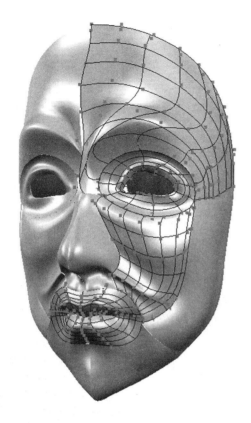

The model made of patches will be harder to use.

This method is called Flexible Enveloping. Flexible Enveloping is the process of choosing a skin mesh that you have already built and assigning any number of IK (and other) deformers to that skin mesh. Just assigning an Envelope is the simple part – then you have to modify the Envelope so that it behaves the way you want it to. This process is called Weighting.

BINDING SKINS TO IK AND WEIGHTING THEORY

Before we talk about the mechanics and terminology of Enveloping, I think it's helpful to understand why Enveloping is so important to character animation. First, let's consider the Holy Grail of all character animation: single-surface models and smooth IK deformation. In a real creature, the skin forms one unbroken (hopefully) surface that wraps entirely around the character, covering it completely. Underneath, a system of muscles and bones bends, bulges and twists that skin into different shapes. No matter what the skeleton and muscles do, the skin just stretches and slides over the bones and muscles underneath. As character animators, that's what we want. If we could build a single surface mesh, either from NURBS patches or polygons, then build a similar system of bones and muscles, we would use Enveloping to bind the skin surface mesh to those bones and muscles underneath. Then, if we got it right, our skin would bend, bulge, slide, and stretch nicely, without any jagged pulling, or sudden gaps in the surface.

FLEXIBLE ENVELOPING TO INVERSE KINEMATIC CHAINS

Enveloping is just a way of deforming a skin with a hierarchy (or hierarchies) of IK chains and other objects. A skin is really just one or more geometric objects, either singly or in a hierarchy. You can Envelope any kind of skin object in XSI – and that includes curves, polygons, NURBS, lattices, cages, and even particle systems.

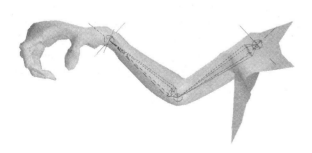

The Bones inside the arm help deform the skin.

The skin can cover just a part of an IK chain, or it can surround the entire IK system. There can be any number of IK bones and joints in an Envelope deformer, and even other kinds of geometry can be used in an Enveloping deformer. Envelope deformers are remarkably versatile.

HOW ENVELOPE ASSIGNMENT WORKS

The way skin deformation works with envelopes is simple to understand, but complex to control. When an IK chain is connected to the skin with the Envelope→Set Envelope command, each vertex or control point on the skin model is assigned to the joints that lie within the skin, in direct proportion to the proximity of that vertex or control point to the joints. Points on the skin that lie one unit from one joint and three units from another will be assigned, or weighted, 75% to the nearer joint and only 25% to the further joint. When the further joint rotates, the Control point moves a bit to follow the location of the joint, but when the nearer joint rotates, that vertex moves a great deal. In this way, each nearby bone in the skin modifies the shape of the skin as the bone's joint rotates. This is called Distance Based Assignment.

As the effector of the IK chain translates through space, all the joints rotate, moving bones, and all the vertices on the skin move to follow them, so the skin remains wrapped around the IK chain. When the IK chain bends, the skin bends as well.

Just connecting a skin hierarchy to an IK hierarchy is simple. After the geometry is prepared, place the IK chain within the model, so that it is in a starting position that makes sense for the object you create. If you use this method to make a hand out of a hierarchy of polygon objects, for example, each finger chain should lie within the polygon mesh for that finger. The IK chains should themselves be parented together into a hierarchy if you use more than one chain, again in a way that makes sense for the model.

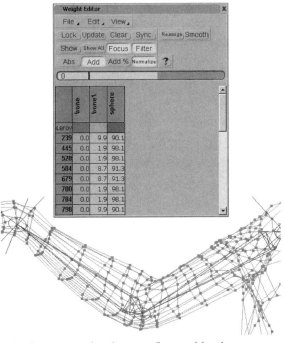

Each point on the skin is influenced by the nearest bones.

You'll want to pay special attention to the location of the joints: they need to lie in the center of the area where the skin should bend.

LOCAL JOINT ASSIGNMENT

When the IK fits within the skin hierarchy you have made, just select the skin hierarchy as a branch (with the Middle Mouse Button and the Space bar), and choose the Envelope→Set Envelope command. Then, pick each bone or other object that you want to be enveloped to the skin. After you have carefully picked each deformer with the Left Mouse Button, right-click to end the picking session and execute the Envelope Assignment command, adding the Envelope Operator to the skin mesh.

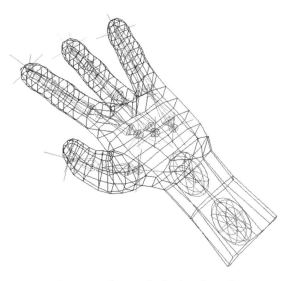

The Bones lie inside the hand mesh.

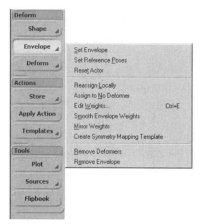

The Envelope Menu has commands for binding and removing skins.

ASSIGNMENT TO THE WHOLE CHAIN

You don't actually have to use all the individual bones in an IK hierarchy; it's a lot simpler to put the whole thing in a big hierarchy and pick in the top as a branch than to try to pick hundreds of smaller bones one at a time. This works the same way: select the skin hierarchy (the stuff you want to deform) and then choose the Envelope→Set Envelope command. This time, pick on the entire hierarchy of IK elements, or just on the individual IK roots if you prefer, with the Middle Mouse Button to add them as branches. When you're done, and have picked all the bones and other IK elements that you want to be considered as deformers by the Envelope Operator, click with the Right Mouse Button to end the picking session, and add in the Envelope Operator.

You'll see that the bones change color, and that the skin becomes color coded to match the bones underneath that area of the skin.

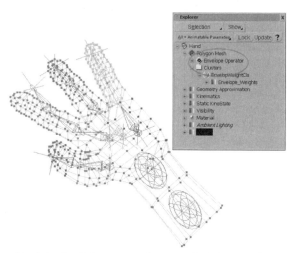

Look in the Selection explorer to find the Envelope operator.

If you select the skin hierarchy and look in the Selection explorer, under the Surface Mesh or Poly Mesh node you'll see that a new operator has been added, called the Envelope Operator. If you click on the operator icon for this Property, you'll see the Envelope Operator PPG with a toggle to mute the envelope, turning it on and off.

The rest of the envelope options are located at the cluster level. If you had a cluster selected when you added the Envelope Operator, only that cluster will be affected by the Envelope Operator. If you had the whole object selected, a new cluster will be created for you, called the EnvelopeWeightCls.

Open it up to check out the options found there: we'll cover them as they are needed and explained in the rest of this chapter.

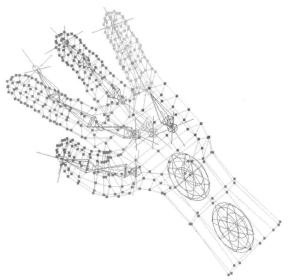

The color of each point on the skin matches the bones underneath it.

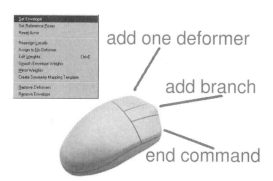

Add all the deformers in with the Left and Middle Mouse Buttons, then click with the Right Mouse Button to compelte the command.

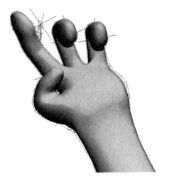

These hands are enveloped to IK chains, which then deform them.

KEEP CONTROLS AND CONSTRAINTS OUT OF THE HIERARCHY

We'll cover this in much more detail in the Chapter 9, "Complex Human IK Rigs", but it bears mentioning here first. If you build a character rig to make it easier to control and animate your character, you should keep those elements separate from the Hierarchy of the IK chains and other deformer objects that you plan to use in an envelope. If you had any of the rig controls in the same hierarchy as the IK, you would, by default, be using those controls to actually deform the skin, instead of using them to control the IK, and letting the IK deform the skin. This would make weighting the envelope much harder, and would lead to unexpected stretching and tearing of the skin. In the schematic view, examine your IK hierarchy and verify that any controls you have driving the IK are in a separate, distinct hierarchy. Since the controls for the IK (called a "rig") can't be in the same hierarchy, but still must drive the IK, that tells us that the roots and effectors of the IK must eventually be constrained to the rig. Don't worry about this now – I'll go into detail in Chapter 9.

CARTOON HAND: AT A GLANCE

TOPICS COVERED

In this short tutorial, you will use a pre-made scene with a simple hand model and some IK, then deform the hand with the IK using an Envelope operator. You'll then examine the envelope weighting to understand how the IK affects the points that make up the hand.

You'll learn how to:

- Add an Envelope Operator to a Skin
- Select and manipulate an IK effector
- Examine the Envelope weight map

MATERIALS REQUIRED

This tutorial will use the CartoonHand scene from the courseware project. The courseware can be downloaded from http://www.mesmer.com/books/xsicharacter.html if you have not already installed it on your computer.

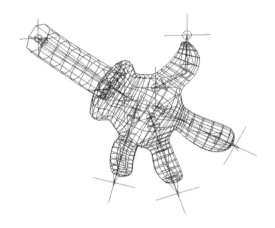

The hand is a single polygon mesh object.

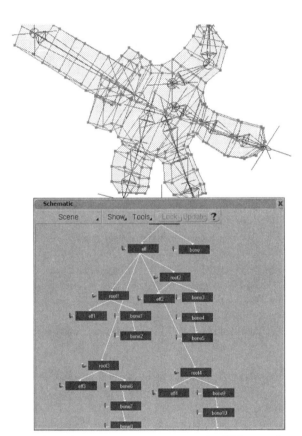

Use the Schematic View to examine the IK hierarchy.

TUTORIAL: CARTOON HAND

This simple and quick tutorial introduces you to the Envelope operator, and shows you how to deform a polygon mesh skin with a hierarchy of IK chains.

STEP 1: EXAMINE THE SCENE

From your courseware project, open the CartoonHand scene. This scene contains a polygon mesh cartoon hand model, with a bit of the forearm still attached, and a separate IK hierarchy for the arm bone, hand bones, and fingers. All the IK is parented together in one hierarchy to make it easy to select and use. Orbit around and select the objects to familiarize yourself with them, but don't change the position of the IK bones or effectors, since they are correctly placed within the hand already.

STEP 2: ENVELOPE THE SKIN

The hand model is the skin, so select it. It's a single object, so selecting it as a node (Left Mouse Button) is fine, but if your skin was a complex hierarchy of elements you would want to select the skin as a branch or tree. Open a schematic view (or explorer) and find the IK hierarchy, but don't select it yet – leave the hand selected. From the Animation module, choose the Envelope→Set Envelope command, and then pick with the Middle Mouse Button on the top of the IK hierarchy in the Schematic or the explorer view. If you pick IK with the Left Mouse Button, that only adds a single IK element, which would be really slow, but when you use the Middle Mouse Button, you are picking the IK as a branch, so all the IK elements below the one you picked on in the Hierarchy are also added to the envelope. Adding IK as a branch is faster, and also safer, since you won't accidentally miss some tiny bone. However, you can also add Envelope deformers (bones and other objects) one at a time if you wish.

Right-click to end the pick session and complete the Envelope command.

Note: You can also add all the bones to a group, then choose the group when you execute the Envelope command. If you have a lot of bones, and plan to envelope/unenvelope often, this can save time.

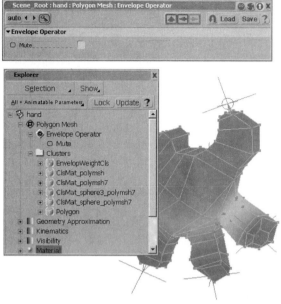

The Envelope Operator actually deforms the hand.

STEP 3: EXAMINE THE RESULTS

You'll know that the Envelope operator has been correctly applied, because the IK and the vertices of the hand model will change color. Each bone has now been assigned a new color, and the vertices that are most directly deformed by that bone have also been assigned that color. This visual feedback is helpful, but it doesn't really tell you how the skin will be deformed. To see the whole story, make sure the hand is still selected, and change your camera view to the Constant shaded mode, then in the Show (eyeball) menu, toggle on WeightMaps. The WeightMap shows how the actual surface of the model is assigned to the IK, and how the influence of the different bones blends along the surface.

STEP 4: FIND THE ENVELOPE OPERATOR

Find the Envelope Operator in the transient Selection explorer (the Selection button in the MCP) so you know where it lives. With the skin (the hand) selected, in the Selection explorer, open up the Clusters folder, open up the EnvelopeWeightCls cluster and then the Envelope_Weight, and see the Automatic Envelope Assignment operator underneath. Click directly on the icon for that operator to pop up the Automatic Envelope Assignment PPG. Here is where the Assignment depth (how many bones are blended for each point on the skin) and the Assignment method are chosen. We'll explore them later. Close the PPG.

STEP 5: USE THE IK TO DEFORM THE HAND

Select one of the IK effectors, which are the nulls at the end of each finger. Now translate that effector to curl the finger bones closed about halfway. See that the skin of the hand now deforms, staying wrapped around the finger bones!

Try some of the other effectors as well. Note that in some places, the vertices of the hand are assigned to neighboring fingers, which causes them to stretch a bit when the wrong finger moves. You'll have to adjust the weighting to fix this, in a later tutorial.

Finally, increase the smoothing on the hand object by selecting the hand, and tapping the plus (+) key on your keyboard. Look at how the WeightMap smoothly shades the new Subdivision Surface!

STEP 6: SAVE YOUR WORK

Save your work for later, so you can fix the weighting. Call the scene MyHandToWeight and save it in your local project, not in the courseware.

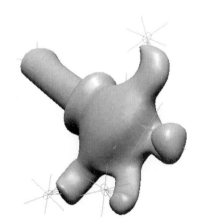

You can now pose the fingers by translating the effectors of the IK chains.

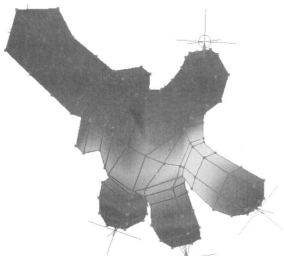

The weight map shows the bone color on the skin surface.

That's it – enveloping a skin is simple. It's making the weight blending look right that's the tough part. Keep reading the next session to learn how to adjust the weighting to make more sense.

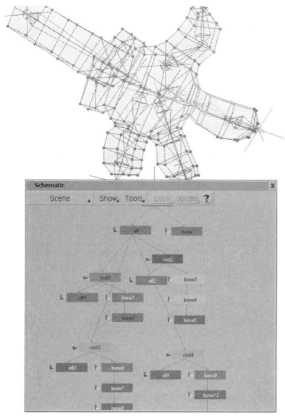

The points of the hand are color-coded to match the bones.

ENVELOPE ASSIGNMENT DEPTH

The default settings for the Envelope command do a good job of weighting the points on the skin to the joints in the skeleton, but there are cases where you'll want to make some changes.

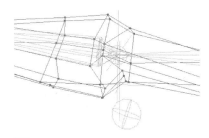

Two-bone blending might be appropriate for fingers, arms, or legs.

By default, only the two closest bones are considered by the envelope operator as it deforms each sample of the skin. That's great for things like a knee, where there is only one bone below the knee and one bone above the knee. For something like a head and neck it wouldn't provide enough blending between nearby IK elements, since the skin around the neck needs to blend around the collarbone, the shoulder blades, the spine, the neck, and the skull. In this case you could increase the Envelope Assignment Depth, to force the Envelope Deformer to consider more IK elements for each sample of the skin. To do this, select the skin, and using the Selection explorer in the MCP open the Clusters/EnvelopeWeightCls/Envelope_Weights/Automatic Envelope Assignment PPG. Increase the Assignment Depth to 4, meaning that each area of the skin will now be influenced by the four nearest bones or other IK elements.

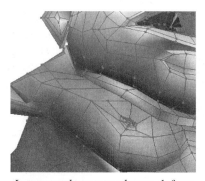

In areas where more bones deform the skin, higher assignment depth is useful.

 Note: An advanced technique here is to lower the assignment depth to 1 for skeletal systems, meaning that there will be no blend at all between bones, then use the Smoothing brush on the assignment weight map, with the Attribute Painter for maximum control, to manually determine just exactly how each the skin assignment blends between each bone.

ENVELOPE ASSIGNMENT METHOD

If sections of the IK hierarchy get too close together, the skin may be shared between joints that shouldn't be considered. For instance, if you build the skin of a hand with the fingers close together, and then put a hierarchy of IK chains in the hand and connect the IK hierarchy to the skin with the Envelope command, the skin of the little finger might be shared between the joints in the little finger and the next finger over. This would make the skin stretch in a weird way when the little finger effector moved.

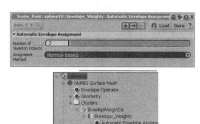

Normal-based assignment is a good idea, but flaky in production.

That's because the skin on each finger is close to the bones in the other hand as well.

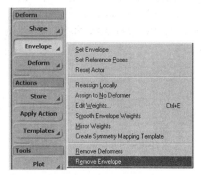

Select the skin, then use the Remove Envelope command to cut loose the IK.

Another way to assign skin samples to be deformed by different IK elements is to use a normal-based assignment, instead of a distance-based assignment. After you envelope a character (but before you move any effectors around) you may safely change the assignment method. Choose the skin hierarchy and open the Automatic Envelope Assignment PPG. Change the Assignment Method to Normal-Based from Distance-Based. Now the envelope assignment operator will look at the normal direction of the skin (so you had better have the normals facing out...) and assign each skin sample only to bones and other IK elements that lie inside the normals of that sample.

This is a great idea, but it doesn't always work: try it out on your model, and if weird tearing and unassigned vertices stretch off oddly, undo the change and go back to distance based assignment.

In cases like this, you can manually control the weighting of the points on the skin to determine which joints affect them. The influence of each bone on each skin sample is called the vertex weighting and is expressed as a percentage, which you can manually change either numerically or with the Generic Attribute Painter tool. The methodology for this process is detailed in the Weighting skins section a little later in this chapter. However, since weighting is a hassle it is always a good idea to consider how the automatic weighting works when constructing the skins, to minimize the manual weighting work that must be done. Building your skins in poses with limbs loosely apart (the natural pose) will be a big time-saver later on in the process.

The starting pose of the skin makes weighting easy or difficult.

ADDING IN NEW DEFORMERS

When you have a character already skinned up, which is to say that you have bound the skin to the IK using the envelope operator, you may find yourself wanting to add more IK bones or other deformers. If you want to simply create a new IK deformer object, like a an IK chain or just a simple geometry object to add a bulge or stabilize an area of skin, you can always add them into the existing IK hierarchy at any time, or just use the Envelope→Set Envelope command to add in a new deformer. Select the skin hierarchy (the envelope) choose the Envelope→Set Envelope command and then pick on the new deformer objects that you want added in. If you already have an Envelope Operator on the skin, a dialog will pop up to confirm that you do want to replace the previous weight assignment with a new weight assignment. Click the OK button, and pick the new objects. When done, right-click and the whole envelope will be re-calculated. This will generate a new WeightMap, so any manual modifications you've done will be lost. You should also try to do this in the base pose of the Envelope, before moving parts of the IK around, because if the skin isn't in the same pose it was when it was first enveloped, the enveloping might work out a bit differently this time (since different bones will be closer to different parts of the skin) and as a result some error seems to creep in. Just like Sade says, it's never as good as the first time.

REMOVING ENVELOPES

It's hard to make permanent changes to the skin geometry while it's enveloped. If you need to re-model the original skin, perhaps adding some additional detail, or modifying the shape of your character, it's easier to remove the envelope operator, make the changes, and then re-envelope it. To remove an envelope operator properly, select the skin hierarchy as a branch and choose the Envelope➜Remove Envelope command. Now your skin will no longer be bound to the IK and other deformers. You can also remove just specific deformers (bones or other objects) from the envelope, leaving the rest alone. When you do this, by selecting the skin, choosing the Envelope➜Remove Deformer command, then picking with the Left Mouse Button on the deformers to remove and right-clicking to end the pick session, the envelope weighting will again be re-calculated automatically.

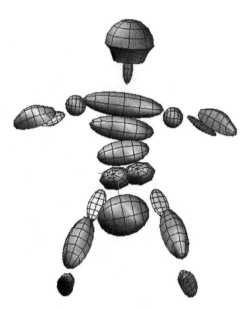

Any object in XSI can become a deformer.

ENVELOPING TO OBJECTS OTHER THAN IK

I mentioned earlier that skins can be weighted and deformed by other kinds of objects than just IK chains. In fact, any object in XSI can function in exactly the same way as an IK chain and can be weighted to influence the skin around it. All you have to do is select the skin, and add the object as a deformer in the same way that you add in the IK: with the Envelope➜Set Envelope command. This means that a small null, a cube, a sphere, or even a more complex hierarchy of models can be defined as a skeleton and used to model or animate deformations of a skin.

One way to use this feature is to add in objects within the skin that deform it in addition to a pre-existing skeletal structure to show effects such as musculature moving under skin, muscles stretching the skin over them, or heavy swaying girth, like a fat character's stomach.

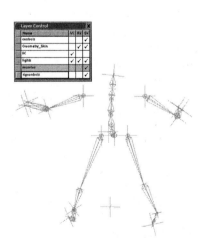

The IK layer won't ever render, and it isn't selectable.

You can add geometry elements directly to the hierarchy of IK so that they will just automatically be added when you envelope the skin to the IK hierarchy, or you can add them separately after the IK has been added to the envelope.

One thing to remember is that the actual shape of the geometry objects really doesn't make any difference in how the skin behaves.

Once enveloped to the skin, the points of the skin are automatically re-weighted to be influenced by proximity to the new skeleton geometry objects. When you translate, scale, or rotate the object, the skin deforms over the top of it.

Another thing to keep in mind is that while IK never renders, these other objects might. You should either change the render visibility of each object, or put all these objects (and the IK) into a layer, and turn off the render visibility of the whole layer so the objects don't show up unexpectedly in the render.

Because the actual vertices of these objects are never a part of the Envelope calculations, and therefore don't have any effect on the motion of the skin, it is a good idea to choose relatively simple polygon objects or nulls.

One fantastic use for this technique is in creating muscle bulges with expressions (the more powerful relatives of constraints) to link them to the rotation of specific joints.

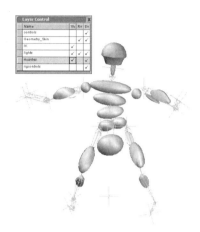

Now the bones have muscles attached, and both muscles and bones deform the skin.

WEIGHTING YOUR SKIN

As I mentioned earlier, enveloping IK chains to a skin is the easy part, and making the skin obey the joints and deform exactly as you have in mind is the tough part. The process of determining exactly how each area of the skin will behave in relation to each joint of each chain is called weighting the skin.

Because each vertex is controlled by each joint according to a percentage weight, the way that the skin deforms is determined entirely by the weighting for each joint on each and every vertex (or CV or sample) of the skin. If your skin model has a great many points, as in the case of a dense polygonal mesh, it can be very time-consuming to edit the weights to your satisfaction. The easiest models to weight are those like single-piece NURBS skins, or Subdivision Surfaces, that have few CVs or vertices, arranged so that more model detail is available near the joints that bend the most.

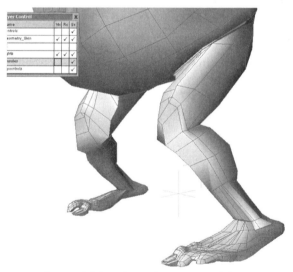

This model has the right amount of detail.

VIEWING THE WEIGHT MAP

When you first assign a chain to a skin as an envelope, the weights of each vertex or control point are calculated automatically. Inevitably, one joint in the chain or chains will be closest for each vertex, and will therefore have the greatest influence on that point on the skin. XSI has a nifty trick that will help you immensely while weighting your skin: it colors the vertex to match the color of that joint. XSI also creates a weight map for the envelope deformation, which graphically shows the blending of the skin between joints by shading the skin in the joint colors. To see this, change your camera view to the Constant view mode (Shaded will also work, but is slower) and then under the Show options (eyeball menu) make sure that Weight Maps is toggled on. Lastly, make sure your object is selected, since by default weight maps only show on the selected object.

Now you can see which joints match which areas of your skin model. Orbit around to see how this looks.

The color of the joints in the IK chains is determined automatically, and XSI always uses the same order of colors starting from the first joint and moving down the chain. The default colors, therefore, may not help you much in cases where IK chains of identical length are located close together, such as fingers and legs. In these cases, it would be more helpful to assign your own colors to each joint, so you can tell from the skin colors which of the two chains is influencing that area of the skin most strongly.

The weight map shows the influence of each deformer on every part of the skin (envelope).

You might, for instance, choose to alternate colors between fingers, and use the same pattern of colors on the left and right arms, to make the resulting weight map easier to look at and understand. You can change the deformer color in the Edit Weights PPG or layout, covered a bit later in this chapter.

HURRY UP AND WEIGHT

Keep in mind that the color system is just a way to visualize the assignment and predict problems with the skin weighting.

There are three primary ways to change the weights on the skin: manual assignment, weight-painting assignment, and bounding model assignment

In this chapter we'll tackle the first two, leaving the bounding model assignment for Chapter 9.

MANUAL IK WEIGHTING

Manual reassignment is useful for assigning points entirely to one joint, or for removing vertices from the envelope altogether. For instance, say you create a human skull, and place a simple single-joint chain in the jaw to move the mouth region. When you test the motion by translating the effector, you will find that the entire head flips and deforms when you drag the effector in the mouth region

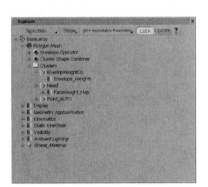

Each object can have many clusters, each with many weight maps.

The solution is to assign all the points in the lower jaw to be deformed only by the jawbone. To do so, tag the jaw points, and then execute the Envelope→Reassign Locally command. Next, click with the Left Mouse Button on the jawbone (check the Status Bar for a prompt). Finally, you must assign the rest of the head to be influenced by no deformer at all. Tag all the points in the head, perhaps by dragging a rectangle around the head and jaw with T and the RMB to toggle the selection, then choose the command Envelope→Assign to No Deformer.

This will result in a harsh line between weighted and unweighted skin vertices. You could correct this by selecting the skin and Choosing the Envelope→Smooth Envelope Weights command, which actually has a persistent operator in the Selection Explorer that you can inspect if the urge strikes you.

Another common scenario for using Reassign Locally is in weighting a tagged region of points entirely to one joint. Imagine that you are assigning a skin to a human model, and you built the skin model and the IK chains so that the legs are side by side. When you envelope the IK chains to the skin with the Envelope→Add Envelope command, the joints from the left leg will partially influence the skin of the right leg, and vice versa, simply because the joints are fairly close together in the model's stance. For each joint on both legs, you must insure that the left foot joint influences only the left foot skin, the right foot joint influences only the right foot skin, and so on.

The process is to first tag the points to be reassigned, on the inside of the left thigh, for instance, and then invoke the Edit Weights command from the Envelope menu.

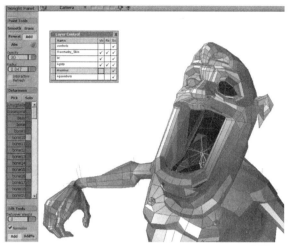

The head is stretched because it's weighted to the jaw and the skull indiscriminately.

Tag the points in the jaw, then assign them manually to the jaw-bone.

This pops up the Weight Editor dialog. The Weight Editor dialog describes exactly how each and every vertex or control point in the mesh is assigned to each and every deformer you have assigned with the Envelope→Add Envelope Command. The Edit Weights PPG gives you the power to look at and change the weight assignment of each and every point on the skin, individually and in groups. You can pick a specific vertex and remove the influence of a specific joint, or you can select a group of vertices, such as the left thigh, and remove the influence on all of them from another joint, such as the right thigh bone, so only wanted joints are considered when the skin deforms.

You can manually specify the ratio of influence of each joint, changing it to an absolute value, or by adding or subtracting degrees of influence.

The lower part of the box is a chart, showing you the weight of each point of each surface to each potential deformer. Rows represent each vertex or control point in the surfaces selected. Columns represent the deformers that are acting on each vertex. The numbers in each box indicate exactly how much weight each point on the surface has to each deformer in the envelope.

When a number is in a light gray box, that point (row) is not at all weighted to that deformer (column). When a point on the surface is weighted to a point or two, it is located in a colored box, with a number indicating the strength of the weight. You can also type weights directly into this spreadsheet-like arrangement.

If you click directly on a row number, you select the corresponding point on the surface in the 3D views. If you click directly on a column heading you select you select that deformer in the 3D views.

With a bone or other deformer selected, and one or more points selected, you can change the influence that the chosen bone will have on the points with the long slider in the Weight Editor.

While adjusting the weights of your character, if you notice that some points are influenced by a bone that should not affect them at all, you can tag those points in the 3D views with the T button, which will activate them in the Weight Editor. Then, choose the bad bone in the Deformer list of the Weight Editor, and drag the slider to zero to remove any influence that the bone might have had on those points.

Setting the influence to zero (0) means that the bone won't deform the points at all, while setting it to 100 means that the points will be entirely dedicated to that bone, and will follow it wherever it goes without consideration for any other deformer.

MIXING WEIGHTS MANUALLY WITH EDIT WEIGHTS

Completely weighting points 100 percent to a single bone, or completely removing all influence from a single bone, are both simple cases. What if you need to adjust the blend of weights on points between two or more bones? Well, the new method is to paint weights, covered in the next paragraph, but you can also manually adjust the proportion of weights on each vertex or CV. The Weight Editor slider is just an input widget – you use it to add or remove influence from a single bone at a time. But how exactly does it add and remove weight? There are several options to help you here. The absolute method will set the weight for the selected bone on the selected vertices to be exactly the absolute value you choose with the slider (or numerically enter). The Add mode will add a percentage given by the slider to the selected vertices, so that if you dragged the slider to 10, it would add 10% more weight to the selected vertices. If the selected vertices already were weighted 45% to the selected bone and you dialed in 10 on the slider, the vertices would now be weighted 45% + 10%, or 55%, to the bone. The Add% mode is more gradual – it adds a percentage of the current weight, so that if the vertices were already 45% weighted to a given bone and you dialed in 10% with Add% mode active, the vertices would now be weighted 45% + (10%*45%), or 49.5%, to the given bone. The Add and Add% modes can also be used with the Paint Weights tool to make it work more gradually and smoothly.

Click this button to show the Paint Weights panel.

ENVELOPE WEIGHTING WITH PAINT

While numerically adjusting the percentage of influence between specific vertices and a given bone is certainly precise, it's not much fun. Painting on weights using the paint tool is a whole lot more enjoyable. The general concept is just the same: select your skin, pick a bone to weight to (or from) and then add or remove the influence of that bone on the surrounding skin areas. What's different is that you get to see the color of the bone on the skin, blended with the neighboring bones, and you get to see the area of the skin where you are making changes with the visual cues of the paint tool. Before diving in, take a few moments to set up your view for maximum feedback.

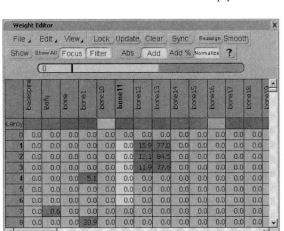

The Paint Weights panel

Open up your enveloped hand model, the one you saved earlier, or use the scene called CartoonHandEnveloped in the courseware project. Show the Paint Weights panel with the button in the lower-left corner of the screen that looks like a paintbrush.

SHADED MODE, CONSTANT MODE

The weight map can be viewed in either Shaded or Constant view. Shaded view looks cooler, but constant is more useful, and faster to display on most graphics cards. As your models become more complex, this can make a difference.

Since painting weights is a visually oriented task, you'll want to maximize your camera view and frame your skin model so you can really see the weight map well.

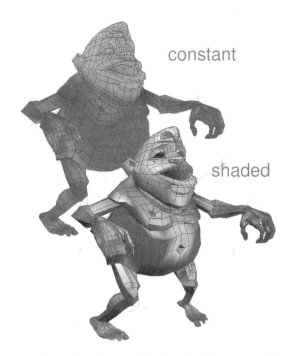

The Shaded mode is cooler, but the Constant mode is easier to work with.

In X-ray mode you can see bones inside skins.

MIXED MODE AND X-RAY MODE

You can also set your display options to show you the skin and the bones laying under the skin. In the Show (eyeball) menu Display Options, find the first Display Options tab and toggle on X-ray mode. Now you can see right through the model. This is helpful when picking bones, since if you can't see them inside the model they might be hard to pick. If you don't like working like this, you can also just switch back and forth between constant and wireframe mode, using the Middle Mouse Button on the View menu to swap between the last two chosen modes.

VIEWING NAMES ON IK

It's not a bad idea to show the names of the IK elements that are unselected, so that if you wanted to you could choose them by name in the Weight Panel UI. In the View→Visibility Options→Attributes tab, under the right column, which applies to unselected objects, toggle on Name. Now the bones and other items will have names superimposed right in the camera view.

ADJUSTING PAINT BRUSH PROPERTIES

Show the XSI Paint Weights Panel by clicking the third button from the lower-left corner of the UI, which looks like a small paintbrush.

Now you can select a bone in the Paint Weights panel, in the scrolling list of deformers, or you can use the Pick button in the Weight Panel UI and then pick on a bone. When you are ready to paint, you can invoke the Paint tool by holding down the W hotkey.

You can also activate the Paint tool from the Property menu, but since you've switched to the Weight Panel UI you can't see the Property Menu without switching views using the view switcher at the bottom of the panel.

While you have the W key down, you can move your mouse cursor over your skin to see the Paint tool. The Paint tool shows up as circle showing the coverage area that stays tangent to the surface as you move it around on the skin.

You can interactively adjust the radius of the coverage area, making the circle bigger or smaller by clicking and dragging with the Middle Mouse Button. The radius will pop up and be displayed in a small gray strip in the bottom of the view window your cursor is in, until you let go of the Middle Mouse Button.

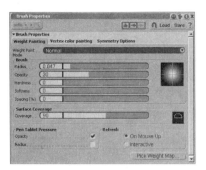

You can adjust how the brush behaves in the Brush PPG.

Show the Paint Weights panel with the small brush button in the bottom-left of the screen.

When you Click with the Left Mouse Button, the paint tool will lay down weight, and when you click with the Right Mouse Button it will remove weight from the area under the paint tool. The amount of weight that it adds or removes varies, starting from 100% at the center of the circle, to 0 at the edges. However, you need to be able to control this in order to do any kind of good work.

SOFTNESS, OPACITY, SIZE, COVERAGE

You will want to lay down and remove weight gradually and softly, building up the effect slowly with a number of strokes for best results. An analogy to painting is that using the Paint tool at 100% is like throwing a bucket of paint on the canvas – you don't end up with much subtlety of light and shade that way. Near the top of the Paint Weights panel you'll find the Opacity slider.

The opacity controls how much weight is laid down with each stroke. You'll want this set low, like 25%, so that you gradually build up weight as you paint on the surface. Here you can also determine whether the brush adds weight, removes weight, or smoothes the gradation of weights on the surface. Leave the drop menu set to Add for now.

There are other, more powerful Brush control options in the Brush Properties PPG. Open the Brush Tool PPG with CTRL-W, or choose Brush Properties from the Property menu in the Animation module.

The Softness controls how the value falls off from the center of the tool to the edges. You can see the changes represented in the PPG on the brush shape indicator. You will want a soft, gradual falloff for most applications.

The Coverage slider changes how far around corners the paint tool works. This is not usually a big concern – leave it at the default.

ADDING WEIGHT TO ONE BONE

The most common way to use the Paint Weights Panel is to add the weight of one bone at a time to areas of the skin around that bone. To do this, change your camera view to show in Constant mode, make sure the View menu is showing weight maps, and select a skin mesh object that you have previously bound to some IK or other deformers. The object should show up with a multicolored surface. If it doesn't, something is wrong. Check that the skin is in fact enveloped, that the View→WeightMaps toggle is on, and that the view is in Constant or Shaded mode. You'll want to be able to see the model and colored weight map as clearly as possible, so maximize your Camera view window and frame the skin object.

Next, locate the bone you want the selected skin weighted to in the scrolling list of deformers in the Paint Weights panel, and click on it to activate the bone. If you switch (temporarily) to wireframe mode, you'll see the bone highlighted in white to help show you what bone is active. Now you have one envelope object selected, and one bone picked in the deformer list. That tells XSI that you want to adjust the weighting of that one envelope (skin) to that one bone(deformer).

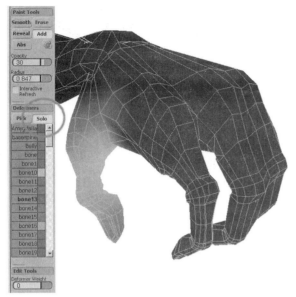

The Solo button displays only one selected bone in the WeightMap.

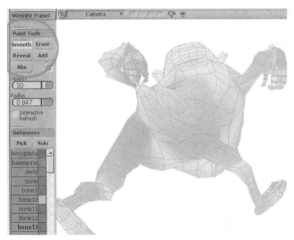

Use the Smooth command and smooth brush to fix problems.

Naming the bones first helps a great deal here; however, if you didn't name your bones, there is another way to choose which one you are weighting to. Set your View style to Wireframe. Click on the Pick button in the Weight UI, and your mouse cursor will change to the pick cursor, indicating that you are in pick mode. Carefully pick the bone you want to weight to, which will briefly flash white, and become selected in the deformer list. Now, since you can only see the bones to pick in the wireframe mode, and only see the weight map to paint on in Constant or Shaded mode, it would seem that you have a problem. However, XSI will automatically switch to Constant view for you when you hold down the W hotkey to engage the weight paint brush.

 Note: There is an X-ray mode option in the Display Options for constant and Shaded mode, but this dims the weight map so much that I prefer to just switch view modes for the bone picking part of the operation.

Now you are ready to paint on some weight. When using the Paint tool, you don't have to tag vertices on your model (although you can). If you are using the CartoonHand model, start with the bone protruding from the wrist. You want the skin on the forearm entirely weighted to that bone, and a gradual blend up into the middle of the palm, where the finger bones will take over.

ISOLATING ONE BONE

It's rather hard to see exactly what's going to happen with all the bones showing in a rainbow of colors on the skin. Wouldn't it be easier if we just saw the one bone we're working on in the weight map? Yes, it would. Click on the Solo button in the Weight Panel UI, and see that now, only the area of the skin influenced by the selected bone is lit up in the weight map.

Use the Paint tool now, clicking and dragging with the Left Mouse Button, to add weight to the area of the skin around the forearm, blending gradually to the center of the palm. If you add more strokes to the area around the end of the arm, it will be weighted heavily to the forearm bone. You can also use the Right Mouse Button to remove weight from the palm are if you lay the weight down too thickly.

When done, use the Pick button to pick the next bone, and work your way through the hand, binding the skin to just the bones that should be deforming it for each finger.

A smooth Joint will bend nicely when animated.

Extreme Poses show off problems in the skin weighting.

POSING MODELS IN BAD POSITIONS

When you first envelope a skin model, you will have already carefully adjusted the IK to fit perfectly within the skin, so no problems with weighting are likely to be visible. In fact, you'll not notice any issues with your envelope assignment until you actually use the IK to deform the skin – that's when problems show up.

So, before you start animating and have to go back to re-weighting, you'll want to use the IK in your skin to pose your character in extreme positions to reveal flaws in your weighting. For instance, you would want to pick up a character's leg as high as it will ever go to see how the blending is going to look in the area from the thigh through the butt and up into the lower back. Then you can fix it with the Weight Panel, put the foot back down, and repeat with the other foot. Gradually work through all the limbs in your character, posing the character in the most extreme position likely to occur, and fixing the weight blending.

SMOOTHING ENVELOPE WEIGHTS

If there is too great a change in how the envelope is assigned from one vertex to the next, there might be an unsightly seam, or a jagged edge in the model when it animates. Using Subdivision Surfaces alleviates this problem a great deal, since the SubD just re-calculates and stays smooth at each position the envelope takes, but it's still a good idea to be aware that the envelope weighting should gradually change across the surface of the model, without too many drastic boundaries between bones. There are two very useful tools in the Weight Panel UI to make sure that weights are smooth: the Smooth brush and the Apply Smooth operator. If you have an Envelope selected (or just a group of vertices on an Envelope selected) and click on the Apply Smooth, XSI will look at each vertex of sample in the weight map and blur the weight between it and the neighboring vertices. This has the effect of keeping regions of same weight intact, while blending the boundaries between areas of differing weights. The result is a nicer, smoother transition between the effects of the different deformers.

You can adjust the amount of smoothing it performs by inspecting the Smooth Envelope PPG on the object in Clusters/EnvelopeWeightCLs/Envelope_Weights.

One technique to explore when enveloping simple characters with IK only in arms, legs, and fingers is to set the assignment depth to 1, so that the envelope Operator doesn't even try to automatically weight the bones based on Normal or Distance, then use the Smooth tool to add in the precise blending that you want. Since the Smooth tool blends based on adjacent samples in the WeightMap, not on proximity in 3D space, it's more likely to do a better job the first time.

PAINTING SMOOTHING ON

You can also smooth just specific areas of the skin using the Paint tool. Obviously, this provides a much higher degree of control over the results than just auto-smoothing the whole character. In the Weight Panel UI, switch the Paint tool at the top to Smooth. You can adjust the amount of smoothing in the normal way for the Paint tool, with the Opacity slider. Now when you click and drag over an area of the skin with the Left Mouse Button, the area of the weight map under your mouse will be smoothed, blurred, and averaged with the neighboring areas.

LOOKING AT EACH SAMPLE WEIGHT

If you plan on exporting the character weighting data – for instance, for use in a Game engine – you'll want to be able to see the raw data before it's exported. You can also change each individual vertex weighting to each bone deformer in this way.

With a skin envelope model selected, call up the Envelope→Edit Weights PPG with the CTRL-E hot key. The Edit Weights PPG is the ancestor of the Weight Panel UI. It has a spreadsheet-like grid, displaying each bone or other deformer along the top horizontal axis and each and every vertex or sample in the envelope down along the vertical axis. The intersection of each vertex and each deformer shows a number for the weight or influence of that deformer on that vertex or sample. You can directly edit these values if you wish.

WEIGHTING LORPHEA: AT A GLANCE

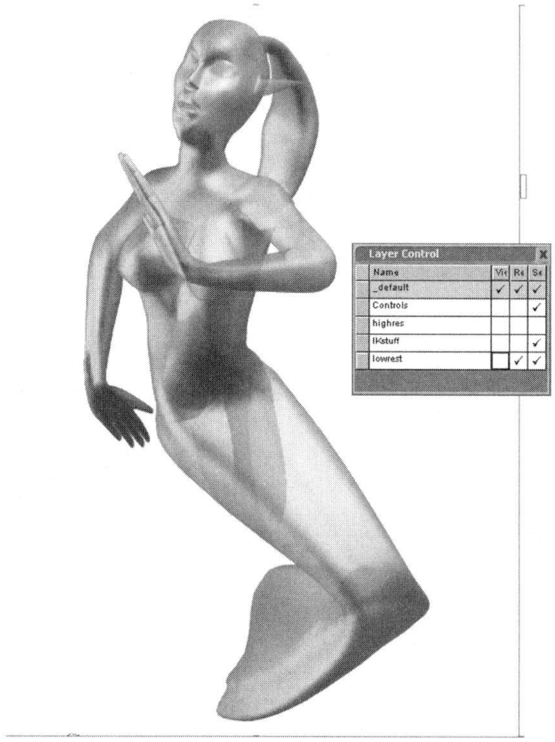

Lorphea courtesy of Jake Kazdal, Sega Japan.

TOPICS COVERED

Lorphea the mermaid (thanks for the model goes to Jake Kazdal in Japan) has a simple skeleton setup, but the default weighting has problems, particularly around her long hair, her ears, and her fingers. You'll fix these with the weight painting and smoothing tools.

You'll learn how to:

- Change assignment depth
- Smooth Envelope Weights
- Paint influence on a skin

MATERIALS REQUIRED

This tutorial requires the LorpheaWeight scene from the courseware accompanying this material.

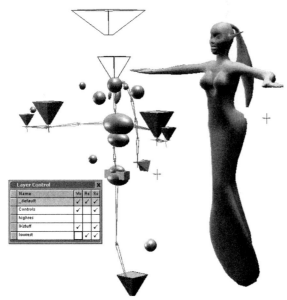

Lorphea and her IK bones and muscles

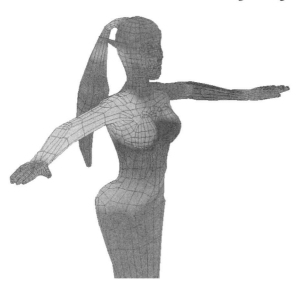

Lorphea is organized into layers for her skin and IK.

TUTORIAL: WEIGHTING LORPHEA

It's easy to add an IK skeleton system to Lorphea, but when she moves she'll have weighting problems. If her long hair – which has an IK chain in it – moves, the points on her shapely bottom will stretch in a nasty manner.

Her face is going to stretch in a foul way when her head moves, and her full bosom collapses frighteningly when she brings her arms in. The solution to these problems is painting a better weight map to bind the skin to the deformers underneath.

Making all the changes you need vertex-by-vertex is certainly precise, but it's awfully slow and not very much fun. Fortunately, XSI has a stupendous new toolset and user interface to make this chore fast and fun, called the Paint Weights panel, the mother of all weight reassignment tools.

In the view switcher at the bottom of the left-hand menu stack, click on the third button (that looks like a paintbrush). This will swap the regular menu stack with the Paint Weights Panel.

The basic idea is simple: in Constant shaded mode, with WeightMaps turned on, you can see the influence of each bone on the skin as a gradation of color, blending from one bone to another. With the Paint Weights panel, you can pick a bone (or other deformer) and then paint the color corresponding to that bone directly on the surface of the model. As you add the color of one bone to the skin, the skin becomes weighted more to that bone and less to the other bones. In this way you simply paint color onto your model to change the envelope binding weight assignment.

Each vertex weight can also be smoothed to the vertices around it, which is a quick and simple solution to many weighting problems.

Because problems in the skin weighting usually become painfully evident only during animation (for instance, you see then that moving the arm causes the belly to stretch), you can scrub the time slider to see different animated poses of your creature, and use this dialog to create a weighting that works for the different poses.

She'll be multicolored when her WeightMap is showing.

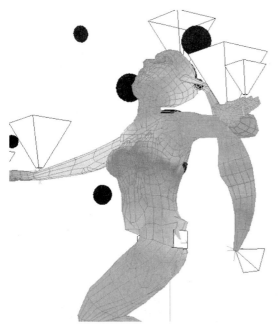

Her bottom is influenced by her hair. Her head is messed up. That's not good.

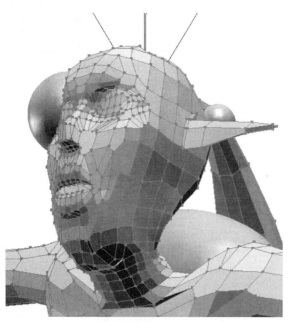

Tag all her head points.

STEP 1: OPEN THE SCENE

Open the LorpheaWeight scene, and look around. Open the Layers box with the Layers→Layer Control menu command in the top-right corner of the Main Command Panel, and see that the IK is on one layer, and the skin on another. Open a Schematic view and see that the IK is in one big hierarchy, to make it easy to envelope.

Set the Camera view to Constant mode, in the View menu toggle WeightMaps on and use the view switcher in the bottom-left corner of the Menu stack to switch to the Weight Panel UI. Now you are ready to paint weights. Switch the view switcher back to the Menu stack and change to the Animation Module for the next step.

STEP 2: ENVELOPE LORPHEA

Enveloping means that you want to bind Lorphea's skin to the IK hierarchy so that the IK bones deform the skin around them. This deformation is called an Envelope Deformation. Select Lorphea, and choose the Envelope→Set Envelope command from the Menu cells in the Animation Module. Now, in a Schematic or explorer view, pick on the IK hierarchy (at the top) with the Middle Mouse Button to add it as a branch into the Envelope Operator. Click the Right Mouse Button when you have it right to complete the command. If you get it wrong, and only add part of the IK, select Lorphea, and choose Envelope→Remove Envelope to restore Lorphea to where she started, then try again. When she's properly enveloped, you'll see a multi-colored weight map all over her body.

STEP 3: TEST THE ENVELOPE

Now you can test the effects of the Envelope. Select the Effector at the end of her long hair, and translate it. See the hair deform correctly, but also see her bottom affected, which is not correct. Leave the hair in a pose that shows the problem. Select the effector in her fluke, and bend her tail, looking for problems. Tilt her head back with the effector in her mouth. See her head bend oddly. We'll fix all these problems.

STEP 4: FIX THE HEAD

The head has a big sphere in it, that is a child of the top bone in the neck. The whole head needs to be weighted 100% to that sphere, since it will act like a skull bone and keep her face rigid. Tag all the points around her head, down to the top of her neck, but not including the long hair. Choose the Envelope→Reassign Locally command, then pick on the skull sphere to assign the points totally to that deformer object. See the face snap back into shape!

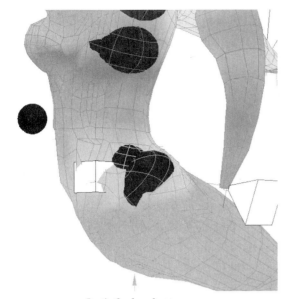

Let's fix her bottom.

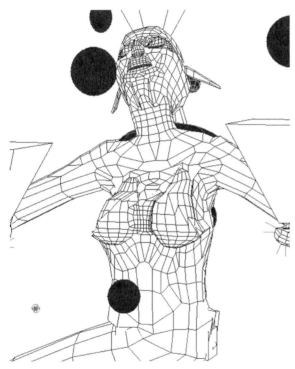

Her chest deflates unflatteringly.

STEP 5: FIX HER BUTT

The points on her rear are stretching towards the end of the hair. There is another big sphere inside her posterior that will act as the anchor for the points around it. You need to remove the influence of the hair, then paint more influence from that object, called "Pelvis", onto the skin around it. Use the view switcher to pop up the Paint Weights UI. Pop up the Brush Properties with CTRL-W and set the Opacity to 25%. Set the Weight Paint Mode to Reveal and close the Brush Properties PPG. Use the Pick button to enter Pick mode, and choose the last bone in the hair. Now you are all set to remove influence on her bottom from the last bone in the hair. Hold the W key to pop up the Paint tool, adjust the Radius to your liking with the Middle Mouse Button, and paint on her butt with the Left Mouse Button. After removing the influence of the hair bone, use the Weight Panel UI to change the Paint Tool Mode to Add and use the Pick button to choose her Pelvis, the sphere in her butt that should be deforming the skin around it. Now you are ready to add influence from her pelvis to the skin. Paint with the W hot key and the Left Mouse Button on her butt, smoothly weighting the skin there more to the Pelvis. You will see the bad vertices that were stretched towards the hair moving back into position during this process. If you have a really fast computer you might try toggling on the Interactive Refresh mode in the Weight Panel UI, so you can see the Envelope operator update in real time as you paint. This is CPU intensive, so if it's too slow to be effective, turn it back off.

STEP 6: EXPAND HER CHEST

When her arms are pulled in towards her body, the sides of her chest collapse in towards her collarbone. That's because her upper arm bones have too much influence on that area. That area should be weighted more to the big sphere located in her chest, named "diaphragm". Use the Weight Panel to Pick the diaphragm, and then click on the Solo button to only see that bone in the weight map. You want the color of that bone to extend through her shoulders, blending smoothly into her upper arms. Paint more influence gradually on her chest and shoulders, blending into the arms smoothly. See her chest expand back to where it should be.

Save your work, because we're going to try a different method next.

STEP 7: DO IT AGAIN

This time, try using the Smooth tool. Open the original scene, and envelope Lorphea again as in Step 2 above.

Before you move any of her IK, use the Selection explorer in the MCP to find her Automatic Envelope Assignment operator, which is in the Cluster Folder, under the EnvelopeWeightCls item, under Envelope Weights. Open it up, and change the Number of Skeleton Objects to 1 bone. Now there will not be any blending at all; each sample on the skin will be weighted entirely to the closest bone.

You can now adjust the effectors to pose her in a bad position, showing all the problems with the weighting.

The magic Smooth tool fixes Lorphea right up.

STEP 8: SMOOTH HER SKIN

Now, if the weight map were smoothed, there would be a better transition from one bone's influence to the influence of the neighboring bone. Click the Apply Smooth button to use the Automatic Smoothing.

Look to see how the envelope changed!

In the Weight Panel UI, change the Paint Mode to Smooth, and manually paint on more smoothing in the areas where you think it's needed.

The Smoothing tool is often a quick way to get the envelope into pretty good shape.

Weighting an envelope properly is all about posing the model in a way that shows the flaws in the envelope assignment, then correcting those flaws. This can be a tedious, time-consuming process, but the new Paint and Smoothing tools certainly ease the pain quite a bit. After a bit of practice, you'll be able to re-weight a character in just a few minutes.

CONCLUSION

In this chapter you learned all about Envelope Operators, how they work to deform the skin around an IK system, and how the weight map shows the influence of each bone on the skin around it. You learned how to add and remove additional deformers from an existing Envelope Operator, you learned how to weight points entirely to one deformer, and how to use the View Switcher to show the Weight Panel UI.

You also saw how the Weight Panel UI and the Paint Property page can be used to Paint values onto the Weight Map of an Envelope operator.

Lastly, you saw how the Smoothing command and the Smoothing Brush work to make good weighting easier.

QUIZ

1. YOU CAN ONLY USE ONE MESH OBJECT AT A TIME WITH THE ENVELOPE OPERATOR.
   a. True
   b. False

2. YOU CAN ONLY USE POLYGON MESH OBJECTS WITH THE ENVELOPE OPERATOR.
   a. True
   b. False

3. HOW MANY IK CHAINS CAN BE USED WITH ONE ENVELOPE OPERATOR?
   a. One chain
   b. Any number, but in one hierarchy
   c. Any number

4. THE ASSIGNMENT DEPTH DETERMINES WHAT?
   a. How many bones deform each sample
   b. How far away the bone works
   c. How strong the bone is

5. CAN REGULAR POLYMESH OBJECTS BE USED AS A DEFORMER, JUST LIKE IK?
   a. Yes
   b. No
   c. Maybe

6. WHAT ABOUT NURBS OBJECTS? CAN THEY BE DEFORMERS?
   a. Yes
   b. No
   c. Maybe

7. HOW MANY DEFORMERS CAN INFLUENCE EACH SKIN SAMPLE?
   a. 2
   b. 1
   c. Many

8. WHAT S THE MOST GRADUAL WEIGHT CHANGE METHOD?
   a. Absolute
   b. Add %
   c. Add

9. WHICH CONTROL HELPS THE PAINT TOOL LAY DOWN WEIGHT MORE GRADUALLY?
   a. Hardness
   b. Opacity
   c. Softness

10. WHAT S THE PAINT TOOL HOT KEY?
    a. CTRL-W
    b. W
    c. P

BOB BONNIOL

CREATIVE DIRECTOR

MONARCH DESIGNS / MODE STUDIOS

Anthony Rossano: Fill us in on who you are and what you do!

Bob Bonniol: I'm creative director and a partner at Monarch Designs and Mode Studios. Monarch and Mode occupy a weird niche in the business of graphic design and content creation. The focus of our business is creating content for projection in live events. If you've ever gone to a concert and seen the wall of eye candy that happens behind the performers, or perhaps been to a Broadway show or an awards show and seen big screens scattered throughout the stage that display any kind of info or video or film sequence, we are the kind of people who put together that kind of media for those kinds of clients, though in general we'd do that sort of thing fort anybody who walks through the door.

ATR: So whoever's paying, huh?

BB: That's exactly right. If you have a commercial that needs eye candy, we can help you there too. But our core market is those people who need to put it on the stage.

Original image from Burn The Floor World Tour. Lighting and Projection Design by Bob & Colleen Bonniol. Composite Texture by Laura Oliver. Image created in Softimage XSI, After Effects, and Knoll Light Factory. Projected via HD video projectors from Christie.

Previsual Picture of Burn The Floor World Tour. Directed by Jason Gilkison, Lighting and Projection Design by Bob & Colleen Bonniol. Image created in Softimage XSI, Arete PYRO, and After Effects.

ATR: Bob, how did you come to the idea of doing digital lighting?

BB: Well, I'm partners with my wife Colleen. Colleen and I both started in the theater, and on the technical crew. Colleen started her career by touring with Bruce Springsteen and Michael Jackson and U2 doing rock and roll lighting. She was a truss-monkey - running around on all of that staging you see at a concert, hanging and focusing lights. At the same time I was actually doing the same thing for Broadway shows, unloading lighting equipment, putting it up, turning it on, and pointing it in the right direction. We both ascended through the ranks to the point where we were actually designing the lighting, working with the artists and conceiving the aesthetic needs of the show, then plotting it out, figuring out how to do it, and what equipment we would need.Colleen diverged a bit and went off from concert lighting to feature film lighting, so we brought that set of skills to the table

ATR: What turned you on to 3D animation?

BB: Well, you know, it's kooky. Colleen and I were both feeling kind of burnt out on the business of working in entertainment and doing lighting design. We were looking around for what would be a cool shift to a different area of entertainment. At the time it was about 1995, and we thought hell, what's happening in 3D seems to be really cool. It was about that time that we were seeing Jurassic Park and therefore a real explosion in 3D media. So we decided that it would be really cool to learn to become 3D animators, and maybe go to work at a 3D animation company. We went to get ourselves training at the fabulous Mesmer. (Ed.: Nice plug, Bob.)

We came out of the class having learned a lot about Softimage 3D. When we got out the other side of the class we found that we had a pretty good understanding of the tool, but my God, what a deep and complicated tool it was. And we felt that we would have to put in a lot more time, and develop our reel a lot more if we were really serious about working for somebody else. So what we decided was we'll just form our own company, and try to apply 3D on our own. And we did! We wanted to be like ILM, or Rhythm and Hues. We did a whole bunch of children's animated show pilots, which were pretty darn good, given our level of skill. Working with producers at that level was something that was foreign to us. It went OK, but then out of the blue, a producer that we had worked with in the past called us and said, "We've heard that you've shifted from lighting into video design," was how they put it, "and would you be capable of coming and doing this show, and designing all the eye candy that goes behind it?" To us that seemed like a perfect amalgam. We thought, "Of course we know all these tools, we know all these people, we know what that situation is like, certainly we can bend our 3D skills in the direction of producing multimedia for concerts and live events." So we did it, and it was a trying experience and a whole new path of discovery, but we came out of it really pleased with what we'd done. Then pieces just fell into place after that, and we just kept getting more and more of those kinds of shows. That's what the studio became.

ATR: Tell me about the creative process. When a client comes to you and says "we want sizzle" how do you go about refining that into something that is accomplishable?

BB: We're big big believers in identifying what the client wants. We initiate a long, in-depth discussion where we examine what they are going to do with the show. We go to the script, we go to the source materials. We try to associate what kind of "sizzle" they want. Then we interface with the other members of the creative team, the scenic designers and the lighting designers and the director and the choreographer, to identify what color palettes will be involved, what lighting choices could be made, and where the projection surfaces will be, what will surround them, what will the performers be doing and why, and what is the psychology of the moment. Then we go off and cook up what we think they need, and develop storyboards, and go back to the producers with them. We say, "This is what we think - we think you want this. Here's what it looks like." Further refinement and dialog follow.

Original image from Burn The Floor World Tour. Lighting & Projection Design by Bob & Colleen Bonniol.
Image created utilizing composited live footage, Softimage XSI, Trapcode Shine, and After Effects.

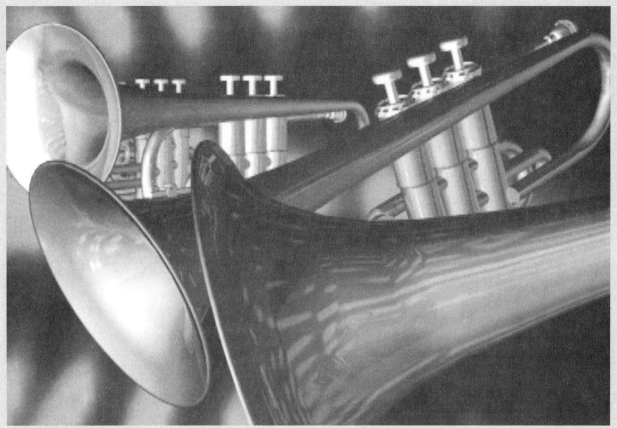

Original image from Burn The Floor World Tour. Lighting and Projection Design by Bob & Colleen Bonniol. Image created in Softimage XSI (modeling by Colleen Bonniol), Trapcode Shine, and After Effects.

ATR: Is it one person at a time or are these group meetings?

BB: As a creative director I find myself having a majority of those conversations with the individual players. I'll speak with the director individually and try to make a creative, psychological, emotional connection with him, to make him understand that I understand what he wants and that I am on his side. I'll try to build that same relationship with each of the individual creatives. Then we do a lot of distance communication, getting everyone together on a conference call, and at that point everybody is on the same page and everybody knows what everybody else's agenda is. It's totally critical in any collaborative effort of any kind that everyone is working toward a common goal.

ATR: Where does this end for you?

BB: I'd like to think the beach in Aruba, but I am compelled to be an artist, in all forms. When I'm not working at the keyboard I'm painting or building little hoo-haws. At some fundamental level I am an artist and I will always want to express myself. I definitely have found that these tools and technologies have allowed me to express myself more effectively than in any other medium. I have to think that no matter what happens I am going to be creating, using this toolset, my entire life. I cannot imagine otherwise.

7 CUSTOM PROPERTIES & LINKED PARAMETERS

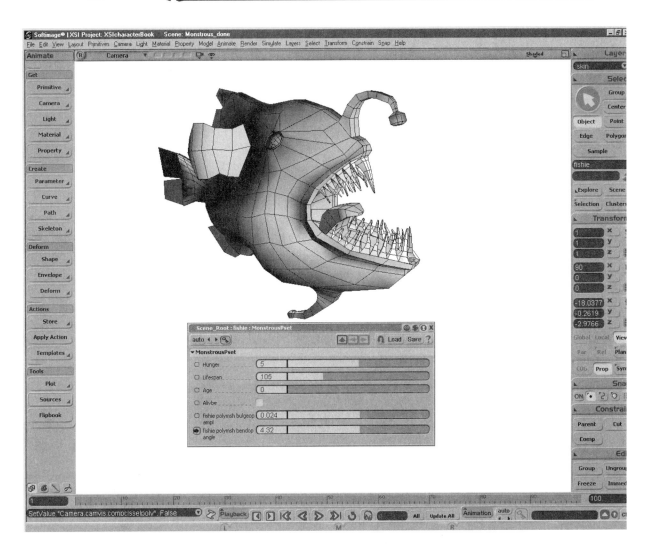

IN THIS CHAPTER YOU WILL LEARN ABOUT:

- How to create your own new Property Pages (PPGs)
- How to add your own properties to objects, and edit them
- How to use your own properties to control other properties
- All about links, and Set Relative Value
- How to use links with Deformation Operators
- How to link IK Bone rotation and other deformations
- How to link IK Bone rotation and Shapes for musculature

INTRODUCTION

In XSI, every object is made up of many different properties. These properties describe the object, and they give you as the animator an interface to change the nature of the object over time. For instance, the material color of an object is expressed as a Property Page (PPG) that contains a number of property sliders, all working in conjunction to determine what the object looks like. Changing the values in the Material PPG over time causes the object to animate the material color over time.

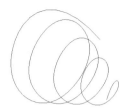

Objects are made up of many properties.

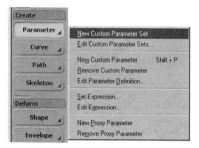

The Create→Parameter Menu

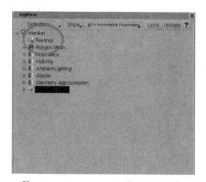

You can see custom Psets in the Selection explorer.

You name your custom property in this dialog.

Each type of object in XSI comes with a number of standard PPGs and properties that describe the features of that kind of object.

So far, you've only used the properties of an object that are the default properties for that type of object, but it is also possible to create your own PPGs, and your own properties, for existing objects. In this way you can extend the definition of the object by adding new features and capabilities.

For instance, you could select a human character and add a PPG called Emotion, and within that PPG, properties called Fear, Anger, Hatred, Peace, and Love.

When you add a new PPG and new properties to an object, they are really just interfaces waiting to be hooked up to something else. When you add a Fear property to the human character model, it won't actually do anything, because you haven't hooked the Fear property up to anything.

You can make these new properties useful by inventing innovative new ways to connect them together with existing properties and even new custom properties.

You might collect custom properties (or existing properties) together into a custom PPG just to make it easier to find what you want all in one place.

You might build one custom property slider that changes several other properties all at once, just to save yourself time and effort.

You might use a link between one custom property and a number of other properties to control them all in an interesting, non-linear way, to make hand animation easier.

You might ultimately write your own expressions to automate complex animation tasks without any effort on your part at all, using custom properties as inputs and variables to those functions.

Custom properties are really just the front end, the interface, to any number of different uses that you can dream up, but the thing to remember is that they are all about connecting one property to another.

CUSTOM PARAMETER SETS

Though the names are slightly different, the concepts of properties and parameters are the same, so for consistency in this book I'll use the term properties, even though the menu commands call them parameters. I'll abbreviate the name to Custom Pset to avoid confusion.

Value Type	Example	Explanation
Boolean	Yes / No	Any question that can be answered True or False
Integer	[2, 38, 1024, -91]	Any whole number, positive or negative
Float	[12.5 , -2.02, .0001]	A floating point number with decimal accuracy
Text	Names, Labels	Any alpha numeric string

Use the Value type that's right for the property you want.

Custom properties must belong to a custom PPG, and PPGs must belong to an object. Therefore, the first thing to do is to decide which object to put the properties on. If you want to add a custom property to a single object, then there is no question, but often you'll be adding custom properties that control an entire character, with a large hierarchy of bones and controls. In this case it is customary to add the Custom Pset to the top element in the character rig hierarchy.

To add a custom PPG, select the object you want it to belong to, and choose the command Create➔Parameter➔New Custom Parameter Set from the Animate module. A small dialog will pop up allowing you to choose a name for the Custom Pset. When you have typed one in that will make it obvious to you later on that this is one you have added, like "MyCustomProperties" click on the OK button to complete the command. Now, if you open a floating explorer view with the hotkey 8, and open up your object, you'll see a new property with a small orange C icon, labeled with the name you chose. If you click directly on the orange C icon for the PPG, it will open up. Since we haven't added any custom properties, it will now be empty.

You can add as many of these custom PPGs as you wish to one object, or distribute them among many objects. If you do have more than one custom PPG, you will have to be careful to tell XSI which one you want to add custom properties to in the next step. To choose which custom PPG you want to add to, select it in the explorer by clicking directly on the name of the custom property.

The Parameter➔Edit Custom Parameter Sets command will show all the Custom Psets on the selected object, in one PPG with a tab for each Pset.

You can delete a custom PPG by locating it in the explorer, right-clicking over it with your mouse, and choosing Delete from the context menu.

ADDING CUSTOM PROPERTIES

All by themselves, the Custom Psets are really rather useless unless they contain some custom properties. Adding custom properties to custom Psets is simple: just select the Custom Pset first in an explorer view, then choose the Create➔Parameter➔New Custom Parameter command, or use the Shift-P hotkey combination. The New Custom Parameter dialog will pop up, so you can tell XSI just what kind of a property you want.

First, choose a name for your custom property that describes what the property will control, like "hipsway" or "volume".

Next, use the Value type drop list to determine what kind of information the property will contain. Text strings are not terribly useful without heavy scripting experience, Booleans give you an ON/OFF toggle box, an integer is a whole number like 5 or 234, and a Floating Point number is a decimal value like 6.43. Use the value type that is right for your property: for instance, a Frame Counter should use whole numbers (Integers) while a scaling factor like "health" might best be a Floating point number.

After choosing a value type, determine the range of values that you want to be possible for the property to represent. For instance, if you have a property for the "age" of your character, perhaps the character is born at age 0 and can't get any older than age 100. In this case you would set the Minimum Value to 0 and the Maximum to 100. Often when creating a scaling value that you'll multiply by another value to increase or decrease some effect, you'll set the minimum to –1.0 and the maximum to +1.0.

If you toggle on the UI Range option, you can provide a different Minimum and Maximum that change how far the slider bar will go up and down to change the value. The user can then over-drive the property by directly entering a numeric value up to the actual maximum or down to the actual minimum.

If you leave the Animatable box checked, a small green animation divot will be added to your custom property so that you can set keys on it, edit it with the Animation Editor and the Dopesheet, or perform other animation tasks with it.

If you check the Read-Only box, the name and slider will be grayed out.

Click the OK button when you are done to add the Custom Property.

If your Custom Pset was open, you'll see the new property pop into the Custom Pset PPG. If it's not open, open the Custom Pset with the Edit Custom Parameter Sets menu command or by clicking on its icon in the explorer.

EDITING CUSTOM PROPERTIES

What if you have added a property and realize after the fact that you need a larger value range, or that you want to change the name? In that case you can mark the custom property and edit it by re-entering all the options that determine the what goes into the custom property.

Mark the custom property by showing the Custom Pset that it belongs to and then clicking directly on the name of the property to edit. That name will turn yellow to indicate that it is marked, and the name of the property will show in the bottom-right corner of the screen in the marked parameter list.

Now choose the Parameter→Edit Parameter Definition command from the Animate module, and re-enter all the data for the property, including the name and value type. When you hit the OK button, the old property will be replaced with the new one.

You can also remove a custom property, by marking it in the PPG, in the explorer, or in the Marking List, and then using the Parameter→Remove Custom Parameter command.

EXAMPLE: MONSTROUS PROPERTIES

Let's say that you want to add some custom properties to a vicious undersea creature that will later be used to automate its animation and responses, creating an automaton, a robot.

Step 1: Open the Monstrous scene from your courseware.

Step 2: Select the Fishie model, and switch to the Animate module.

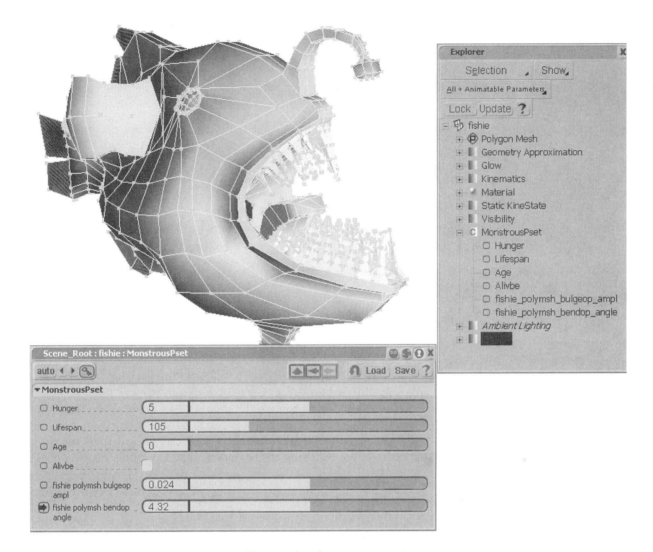

The completed custom properties

Step 3: Create a Custom Pset with the Parameter→New Custom Parameter Set command.

Name the Pset "Monstrous".

Open up the now-empty Pset with the Parameter→Edit Custom Parameter Sets command, and click to the Monstrous tab.

Step 4: Add a Property called "Hunger" with New Custom Parameter. Make it a Floating Point value between 0 and 10, with a default value of 5, so the fish will be born hungry.

Step 5: Add a Property called "Lifespan", as an integer, with a minimum of 100, a maximum of 120 and a default of 105 so that all fish born of this one will have life spans within this range.

Add a Property called "Age", as an integer, with a default of 0, and a Max of 121.

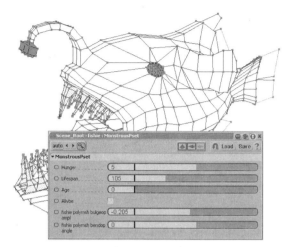

Now the Bend Angle and Bulge Amplitude sliders are in the custom Pset.

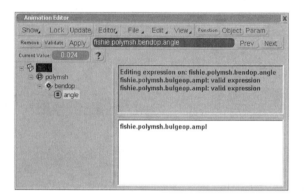

Dragging the source prop onto the target prop connects them with an expression.

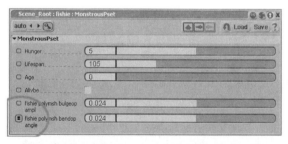

Now the Bend Op is connected to the Bulge Op.

Make another called "Alive", making it a Boolean. This way you can have a toggle showing whether the fish is alive or dead.

Step 6: Play with the sliders and the check box. Cool, but they don't do much yet.

That's it – that's all there is to making custom properties. Save your work for use in future exercises.

COLLECTING PROXY PROPERTIES

Custom Psets are also good for collecting properties that live in different PPGs all into one Custom PPG to make them easier to work with and animate. For instance, the monstrous fish has a bend deformation that makes the tail swing back and forth, and a bulge op that can make the fish pulse in a disturbing manner. The problem is that these are inconvenient to use in different PPGs. Wouldn't it be nice to collect the Bulge Amplitude and Bend Angle sliders into the same Monstrous Custom PPG so you could animate the sliders together without hopping around too much between PPGs? Well, you can, by making a copy (or Proxy) of a parameter and placing it in another Custom PPG. The way to do this is to open the target Custom Pset and lock it open. Then open the PPG that has the parameter you want to copy, click directly on the green divot, and holding down the Left Mouse Button, drag it over the Custom Pset and let go. The Property will be copied to the Custom Pset. Let's do this for the Fishie:

Step 1: Open the Monstrous scene.

Open the Custom Pset you made earlier, or make another one. Open that Custom Pset and lock it open with the keyhole icon at the top right corner of the PPG.

Step 2: Open the Bend Op. Open the Bend PPG, find the Bend Amplitude Angle slider, click and drag the green animation divot next to the word Angle over the other Monstrous PPG (the Custom Pset) and drop it into the blank gray area at the bottom of the Pset (note: drag-and-drop doesn't work in Irix or Linux). A Proxy slider will be added, named "fishie polymesh Bend Op angle". Close the Bend Op PPG, and try out the Proxy slider to see that it works just fine.

Step 3: Proxy the Bulge Op. Same process: open the Bulge, drag and drop the green Amplitude Divot onto the bottom of the Monstrous PPG.

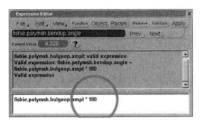

A simple expression makes the bend 180 times bigger than the bulge.

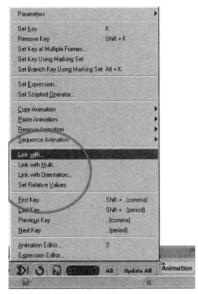

Start by using Link With, then Set Relative Values.

LINKS AND RELATIVE VALUES

You've added new custom properties, and you have even copied existing properties into the custom pages, but you have not yet connected any properties together, or found out how to use the new sliders you have made to drive other properties. It's time to see how that can work.

The simplest thing to do is to connect one property to another with a direct expression. This will simply create a formula that makes one property always equal to the other. This can be done by dragging and dropping. To make one property equal to another, just drag the master property green divot directly on top of the slave property green animation divot and the appropriate expression will be generated to hook the two properties together. In the example of the Fishie and its Monstrous Properties, it would be nice to connect the Bend Op to the Bulge Op, so that when you drag the Bulge Op amplitude proxy slider it would also change the Bend Op angle slider.

Step 1: Open the monstrous Custom Pset, and click and hold down over the Bulge Op green divot, then drag it up over the green Bend Op divot and let go. The Bend Op divot will change to a black equals sign (=) icon to indicate that an expression has been added. Now when you drag the Bulge Op slider, the Bend Op changes as well.

Step 2: The problem is that the scale of the Bulge Op slider goes from about -0.5 to +0.5, which isn't very much of a bend angle. It would be nice to change the relationship between the two sliders.

Right-click over the Expression icon on the Bend Op slider, and choose Expression Editor from the context menu. This shows the simple expression being used to link the two properties. In the white area, after fishie.polymsh.bulgeop.ampl type "* 180" without the quote marks, and click on the Apply button in the top of the Expression editor. The Expression language is covered in detail later in this material, but it's easy to see that we have just scaled up one value by 180. Now the sliders have a better relationship.

LINKS

In the previous example, a linear expression connects the two properties. The more one slider changes, the more the other changes, in a direct relationship. A more complex way of connecting one property is called a Linked Parameter. A link creates a relationship between one property and another that is not necessarily linear. In fact, Linked Parameter uses a function curve in the equation describing the relationship between the two properties, so that as one property changes, the other changes as a function of that curve. You can even edit the function curve in the Animation Editor.

The best part of working with Linked Parameters is that they can be used without editing any formulas; you just show XSI what the relationship is like in different cases, and XSI generates the curve to describe that relationship.

Each animatable parameter can be linked. If you right-click on a green animation divot, or look in the Animation menu at the bottom of the screen, you'll find three options for defining links: Link With, Link with Multi, and Link with Orientation. Link With connects any one property to any other property, Link with Multi creates a one-to-many link, and Link with Orientation connects any one property to the orientation (rotation) of any other object. Link With is the most flexible, but you can use Link With Orientation to quickly link the behavior of character deformers to IK skeleton bone orientations.

Remember: links create a relationship between a very specific property on one object and a very specific property (or properties) on the same or another object. You have to be careful to know what property is currently marked when using the Link With command from the bottom Animation Menu. It's probably a good idea to use the linking commands from the green animation divot right on one property, so you are sure that you are applying the link exactly the way you want. When you're a pro you can use the links with the Marked Parameter Set and the bottom Animation Menu.

To see the power of links, try the following exercise.

LINKED SPRING: AT A GLANCE

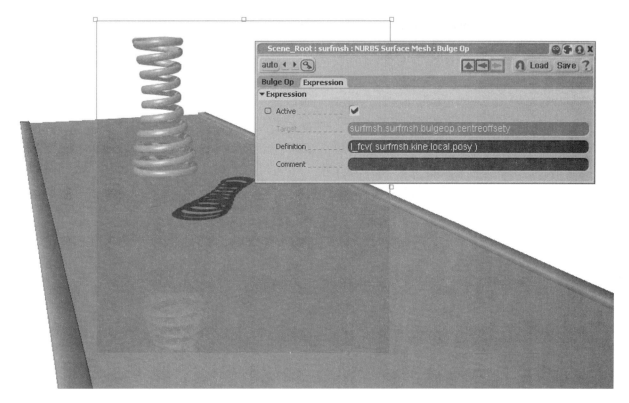

TOPICS COVERED

In this tutorial you'll see how to link one property or parameter to another property, so that when you change the master property, the linked properties also change, automatically.

You'll learn how to:

- Create a link between properties
- Set different relative values to define the relationship between the properties
- Animate one, and see the result on the other.

MATERIALS REQUIRED

You will need the linked_spring scene from the courseware that accompanies this book, available at http://www.mesmer.com/books/xsicharacter.html.

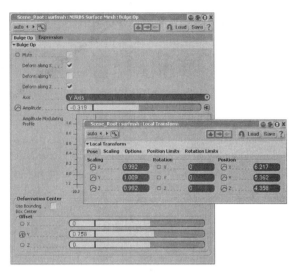

Open both PPGs, using the lock icon to keep the first one open.

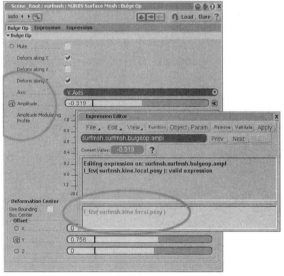

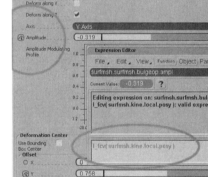

Bulge Amplitude is now linked to local position in Y.

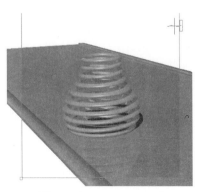

The spring, compressed

TUTORIAL: LINKED SPRING

The Linked Spring scene contains a coil spring that you'll need to animate bouncing around on the flat roadway. However, using links, you'll set up the spring so that the Bulge deformation that is on the spring activates automatically, and changes depending on where the spring is in space. When the spring gets close to the ground, the bulge will expand, as if the spring is compressing and growing wider as it hits the ground.

STEP 1: EXAMINE THE SCENE

Open the linked_spring scene, and find the Bulge Op on the spring. Open the Bulge PPG, and lock it open.

STEP 2: LINK THE BULGE AMPLITUDE AND THE LOCAL TRANS Y

You want the bulge to operate so that the spring is fat when it hits the ground, and skinny in the air, with a few vibrations between fat and skinny as it moves up and down.

First, set up the link. Right-click over the green divot next to Amplitude in the Bulge Op and choose Link With. In the explorer that pops up, find the spring and click directly on the name of the Kinematic Local Transform Position in Y. This tells XSI to connect the Bulge Amplitude to the Local Position in Y of the spring. You'll see the Green animation divot replaced with a black and grey L icon, to show that the property is now linked. At the top of the Bulge Op PPG, you'll see two more tabs, for expressions. If you click on the second one you'll see that an expression has been added to connect the target (the Bulge Op Amplitude) with the spring.kine.local.posy using an Fcurve (function curve) to vary the relationship. The current value of that Fcurve is also shown there.

STEP 3: SET SOME VALUES

You've created the relationship between the Bulge Amplitude and the PosY, but you haven't told XSI what the Amplitude should do when the PosY changes. To do that, select the spring and place it up in the air a ways. Drag the Amplitude slider to -0.5 so that the spring is squished inwards.

Now you've changed both sides of the equation: the posY and the Amplitude. Save this setting by right-clicking on the Link icon in the Bulge PPG and choosing Set Relative Values to show XSI what the Bulge Amplitude should be when the Spring is up in the air like this.

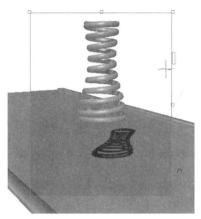

When the spring is in the air you want it skinny.

STEP 4: SET ANOTHER VALUE

Now move the spring to be on the ground, and set the amplitude of the bulge to be 0.6, so it's fattened out. Set another Relative Value to show XSI that when the spring is on the ground, you want the bulge fattened out. You can set more relative values if you want; just move the spring, change the amplitude, and set relative values. Defining a relationship in this way is like training a dog: you show the dog what to do and when to do it, and the dog links the behavior you want to your voice command to do it. What XSI really does is create an animation curve that describes the value of the target property as a function of the linking property. When you use the Set Relative Values command, you're setting new points on that curve.

STEP 5: TRY IT OUT

Now, select the spring, and translate it up and down. See that the spring bulges in and out automatically as it moves in space.

Links are a simple but powerful way to connect one property to another, in a way that allows for more flexibility and differing results than a simple linear relationship. As you'll see in the next section, links are a good way to save effort as well, by linking a bunch of properties to the same slider so you can control a lot of different objects all at once.

LINKING IK TO CUSTOM SLIDERS

You now know that you can use links to connect one property to another. This also applies to custom properties. You can link existing regular properties to the custom sliders that you create in Custom Psets. For instance, you might create a slider called 'lights' and then link the intensity and falloff of a whole bunch of lights in a theater scene to that one slider so you can animate them all at once more easily, just like using a traditional lighting board. The workflow for linking multiple objects is a little bit harder: you must use the marking list and the selection list in conjunction with the Linking commands.

One great use for this is the technique of linking bone rotations to a slider, so that complex FK poses can all be connected to one slider. In the following exercise, you'll use marking and Link With to link a bunch of bones all at once, in a series of poses.

MONKEYS PAW: AT A GLANCE

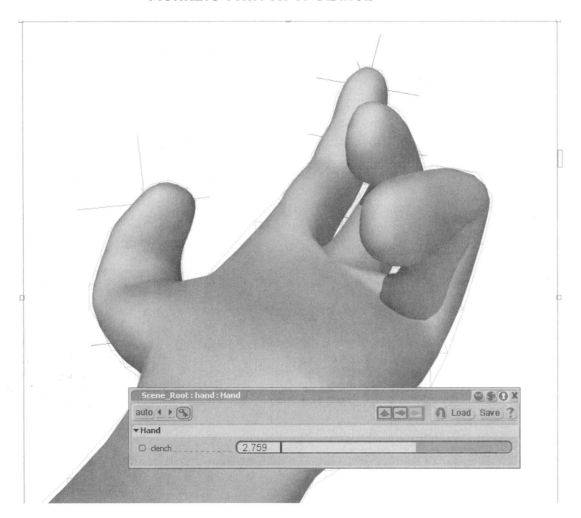

TOPICS COVERED

In this tutorial, you will link the joint rotations of all the fingers in the monkey's paw to one custom slider, then you will set the monkeys paw in four different poses and set the relative values to connect those poses to different points on the slider. In this way, the slider will control the poses of the hand.

You'll learn how to:

- Mark several objects and properties to work on them all at once
- Connect many objects to one with a Linked Parameter
- Set multiple relative values at once
- Simplify IK animation with custom sliders

MATERIALS REQUIRED

This exercise uses the Links_MonkeysPaw scene from the courseware.

TUTORIAL: THE MONKEY'S PAW

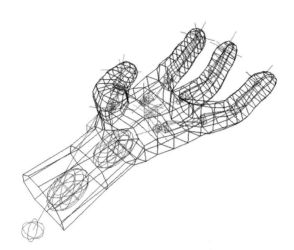

The paw is already enveloped. Find the IK effectors and test them.

In this tutorial you will explore a simpler way of accomplishing hand animation, by driving the IK effector which in turn drives the rotation of a number of joints, all with a single custom slider.

Many times, people spend way too much time building an elaborately articulated finger system, driven by IK, for a character that will never do much at all with his hands. Animating with a whole bunch of IK in the hands is quite difficult and time consuming, so we have an opportunity here to build a better system.

In this system, one slider will control all the finger effector locations in the hand. There will be four poses possible for the hand – starting with all the fingers stretched wide out, then to a slack hand, then to just the index finger pointing out, and finally to a closed fist. You'll be able to animate smoothly between all these poses with a single slider.

STEP 1: EXAMINE THE SCENE

Open the Links_MonkeysPaw file and look at what you have there. The hand is already enveloped to the Finger IK. The first bones of the hand IK have joint rotations set to keep them from changing, so all the action will happen in the second and third joints. The Schematic is open so you can easily find and select the effectors.

STEP 2: ADD A CUSTOM SLIDER

You need a Custom Pset and a Custom Slider. Add a Custom Pset by selecting the hand and using the Property→New Custom Parameter Set command from the Animate Menu.

Name the hand Pset "MonkeysPaw".

Open the MonkeysPaw Pset, and add a slider called "Clench" to it with the New Custom Parameter command. Make the Value type Floating Point, with a minimum value of 1 and a maximum value of 4.

Lock the Pset open so it won't go away unexpectedly.

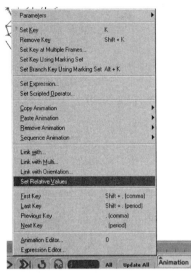

The Relative Value command is in the Animation Menu.

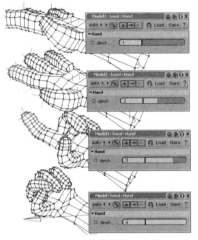

The hand and slider in the next position

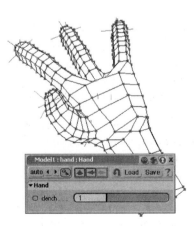

The hand and slider in the first position

STEP 3: LINK THE BONES TO THE SLIDER

You want to link each of the finger bone rotations in the hand to the same slider. Although you're going to link all the bone rotations, you'll be setting the bone rotations by manually translating the effectors. The effectors make it easier to pose the fingers, but the animation will be more sly if the bone rotations are linked. The link commands will apply to whatever elements are selected, and only on the marked properties of those selected elements. So, select all the finger bones, either with careful regular selection or with the IK chain filter in the MCP, and mark all the finger bone rotations, by clicking to activate the rotation cells in the MCP. The Marked Property feedback line will say "kine.local.ori". Immediately lock the marking list with the little keyhole icon. Now, with all the bone rotations marked, choose the Animation→Link With command from the timeline Animation Menu, and choose the new "Clench" custom property slider that you just added, so that the bone rotations are now linked to the slider.

STEP 4: SET THE RELATIVE VALUES

Now you need to train XSI. You'll first set the slider in the first position, at 1, and position the effectors to stretch the fingers out fully as if the hand is palming a basketball. When you have all the effectors in the pose you like for the first slider position, select all the finger bones again, verify that the orientations are still marked, and choose Set relative Values from the Animation Menu. When you use a command from the Animation Menu, it will be applied to the selected items and the marked properties only. That's why it is important to select all the bones and mark the rotations each time before you choose the Set Relative Values command.

STEP 5: SET THE NEXT POSE... AND THE NEXT... AND THE NEXT

Now you have one pose of the fingers stored on the slider. We need to add three more. First, change the slider to the second position, 2, and pose the effectors in a slack hand shape, as if the hand was hanging loose, fingers slightly bent. Select all the bones, mark the rotations, and set a relative value. Now you have two relative values. Slide the clench slider between 1 and 2, and you should see the hand change poses. Do it again: set the slider to 3, and curl all the fingers except for the index finger, as if the paw is pointing at something. Select all the bones, mark all the rotations, and set a relative value. In the fourth slider position, save a relative value with the hand clenched into a fist.

STEP 6: TEST AND ADJUST

Now try out the slider, seeing that the complex IK poses of each finger are all linked together to the one slider. You can adjust the fingers now, adding new poses in between the major ones, or refining existing poses, by selecting the effector you want to change, moving the clench slider, posing the effector and setting a relative value on the bone rotations.

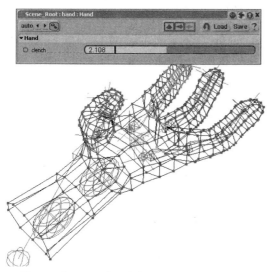

This is the completed Custom Property Set.

In this case, setting one slider to drive a whole bunch of IK bone rotations is a huge time-saver, but you can use this technique to link any combination of properties to a custom slider, or to any existing slider. The possibilities are endless.

LINKING MUSCLES TO BONES

Actual human bodies are shaped by stretching a skin (an envelope) over bones, just like IK in XSI, but in humans there are also muscles and other softer tissues underneath the skin, attached to the bones, that influence the shape of the skin stretched over them. We can create these sorts of soft tissues and muscles in XSI as well, by adding geometry objects to the IK hierarchy. Then, when a character model is enveloped to the IK hierarchy, the geometry objects are considered as deformers just like the IK bones are.

That's great, but it would be even better if the muscles and soft tissues could slide on the bone, and change shape to flex and relax as the bones they are attached to rotate.

Well, you can build these sorts of systems, and create dynamic actions for the muscles simply, using the Link with Orientations command. The Link with Orientation command is a special type of link that creates a relative value equation automatically, and then gives you a slider for an Interpolator to control the strength of the relationship.

The character Ethelred pictured here has such a collection of objects parented into the IK hierarchy, as children of the bones. For instance, the balls above the character's hips will stabilize the skin blending over the area from the base of the spine to the tops of the thighs, just like your own buttock muscles do.

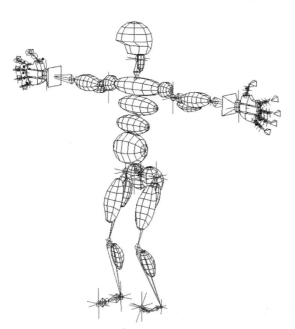

Ethelred has muscles linked to bone rotations.

The muscle-shaped objects on his upper arms act like musculature on top of the IK bone. When the muscle gets shorter, it bunches up the skin around it. When the muscle slides up the bone, it drags the skin around it relative to the bone.

 Note: In a perfect world we would be able to determine how much the skin slides over the muscle compared to how much the skin stays bound directly to the muscle, but in the regular IK enveloping system that's not possible.

It is theoretically possible to use a cloth simulation to get this sort of look, but the cloth has no shape memory, so the skin doesn't tend to regain its original shape. You can also experiment with using ShrinkWrap to deform a skin over musculature, which works well on simple examples, but is not practical on complete characters.

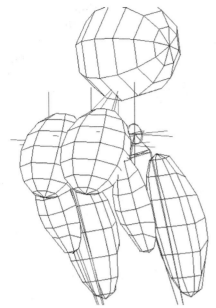

Ethelred's back end, showing his musculature

Here in this book I am using small polygon spheres that have been sculpted to resemble muscles, but the actual shape of the object is not important. Only the location and direction to the object center is considered by the Envelope Operator.

The muscles are then made children of the bone segment they will slide on, and a linked property is used to associate different poses of the bone with different orientations of the IK joint.

In the case of a biceps, for instance, when the elbow joint is outstretched, the muscle is thinner, and closer to the elbow. When the elbow joint is rotated to the maximum angle, then the biceps is flexed, thicker, and translated higher, toward the shoulder.

In the following quick exercise you'll see how to do this.

Step 1: Draw a two-bone IK chain in the form of an arm. Name the first bone "upperarm" and the second bone "forearm" so you can find which one you want, later.

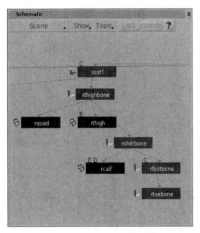

The muscle is a child of the IK bone.

Step 2: Get a primitive sphere, and push and pull points to make it into a muscle shape. This is purely cosmetic, and will not affect how the muscle works. Make it about the right size to fit as a biceps on the arm bone, then freeze the operator stack and freeze all the transformations. Make sure the center is within the biceps with the Transform→Move Center to Vertices command.

Step 3: Attach muscle to bone. Move the muscle to the upperarm bone, and orient it correctly. A quick way to do this is to constrain the position of the muscle to the bone, adjust the position with the Comp button in the MCP on, then relax the constraint once the muscle is in the right place. You can orient it by constraining the orientation, turning on Compensate, rotating the muscle, turning off Compensate and relaxing that constraint as well. If you have a lot of these muscles to place, this can be a time-saver. You can also simply place the muscle in the right spot manually for this exercise.

Step 4: Make the muscle a child of the upper arm bone. Now the muscle will move as the bone rotates.

Step 5: Link the Scale of the muscle to the Orientation of the forearm bone.

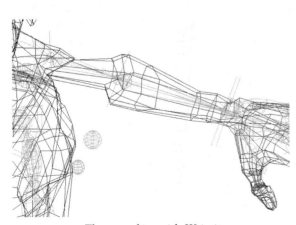

The arm skin, with IK in it

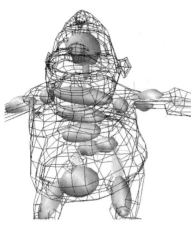

The actual shape doesn't make any difference at all.

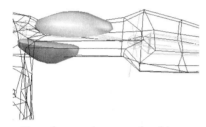

Now the arm has muscle objects.

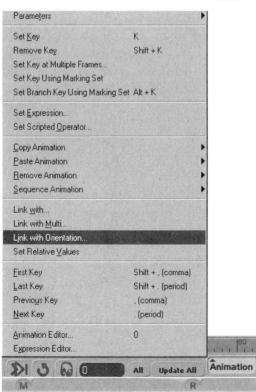

Link with Orientation is a special link.

Using the IK effector, bend the arm to the maximum rotation that the elbow will ever have. Select the muscle, and display the Local Transform PPG. Right-click over the animation divot for the axis that is perpendicular to the bone, in this case local Y, and choose the command Link with Orientation. Now choose which bone to link it with, the forearm, from the explorer that pops up. Two new tabs have been added to the Local Translation PPG: an expression and an interpolator. The expression changes the scale in Y by a factor based on the orientation of the forearm bone you chose. If the muscle scales too much, reduce the Interpolation value. If you want the muscle to change more, increase the Interpolator. If the Muscle is changing opposite to the way it should, right-click over the Link icon in the PPG, and this time have the arm stretched out before linking the muscle scale in Y to the orientation.

Step 6: Link the local translation of the muscle to the orientation of the bone

This time, use the Local Transform Scale property (X is the correct local direction for me, but yours might differ depending on how you modeled the muscle). Use the Link With Orientation command to connect the muscle to the upperarm bone. Again a new Expression and Interpolation tab are added to the Local Transform PPG. Adjust the Interpolator.

Step 9: Test the muscle. Select the arm effector and translate it, bending the arm and straightening it out. You should observe the muscle changing size and location as the arm flexes! In this way you can use linked parameters to connect the effects of changing musculature to the orientation of the joints in a character.

Step 10: What if you could do the same thing with the Link With command? You would just have to set the Relative Values yourself. Start over with a fresh scene, or remove the Link from the muscle elements with the Remove All Animation command in the muscle PPG, in the Animation Divot for the axis that is linked. First, Link With both Scale and Translation on the Muscle to the Forearm Rotation in Z. With the arm straight out, set the current scale and rotation relative values, by marking the Scale cells and choosing the Set Relative Values command from the Animation menu, then marking the Translation cells and executing the same command. (You could get tricky and mark both scale and translation, lock the marked list, and execute the Set Relative Values command only once.)

Now, bend the arm 90 degrees, and scale the muscle to bulge out. Set a Relative value in this pose.

Translate the muscle up in the local axis along the upper arm towards the shoulder. Set a relative value on the translation, linking it to this pose of the arm as well.

Test and adjust. This method gives you more control, but is not as automated.

Step 11: Extra credit: Since you can link anything with orientation, you can link the amplitude of a Push operator to the orientation of a bone. And since you can modulate the intensity of a push operator with a weight map, you can have the push apply itself unevenly on a model. And since you can paint a weight map in any way you choose, you could effectively paint a deformation onto an object, then link that deformation with a given pose of an IK element. For example, if your character has a smooth arm, and when it flexes you want to see veins pop and sinew stretch, you could make a cluster for the area, fire up the Paint Push Tool, and carefully paint in the new detail. Then, link the Push Op Amplitude slider to the bent orientation of the elbow joint. When the elbow bent, the new painted in detail would emerge from the model! You can go at least one step further than this, by painting a Vertex Color map to cover the area (or the whole character) then hooking up a Vertex_rgba node to the displacement in the Render Tree, adding additional Displacement and Subdivision in the Displacement Tab of the Geometry Approximation PPG, adding an Intensity Node between the Vertex_Color Displacement Map and the Material node, and then linking up the intensity slider to the orientation of an IK bone (or anything else…). Since a Vertex Color map – not a weight map – is required, the technique works only on polygon meshes. This gets you potentially infinite surface detail, controlled by any number of displacement maps on any number of clusters, and all the detail would be created at render time so you could animate with a lighter model. Try it out and send me a picture of the results…

POSE-BASED SHAPE ANIMATION

When IK elements in an envelope change the shape of a skin, the vertices on the skin actually just translate and rotate to follow the bones. In many cases, skin doesn't actually do that. For instance, when you lift your arm above your head, the skin between your shoulder and your chest doesn't rotate at all – it just slides up and stretches more tightly over your ribs and fatty tissues. The shape of your pectoral muscle actually changes shape in a way that can't be determined just from the rotation of the shoulder. The only way to really get the proper look for how the skin changes when the shoulder rotates is to have several different shapes for different poses of the shoulder, sculpted into the right artistically pleasing form for the skin and the musculature to be in for that shoulder pose.

This method gives the sculptor immense control over how the skin on the envelope behaves.

In XSI this concept of changing the shape of the envelope based on different IK orientations is called a pose-based deformation, and is set up with the Shape→Link With Deform command in the Animation Module. Pose-based deformations are really just cluster shapes, dropped into the Mixer (in a shape track) with a custom slider to control the relative strength of each shape.

Creating the pose-based deformation is easier than explaining it, so try the following tutorial.

THE STRETCH: AT A GLANCE

TOPICS COVERED

Skin around a shoulder moves in a very particular way, due to the changes in the shape of the muscles and the stretching of the skin when the shoulder moves. We'll use a Linked Shape deformation to automatically connect several shapes with the orientation of the shoulder. This method can also be a good way to fix enveloping problems.

You'll learn how to:

- Use cluster-based shape animation
- Set up an auto shape deform
- Link shapes to IK poses

MATERIALS REQUIRED

This tutorial uses the ShoulderShapes scene from the courseware.

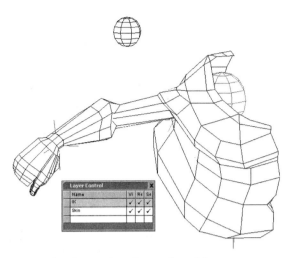

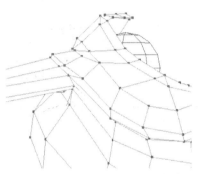

The skin is already enveloped for you.

Make a cluster for each linked deformation.

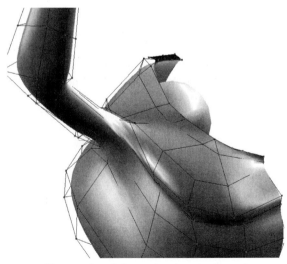

The regular deformation just isn't good.

TUTORIAL: THE STRETCH

When your character flails his or her arms around, you'll want the skin to look as if it's sliding over a series of muscles that are stretching out and bunching up as the arm moves. The best way to do this is with shape animation linked to an IK pose.

STEP 1: LOOK AT THE SHOULDER

For simplicity, only the shoulder, the arm, and a bit of the belly are in the scene. A simple two-bone chain is bound and weighted to the skin. You can move the arm with the effector near the wrist.

STEP 2: MAKE A CLUSTER

Although this will work on the whole model, your scene will be lighter and play faster if you put the deformation on a cluster. So, tag all the points in the shoulder area, and the skin of the breast, and a row of points on the chest and back, and make a cluster with the Cluster button in the MCP. Tap the Enter key to call up the Cluster PPG, and name it "Shoulder".

STEP 3: LINK THE CLUSTER TO THE UPPER ARM BONE

The shoulder skin moves when the upper arm bone rotates, so we'll want to link the cluster to the upper arm bone. The pose that the arm is in will become one of the shapes XSI uses when you link it, so move the effector on the IK to place the arm back in the starting (down) position. Make sure the Shoulder cluster on the skin is selected (use the Cluster explorer in the MCP) and choose the command Shape→Link Deform with Orientation, then pick on the upper arm IK bone and right-click to complete the command. You have now established a relationship between the quaternion orientation of the upper arm and the shape of the cluster.

STEP 4: SET A NEW POSE

Now, lift the effector to place the arm up, as if the creature were reaching up to get something off a high shelf. See how the shoulder is creased on top? That's bad; it should bulge as the muscle under it contracts, instead of rotating under the shoulder. Model the skin around the shoulder into a better shape, using the M or T hotkeys to move and tag/transform points. Also pull the skin of the breast area up to the shoulder a bit, and make it thinner, as if it was stretched. Make any other changes you want, to imitate what the model should look like with the arm up. Now select the cluster again (or even a single point in the cluster) and choose the command Shape→Save Deform Key. This creates a new shape for the cluster, adds it to the shape Mixer, and hooks up another slider to control the amount of deformation, then finally links that shape Mixer to the quaternion orientation of the upper bone.

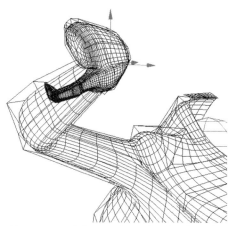

This is a much better shape for the shoulder.

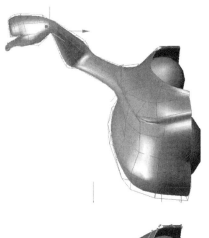

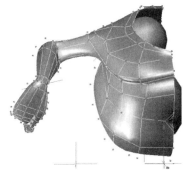

The arm looks good in all kinds of different poses.

STEP 5: TRY AND MODIFY

Now when you use the effector to move the arm, the skin should also change shape.

You can adjust how the different cluster shapes combine by changing each one's falloff. To see that in action, open the Falloff PPG by selecting the skin and looking in the explorer for PolyMesh→Clusters→Deform Falloffs. If you don't seem to be getting the effect you modeled in, increase the falloff and move the arm again. Often, high values near 7 or 8 work best.

STEP 6: DO OVER

See how that worked? Now you'll want to do it again, this time with three or four poses for different states of the shoulder. You can remove the prior effect by locating the Cluster Shape Combiner operator on the skin, clicking on it in the explorer, and using the Delete key on the keyboard. Now set different shapes for the arm: a pair for front to back, then a pair for up and down.

Since you can have as many clusters on a model as you want, you can use this technique to localize subtle changes in the shape of the skin for each muscle group. Each area of the skin can therefore be given different shapes to correspond to changes in the pose of the IK. This technique is a good way to correct weighting problems, to simulate the changes in the shape of muscles of sliding skin over muscles as limbs stretch out.

CONCLUSION

In this chapter you learned a lot about connecting cause and effect in XSI. You learned how to make your own custom PPGs and your own custom parameters. You discovered that properties from different PPGs can all be collected in one easy to find Pset, using Proxy Parameters. You saw that properties can be tied together with drag and drop. You explored linked parameters, and how they create a non-linear relationship between properties. You learned how one slider can drive the behavior of many IK chains, simplifying hand animation. Finally, you used pose-based deforms, to link different shapes in a cluster combiner operator with different positions on an IK bone.

QUIZ

1. **HOW MANY CUSTOM PPGS (PSETS) CAN AN OBJECT HAVE?**
   a. Two
   b. Four
   c. As many as you want

2. **WHEN MAKING A CUSTOM PROPERTY, WHICH IS AN INTEGER?**
   a. 4.2
   b. 17
   c. -4

3. **DRAGGING ONE PROPERTY ON TOP OF ANOTHER CONNECTS THE TWO WITH:**
   a. An interpolator
   b. An expression
   c. A cluster combiner

4. **HOW MANY RELATIVE VALUES CAN A LINK CURVE HAVE?**
   a. Two
   b. Four
   c. As many as you want

5. **LINK WITH ORIENTATION LINKS A PROPERTY TO:**
   a. Muscle Pose
   b. The quaternion orientation of an object
   c. Trans Y

6. **LINK WITH LINKS ANY PROPERTY TO:**
   a. Bone orientation
   b. Any other property
   c. Another link

7. **CAN YOU LINK A BULGE DEFORMATION AMPLITUDE TO THE SAME OBJECT S TRANS Y?**
   a. Yup
   b. Nope
   c. I Dunno

8. **CAN YOU USE LINK TO MODIFY THE SCALE OF A MUSCLE ENVELOPE DEFORMER?**
   a. Yup
   b. Nope
   c. I Dunno

9. **WHAT CAN YOU NOT LINK TO AN IK ORIENTATION?**
   a. Weight map amplitude
   b. The Cluster Shape Combiner
   c. Render Frame Number

10. **POSE BASED DEFORMS WORK BEST FOR:**
    a. Fixing weight problems
    b. Sliding skin, bulging muscles
    c. Both

8   HUMAN CHARACTER MODELING

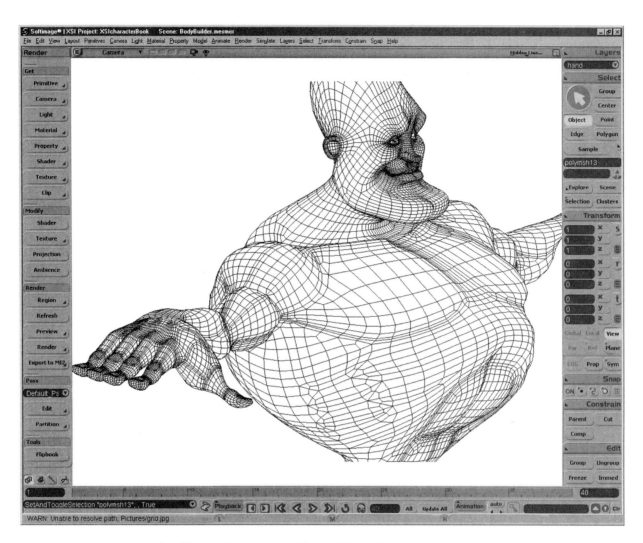

IN THIS CHAPTER YOU WILL LEARN ABOUT:

- How to think about organic modeling
- Polygon modeling techniques
- Subdivision Surface techniques
- How to use the Rotoscope view
- About good modeling poses
- How to maintain proportions
- How to build arms, legs, hands and feet
- How to build human torsos and heads
- Finished assembly and model cleanup

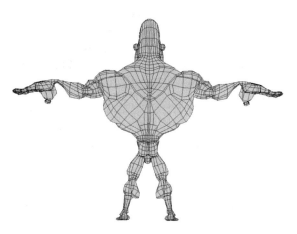

A good pose makes the eventual skin bending look better.

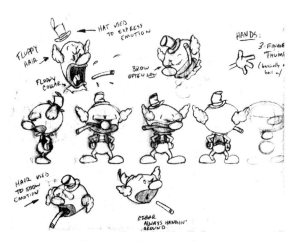

Francis's character sheet

INTRODUCTION

Modeling is really the process of building, from scratch, new shapes that help carry your ideas to the audience. What your models look like is a big part of how they will communicate when they are on screen. As a result, modeling is an artistic pursuit, and in no case is this truer than when modeling characters. The final form of the character – whether human, animal, or other – has a lot of impacts. Will the form have appeal? Will audiences like looking at it, be scared by it, or simply not be engaged at all by it? In addition, there are technical considerations. Will your character be easy or difficult to rig up and weight? When weighted, will the character be able to move in a convincing manner?

Will the character be able to touch his toes, for instance, or reach behind his head?

The exploration of all these questions is a matter of art. Creating a good character is closer to sculpting than drafting, and a general understanding of musculature, form, contour, and pose will help.

Fortunately, XSI has some fine tools to make your modeling tasks more fun, more rewarding creatively, and a lot easier.

In the past, complex characters were most often quilted together from a patchwork of NURBS elements. This process was counterintuitive at best, frustrating and unproductive at worst. In XSI it is probably a good idea to skip NURBS entirely for models as complex as characters, and turn instead to modeling with Subdivision Surfaces.

Every polygon object is really a subdivision surface in XSI. With a Poly object selected, you can interactively refine the surface with the plus (+) key on your numeric keypad, and reduce the detail with the minus (-) key. You never have to worry about the creation of the final surface, because that's done later, by increasing the subdivision level to become perfectly smooth. Your job is simply to influence the final result.

Since you are working on a polygonal cage, you never have to worry about keeping a rectangular topology. You can create areas of high detail and low detail, and add and remove vertices and edges at will.

BUILDING A GOOD POSE FOR WEIGHTING

The pose you choose to build your character in has a great impact on how easy or difficult the envelope weighting will be, and also on how nicely the skin flexes and stretches when animated.

Francis is drawn flat front and back to ease modeling.

Often the ease of the modeler works against the final quality of the deformation when the character is animated. For instance, it's easier to model a character in a stretched out pose where the arms and legs are all perfectly flat within one plane, but such a pose is unnatural and not lifelike in animation.

The best pose to end up in (at the end of your modeling process) is one where the character is standing loosely, with each major joint bent to an intermediate position, midway between the most rotation and the least rotation that the joint will ever have.

A model created in this loose middle pose will have a more natural aspect when animated, and less extreme weighting problems since the perfect pose is halfway between the two extreme poses.

If your reference material is drawn in a more orthographic manner, build the character using the reference material, then at the end of the process throw out the reference material and sculpt the model to the loose pose, where it will look more natural and lifelike.

USING REFERENCE MATERIAL WITH ROTOSCOPE

Many beginners sit down in front of the computer, get a primitive cube, and wait for some sort of inspiration to strike. Failing that, the beginner just starts noodling around with the model, hoping something good will just happen by itself. This is the Million Monkeys method, which states that if you put a million monkeys in front of a million typewriters, eventually one of them will crank out an original work of staggering genius. This method is a little too hit-or-miss for my tastes. Another way to approach the task is to actually plan what you want, research the forms it could take, and then produce or obtain reference material to guide your efforts.

This can be photographic reference material, illustrations, or material from books. Anything you can get your hands on by scanning or downloading can become reference material.

For human reference, you should purchase a set of books:

Burne Hogarth's "Dynamic Anatomy" and "Dynamic Figure Drawing"

Gary Faigin's "The Artist's Complete Guide to Facial Expression"

Eadweard Muybridge's classic "Complete Human and Animal Locomotion"

If your reference material is drawn with perspective and foreshortening it is much harder to intuit accurate proportions, so it is often a good idea to draw your own reference material. When working on a commercial project, you should definitely have construction illustrations made to ease your modeling tasks. The construction drawings should all be made to the same scale. There should be front and side views at a minimum.

For instance, Francis the Clown started out with a clown bio, a name, and a description of his personality. Then an illustrator (thanks, Theron Benson) drew different versions of Francis, until we liked the results.

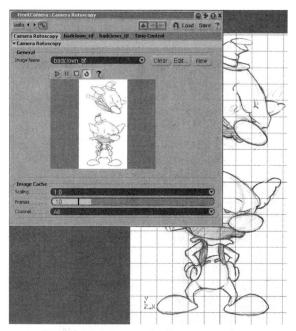

Load an image into the Rotoscope plane.

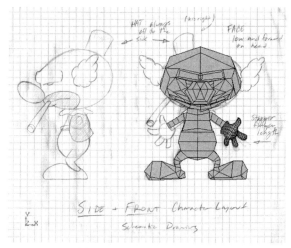

Modeling using the Rotoscope view

Next, Theron drew versions of Francis in orthographic poses, to make modeling easier.

Finally, I scanned Francis's construction drawings. The scans should be sized to fit well on-screen, no bigger than 700*400 at 72 DPI. The backgrounds of the scans should be color corrected to a subtle gray color, so that wire frames in either white or black will be visible against the scan. The scan should be saved as a JPEG file, and placed in the Pictures folder in your XSI project.

Now you can use Rotoscope view mode to see your reference material while you model. In the Display drop menu from the top-right corner of your Front view choose the Rotoscope Options command to see the Rotoscope dialog. If you already have imported your reference as clips, you can choose the image you want from the Clip drop menu. If you have not yet brought the clip into your scene, use the New➔New From File button in the Rotoscope Options PPG to browse your filesystem and choose the reference material you want in the Front view.

If you need to crop the image, flip it, or adjust the background to be gray, you can Alt-right-click over the image and use the FX tab of the Clip Properties PPG to make the edits you need. These changes are dynamic and non-destructive, which means they won't affect your image on disk.

When done, close the Rotoscope Options PPG, and back in the Display drop menu, toggle on Rotoscope mode.

Now, no matter what view mode you are using (wireframe, hidden line, shaded, etc.) your reference image will be pasted behind your scene.

Repeat the process in the Right view to bring in the side reference material.

KEEPING PROPORTIONS WITH ROTOSCOPE

If you are using two images, one for the Front and one for the Right, it is extremely important to understand the relationship between the scale of the 3D model and the images, and also the relationship between the scale of one image and the other image.

For instance, if you are modeling a head, you need the side reference image to be the same size relative to your scene that the front image is.

When you zoom in with the Z hotkey in the Roto mode, you are changing that relationship, which would be bad. So, you need to set the relationship correctly the first time, then lock the Zoom to the Rotoscope image size on screen, so that you can zoom around while modeling without screwing it up.

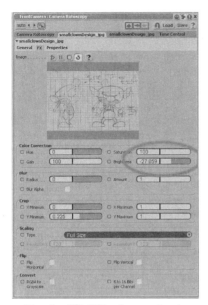

Use the ClipFX tab to make the image easier to see over.

To make your life easier, there should be an element in each reference image that is the same size, which you can use to match the scale of the front to the right with. If you look at the Francis images you'll see a square around each one. That square is the same size relative to Francis in each.

If you view both images (one behind the Front view, the other behind the Right view) you can then get a primitive cube, and use the Z hot key carefully to match the cube in the 3D view to the exact scale of the square in the images. When the cube matches the square in all views, the scale of each view is matched perfectly between both views. Now, quickly, before it gets screwed up, lock the scale with the Zoom icon in the top of each of the Rotoscope views (it looks like a small magnifying glass).

Now you can model while looking at the reference material, pulling and pushing points to fit the illustration.

If your illustrations are really good, you can look forward to quickly creating an accurate 3D model. However, it is sadly common that the 3D model lacks some of the appeal and life of the 2D illustration when created this way. At a certain point near the end of the process, you'll want to turn off the Rotoscope reference and add back in the life and sparkle to the character by looking only at the 3D version while modeling.

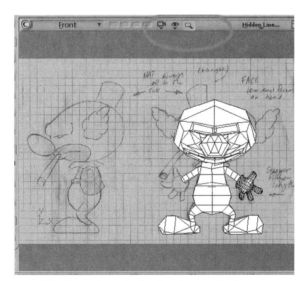

The Zoom icon locks the view to the image.

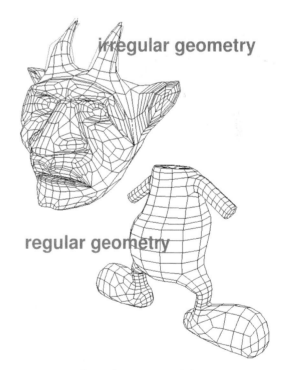

Regular polygons smooth better.

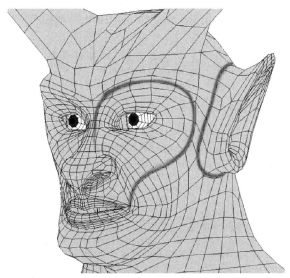

Edge loops are rings of edges.

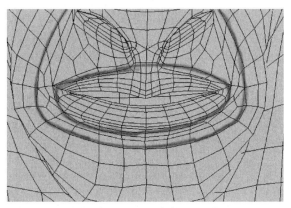

Muscles surround the mouth.

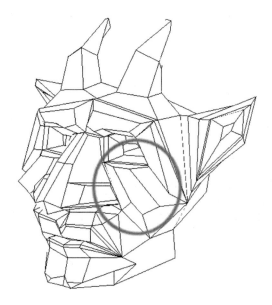

Contours are sharp changes in elevation.

MODELING TECHNIQUE

When modeling with Subdivision Surfaces (SubDs), you are freed up to work in a way that more closely imitates how a physical sculptor might work. You can start with a simple primitive form, and gradually refine it, bit by bit, until you become satisfied with the results.

It is helpful to imagine that you are not actually working to create a surface, right at the start, but rather to follow this progression of steps:

First, block in the form, paying attention to proportions, with large volumes of space

Second, analyze the results you want. Find contours, and add them to the form.

Third, add in articulation detail where parts need to flex most (joints, etc)

Fourth, refine the surface, adding in fine details, creating areas of higher density.

Fifth, remove unwanted details, and refine the contours.

Last, examine the model and clean up bad polygons, open edges, etc.

The process of sculpting is one of progressive refinement, starting with the general and moving to the particular. You will be done only when you decide that you are done, when you decide to move on to another task.

Remember that you can always decide to come back to the model later, or even throw it out and start over again. It's always better the second time.

KEEP IT SIMPLE

"Keep it simple" is good advice in many situations, but it has never been truer than in SubD modeling. Remember that the finished surface will have much more detail added automatically. Your job is just to define the form and the contours.

In polygon modeling, simplicity means keeping the polygon count low, and keeping the polygons regular. Large areas with very few polygons will smooth out very nicely. Never add an edge or a polygon if you don't have a reason, and conversely, remove any detail you are not sure you need.

In general, it's a good idea to use four-sided polygons whenever possible. Feel free to also use triangles freely, but you should avoid using polygons with more than four sides, although XSI will still create a proper Subdivision Surface. Polygons with more than four sides tend to create strange tessellation patterns in the SubD, generating odd contours you didn't intend.

Also, if you try to use four-sided polygons it will be easier to define closed loops of edges that connect back together, which makes nice musculature.

When more than four four-sided polygons come together at one time, you'll end up with a vertex with more than four edges radiating out from it. This type of vertex is often called a pole. Poles are good places to start and end contours (sometimes called edge loops in other programs) if the contour doesn't form a complete closed loop. Keep the number of poles down, and place them where skin would normally bunch up, like the corners of the eyes or the mouth. Avoid their use in large flat areas where tessellation artifacts might show up.

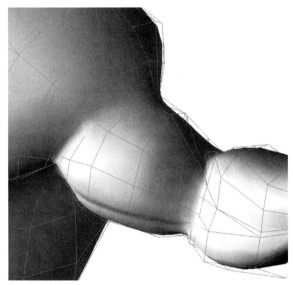

This muscle has no contours.

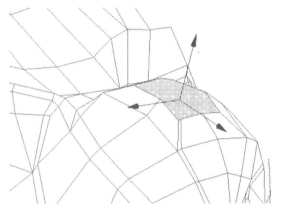

The Extrusion method of building elevation

The Split method of building elevation

EDGE LOOPS, CONTOURS, AND POLES

The outside edges that separate one mass from another are called contours. You can make the contours harder either by adjusting the Edge/Vertex Crease value in Modify→Component or, better yet, by simply adding another similar contour close to the original. When the final subdivision is created, it will interpret contours that are close together as more dramatic changes of direction in the surface with a harder edge, and contours that are far apart as soft, uniform smooth shapes.

These contours show the direction and shape of the muscles underneath the skin. Sometimes they form closed shapes called edge loops that circumnavigate muscles. Sometimes they form contours that start at a pole where the muscle is anchored, and progress along the surface to end at another pole, creating a crease in the surface, like a wrinkle.

In the face, the important muscles to understand are the muscles of the brow, around the eyes, around the mouth, and anchoring the mouth to the checks and jaws.

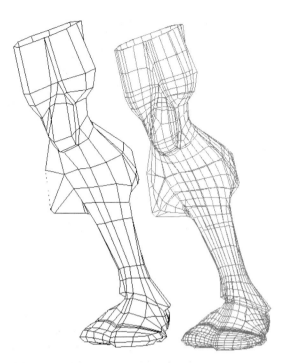

This knee has enough detail to bend well.

MODELING FOR EXPRESSIONS AND LIP SYNC

The topology of the polygon mesh that you build will have an effect on how that surface can move when it is finally animated. For instance, if you don't build enough detail into the mouth you might not be able to make all the mouth shapes you need for lip sync. On the other hand, if you build too many contours around facial features, you'll have too much work to do when creating the shapes and the face might not stretch nicely.

It is very important to understand the structure of the muscles that you are trying to simulate. When your model moves, you'll just be pushing vertices around to stretch the skin, but when a real creature moves, something more complex happens. Generally there is a skeleton layer that provides structural rigidity. On top of that skeletal layer lies a muscle layer, and it's these muscles that attach to the skeleton and then push and pull the skin into different shapes for emotions, facial expressions, lip sync and poses. If you understand how the muscles might be arranged in your creature, you can build the topology of the polygon mesh to push and pull well in the directions that the surface would if your creature was real. Look at the aforementioned reference material in the books from Faigin and Hogarth to see where the muscle masses are, and how they contract and move.

BUILDING MUSCULATURE

In a simple example, the biceps is a large muscle that attaches to the forearm inside of the elbow, and anchors at the other end under the armpit. When the biceps contracts, it bunches up to become shorter, and slides up the arm bone under the skin towards the shoulder. So, to build a surface that will show the contour of the biceps and will also animate well, you need to draw edges around the outside shade of the muscle. However, if all you drew in were the contours around muscles, the model would still end up perfectly smooth and round. That's because there need to be high spots in the contours to fill out the shapes. Changes in elevation, separated by contours, will come out as bumped-out (relief) forms on the smoothed model. Depending on the level of detail you require, there can be concentric contours at different elevations on the model, just like a contour map of a landscape, or just one or two vertices in the middle of the form bounded by the contour, connected by edges to the edges in the contour.

Because quads smooth out so nicely, an automatic way to create contours and elevations is to select one or more polygons on the model, then use CTRL-D to extrude the polygons, and in local mode, scale them in X and Z to shrink the contour. Now you'll have two edges running in a loop, parallel to each other, to create a harder change of direction in the surface. Use CTRL-D again, and this time scale the contour in X and Z, but also translate it in local Y out from the surface along the normal direction, to create a change in elevation. Now, when you look at the smoothed shape by increasing the smoothing with the plus (+) key on the numeric keypad of your keyboard, you can see a strong contour running around a change in elevation, as if there was a muscle underneath the skin at that point.

When you create shapes for the movement of that biceps muscle under the skin, you can animate the points in the elevation to get higher, while moving all the points of the contours so that the shape bunches up and moves towards the shoulder.

BUILDING DETAIL AROUND JOINTS

When your character needs to bend an arm or a knee, that joint needs to deform in an attractive manner, which is not exactly automatic. In the case of a knee, if you don't have any contours running around the knee at the bend, then there will simply be no points there to rotate around the joint as the knee flexes. If you don't have enough detail – and in the right configuration – around the knee, it will tend to collapse when the joint bends. At an absolute minimum, you need one contour running generally around the top of the bending area, and one contour running around the lower boundary of the bending area. These upper and lower bounds isolate the bending and flexing of the skin to just the area between them. The vertices of the upper bound should be weighted almost entirely to the upper bone, and the lower bound to the lower bone. In the middle, between the two bounds, you can add more contours to define the shape that the joint takes on as it flexes.

BODY PARTS

Talking about modeling is all very well, but it doesn't help quite as much as actually seeing something come together. For the rest of this section we'll go through the process of building a human figure.

To best use this section, just follow along, looking at the sequence of images to see how the shapes change from one to the next, read the short captions, and follow along.

We'll start with good proportionate drawings to help us with scale and shape courtesy of Elliot Rosenstein. Elliot has drawn the body parts to aid us in our modeling tasks. These images were scanned at relatively low resolution, and color corrected to a gray background so that both selected meshed (white wireframe) and unselected meshes (black wireframe) will be easy to see against it.

Let's break the figure down into small parts that we can tackle one by one without becoming overwhelmed, starting with the easy stuff to warm up, then finishing with the most difficult parts, the hands and the face. Finally, we'll assemble all the parts and merge them into one big mesh.

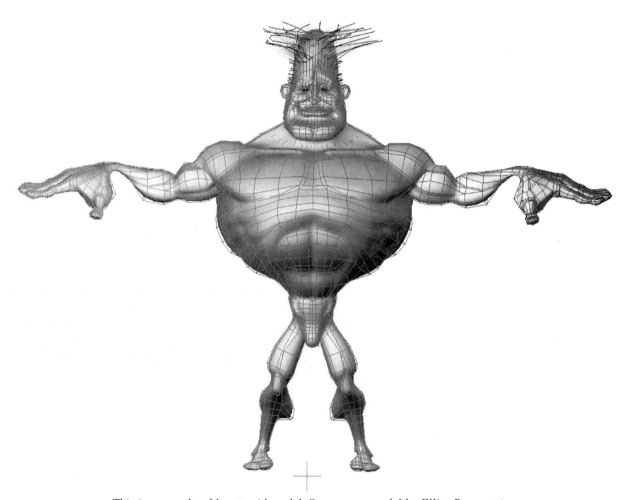

This is a completed humanoid model. Sssuperguy model by Elliot Rosenstein.

Sssuperguy drawings by Elliot Rosenstein

Remember the process of SubD modeling: first block in volumes and proportions, next add contours, and finish with surface detail. After each part is done, place it on a layer, and save the file with a different version number so that you can always go back to a previous revision, and so that you end up with multiple versions of the file just in case something goes wrong or one version becomes corrupted or lost.

ARMS

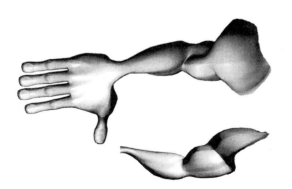

In the Front and Right views, toggle on the Rotoscope view and load the armfront.pic and armright.pic images, courteously drawn by Elliot. The reference material is drawn without foreshortening to make it easier to see the correct proportions, and the pose is loose and unflexed.

The Front and Side Rotoscope material for the arms

FIXING ROTOSCOPE SCALE

Both images were carefully scaled to have the same size, so that the arm is the same length in front and side view. As soon as you load the images into the Roto views, lock the Roto Zoom with the small magnifying glass icon in the top titlebar of the front and right views. This will lock the proportions to be the same in both views.

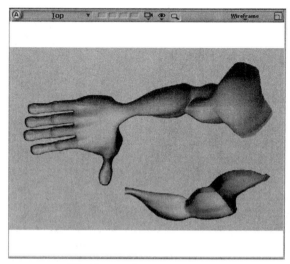

The Roto reference in the view

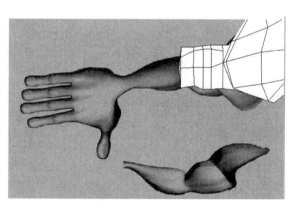

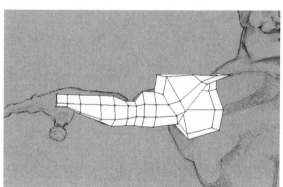

The black rectangle around the image is exactly the same size in each image, so that if you make a mistake and accidentally zoom in one or the other views without the Roto Zoom lock on, thereby screwing up the proportion between the two images, you can get a default cube, scale it up to match the size of the black rectangle in one image, then carefully zoom or dolly in the other view until the cube is also the same size as the black rectangle in that view. When the cube is the same size in the front and right views you may be certain that the scale of the two views is the same, and that you can continue to work.

START WITH A PRIMITIVE

The arm section we want to build runs from the shoulder to the wrist, and is a very simple shape. Start with a six-sided polygon cylinder, cut the top and bottom off, and scale to fit the dimensions of the arm. Remember that the SubD cage must be larger in diameter than you want the finished surface to be. You can imagine that the finished model will shrink 10% or more when you subdivide it, so make it a bit bigger than the reference material of the arm.

Add a row of edges so that there are two in the middle of the cylinder, and tag and move them so that one set is just above the elbow and the other just below.

Add another set of edges halfway down the forearm, and one in the middle of the biceps.

Rotate the vertices around the arm to twist the contours to look like the contours of your own arm and then pull vertices away from the surface to define the high points of the forearm, and the biceps.

Pull the points of the shoulder end, and add in a few more edges to round out the shoulder. Make sure you have an edge loop around the shoulder muscle, and one around the biceps.

Create a layer with the Layer menu at the top of the MCP, name it arms, and put your arm on that layer. Make that layer invisible so the arm is out of the way.

Save your scene with some name like "bodyparts1".

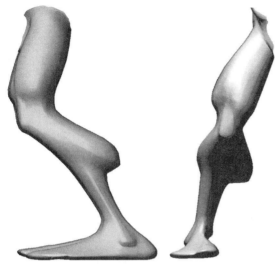

The leg reference material

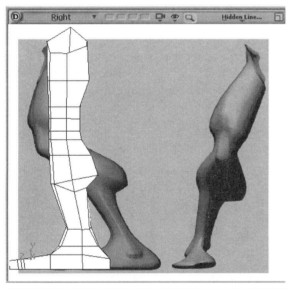

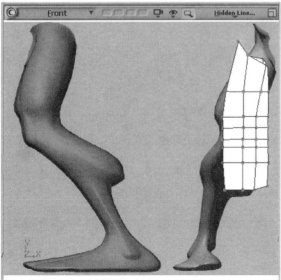

LEGS

Next is a leg. In the Rotoscope Options load up the legfront.pic and legright.pic images into the Front and Right views, respectively. Start again with a six-sided cylinder.

Add in the edge detail on either side of the knee. Add in a row of edges mid-thigh, one mid-calf, and one below the calf but above the ankle.

Using the Front and Side views, move the vertices of these cross sections so that the cage blocks out the volume of the leg, and matches the proportion in both views.

Pull up the vertices of the top of the cylinder to make the outside top of the leg where it meets the buttocks, and pull down the inside area to meet the crotch. The top edge of the leg should look like the leg ends at the edge of a pair of tight underwear. After you have defined the edge, select the flat polygon shearing through the face of the buttock, and extrude it to create a blocky volume for one half of the posterior. Add in a parallel edge near the centerline to define the centerline.

DEFINE CONTOURS

Now, think about the muscles and contours of the leg. Where are the high points? What contour surrounds the high muscled points? Modify the vertices by rotating them around the leg to make a low-res version of the contours, then add more detail where necessary. Keep checking the Front and side views to make sure the volume and proportions are correct, and evenly larger than the surface you eventually want.

Where there is now a flat polygon that needs to become a bulge, split the polygon in a cross shape and pull up the middle vertex. This method creates areas where the resolution of the surface changes dramatically. If you don't like this, rather than splitting the polygon to create a high vertex in the middle, CTRL-D extrude the polygon away from the surface and scale it down in local X and Z to make the high spot. This method keeps all the edges connected, but generates more polygons.

Add a kneecap by extruding the flat polygon there. You can add creases behind the knee by creating parallel edges there.

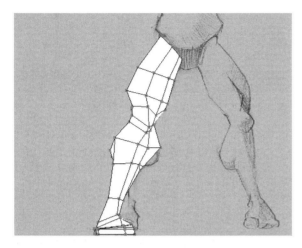

Do a last pass adjusting the contours, and adding parallel edge loops where you want particularly defined muscles.

When done, smooth up the surface by increasing the polygon smoothing with the plus (+) key on your numeric keypad. Put the leg on a layer all its own, and save the file with a different number, like "bodyparts2".

TORSO

Use the Roto options to swap the leg images for the torsoright.pic and torsofront.pic so you have some good reference material.

Because the torso is more or less symmetrical, you just need to build half of it. Set this up as follows.

START WITH A PRIMITIVE

Get another six-sided cylinder. Scale it slightly wider and thinner so that it matches the width and breadth of the torso in the Roto images.

Cut off the top and bottom.

Add in more top-to-bottom detail, either with the Geometry operator or by selecting parallel edges and splitting them with Shift-D. Four sections, top to bottom, are a good start.

The torso reference material

Adjust the edges bounding the chest and back, and make that portion broader than the shoulder.

Now chop it in half by selecting all the polygons on the right half of the cylinder and deleting them.

Also delete all the polygons of the top and bottom caps, because you'll want the top to connect to the neck and the bottom to connect to the legs.

Freeze the model, and toggle on Immediate mode now. Also Freeze all the transformations.

MIRROR LEFT AND RIGHT

Make an immediate Instance (with Duplicate/Instantiate➔Instantiate Single) of that first half, and scale by –1 across the plane in which you want the body mirrored, probably X if you built the torso facing the Front view. Now select the original and assure yourself that modifications to the original are reflected in the other half.

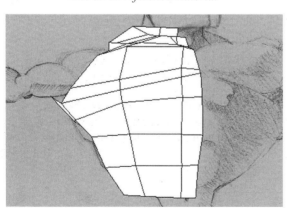

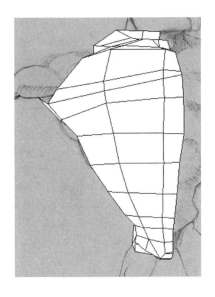

SCULPT

Scale the proportions of the torso to match the front and side views.

On the bottom, pull up the outside and down the inside to match the shape of the crotch and hip. Imagine that the leg will attach here, and make the edge of the shape look like the bottom of a bikini line.

Look at the reference drawing and see where the contours should be. Adjust the vertices so that they line up with those contours.

Adjust the shoulders to be broader on top. Extrude out the shoulder to bulge on top and to extend away from the body. Cut an open hole in the shoulder to attach the arm later.

Define the bottom outline of the pectoral muscle. Add a line of parallel edges to create a rapid change of contour at the bottom of the pectoral that will define the shape.

ADD DEFINITION

Add more parallel edges to define the musculature of the stomach.

Pouch out the fatty skin on top of where the kidneys would be, directly above the bottom edge.

On top, refine the contours of the collarbone, with depressions and corresponding sinews running up into the neckline.

On the back, flatten out the space between the shoulder blades and provide the re-curve of the lower back. Create the contours that surround the shoulder blades, and make sure they link up with the contours around the shoulders.

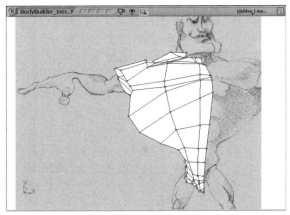

MERGE THE HALVES

When done, make certain that the vertices that form the centerline are exactly on center by tagging them all and scaling them to 0 in global X.

Merge the left and right halves. Freeze the result, and make a layer for the torso, then hide the construction halves.

Smooth the torso and examine it to see that it matches the scale and proportions correctly. Make any further modifications you need to bring it into line with the reference material.

Save your work.

FEET AND TOES

As usual, replace the images in the Rotoscope plane with new ones from the Pictures directory. This time we'll use the Top view and a Right view, since the frontal view of a foot doesn't give much information. Load the foottop.pic and footright.pic images into the Rotoscope Options PPG for the corresponding top and right views. Toggle off Rotoscope in the front view so it won't be confusing.

Feet are difficult, so a few words here about what will be important are in order. As usual, the first thing to make will be the overall blocky shape. If the proportions are right, then the contours of the ankle will be easy to add. The toughest part is the organization of the contours stretching from the top of the foot to the toes, which are fairly simple by themselves.

DEFINE THE VOLUME

Start with the volume of the foot. The foot is basically a rectangular block, wide and flat, tapering down to the toes. It becomes slightly thinner and arched in the middle. Get a Primitive cube, and scale it to fit all the way around the illustrations of the foot in the Top and Right Roto views. Use the Geometry PPG for the cube (Immediate mode must therefore be off temporarily when you get the cube) to add regular subdivisions. Add four more subdivisions along the length of the foot, so that the foot has five sections front to back. Add two more subdivisions across the width of the foot, so that it has three sections left to right. Add no more subdivision from top to bottom.

Tag points one row at a time, and moving them in Global space so you retain perfect accuracy, translate them back and forth along the foot to adjust the position of the cross sections. Move one close to the back to define the heel roundness, the next in front of the ankle, two at either end of the arch, and the remaining cross section near to the toes.

Now adjust the cross sections that define the width of the foot, so that the middle section of the foot is much wider than the sections at the edges.

SCULPT

You can now freeze the operator stack, turn on Immediate mode, and begin sculpting the vertices to match the proportions of the illustrations. In the Right view, tag groups of points that run across the foot and translate them in drag mode to a position just above the edge of the foot in the illustration. Since you tagged a rectangle you'll get all the points running away from you in the axis perpendicular to the view you made the selection in. This ensures that all the points in that section of the contour get moved uniformly. Moving each point by itself would take longer and be messier.

Continue this process in the Right and Top views to match the proportions of the drawings, leaving a little extra bulk so that when the SubD shrinks the surface it will match the foot illustrated in the Roto images. In the Front view, imagine how the contours of the foot change, being slightly taller in the middle of the foot. Make adjustments there as you see fit.

Adjust the front of the foot in the Top view to place the leading edge at the furthest solid point of the foot, before the toes sprout out, and make sure that the edge curves back, being most forward at the big toe's side and curving back to the little toe's side.

SPROUT TOES

Five toes need to be built. The easiest way will be to adjust the front of the foot, which now has three polygons facing forward, so that the outside polygons are very thin and pulled slightly back towards the heel. Then, divide the single front-facing polygon into five slices with new top to bottom edges. Use the Add Edge tool, so that the toes are less regular, and you can vary the width of each toe from big to small.

Now the plan is to extrude each toe separately, so that it does not connect to the neighboring toe. Imagine the shape of each toe, and give each about four segments, with two segments close together to form the first knuckle and two to form the second knuckle. Repeat with all five toes, unless your figure has been mauled in a tragic farming mishap.

THE ANKLE

Now build the ankle. Locate the polygon facing up on the top of the foot, next to the heel, and pull it up away from the surface a little ways. Now extrude it in local Y so that it pops up from the surface. Select the sides of this new smooth ankle section, and extrude them, making the resulting polygon smaller and translated out in local Y from the surface. Adjust the vertices of this new ankle area to make it less regular, and to make the back thinner than the front, as if a thin tendon ran from the top of the ankle, smoothly blending into the width of the heel.

From the front of the ankle, arches need to be artfully extended over the front of the foot to connect to the toes, as if there were tendons connecting each toe to the top of the foot.

You can create double edge pairs here, and pull them away from the surface a bit to define the contours of the muscles and tendons that lift the toes.

Now the process of progressive refinement is up to you. Smooth the foot, look at it, identify things that don't look quite right, and make small adjustments to the shape until you either like it a lot or run out of time. It's a good idea to get other people to look at the model. They'll see things you didn't because you've been looking at it for so long (or they might just tell you that it's perfect and you shouldn't change a thing).

When done, make a layer for the foot, save the file with a new version number, and move on to the next body part.

HANDS AND FINGERS

Hands and fingers are a real challenge to sculpt in any medium, and building them in 3D is no exception. At this point you should be realizing that the problem is not the usefulness of the toolset, but rather the challenge of creativity, of accurate perception, and understanding physiology.

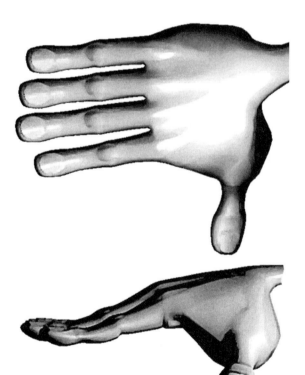

The hand reference material

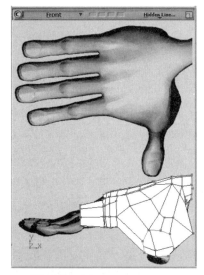

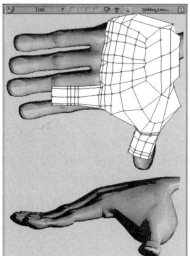

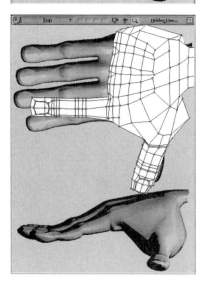

Set up your Roto views with the handtop.pic and handside.pic images

Let's break the hand down into four small projects: the palm, the thumb, the forefinger, and all the other fingers.

THE PALM

First, build the palm, starting with a primitive cube having two subdivisions. Scale the cube to the rough size of the palm. As usual, tag and move the points of the edges to match the shape of the reference material. Also be sure to tag points in the interior of the cube and adjust the thickness of the cube to have a slight concavity, just like your palm. Make the palm thicker at the wrist, and thicker yet in the meaty area at the base of the thumb.

Rotate the points near the edges of the hand to give it the characteristic curved surface, as if it was slightly cupped.

At the front of the palm, where the fingers will connect, divide the front facing polygon into four unequal slices. One at a time, select each of the resulting polygons, duplicate it, scale it down just a bit, and delete it to reveal a hole for the finger to attach to later.

ONE FINGER

Next, build the forefinger because it can then be modfied for the thumb and the other fingers. Let's get tricky this time, and start with a revolved curve. In the Right view, draw a NURBS curve over the hand image, dropping two points near the finger tip, two points on either side of each knuckle, and end the curve at the knuckle of the hand. Move the curve to a position near the Z-axis and revolve it. In the Revolution PPG, set the axis of revolution to the correct axis, and give it 6 U subdivisions. Adjust the position relative to the axis to make the finger the right thickness. Don't worry about the open tip, because we'll patch it with a polygon later.

Now tag rows of points and rotate them to bend the finger slightly into a comfortable, natural pose for your own index finger. Make any other adjustments necessary to the rough volume of the finger, making sure it tapers slightly in height towards the tip, but doesn't change much in width.

When you like the proportions, use the Create➜Poly Mesh➜Nurbs to Mesh command to make a polygonal copy of the patch finger. A bare minimum of detail is needed, so leave the NURBS To Mesh PPG set to 1 Step in U and V. Freeze the polygonal version, hide the NURBS version, and move the polygon finger back over the hand Roto image so you can continue work.

Patch the hole in the front of the finger with the Add/Edit poly tool.

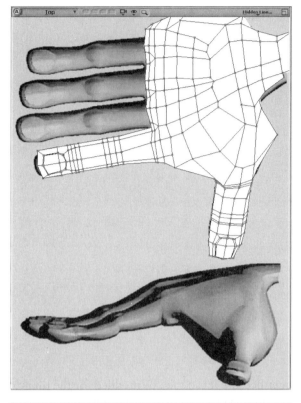

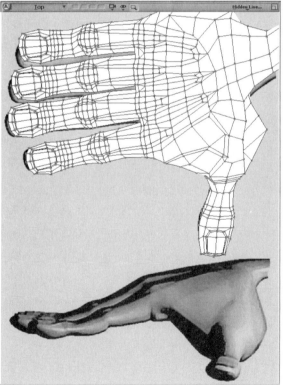

The next task is to define the contours of the finger, making the bulges under the finger in the fatty parts between the knuckles. You may try splitting the edges all the way around between the tip and the first knuckle, then move the points on the bottom to puff out the bottom. Smooth the surface to examine the results. On the middle section try a different method. Select the three bottom-most polygons between the first and second knuckles, and extrude them all together. Scale the new polygons down a bit and translate them out in local Y. For the biggest section nearest the open end, try yet a different technique. Select the three bottom-most polygons between the second and third knuckles, and use Shift-D to split those polygons in an plus pattern, or better yet, and X pattern. Now you can translate the center vertex down and away from the finger to pouch out the puffy part of the finger pad. Smooth up the finger and examine the results, choosing which method you prefer, then Undo back to before you subdivided anything and use that technique for all the finger contours. Repeat this process to create the wrinkles on the top of the finger over the middle of the first and second knuckles.

For the fingernails, select the top fingernail polygon and extrude it with CTRL-D. Sculpt it into the shape of a fingernail, bringing the front forward a bit. Extrude it again, translating the new polygon in local Y by just the thickness of the fingernail. This creates a thin polygonal border across the front edge of the nail. At the back edge of the nail, select all the points and sink them into the flesh a little bit. You may add more detail to the fingernail if you wish to refine the shape.

THE OTHER FINGERS

You can now use the forefinger as the basis for the other three fingers. Move the local center to the open end at the base of the finger with Transform→Move Center to Vertices, then duplicate the forefinger, and scale each finger to match the sizes in the reference material. By tagging and rotating the sections of each finger, customize the bend of each finger to be slightly different, and also adjust the width of each finger, particularly at the tip. Look at your own fingers to see how they differ from each other.

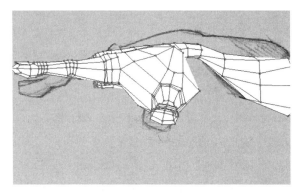

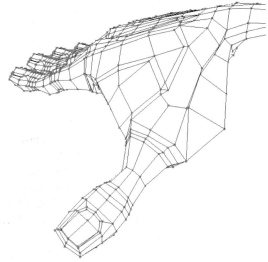

THE THUMB

The thumb is like a finger but with one less joint. You can duplicate another of your fingers, then select all the polygons of the first segment and delete them all. Scale the thumb to be proportionately thicker and broader. Move the thumb to the general area where it will attach to the hand, and rotate it to position, then use the M key to draw the open edge, making it extend into the palm.

ASSEMBLE THE HAND

Each finger or thumb must be hooked up to the palm. To merge a finger to the palm properly, there must be an open hole on the palm that matches the open hole at the base of the finger. Select each of the fingers and position them appropriately. If there are differing numbers of vertices on the palm opening and the finger opening, add some vertices to the palm opening, and add edges to connect the new vertices in a way that makes sense for the webbing between the fingers.

Next, tag all the points around the opening in the palm, and then turn on Snapping, with the Snap to Tagged Components. Move the points of the open end of the finger to snap to the palm. Repeat this with all the fingers and the thumb, then select them all at once and merge the whole selection – palm, fingers and thumb – into one object. Freeze and name that new hand model. Put it on a layer, and clean up the construction elements and spare finger parts. Resave your work.

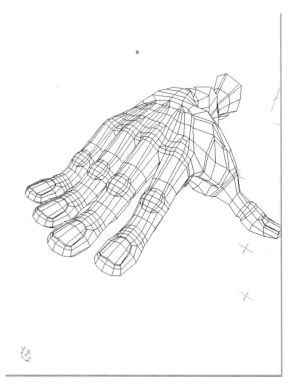

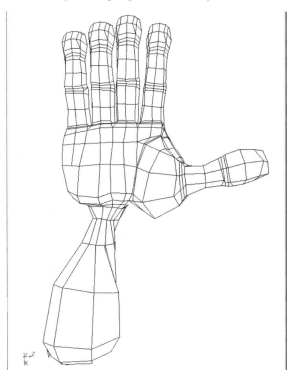

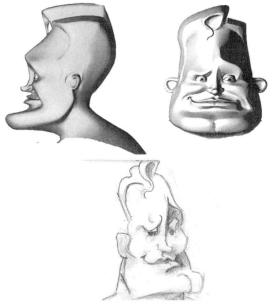

The head reference material

HEAD AND FACE

We spend most of our lives staring at human heads. Without thinking too carefully about the heads we see we have built up a complex set of rules that govern what does and does not look human. If we see a head where the width of the eyes or the position of the mouth or the location of the brow doesn't fall within the acceptable human range of values we'll immediately think that the face looks wrong. However, if we are attempting to create a realistic human face we have a tremendous challenge before us. The closer we get to perfect, the more "dead" the face is likely to look. That's because just getting the proportions correct isn't quite enough to bring the face to life. Taking that extra step to life-likeness means adding variation back to the face, within the accepted ranges. Talented classical painters know that the length and position of the nose can be modified to add character to a face without making the head look unreal, for instance. Another technique is to model the face in some slight expression, rather than completely slack. Think about the Mona Lisa, or add small laugh lines, or crinkle the eyes a bit when you are done. Of course, if your character doesn't need to be realistic your modeling job is much easier, and your character is likely to have more appeal. Paradoxically, the less human the character is, the more it is likely to look alive and express powerful emotions. In my opinion, examples of unsuccessful accurate characters would have to include the people in the film "Final Fantasy: The Spirits Within", while examples of highly successful, emotionally interesting characters would include the characters from "Monsters, Inc".

INITIAL VOLUME

Most of the struggle in modeling human faces is a matter of starting with the correct proportions.

For a thorough understanding of the physiology of the face, refer to the books by Burne Hogarth and Gary Faigin I mentioned earlier.

As usual, load the appropriate reference material into your Roto views. Put the head-front.pic in the front view and the headside.pic in the side view. Get a primitive cube to start with. You'll be adding a lot of edges and vertices to this primitive cube, and to concentrate on the form you'll be ignoring the usual rules of good polygon modeling, like keeping the polygons regular, planar, and not leaving edges terminating randomly. Don't sweat about this stuff, it'll be fixed up at the end. You should also use Immediate mode for this portion, because there will be hundreds of modeling operators on the cube if you do not.

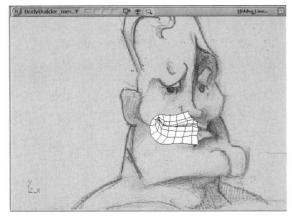

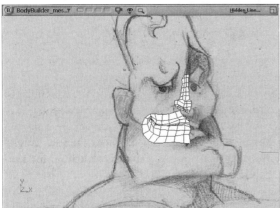

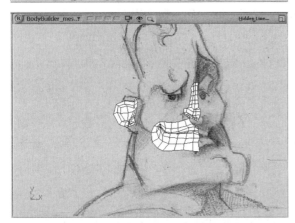

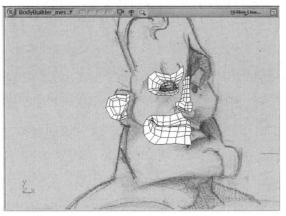

The initial shape chosen to make the primitive will either assist or hinder you in refining the shape. In this case, a cube isn't quite right. The face is not completely flat in front, but rather has planes slicing off the sides at some angle, and the head domes a bit, rounding out the top of the skull. First make these modifications to the cube before adjusting the proportions.

Select the left vertical edge in the front view and extrude it with CTRL-D, which will add edges around it. Now select just that original edge and delete it to leave a flat planar polygon at a 40-degree angle to the front of the cube.

Select the top polygon and extrude it, lifting it a bit in local Y to dome out the top.

MIRROR LEFT AND RIGHT

The head is more or less symmetrical, so take advantage of that fact by modeling only the right side of the head (the left side facing the Front view). To do this the skull needs to be split in half down the middle. Select all the edges crossing the center of the skull and split them with Shift-D.

Select all the polygons with the select by rectangle tool (Y) on the side of the skull to the right in the Front view, and delete them. Turn on Show➔Boundaries to verify that you have an open edge running down the center of the skull. Make an instance of the skull, and scale it by –1 in global X to create the other half. Now you can model on the original and see the results on the instance. It might be a good idea to change the wireframe color of the instance or even make it temporarily unselectable so you don't accidentally make changes to it instead of the original while working.

FINISH PROPORTIONS

Use the technique of tagging vertices and dragging them to scale the skull to surround the head in the Rotoscope reference illustrations. Remember that the skin will shrink quite a bit, so make the skull larger than the reference. Clearly, there is not enough detail in the skull to match the proportions, so that's the next task.

PLANES OF THE FACE

The face is divided into major sections. The head must be chopped up to recreate these.

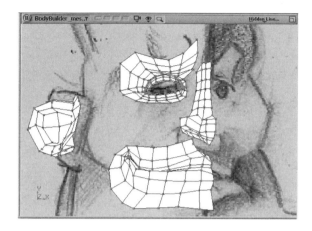

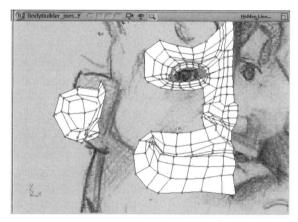

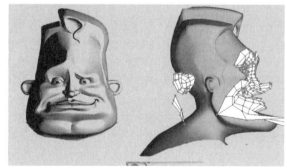

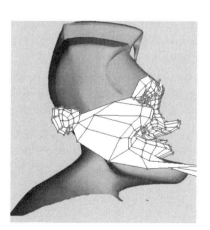

First, divide the head between the forehead and the face. The lower part of the face, including the brows, should be between two-thirds and one-half of the total height of the head. Split the skull edges all around the middle, then tag them and lift them a bit to get between halfway and two-thirds up the face.

The brows have a bit of height, so split the lower face again (just the two front-facing planes) and lift up the edges so that you have a brow portion.

Below the brow, the face is divided in half by a line under the bottom of the node. Again select the edges of the two front-facing planes of the head and split them exactly in half.

The bottom portion of the face is further divided exactly in half by an imaginary line running through the opening between the lips. Add a horizontal edge in the middle of the front-facing polygon by splitting the two parallel edges. Move that new edge up ever so slightly to give more room for the bottom lip than the top, and bevel that edge to create edges around it then select just the center edge and delete it to create a hole for the future gap between the lips.

Select the three bottom edges that now define the chin, and bevel them to create a few more edges.

SCULPT

Now that we have some more detail, again tag points and drag them in the side view first, then the Front view, to match the proportions of the reference material.

Now imagine that you are building the skull that will support the muscles and skin of the face. By considering the skull you can focus on the major forms under the face and get them right while the head is still simple.

EYE SOCKETS

Look to the area for the eye socket. Each eye socket should have six vertices defining it, and should wrap around the corner from the front to the side. Make your skull so.

Next, sink the eye socket into the skull by selecting the big six-sided polygon, extruding it, scaling it down a bit and translating it into the skull. Do this again for good measure, then delete the original polygon (which is now at the center) to create a hole in the skull. You'll pop eyeballs in there later.

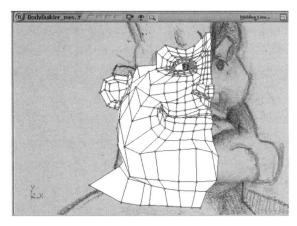

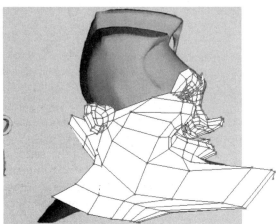

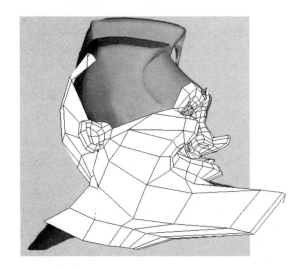

The eye socket should bend in half, with the corners pulled into the head more than the top and bottom, which form ridges to protect the eyeballs. Leave plenty of space, about one eyeball length, between the eye sockets for the bridge of the nose.

EYEBROWS

Let's do a little work on the brow. Slit the edges in the middle of the front span, so you can tag them and drag them up a bit to arch the brow. Split the inside edges of the brow again, then tag then and move them towards the midline for future use in the bridge of the nose. Select all the polygons of the brow and extrude them slightly away from the face. Tag the center points and pull them into the head a little to make the indentation in the middle of the brow over the nose.

NOSE

Move on to the nose. The nose is a pyramid rising from a triangle in the face. Using the add edge tool, draw some edges to define a triangle that will lie in the base of the nose. Now feel your own nose. Mine has a flat top that connects to the brow. Add vertices and an edge parallel to the center line. Now tag the two points where the tip of the nose will be, and pull them away from the face, using the Roto image in the Right view for reference.

Make the nose flat on top. Add edges to fold back the flat area under the nose, then select the new polygon there and extrude, shrink, and translate it to form a simple hole for the nostril.

MOUTH

The mouth is an important area, because it has to be built in a way that will also be animatable. In general, the mouth area should be built according to the construction of the musculature that underlies the lips. That muscle is a circular band of tissue that contracts to close the lips in a pursed mouth shape, but there are also muscles stretching from the corners up to the cheeks and down to the back of the jaw, to pull the mouth open in a smile or a grimace. The edges that are added should mimic the construction of these muscles.

Add two more concentric rings of vertices and edges surrounding the mouth, not worrying about the shape quite yet. From the corners of the mouth, define the edges that stretch back and up to the cheek, and those that stretch back and down to the jaw.

Connect all the vertices in the concentric circles around the mouth together with edges to form lots of little square polygons, with a few triangles thrown in at the corners of the mouth.

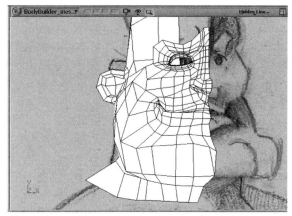

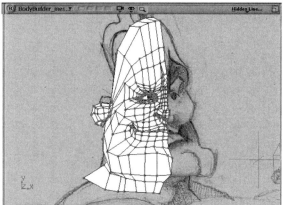

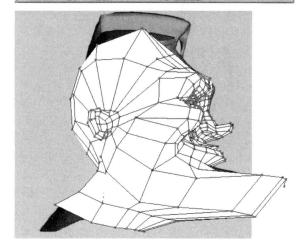

Next, define the shape of the lips by just moving around the vertices we just made. Put your finger on your top lip and feel the shape under your nose. The top lip ends just under the nose in a ridge with a divot in it, creating a shape like an archery bow. The bottom lip has a gentle curve without the divot. The bottom lip is therefore fuller and has a plumper curve. The transition between the skin of the face and the skin of the lip is a hard boundary, so create another edge loop at that point, close to the nearest existing edge loop, so that the boundary will be dramatic when smoothed by the subdivision operator. All the points of that boundary, and all the points inside that boundary, are pulled away from the face somewhat, making the lips just out under the nose.

EARS

Ears help define the shape of the face, but the actual topology of the ear just isn't that important. On the side of the head define a rounded eight-sided polygon in the approximate area of the ear, shrink it to the size of the base of the ear, then extrude it, scale it bigger and pull it out slightly. Extrude (duplicate) the selected polygon again, then again, shrinking the last one and pulling it in a bit to form a cone. Repeat this to create a cone with several interior contours. Connect all the vertices around the ear to make lots of quads, then just sculpt the vertices to shape the ear, making the lobe bigger and fatter and the top rim thinner. Stick your finger in your ear to feel the thickness of the rim and the number of contour changes before it joins the side of your head.

CLEANUP

Clean up the eye sockets, and extrude the top of the eye socket to form an eyelid.

Next you need to fix up all the bad geometry that was created while working on the general form. While the Subdivision Surface operator will gladly smooth just about any kind of polygons, using a combination of four-sided and three-sided polygons whenever possible will result in a more orderly mesh, with easier to find edge loops you can exploit to create stronger contours. Look over your model and use the Add Edge tool to connect the dots, making lots of tris and quads. When you add an edge, consider that it might become a contour, and think about how that contour runs in the actual face. Try as much as possible to mimic the lines, contours and wrinkles in a face. Even if you are making a character with smooth skin, imagine where the wrinkles would be on an old person, and use that thought to guide you.

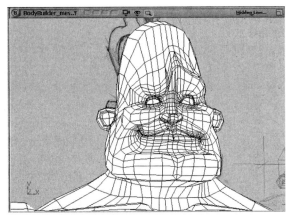

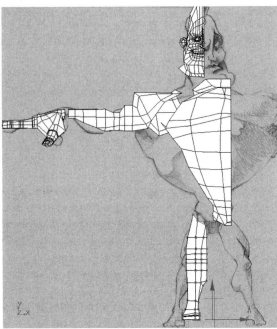

Put the parts near where they will end up.

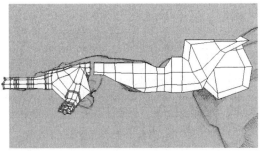

Scale the hand to match the arm.

You can increase the polygon smoothing during this phase to see what you are getting, and look for areas where the resulting surface doesn't look uniformly subdivided. Areas of inexplicably higher detail often indicate that you have a weird arrangement of multi-sided polygons. Clean those up if you can.

PROGRESSIVE REFINEMENT

The last step in the modeling of the face is to look at your work, and add the details that are specific to your own character. If his nose is bigger, make that happen. If his eyes are small and beady, shrink the eyes and sockets. If the character is a happy one, add in a slight permanent smile. Add in wrinkles, add in changes of contour in the face, adjust the height of the cheekbones, modify the slope of the head from top to bottom. Change the size and thickness of the lips, the diameter of the mouth, and the length and protrusion of the chin. All these things and more make each face unique.

To complete the head, verify that all the points along the center line are indeed precisely on the center axis by scaling to zero in X. Merge the two halves of the face together, and freeze the result. Make a few changes to the head to make it less symmetrical, which will help in the life-likeness. Cut a hole for the neck, and adjust the back of the skull and the top of the skull to suit your needs.

Put the head on a layer, and delete the extra halves. Save the file.

IT S ALIVE!

With all the parts of your character built, it's now a matter of stitching the whole creature together. As usual, it's really important that the creature be assembled with the right proportions, and since each component was made separately, it's likely that the scales don't actually match. You need to build a simple guide to help with human proportions.

PROPORTIONAL TEMPLATE

The head is the basic unit of human measurement. Get a cube, and freeze it. We'll call this cube one head unit. Lift it off the ground plane a ways.

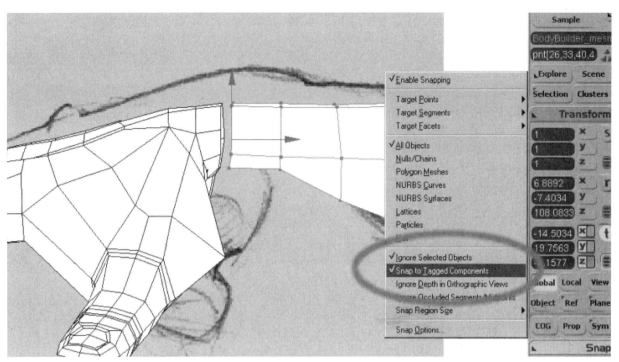

Using Snap to Tags makes this precise work foolproof.

The human body actually has a range of possible head-to-body proportions. Rather short and squat people might be 6.5 times as tall as their head, while tall thin people might be 7.5 times as tall as their head, and superheroic head-to-body proportions are usually even more. Let's choose to make this person 7 times as tall as his head. Duplicate the cube again for the neck, and scale it to 0.3 in Y, and somewhat smaller in X and Z. Place it below the head. Duplicate the head again, this time for the shoulders, and translate it below the neck. Duplicate the head again, and scale it to 1.7 in Y for the chest and belly. Repeat again with one head height for hips and butt, one for upper legs, one for lower legs and feet. Scale the width of each cube to help you visualize this stack of cubes as a human figure.

If you wish to be more precise, you can get a new reference image of your own choosing showing a standing human so you can match the proportions more exactly.

Now you can use this stack of cubes to scale the various body parts you made so that the torso is the right size compared to the legs, compared to the head, etc.

Unhide the head layer. Select the head, scale it and move it on top of the head cube in your proportional template. Repeat with the torso, one arm, one leg, and one foot.

Now each needs to be stitched to the other.

STITCHING THE HAND AND ARM
Carefully position the hand as close as possible to the opening of the arm. Scale the hand until it looks right compared to the arm. The arm should be about three hands long, from the shoulder to the wrist.

Merge the leg and foot, and scale to match the proportional template.

Count the vertices all the way around the wrist, then count those on the open part of the hand. It would be best if the number matched. You can add more detail to the wrist to match the detail on the opening of the hand. If you don't want to do this, it's also OK to attach more than one vertex on the hand to a single vertex on the arm.

Tag all the points on the open end of the arm. Turn on Snapping on Point, turn off any other snapping options, like Snap to Grid, and in the Snap menu, toggle on Snap to Tagged Components.

Select the hand. Now you can adjust vertices with the M key on the edge of the hand, and they will snap to the open vertices on the arm very easily and precisely.

Use the hidden line view style for this so you can easily see if you snap to a vertex that you didn't intend to snap to. Orbit the hand while working to get a good view of the work.

When the vertices are all lined up properly, use Create➔Polymesh➔Merge to make a new object out of hand and the arm.

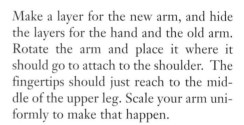

Make a layer for the new arm, and hide the layers for the hand and the old arm. Rotate the arm and place it where it should go to attach to the shoulder. The fingertips should just reach to the middle of the upper leg. Scale your arm uniformly to make that happen.

Now the arm matches the scale of the rest of the body.

STITCH THE OTHER PARTS

Repeat this process for the other parts. Stitch the foot to the leg (matching the scale first). The leg should be about three feet long, from inseam (the crotch attachment) to the top of the ankle.

Of course, this will vary somewhat depending on what size shoes your character will wear and how tall he is. Scale the finished leg to match the proportions in the proportional template.

Scale the torso to the template, then stitch the leg on, and then stitch the arm on.

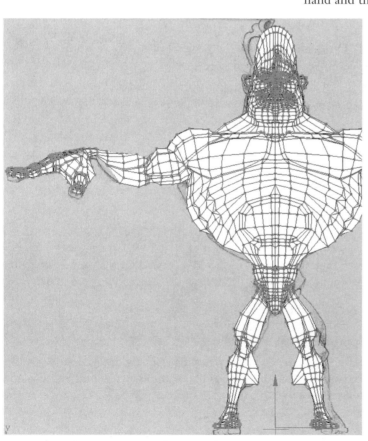

Stitch the torso onto the leg and shoulder.

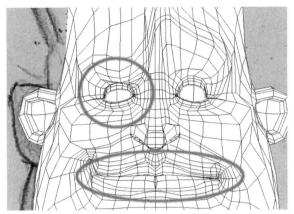

The eyes and mouth should be the only open boundaries.

Mirror the new arm/leg/torso for the other side of the body, verify that the centerline is perfectly on center, and merge the two sides together.

Stitch the head on.

Put the completed figure on a new layer, and hide everything else.

Make sure that Show Boundaries is on in the camera view, so you can see open edges in light blue.

There should be open edges in your eye sockets, under the nose, and in the mouth, but nowhere else. If you see open edges in places where there should be none, it means that your edges didn't seal up properly when you merged one part to another. Fix this right away by either re-doing the guilty merge, or by deleting the offending vertex and then re-patching the hole with the Add Polygon tool. You really want the mesh to be good at this point, because it will be very time-consuming to backtrack and fix this later.

Save your file, and pat yourself on the back. You are done for now. You can always go back to modify the character further, adjusting proportion, refining contours and muscles, and whatever other changes you may want to make.

SMOOTHING CHARACTERS

You can smooth up your character in two ways. If you simply use the plus (+) and minus (-) keys on your numeric keypad, the subdivision smoothing will be done dynamically in the Geometry Approximation PPG.

This has the advantage that you can always turn it up or down to suit your current needs. If you choose this method, you'll be able to envelope and weight using the low-resolution polygon mesh, and the weight maps and skin assignments will be properly propagated to the higher-resolution subdivision surface. If you add materials and textures, those too will be propagated to the smooth subdivision surface, and the character will behave well. This is the simplest method, and probably the best in general.

The other option is to select the character and use the Create→PolyMesh→Subdivision command to make a totally new object that references the character you modeled. This new object will actually have vertices for all the detail added by the subdivision surface, which is an advantage if you need to modify those vertices and a disadvantage if you just want the subdivision surface to be generated and then left alone. In this case you can also change the method of subdivision from Catmull-Clark to Doo-Sabin, which retains the original form slightly better, and allows for the creation of multi-sided polygons in the subdivision surface mesh. One big problem with working this way is that no materials, textures, or weight maps will follow from the low-res version to the high-res version, which means that you'll have much more work to do in texturing and weighting the new higher density mesh.

If you can, stick with smoothing your character using the plus/minus (+/-) key method. It's easier, faster, and lighter for your computer.

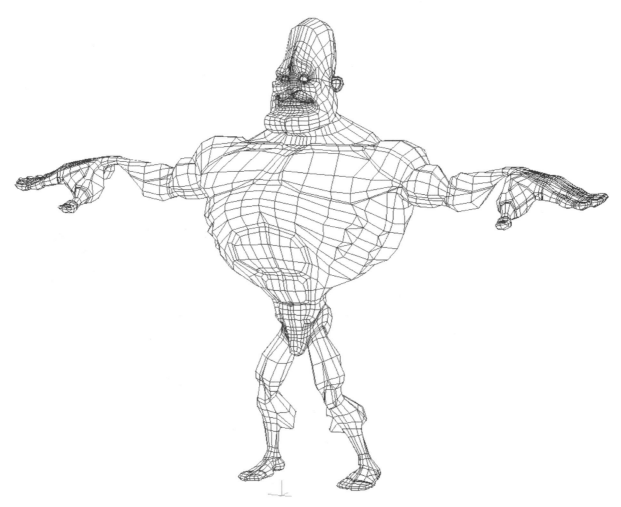

The completed character with no subdivision smoothing.

CONCLUSION

Subdivision Surface modeling is really just glorified polygon modeling, with a few extra tricks thrown in. Because low polygon modeling is all about keeping the detail simple, it makes for very efficient workflow for the modeler. Because the Subdivision operator has the job of final smoothing, we can emancipate ourselves from even worrying about the final surface, and concentrate on the important things: volume, proportion, and contour.

Even though the tools are not hard to master, the task of modeling a human is not at all easy. In fact, it's no easier in XSI than it is in clay, though perhaps it's a bit easier than working in stone. The point is that the quality and appeal of the finished result relies almost entirely on your artistic skills, your vision, and your ability to work methodically. Modeling, like sculpting, is an art, and only by study and practice will you be good at it. So, keep it up! Do it over and over and over...

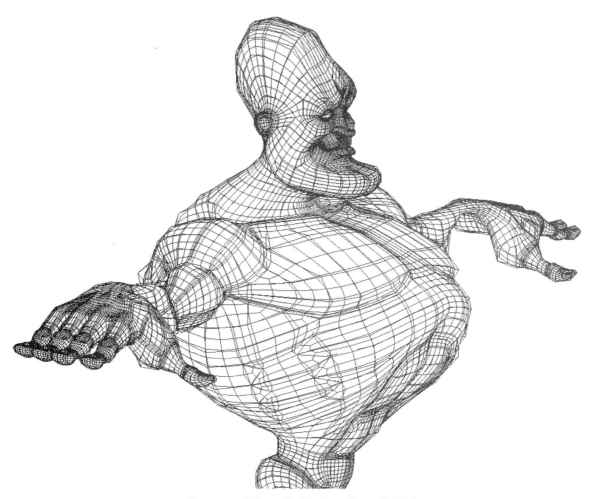

One step of Catmull-Clark surface subdivision

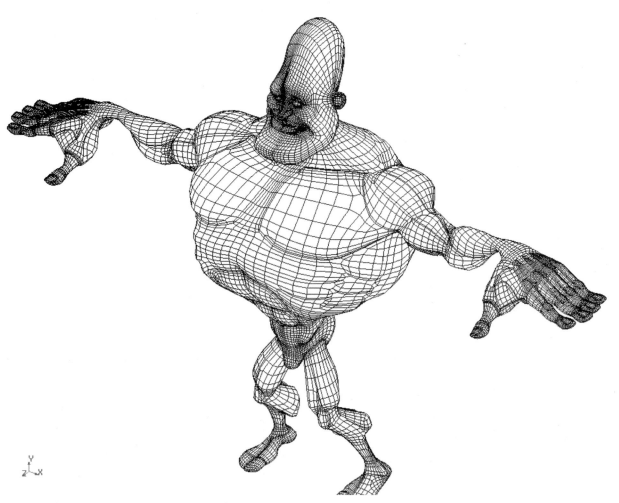

One step of Doo-Sabin, using the Subdivision operator

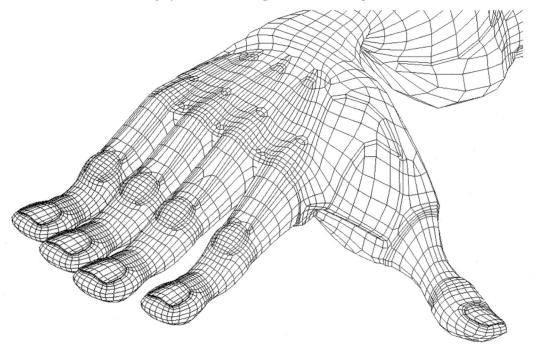

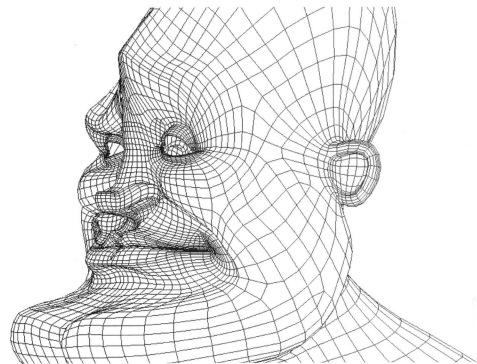

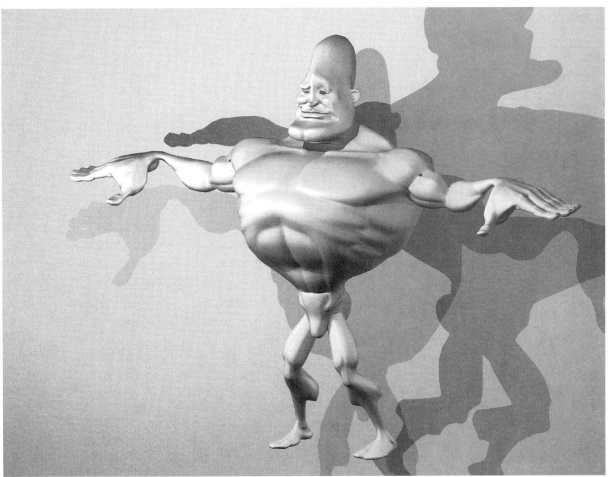

A very smooth character, rendered out

QUIZ

1. WHICH IS EASIER TO USE IN MODELING PEOPLE?
   a. NURBS
   b. Polygons
   c. Implicits

2. WHICH MUST ALWAYS HAVE FOUR SIDES?
   a. Polygon mesh
   b. NURBS patch
   c. Implicit primitive

3. CAN YOU TEXTURE SUBDIVISION SURFACES?
   a. Yes
   b. No
   c. Maybe

4. WHAT IS THE HOTKEY TO INCREASE THE SUBDIVISION ON A POLYGON MESH?
   a. S
   b. Alt-I
   c. +

5. WHICH VIEW STYLE CAN HAVE A ROTOSCOPE REFERENCE IMAGE?
   a. Shaded
   b. Hidden
   c. All of them

6. WHAT IS THE BETTER POSE TO MODEL IN?
   a. Arms and legs straight out
   b. Arms at sides, feet together
   c. Limbs lightly bent, body crouched

7. WHAT DOES NOT BELONG HERE?
   a. Vertex
   b. Loop
   c. Edge

8. WHAT IS THE RIGHT MODELING ORDER OR WORKFLOW?
   a. Proportion, Surface, Contour
   b. Volume, Surface, Contour
   c. Volume, Proportion, Contour

9. WHICH SUBDIVISION METHOD CAN PRODUCE 5-SIDED POLYGONS IN THE RESULTING SURFACE?
   a. Doo-Sabin
   b. Catmull-Clark
   c. Either one

10. HOW DO PEOPLE BECOME GOOD AT MODELING?
   a. Born with raw talent
   b. Fast computer, good graphics card
   c. Hard work, practice

9

COMPLEX HUMAN IK RIGS

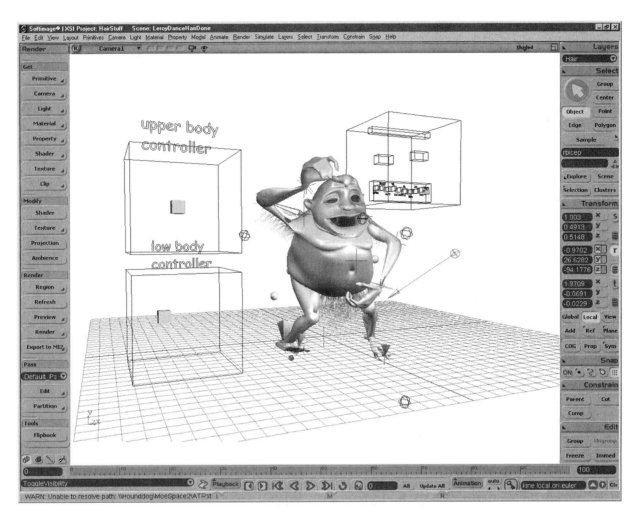

IN THIS CHAPTER YOU WILL LEARN ABOUT:

- How to build simple and complex IK chains
- Determine and animate the resolution plane of each IK chain
- Connect IK Chains together with constraints and clusters
- Organize your work with Layers
- Where to put custom controls (Psets)
- How to make each character a Model
- Pump up your character with automatic muscle bulging
- Build complete IK rigs to ease and speed animation tasks

INTRODUCTION

Up to this point, we have discussed specific tools for building IK chains and binding models to them. Now it is time to talk about strategies for animating the resulting characters.

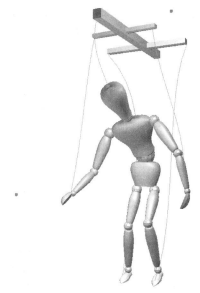

The puppeteer controls the rack, the rack drives the puppet

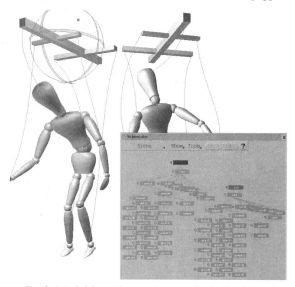

Each Model has identical parts. Only the Model name is different.

The Model Menu commands

In the simple examples so far, we've used simple IK chains parented together, and we have animated the position of the effectors of those chains by setting translation keyframes. Although that was sufficient for demonstrating the IK effects and weighting the skin, it won't be near enough to construct a seriously productive IK system for flexible character animation.

You can certainly connect IK chains together by making one the parent of another to build up a full skeleton. With that system the character could move his hands and legs, but it would be difficult to move his whole body with them. If he needed to walk in anything other than a straight line, forget it. If the animation then needed to be edited, tough.

This is all because of two distinct problems with that setup. First, there are no useful hierarchy of controls over the IK chains themselves. Second, keyframes are being set directly on the effectors relative to the root of the IK chain, so they can't move locally to the model itself as they should. In the following sections, we'll discuss exactly how to build IK chains that meet our exacting production standards.

CONTROL RIGS

A good IK system must be flexible to handle different situations, easily editable so changes can be made later in the game, and structured to make sense in terms of how the creature you are imitating is put together. The fundamental problem to overcome in constructing the IK system is that you need many different ways to attach skins, chains, nulls, and effectors together so they all interact in a natural way. Such a system is called an IK control rig. After that rig is built, it can be reused with many different characters, and passed around to the animators who will actually set the keyframes.

A good control rig automates complex relationships in the character, while still allowing the animator to manually change those relationships if they want to. In other words, the rig should make it possible for the animator to ignore details, but not prevent the animator from doing anything they might want to do.

To easily visualize what we are trying to accomplish, think of a marionette puppet system. A marionette has a physically-based IK system with the limbs constructed of short wooden pieces hinged together. The end of each limb is nailed to a thin wire or string that extends to a wooden puppet rack. The rack is composed of several wooden pieces, so that each limb is tied on the end of a different piece of wood. The puppeteer actually controls the rack, which moves the hands and feet.

No part of the IK construction process is as critical as a firm understanding of the benefits of a control hierarchy. Basically, in a properly constructed IK system, you will never actually move any of the IK chain effectors themselves; you will always move controls that drive the effectors through constraints.

Setting explicit translations on the effectors themselves is a very bad idea. When you set an explicit translation keyframe on an effector, you are specifying a precise translation in space relative to the root of the chain at that point in the timeline. What happens if you want to move the root of the chain in one direction and the end of the chain in another? That would be very difficult without a control hierarchy. What if you want to move an IK parent, like a pelvis, without seeing the children of the hierarchy, like the feet, move as well? You are going to need a control hierarchy for that.

MAKING A MODEL

If you wanted two characters in the same scene to have the same control rig construction, you'd have to do something to ensure that the names of the rig elements did not conflict. Fortunately, XSI has a system to resolve this that carries with it a number of other advantages. If you make the control rig, the IK, and in fact everything that goes with each character into one "model" then the namespace of the model is separate from other model namespaces, and the elements inside these models may therefore be named the same things. So if you had two characters, Bill and Julie, Bill's right arm controller might be called Bill.RightArm while Julie's might be called Julie.RightArm.

Even better, Bill would have his own Mixer, and Julie would have her own Mixer, so the animation from one to the other would not get confused, and animation could be dragged and dropped back and forth easily because the names on everything inside the Mixer would be the same.

To make a model, select everything you want inside, the rig, the IK, any lights, or whatever else you want bound up together. Then in the Model module use the Create→Model→New command. Look in the explorer to see a new model icon as the root of all the stuff you had selected.

MAKING A MODEL SHAREABLE

One other benefit of a model is that it can be stored outside of your scene, in a separate file called an emdl file. Emdl files are stored in the Model directory of your project. When you store a model externally like this, the model can be referenced by other scenes. The advantage of this is that the original model file can change, and the results of that change will then be seen in all the scenes that reference the model file. You could use this to your advantage by setting up starter models stored externally for scene elements that are not yet finished, then collecting the referenced models into an assembled scene. As you, or other people, continued to work on the individual models, the assembled scene could be updated to reflect all those changes. Referenced models are a way to manage many people working in concert on a single scene.

To accomplish this, you must start by creating a model. In the Model property page, you must change the Storage option to External, and change the name of the model to "MyModel". Now, with the model selected, chose File→Export→Model to save the model externally, with the name "importme". Also save the scene file that the model was built in, since you will use that scene to modify the referenced model. Call this scene "ModelScene".

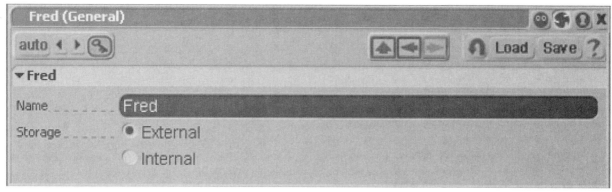

Make the Model sharable in the Model PPG

Exporting an external Model writes it to a separate file on disk.

Now you can start a new scene, and bring the referenced model into it with the File→Import→Referenced Model command. After you see the referenced model imported into the new scene, add a few more elements of your own just to differentiate this scene, and save it as "AssemblyScene".

This assembly scene now contains a reference back to the stored model that is saved externally on your disk in the Models folder.

You can make changes to that original referenced model, and see the changes reflected in the AssemblyScene. To see this in a clever way, launch two versions of XSI, and see the changes flow between them. Launch a new copy of XSI in the normal fashion.

Open the ModelScene into this copy, leaving the Assembly scene in the previous instance of XSI.

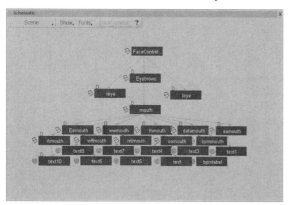

This is a hierarchy in the Schematic view.

Make some changes to the model you saved, by changing the shape of objects, adding color, or adding new elements to the Model hierarchy. Now, you must manually update the exported model to disk, so select the actual model in the explorer, named MyModel, and use the command File→Export→Model again, to write the model out once more with exactly the same name as before.

Now the Model on disk has been updated. Switch to the AssemblyScene version of XSI. It will still be showing the previous version of the Model file, since it has not yet been told to update.

Select the referenced model as a branch or a tree, and choose the Model→Update Referenced Model command to tell XSI to look to the disk for changes. You should now see the changes you made updated in the Assembly scene! This is a great way to bring a lot of work together in the beginning to rough out the scene, then progressively refine it.

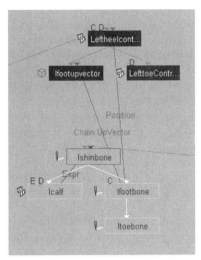

These are constraints in the Schematic view.

This is a control hierarchy for a pair of legs.

HIERARCHY VERSUS CONSTRAINTS

You already know how to parent objects together into a hierarchy. Hierarchies are great because the child object inherits all the transformations of the parent object, allowing motion to be layered on top of motion on top of motion. Using a hierarchy, you could first animate a finger curling, then the hand parent waving, then the arm waving, then the person jumping up and down, and then the ship that the person is on sailing away. The actual motion of the little finger would be a combination of all these motions. Another advantage is that the child does not have to be located in the same point in space as the parent to be transformed. The only downsides of hierarchies are that the child gets all the transformations from the parent, not just ones you might want, and that the child can never have more than one parent. That's where constraints come in. With constraints you can choose which of the transformations (S, R, T) you want transferred from one object to another, and an object can be driven by many constraints at once. To pin one item to another in space, you would constrain the translation, using a Position Constraint, an Object to Cluster Constraint, a 2-Point Constraint, or perhaps even a Path Constraint. To control the rotation of an object, you could use the Orientation Constraint or a Directional Constraint.

Constrain→Position hooks objects together in space, Constrain→Orientation controls the object rotation, and Constrain→Direction makes one object point at another at all times. Constraints allow you to pick and choose which transformation data you want from one object to drive another object. Expressions can take this farther and automate simple actions and relationships in the IK system. There is pretty much no downside to constraints.

It helps to think about the control hierarchy as the strings that operate the marionette. The effectors of the marionette are nailed onto tiny controls that are parented by strings onto the control rack. Above the controls for the effectors are more controls in a hierarchy to make up that rack. That's a control hierarchy, and it works the same way in Softimage|XSI as it does for a marionette.

Control hierarchies have another important function: they abstract one layer of movement from another, because each level of the hierarchy can have its own animation or not, depending on the needs. Thus, each new control level in the hierarchy gives you more flexibility and control over your model.

You can layer the effectors in a hierarchy by function to illustrate this. The effectors of the feet are controlled by foot controls. The foot controls are controlled by a pelvis control.

The Strategy of the Hierarchy

The hierarchy can do quite a few things for you, so you need to think about what you want before you hook things together with the Parent button. Remember that you can hook up the hierarchy from the top down, or from bottom up. Top-down means that you select the parent object, then activate the Parent button in the MCP and pick the children with your Left Mouse Button. Bottom-up means selecting the child object, activating the Parent button, and picking the parent object with your Middle Mouse Button.

Reusability

The hierarchy abstracts the animated elements from the actual IK chains. This means that the rigs you build will be reusable for a wide variety of characters. When the time comes to skin up a new character, you can just pull in a stock character rig, delete all the IK chains from it, move the controllers around to match the new proportions of this character, then draw in new IK Chains, hooking them up with constraints. Since a lot of your effort went into setting up the rig, this saves a lot of time.

Easier Enveloping

Once you're ready to envelope a character to all the IK you set up, it's important to keep the control hierarchy separate from the IK hierarchy. You must make sure that the IK chains and associated deformers are never in the same hierarchy as the controllers. The two should be totally separate. You can test this by selecting the top of the control hierarchy as a tree (Space bar and Right Mouse Button). When you do this, no IK should become selected. If it becomes selected, you have some contamination between your IK and the control hierarchy. Find it, and cut the IK loose from the controls.

If your IK is in the same hierarchy with the controls, you'll find it tough to envelope the skin to the IK without accidentally getting the controls added in as deformers. If that happened, moving the controllers would deform the skin, when what we want is for the controller to move the IK which deforms the skin.

Easy Selection

When you finally have a complex character all rigged up and ready to animate in a scene, you'll often find the whole assemblage of little black lines on the screen confusing, like a rats' nest of straight black hairs. The roots and effectors of IK chains are particularly hard to see since they look so much like nulls or other short line segments. Trying to even find an effector in a scene is just too hard to be productive. Since you build your own controllers, you can make them easy to spot, big enough that they won't blend in, distinct enough that they are easy to select, and with a helpful shape that visually directs you to the position of the driven element.

You can even change the colors of the controllers with the color palette layout switch in the bottom-left of the UI, or change the display method on the controllers themselves in their Display PPG; for instance, to make them display in wireframe even when the rest of the scene shows in hidden line.

AUTOMATIC ANIMATION AND LEVELS OF CONTROL

When you animate a parent object in a hierarchy, the children of that object inherits the animated transformations. This means that when you animate your legs controller, both individual right and left leg controllers will inherit that motion. It's obviously easier to animate one object than to animate two. In this way, building a hierarchy that makes sense for your character will save time. However, the hierarchy should not prevent you from animating each element separately. For instance, the previous example would only be useful if the character was hopping up and down with both feet at the same time. If the character wanted to move one foot independent of the other, you would then select just one foot and animate it, at a lower level in the hierarchy so that the transformations would not be shared to both feet. This concept is called Level of Control. You want to make it easy, but not prevent fine control.

EASIER ANIMATION

Since you'll be moving the character with the control hierarchy, it stands to reason that you will also be setting keyframes on the control hierarchy. You will also be storing animations on the control rig that can be used in the Mixer. Since that is true, time can be saved by using the hierarchy to store actions and save poses. If you select an entire hierarchy and choose the option Action➔Store➔Marked Parameters – Current Values, the transformations of each element in that hierarchy will be stored all at once. If you select a hierarchy as a tree then use Store➔Fcurves – Animated Parameters, then XSI will search through the tree for you, finding all the things you've keyed, and extract those animation curves to store in a single action. As you can see, having all the elements that you animate collected and organized into a hierarchy will save you a lot of effort.

ANIMATION RE-USE

You will eventually be saving animation as action clips, for use in the Mixer. These action clips are easy to save to disk as well. As a result, if you stored action clips on a generic control rig, you could recover them for use later on a completely different character, as long as that character used the same control rig. In fact, the control rig just has to be similar, since XSI can re-map animation in a clip between different elements. So, if you create a reusable control rig, you'll also be able to create a library of animation clips that might find use later.

BUILDING A SIMPLE CONTROL RIG

The previous description was a little abstract. The actual implementation is a lot easier. The plan now is to create a simple control rig for a pair of legs, to make it easy to animate them, easy to move them around in the scene, and easy to store animation actions.

Throughout this chapter you'll will build on your work, making it better and more sophisticated, so keep your work here, take the time to make it look good, and keep it organized.

*The center of the control is at the
point of the pyramid.*

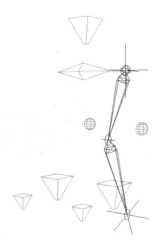

A simple 2-joint IK chain

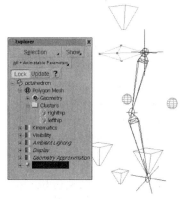

*Now the root and effector are con-
strained to controllers.*

The first step is to build a template control object that will be used to make the elements of the rig. I'm going to use polymesh cubes in this example because they make it plain that geometry has nothing to do with creating a control hierarchy for animation. In real-world production, technical directors often set up the rig with nulls, cones, implicits, or other objects. I use cubes that are modeled into inverted pyramids, because they are easier to see onscreen than controls and, therefore, easy to pick and set keyframes for in the animation phase.

To make the pyramid, get a polymesh cube and tag the four lowest vertices. Scale them down to almost a point. In center mode, move the center of the cube to directly below the tip of the pyramid, as if the pyramid was pointing to the center. Change back to Object mode. Name the pyramid "controller". This controller will be the template for a lot of others that will be made by just duplicating this one.

In the Right view, draw a two-joint 2D chain in the shape of a leg, with the knee rotated slightly. This will be the left leg, so shift it in negative X a few units.

Select your controller pyramid, and make a copy of it. Name it "leftHip". Place it near the root of the left leg. Select the root of the chain as a branch (Middle Mouse Button and Space bar) and then choose the Constrain Position command from the lower part of the MCP on the right edge of the screen. Pick the leftHip controller to complete the command. The IK chain will now jump to the position of the controller.

Duplicate your Controller again, and name it LeftHeel. Move it near to the effector. Select the effector, and use Constrain Position again to snap the effector to the LeftHeel controller.

Try both controllers out. When you select the leftHip controller and translate it, the top of the chain should move. When you select the LeftHeel controller and move it around, the effector should move. If this isn't the case, you've done something wrong, like constrained the objects in the wrong order. The IK elements should be selected, then constrained to the controllers.

By default, the IK solver type is set to the SI3D solver. As mentioned before, the XSI Solver has more options, so for each and every IK chain you build, select the first bone, open the PPG with the Enter key, and change the IK Solver Behavior to the Softimage|XSI Solver and the Solver Angles to Use Preferred Rotations. If you neglect to set this for each chain you add, you may experience unexpected results and a difficulty in control.

Repeat this process to build the right leg. While there are a few Duplicate Symmetry options, including one in the Skeleton menu, it's a better idea to build each one from scratch so you know it's right.

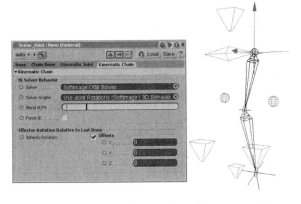

Be sure to always change the solver type to the Softimage\XSI Solver.

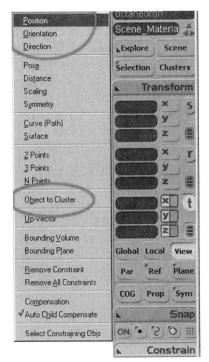

The Constrain➔Position menu cell

Now a hierarchy of the controllers must be built. Make one more duplicate of the controller and name it "hips". Move it to the center of the legs, up in the air between the leftHip and the rightHip. This controller needs to be the parent of the two hip controllers, so that when it is moved as a branch, both the left and right hips also move. Make it so.

Now each hip can be moved independently, or together, depending on what you want to animate.

Consider the heel controllers. If they were children of the hips, then every time that the hips moved, so would the heels. That would be bad, because it would be hard to move the two independently. When the hips moved, the feet would slide along the floor.

So, create another controller, place it between the heel controllers, and call it "feet". Make it the parent of the two pyramid heel controllers. Now you can animate the feet separately, or together.

There is still a problem, because the hip hierarchy of controls and the feet hierarchy of controls are not themselves connected in any way. There needs to be some controller above both of them, so that they can be hooked together in a way that leaves each one autonomous of the other. In other words: a hierarchy where the feet are not children of the hips.

Create another controller duplicate, called "COG" for center of gravity. Make it the parent of the hips and the feet.

Take a look at what you've done. There is a hierarchy of pyramid shaped controllers connected together with a parent-child relationship. The child controllers will inherit the scale, translation, and rotation of the parent controllers.

Then there are some loose IK chains, which are bound to those controllers with position constraints.

Try moving the controllers of the feet one at a time, or the controller of the hips as a branch, to see how you can control this puppet-rack-like arrangement. Select the hips and translate it up and down to see the legs bend. Try rotating the hips (in Branch mode) around the Y-axis to see how the rotation drives one Hip Controller forward and the other back. Experiment to get the full idea, and if you want, set explicit translation keys for first one foot moving forward, then the hips, and then the other foot, about every five frames. Remember to set a keyframe for each foot controller and the hips at each new point to keep the back foot planted while the front foot travels.

This simple rig has one other advantage. You can pick up the whole rig and move it somewhere else, or even scale it up (though you would have to lengthen the bones on the IK chains). Try this out by selecting the COG controller as a branch or tree, and translating it somewhere else in the scene. You should see all the other stuff, controllers and IK, move with it!

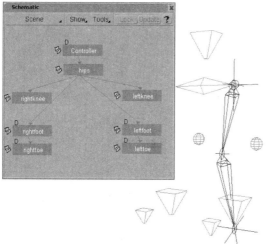

The hips are the parents of both leg controllers.

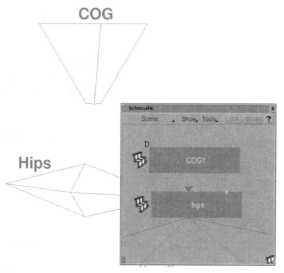

The COG is a level above the hips, and a level above the heels.

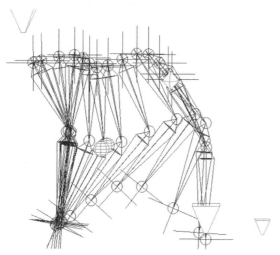

Key each foot and the hips every 15 frames.

If you make an error and wish to remove the constraint on an object, like the effector of an IK chain, select the constrained object (the slave object, the one that moves automatically) and use the Constrain→Remove All Constraints command to cut it loose.

For extra credit, pace up and down the nearest hallway and pay attention to the position of your pelvis relative to your feet at each point in your stride, and also to how your hip swings forward as you step forward. Generally, your pelvis remains centered between your feet at all times, and rotates slightly around Y as each foot steps forward. Because your legs are a fixed length, at your most extended point in each stride, your legs form a triangle with the floor, and your hips are lower (closer to the floor) at that point than at any other time in your stride. All these behaviors of the pelvis are easily set up with an expression, so they happen automatically as you move the feet of your creature.

USING CLUSTERS WITH IK

A variation on the constraint connection method is to use cluster constraints. Using this technique, you can hook objects together with physically rigid objects, such as cubes and octahedrons (or any model). The idea is to build an internal structure for your creature with solid geometry, and then attach the IK chains as appropriate.

Since you can have as many different clusters as you wish on an object, (limited by how many vertices it has) you can make up more flexible methods of constraining IK just where you want it.

Let's modify the hierarchy from the previous example to use a geometry object with cluster constraints to function as the hip. This will simplify the hierarchy a bit.

Get the pair of legs you just built, or make another pair. Delete the hips controller, and the leftHip and the rightHip.

Get a primitive circle, and adjust the number of points on the circle to be four, then freeze it. Scale it and move it between the legs, where the hip would be.

You want to define four clusters on this object: one for each hip socket, one for the spine, and one for the crotch. To make this easy to do, pop up a floating explorer with the 8 key, then frame the circle with the F key. Lock the explorer, and expand the Polygon Mesh→Clusters folder. There are no clusters now, but there will be soon. Name the circle "hips".

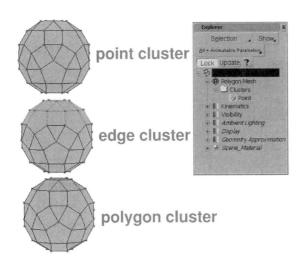

point cluster

edge cluster

polygon cluster

A cluster is a group of components that is saved with a name for future reference.

A circle with four points, scaled to be pelvis-shaped

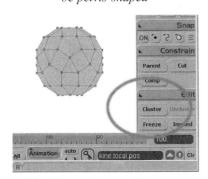

The Cluster button only appears when you have components selected.

Creating clusters is easy. Tag the one point on the left corner of the hips with the T hotkey, and in the MCP look to the bottom to click on the Cluster button. You should now be able to expand out the Clusters folder in the MCP, and see the newly created cluster. Tap the Enter key to pop up the General PPG for the new cluster, and name it "leftHip". You can also right-click over the cluster in the explorer to get a context menu that includes the ability to rename the cluster.

Now tag the other side, make it a cluster in the same way, and name it "rightHip". Make the top point into a cluster called "spine' and the bottom point into a cluster named "crotch".

Attaching the IK roots to these new clusters works differently that when you did the Constraint by Position. You really must have the explorer up, showing the clusters, and Locked, so that it doesn't recycle when you select the IK root.

Select the IK root, the top of the left chain, and choose the command Constrain Object to Cluster from the Constrain menu in the bottom right MCP. Now pick on the leftHip cluster in the explorer to finish constraining the IK root to the leftHip cluster.

Select the other IK chain and use Constrain Object to Cluster to attach it to the rightHip cluster. We won't do anything with the other clusters just yet.

Check your work by loading the scene HumanIK1 and comparing it to your own work.

If you make a mistake, and accidentally constrain something incorrectly, the best way to remove the errant constraint without damaging everything else is to identify which object the constraint went on (this object was selected when you made the mistake), then open a Schematic view and frame the object. You should see a line running from the constrained object to another object, with the name of the constraint on it. (If not, make sure the Show menu has Constraint Links checked to be visible.) You can select the Constraint by clicking on the name of the constraint in the middle of the blue line connecting the contrainer and the constrainee, and delete it with the Delete key on your keyboard.

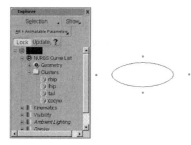

Now the circle is named hips, and has four clusters.

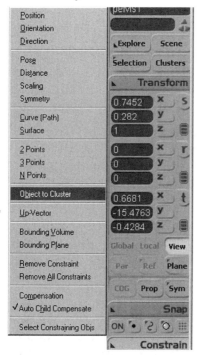

Use Constrain→Object to Cluster to snap an object onto a cluster forever.

THE COG AND GPS

All the animation in the rig must be stored relative to some other object. In fact, everything in the rig is ultimately relative to whatever element is at the top of the rig hierarchy. This part of the hierarchy will stay put in space as the rest of the character animates away from it. We can call this element at the top of the control rig the GPS, for global positioning system. It's what all the animation on the character will ultimately be relative to. This can be very important for game development or other cases where the actual location of the final IK effectors must be cooked down and exported, but it also just makes your work easier. You can animate the character with the GPS at 0,0,0 then pick up the whole rig and put it somewhere else in the scene, like on a boat or a plane.

The COG is a similar idea, and stands for center of gravity. The COG is the next element in the hierarchy down from the GPS. Imagine that if your character decided to take up competition high diving, that the character rig would have to be able to twist and rotate as the character dove into the water. The COG would be the pivot point around which the body spun. If the character walks forward, it will walk away from this center point.

Add the COG and GPS to your leg control hierarchy (your legs might already have a COG – in that case, just add the GPS). First, get a primitive null and name it GPS. Leave it at the global origin, 0,0,0. Get another object – this time an implicit sphere, which will help remind you that it is a pivot – and name it COG. Make the GPS the parent of the COG. Make the COG the parent of the hips.

The GPS and everything below it can be made into a model if you wish.

Save your work.

CONTROLLING THE RESOLUTION PLANE

Right now the legs work just fine as long as they walk straight forward, and you never try to select the whole rig and rotate it. If you do try to turn the body, you run into a severe problem, which is that there is no way of controlling which direction the knees are pointing. Without being able to point the knees, the direction that the character walks can't ever be changed. You must learn to control the knee direction, and to do that you need to practice some terminology and add some controls to the rig.

Back in the IK chapter I explained that the orientation of the IK chain was called the resolution plane, and that the resolution plane was always perpendicular to the local Z-axis of the first joint in a 2D chain like these legs. So, if you can control the local Z-axis, you can control the resolution plane, and therefore which direction the knees point.

Get an implicit primitive sphere, and scale it down to be small enough so that it doesn't obscure anything on the screen, but large enough to easily select. Leave it at 0,0,0, freeze the transformations, and name this object "resplanecontroller". This will be the template for the many resolution plane controllers you will need to make in this chapter.

You can remove a constraint with the menu, or in the Schematic.

Duplicate it and name the duplicate "leftKneeController".

Move the leftKneeController behind the left knee, in line with the current resolution plane of the IK leg.

Next, create an up vector constraint on the first joint of the leg, using the leftKneeController as the picked reference. Select the first joint of the leg (the one next to the root), and choose the Skeleton➔Chain Up Vector command from the Animate module. Pick on the implicit sphere you named leftKneeController.

The knee should stay pointing forward, and now be directed in the opposite direction from the implicit sphere. If the knee snaps backwards, the sphere will need to be in front of the sphere. Either front or back is OK, but if the knee flips it indicates that you have built your legs facing backwards, in the negative direction along whichever axis they are aligned with (negative Z, if you built in the Right view).

The kneeController should be placed far enough away from the top of the IK chain that no matter where the effector is, it will not go on the opposite side of the Controller. If the IK effector can move from being in front of the resplanecontroller to being in back of the controller, the chain will flip suddenly as the effector goes past the controller. This is normal; just be careful to keep the controller far enough away from the IK chain that this does not happen.

Now the most important question must be considered: where should the leftKneeController be attached in the control rig hierarchy? If it isn't attached at all, it won't move with the character when it's animated, and thus would be very difficult to use. The leftKneeController needs to be put somewhere that will make animation easiest and most automatic, without sacrificing any flexibility later on.

The best place to add the resplanecontroller would generally be as a child of whatever rig object is driving the root of the chain that the controller is also affecting. In this case, the leftKneeController should become a child of the hips. That way, when the hips are rotated in Branch mode, the knees will automatically be pointed with the hips. When the hips are animated forwards and backwards, the controllers will also move with them, keeping position relative to the IK chains they control. However, attaching them to the hips doesn't sacrifice any flexibility, because you can also animate the controllers relative to the hips to make the knees flap around, changing the resolution plane of the leg, as if your character was practicing his golf swing.

Make the hips the parent of the leftKneeController, then make another duplicate of the controller template object and repeat the process for the right knee so that the resolution plane of each is controlled by an implicit sphere in the control rig.

Check your work by loading the scene HumanIK2 and comparing it to your own work.

ORGANIZING WITH LAYERS

The layer control panel is a useful tool for working with control rigs. If you think about it, you want your control objects to be visible and selectable, but you don't want them to render in the final scene. You want the IK chains and other deformer elements to be visible and selectable until you do the weighting, and then you'll want them to be invisible and unselectable.

The resolution plane is the orientation of the whole IK chain in space.

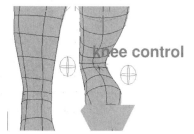

The KneeController is an up vector on the first bone, located behind the knee.

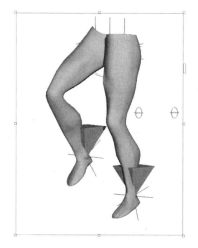

Two finished legs, with KneeControls.

You want the envelope (the skin) to be visible and selectable until you finish adjusting weighting, then you want it to be visible but unselectable.

Open your legs scene and put all the control rig elements on a separate layer called "control rig".

Make a third layer (remember that the default layer still exists) called IK. Select all the IK chains, perhaps with the Chain Element selection filter in the MCP, and move it all to that new layer.

Make one more layer for the envelope, which doesn't exist in your scene at all yet.

Remember that when you add elements they will go to the currently active layer, which might confuse you if that layer happened to be invisible. So, to make sure that doesn't happen, use the drop menu in the MCP to make the Default layer the active layer.

Save your work.

WHERE TO PUT CUSTOM CONTROLS

When you get farther along in the creation of a character, you'll be making custom controls, sliders, and expressions to automate the physics of the character. What needs to be considered now is where to place those custom controls. If the custom controls are added to the control rig hierarchy, they will be much easier to animate. That's because all you'll have to do is set keys on the control rig and on the custom controls, then use the Store→Fcurves – Animated Parameters command which will search through the entire selected hierarchy looking for animated properties, and then bind all those animated properties it finds into a single Action clip.

So, placing the custom Psets on the control rig is a good idea. The remaining question is simply where on the control rig to place the Psets. Since they can be anywhere, it makes sense to put them somewhere easy to remember, and easy to get at. By default, you should choose to add them to the top element in the control rig hierarchy, which in this example is the GPS null.

Select the GPS null, and use the Create Parameter→New Custom Parameter Set command to add a custom property page called "CustomControls". Look at the explorer view to verify that it has been created. We won't do anything with it yet, but it's always a good idea to think ahead.

LIMITING RANGE OF MOTION

Your pair of legs now can walk, jump, or run, but it is also true that they can be posed in unrealistic ways. For instance, there is nothing stopping you from swinging them up and over the body in a complete circle.

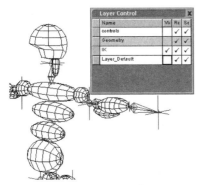

Organize your IK and rig into separate layers.

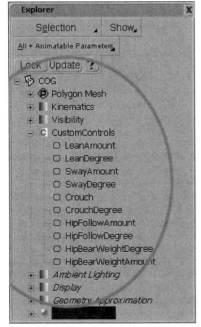

Placing custom controls at the top of the rig hierarchy makes them easy to find and key.

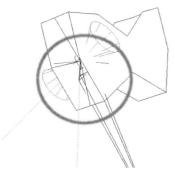

Limiting joint rotation is not always a good idea.

A natural urge for the technical director is to prevent that from happening, by limiting the possible rotation of the joint. While that is certainly possible, using the Rotation Limits built into each joint in the Joint PPG, it is not a good idea.

If you assign rotation limits to a joint – for instance, the top of the IK chain – the chain will stop rotating suddenly and unexpectedly when it hits the limit you set. If you are not very careful how you set those limits, the chain may have a tendency to pop around the limits that you set, or become difficult to pose where you want it.

Real animators solve the problem of limiting how the character can behave by just being careful how they pose the character. If you really want to have hard limits on the behavior of a chain, it is a better idea to use bounding volume constraints, not rotation limits. To try this method out, get a primitive implicit sphere, and scale it up to surround just the bottom half of the left leg. Make this sphere a child of the Hips controller, so that it will move with the Hips when they are animated.

Now select the leftHeelController (which should be inside the implicit sphere) and use the Constrain→Constrain Volume command to add a volume constraint operator to the LeftHeelController. Try selecting and translating the LeftHeelController. See that it will not ever leave the bounding volume of the implicit sphere. You can now scale and position your sphere to limit the range of motion of the heelController, and therefore of the leg.

At this point you may be thinking "Hmmm… could I use this for floor and collision detection?" Good question. The answer is yes.

IK CONTROLS FOR FEET

Look at your HumanIK2 scene, or load a fresh copy from the courseware. The goal is now to expand on this rig, add in more details, and build towards a complete human skeleton. The first step is to complete the simple foot controls for the ankle, as well as the parts of the rig that will control the side roll of the foot.

In the Right view, draw a two-joint 2D IK chain starting below the heel controller, and ending at the length of the foot. The second joint will control the bend of the shoe or foot on the character. Make sure you draw the IK chain with a slight bend upwards at the toe, to set the correct inside and outside of the preferred axis. Select the root of that chain, and constrain it by position to the leftHeelController. The foot bones should be a bit under the heel, so activate the Comp button (short for Constraint Compensate) in the MCP and then translate the IK chain down in Y a bit, to offset the attachment point of the constraint. Turn off the Comp button right away before you accidentally use it again. Name the new IK chain "leftFoot".

Make a new duplicate of the pyramid-shaped controller template, scale it to about half size, name it lefttoeController and place it in the general vicinity of the effector of the leftToe IK chain. Select the Effector and constrain it by position to the new, smaller lefttoeController.

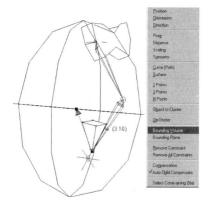

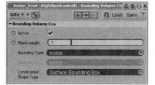

Now the heel controller cannot leave the implicit sphere volume.

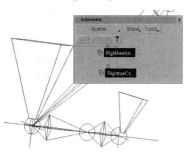

The toe controller is a child of the heel controller

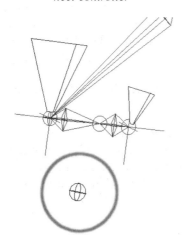

The ankleControl keeps the foot roll under your control.

Now the position of the IK in the bottom of the foot is controlled, but not the orientation of the foot. In other words, nothing controls the roll of the IK in the foot from side to side. If you don't build this ability into your rig, it is inevitable that something will go wrong and the foot will go upside down and you won't be able to do a thing about it. So, make another copy of the implicit sphere you are using as a template for the up vector constraint, and move it directly above the foot. Name that new sphere the "ankleController". Select the first joint of the leftFoot IK, and use the Skeleton➔Chain UpVector command, then pick the ankleController to make sure that the Foot IK chain will always point up at the ankleController part of the rig.

The new pyramid and sphere controllers we just built are not yet part of the rig hierarchy, so we need to add them in. If the larger controller is the heel, then it makes sense that both the toeController and the ankleController would be children of that heel. Make it so.

Repeat this process for the rightFoot, creating IK and controls to drive the end effector and to control the resolution plane of the foot. Make sure you hook up the controls into a hierarchy, with the new control objects as children of the heel controller.

Save this rig in your own project as HumanIK3.

This is a simple foot rig that will be controllable. It doesn't do any fancy auto rolls as feet lift or anything like that. We'll add some automatic features to it later when we write expressions to automate the physics of the rig. If you wish to explore other foot rig construction, investigate Michael Isner's interesting foot roll in the Primitive➔Model➔Rig - Man IK hierarchy.

CONTROLLING LEG IK WITH TWO CONSTRAINTS

If you open your own HumanIK3 scene, or the one included in the course materials, you will note that if you properly select the heel controller of one leg as branch, so that all the downstream controllers of the toe and ankle are also selected, you can move the Heel controller around to flex the leg. You can also point the knee in any direction that you wish by acting on the kneeController. You can also now roll the foot side to side by acting on the ankleController. However, if you move the foot out to the side of the body and lift it up a ways, you'll notice that the ankle does not rotate by itself in the same way that the human ankle would.

In a human, the ankle always rotates to keep the foot perpendicular to the direction of the hip. Think about it: as you lift your leg, as if in a side-kick, your foot also rotates, going from flat to the floor when the foot is down, to flat against the wall when your leg is out horizontally. If you were making a side-kick, you would then control the angle of the ankle slightly to extend the heel out, protecting your toes.

This is an example of how your rig needs to be both automatic and flexible to adjust. In general you'll want the ankle to turn over on its own as the foot lifts, but you will also want to be able to animate it yourself to get the look you want.

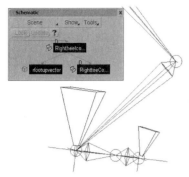

The heel controller is the parent of both the toe and ankle controllers.

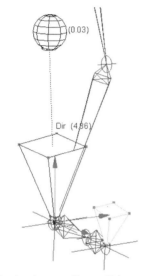

The heel controller will be constrained to point to this sphere near the hip.

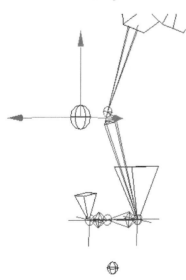

Now the Y-axis of the controller points to the FootOrientation sphere.

This is possible by constraining the direction of the heelController. If you consider the hierarchy, you'll note that the ankleController, which actually does the work of turning the foot over, is a child of the heelController. Therefore, if you were to select the heelController and rotate it, the ankleController would move in space relative to that heelController. We also know that the Direction Constraint is there to help control the orientation of objects, just like the heelController.

Another rig object is needed to aim the heelController at, however. This object will be placed near the hip, slightly to the outside of the body. When this is done, the foot will always stay perpendicular to that control object automatically, and you'll be able to adjust the angle of the foot to the ground (technically called the camber) just by moving that controller around.

To do this, make another copy of the implicit sphere template, name it "leftFootOrientation", and place it above and outside of the left side of the hip.

Select the leftHipController, and examine the local axis by just activating the Translation cells and clicking on the Local mode. This pops up a local axis display so you can see what axis is pointing in the direction you want. What axis is pointing up from the foot towards the hips? If you made the controller template and then froze all the transformations, the local Y-axis should be the one you want, so keep that in your mind for a moment. Now with the heelController selected use the Constrain→Direction command, and then pick on the new leftFootOrientation control object. The foot will most likely snap to a strange angle, because you need to verify which axis is being pointed at the leftFootOrientation controller.

With the heelController still selected, look in the Selection explorer, within the Constraints folder under the Local Transforms properties, and click on the icon for the Direction Cns. Look in the Align Axis area. There will be a one (1) in the axis that is being oriented, and a zero (0) in the others. Move the digit 1 to the Y-axis, and make sure the others are zero, to set the axis of orientation to local Y. Now see how the foot is oriented.

You still need to consider where to place the new leftFootOrientation controller in the control rig hierarchy. You really want this controller to move automatically when the hips move, but also be independently animatable, so it seems as if that direction controller should be a child of the hips. Make it so.

Repeat the process for the other foot.

Now select either heel controller as a branch, and move it around. Note that the foot stays properly oriented, aiming at the hips now. You can also move the footOrientation controller manually to adjust the roll of the foot.

Save the file as HumanIK4.

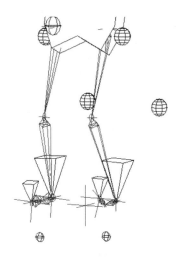

Two completed feet and legs, with rig and constraints

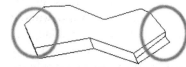

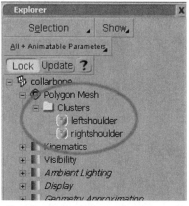

Duplicate the hips and rename all the clusters for the collarbone.

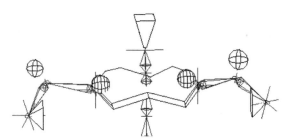

Add in the IK with position constraints and Object to Cluster constraints.

IK Controls for Arms and Hands

The structure of the upper body is very much the same as the lower body, at least up to the wrists. Follow this recipe to build the upper body, ignoring the spinal column for the moment.

You need a collarbone to hang the arms on. The fastest way to make one is to duplicate the hips, change the name to "collarbone", and lift it up in the Y direction to the approximate location of the collarbone on a character.

When you duplicate an object, the clusters are retained, and the object is connected in a hierarchy as a child of the same parent as the original object. Select the COG in Branch mode (Middle Mouse Button) to verify that both the hips and the new collarbone are selected. If not, select the collarbone and use the Cut button a few times to make sure that it isn't in a hierarchy at all, then make it a child of the COG, so that if your character needed to, both the upper and lower body could rotate around the center of gravity.

You'll want to rename the clusters on the collarbone, which now have the same names as the clusters on the hips. The quickest way to do this is to select the collarbone, then use the Clusters explorer in the MCP to select one cluster, say, the leftHip. Tap the Enter key to pop up the general PPG for the cluster, and change the name to "leftShoulder". Repeat this technique to change the name of the rightHip cluster to "rightShoulder".

Duplicate the pyramid controller template to make the leftWrist and the rightWrist. Make both the children of the collarbone. Make two copies of the implicit sphere controller, for the leftElbow and rightElbow, and make them children of the collarbone as well. Move the new controllers to the appropriate sides of the body.

In the Right view, draw a simple two-joint 2D chain, change it to use the XSI Solver type as you've done before, and then hook it in to the control rig using constraints as you did with the legs. Select the root, and use a Constrain→Object to Cluster to hook it to one cluster on the collarbone, then select the effector and use Constrain→Position to hook it to the wrist. Select the first joint and use the Skeleton→Chain Up Vector command to constrain the direction of the elbow to the elbow controller. Move everything around a bit to make it look nice afterwards. If your IK wasn't long enough, or was too long, just open the Bone PPG and adjust the Bone length. Do not scale the bone using the Scale transform cells.

You won't bother with creating an automatic orientation for the wrists like you did for the ankle, since your wrists move around on their own so much more. You'll just have to orient them and save keyframes manually. The Wrist controller is simply to place the location of the wrists in space, as if the character was waving his arms, or flapping his wings. The more complex and subtle twists of the forearm and wrist will be covered separately.

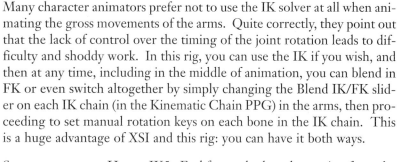

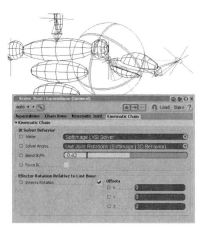

Each chain can be animated with both Inverse and Forward Kinematics.

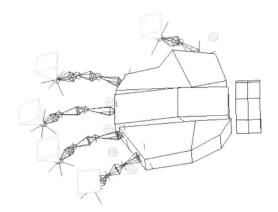

This a completed hand rig.

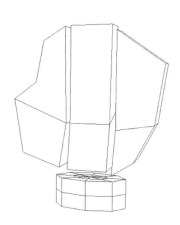

The cylindrical wrist will become the parent of the hand assembly

Many character animators prefer not to use the IK solver at all when animating the gross movements of the arms. Quite correctly, they point out that the lack of control over the timing of the joint rotation leads to difficulty and shoddy work. In this rig, you can use the IK if you wish, and then at any time, including in the middle of animation, you can blend in FK or even switch altogether by simply changing the Blend IK/FK slider on each IK chain (in the Kinematic Chain PPG) in the arms, then proceeding to set manual rotation keys on each bone in the IK chain. This is a huge advantage of XSI and this rig: you can have it both ways.

Save your scene as HumanIK5. Feel free to look at the version from the courseware to make sure you have it all right.

IK AND CONTROLS FOR HANDS

Hands are quite complicated. There are, according to www.wrist-hand.com, more than 25 bones in each hand. That's more complexity in each hand than you'll need in the entire rest of the body. You need to decide how important a full range of motion really is to your character, and whether building it justifies the cost in time and model complexity. If your character's hands won't be seen much, keep the construction simple and animate them with shapes or deformations. However, if your fingers must do the walking, or your character must play piano without flaw, or rhythmically tap his fingers on a table, you might need some IK. In this example I'll build a fairly complex hand rig that you may choose to simplify for your needs.

As is usual for the upper body, good character animators tend to prefer to use Forward Kinematics to animate the fingers, which means setting rotation keys on the finger joints, rather than position keys on the finger tip controllers. You'll build the ability to use both or either method.

The wrist is where the action of the hand starts. The wrist rotation twists all the bones of the hand, and therefore the fingers as well. You need to build the rigid part of the wrist and the meaty parts of the hand.

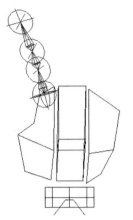

Draw one finger, then duplicate it for the others.

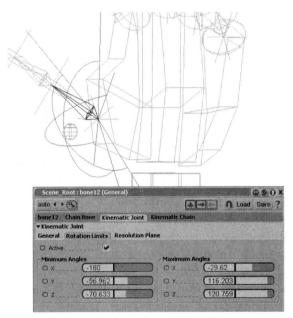

Rotation limits make sense on fingers.

Each finger is a different length – adjust the bone lengths.

Get a primitive polygon cylinder, and shorten it up in Y, then squash it in Z to take on the proportions of the cross section of the wrist. Freeze the transformations and the operator stack. This will become the rigid part of the wrist that anchors the skin there. Above the wrist lies the palm. The palm is essentially split into three pieces lengthwise, so that you can fold your palm, touching your pinkie to your thumb. Make three polygon cubes, one for the section of palm running from the wrist to the smaller two fingers, one for the middle section, and one between the wrist and the thumb. You can sculpt these a bit if you wish just for form, but the shape will have no effect on the results. Freeze the transforms and the operator stack. Move the pieces into position above the wrist as shown. You want the two outside parts to be able to rotate around the middle, so move their centers to the center of the middle cube, and make the center piece the parent of the two outside pieces. Make the wrist cylinder the parent of the middle portion so that they are all now in a hierarchy. You will probably never have to animate using these parts, but just in case your character needs to cup a hand, they'll be there.

The IK of the fingers attaches to these cubes. Your hand should be facing open in the Front window, so draw an IK chain, using the Skeleton→Draw 2D Chain command in the Right view. Make three segments, running from the knuckle to the midsection to the fingertip. Look at your index finger as you work to get the right proportions for the bones, and the correct, slight curve inwards. You'll set up this finger, then duplicate it for the other three fingers. Change the IK solver type to Softimage|XSI in the Kinematic Chain PPG, and prepare to set some rotation limits on the first joint. Rotate the first joint in the preferred axis, Z, to the most extended position you could ever have, slightly more rotated than straight out flat.

Look at the Z Rotation cell in the MCP to see whether that was making the local rotation of the joint greater or smaller. Remember that if the number is already negative, like -86, it might look like it's getting bigger when it's actually getting smaller, like –178. Use the Skeleton→Set Minimum Rotation Limit menu command to add rotation limits for most negative rotation of this pose. Now rotate the first joint in local Z to a pose that is bent 90 degrees positive from the previous minimum, as if the character was walking on his knuckles. If you cannot rotate in Z any more, perhaps the rotation limit became set incorrectly. Open the Rotation Limits tab of the Kinematic Joint PPG for that first bone to check it out.

When you have the joint rotated to the other extreme, set the Skeleton→Set Maximum Rotation Limits. The problem with this is that the rotation in the other axes just got set too strictly. There should be some play in the Y-axis so that the finger can wag back and forth from the knuckle. Select the bone, tap Enter to pop the Bone PPG, and adjust the Rotation Limits for the Y-axis to have +/- 20 degrees of play on either side.

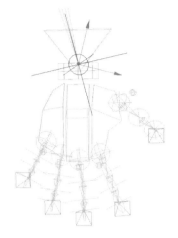

Now the wrist is aligned with the wrist controller, palm down, fingers out.

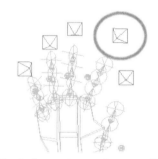

Each fingertip needs a small controller to drive the effector of that finger.

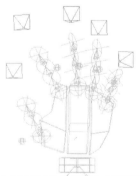

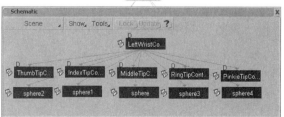

The hand rig looks like this: wrist controller parent of all the fingers.

Name this finger "indexFinger". Leave it where it is for now.

Duplicate the finger, and use the bone length PPG to adjust the size, making it a bit bigger to match your middle finger. Name it "middleFinger". Repeat for the remaining two fingers, "ringFinger" and "pinkieFinger".

Now you may distribute the fingers to the correct locations, at the ends of the three polygon cubes you made earlier. The smaller two fingers go above the outside palm side, and the larger two fingers go on the middle section. Note that the fingers do not start the same distance from the wrist. Make the polygon sections the parents of the fingers. Select each finger as a branch from the root and splay them a little by rotating them out from each other.

Make a two-joint chain for the thumb, place it to the side of the third section, make it a child of that section, and orient it in a way that pleases you.

You may now select the wrist object as a tree, which will select everything in the hand you just built, and move it to the position of the wrist controller in the control rig. Rotate the whole wrist so that it is facing straight out from the body, palm down. The better the hand assembly is oriented along the global axes now, the easier it will be to hook up. Select the Wrist as a branch again, and constrain it by position to the wristController. It will jump in space slightly.

Duplicate the pyramidal controller template, and make it much smaller. Move it over the index finger tip, and name it "indexTipController". Check the accompanying images to ensure that your finger and controller are oriented correctly. Duplicate the pyramid for each digit, changing the names appropriately to "middleTipController", "ringTipController", "pinkieTipController" and "thumbTipController".

Make each of these a child of the wristController, so that when the wrist moves or rotates, the fingers will change orientation correctly.

Constrain the effector of each finger chain by position to the appropriate finger tip controller. Now the base of the finger IK chains are controlled because they are children of the hand and wrist assembly, and the effectors are controlled with position constraints to elements in the control rig.

Save your work as HumanIK6.

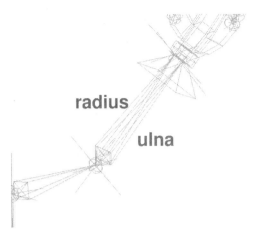

There are two bones, the radius and the ulna, in the human forearm.

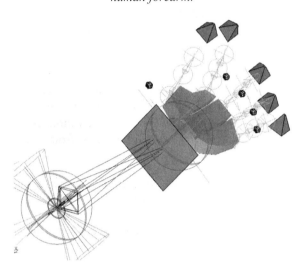

The orientation of the wrist assembly will be driven by the orientation of the wrist controller.

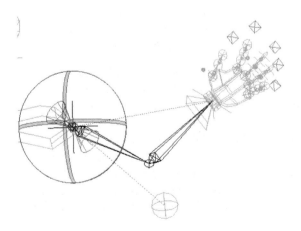

Normal two-bone IK hierarchy for the forearm

IK AND ROTATION FOR FOREARMS

Unless your character is some sort of robot, with a bearing race around the wrist to rotate the hand, you'll need to carefully examine how the rotation of wrist deforms the skin of the forearm. Look at your own arm, and rotate the wrist. The skin around the wrist doesn't twist as the wrist turns over, the skin all the way along the forearm gradually twists, distributing the change along the entire length of the forearm.

You can simulate this easily, which will make your hand animation much more fluid, and easy to deal with. As an added bonus, the weighting of the envelope around the wrist will be better.

The secret is simply that you need two bones in the forearm, just like humans have in our real forearms.

Both bones should start at the same place in the elbow, but should connect, via constraints, to slightly on either side of the wrist structure you just built.

That means that the effectors of the forearm bones will not be driven by a position constraint to the WristController part of the control rig; instead, the effectors of the forearm bones will be made children of the wrist structures, and then the wrist structure will be constrained by both position and orientation to the wristController.

Let's get started. Make sure the wrist assembly is located right where you want it, with the center of the wrist cylinder, which is the parent of that hierarchy, near the center of the wrist controller. Take a look at those centers, by turning on the Show➜Centers option in the Show (eyeball) menu for the camera view.

You want the wrist to rotate when the controller is rotated. That's easy, you can just add an orientation constraint. Before you do that, though, you need to know which axis on the wrist to match to which axis on the controller. Make a mental note of which is which in your scene. In mine, I want to orient the Y-axis on the wrist cylinder to the Y-axis on the controller. With the wrist assembly selected as a branch, use the Constrain➜Orientation command, then in the PPG for that constraint, adjust the oriented axis to be what you want.

The wrist assembly should also be constrained in space to the controller. Make it so.

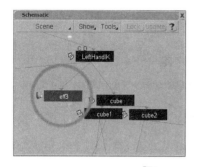

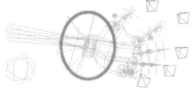

Now the effector is a child of the wrist assembly.

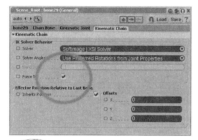

Force IK means that the effector moves relative to the new parent, even without keys set on it.

You now have the wrist assembly controlled by the wristController, but you haven't done anything about the bones in the forearm yet. Pop open a Schematic view, and look at how the forearm IK is currently organized.

The effector is a child of the root, which is normal, and then is constrained by position to the wristController. Select that effector and remove the position constraint with the Constrain→Remove Constraint command.

In XSI, the effector doesn't actually need to be in the same hierarchy as the root. Exploit this fact by selecting the effector, and then cutting it. Now you have a totally loose effector that still works as usual, driving the rotation of the bones. Move the effector to the middle of the cylindrical part of the wrist assembly. This is where it would attach if you did not want the forearm to twist.

Now move the effector away from the center slightly, towards the thumb side of the palm, still inside the cylinder. Make the cylinder the parent of the effector. Name this bone the "radius".

Now you need to draw another single-bone IK chain, starting from the elbow and ending at the wrist, on the other side of the wrist cylinder from the first effector you made. Select the root of this new IK chain, and make it a child of the upper arm bone by using the Parent button and the Middle Mouse Button. Select the new effector and cut it from the root, and then make it a child of the wrist cylinder as well.

One last thing must be done to make the effectors follow this new parent. Select the first bone of the two-bone arm chain, and tap Enter to pop up the Chain Bone PPG. In the Kinematic Chain tab, toggle on Force IK to make the IK solver work in this new configuration. Repeat with the other one-joint chain you built.

Now try out your assembly. Select the pyramid-shaped wristController and rotate it in Local mode to gently rotate the wrist. The whole wrist assembly, fingers and all, should now spin, and the bones should twist slightly about themselves. Return the wrist assembly back to a flat, palm-down position, and repeat the process for the other side of the body.

When you are done, name your scene HumanIK7, and if you wish, examine the HumanIK7 scene from the courseware to see if your scene is built the same way.

IK AND CONTROLS FOR SPINAL COLUMN

The spine of your character should be made with a 3D IK chain. That chain should have just enough segments to describe the curve of the spine, but no more. Keep the number of bone segments as low as possible to simplify things.

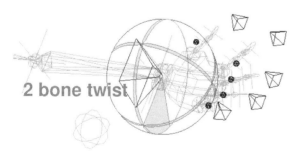

2 bone twist

Now the twist of the wrist takes place gradually all along the forearm.

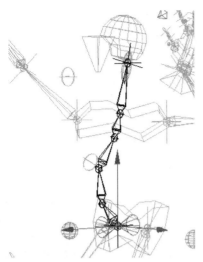

The spine goes bottom to top, from the hips to the collarbone.

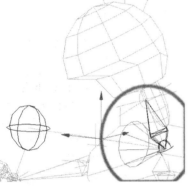

Now the IK chain has two roots and one effector!

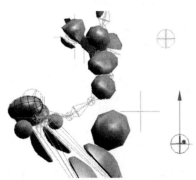

The BellyControl sphere points the gut in the right direction.

In the Right view, draw a 3D chain, starting at the base of the spine, near the top of the hips controller. Drop three bones in the belly and chest, then end one more bone right in the middle of the collarbone, end another bone at the base of the neck, and a last bone at the end of the spine, slightly inside the skull.

Change the IK solver type and chain behavior to Softimage|XSI Solver and Use Joint Rotations.

Select the root of the spine, and constrain it to the top cluster in the middle of the hips. Using the top cluster instead of a position constraint to the center will help the character bend at the waist convincingly.

Select the bone that starts at the center of the collarbone and progresses up the neck. Choose the Constrain by Position command, and pick the collarbone. This causes something special to happen. That bone now becomes a Pseudo-root, which means that the IK spine is now controlled by a root at the top and at the bottom. Make another duplicate of your pyramid shaped controller template and name it skullController. Move it near the effector of the IK spine that sticks out of the collarbone, and then constraint that effector to the new skullController. Make the skullController a child of the collarbone so that by default the head will move with the collarbone, which will move with the hips.

Now you need to control the twist of the spine, with a few up vector constraints. Later, when you build expressions to automate some skeletal physics, you'll cook up an expression to do an even better job of spine twisting.

Make a copy of your implicit sphere template object, scale it down a bit, name it "bellyControl", and move it in front of the character's stomach, directly on center. Select the first bone at the base of the spine, choose the Skeleton→Up Vector command, and pick the new bellyControl to complete the command. Make the bellyControl a child of the hips, so that by default the belly points in the direction of the hips. Make another implicit sphere copy, name it "headControl", and move it up to the neck level, in front of the rig.

Select the first bone above the collarbone, the PsuedoRoot bone, and again constrain the up vector of that bone to the headControl. Make the headControl a child of the collarbone.

Save your work as HumanIK8.

BUILDING IN RIGIDITY

Now you have a good control rig that will move the IK around, but if you look at the IK itself, you'll notice that all you've really added are limbs that bend. There are a lot of other skeletal structures in the human body that exist to add rigidity to the finished person, that protect internal organs, and that provide structure and support for muscles and flesh. If your character doesn't have these skeletal elements as well as his long bones in the arms and legs, the character will be prone to squash and deform in places you don't want, when his arms and legs bend.

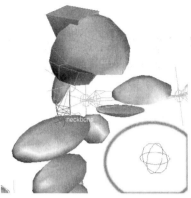

The HeadControl is an up vector constraint to aim the neck.

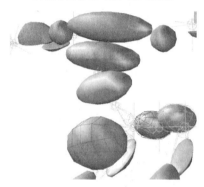

This sphere will become a deformer, controlling the swell and jiggle of the gut.

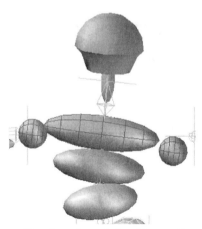

The clavicle and shoulders will help deform the upper chest.

Since XSI can use any geometry object as an IK deformer, the plan will be to use primitive shapes that you scale and rotate to help visualize the internal structures you are building. The actual shape and size of the object will make no difference in the end, since the skin around it will be weighted by distance to the center of the object, but you can still make objects that help you see how the body is put together.

Start with the belly. Get a primitive sphere, scale is down to fit within the belly region, freeze the transformations, and place it in front of the spine near the first bone. Make it a child of that bone. Now the sphere will move with that IK bone, and will also become a deformer when the skin is eventually added to this rig. You will be able to deform the belly by moving the sphere, scaling the sphere, or rotating the sphere. Name the sphere "belly". Add another sphere, slightly wider, to the middle of the torso, slightly in front of the spine. Name it "diaphragm" and make sure it's a child of the nearest convenient spinal bone.

Make one more sphere, rather wider still, and name it "clavicle". Make it a child of the bone in the middle of the collarbone.

The shoulders are a particularly vulnerable area, and quite hard to weight appropriately, because when the arms swing in they tend to collapse the chest skin, and contort the skin around the shoulders. You can minimize this by adding some structures in the shoulders to help hold the skin down. Make two more smaller spheres, and place one at each end of the clavicle, about where the shoulder joint is. Make these spheres children of the clavicle. Since the clavicle is itself a child of the IK spine, all three spheres will become IK deformers later on.

Now add a pair of pelvis structures. Place small spheres near the outside of the hips controller, about where the hip sockets would be. Make each a child of the Root of the spine IK. These will help stabilize the skin as it stretches between the legs, the buttocks, and the lower back.

Finally, you need a skull for this creature. Take a polygon sphere, and model it into a rough skull shape. Freeze it, and place it atop the last bone in the neck. Make it a child of the Effector of the neck IK. This structure will help provide rigidity for the skin around the scalp and the ears, so it won't stretch oddly when the arms move.

Save your work as HumanIK9.

BUILDING SOFT TISSUES

When you have built an IK system and properly weight it to the skin you create, the skin moves with the IK system and bends at the joints in the system. Basically, the IK system provides the bones and joints to hang the skin on. However, in humans and most other creatures, there is a layer of musculature between the skeleton and the skin that also deforms when joints move, bending, bulging, and rippling the skin. You now need to build in this layer of soft tissues into the character. The concept and method is the same as for building the rigid elements, but in this case you'll actually be building things that you'll link, express, and animate later to change shape as the rig moves.

These spheres in the butt function like gluteus muscles.

A simple sphere in a muscle shape. Make sure its transforms are frozen.

Since most of these elements will be muscles, it will make sense to build a template muscle shape that's set up just right for what you want, then duplicate it each time you want a new muscle.

Start with a low detail polygon sphere. Tag the lower half, and in global mode scale it to become flat, so you now have one half of a sphere. Scale the sphere to be wider in X, and quite narrow in Z, as if it were a muscle bulge. Manually modify the end pointing in negative X just a little so you can visually tell which are the front and the back sides. Freeze the operator stack and Freeze all the transforms. This is now the muscle template.

Let's start with the Legs. You want a quadriceps muscle on top of the leg bone and a thigh muscle on the underside of the bone. Duplicate the muscle template, and name the new muscle "leftThigh".

The muscle should be aligned with the bone exactly, so the easy way is to use the Transform➔Match All Transforms command. (If you didn't freeze the transforms on the muscle in the previous paragraph, the muscle will now change shape badly.) Now move the muscle slightly from the center of the bone to the top side and slide it along the bone using local transforms, to where the thigh muscle should be located, and make the bone the parent of the muscle.

Make another copy of the muscle template, and line it up under the same bone with the Transform➔Match All Transforms command, or just move it manually. Also make it a child of the bone. Now these muscles will become IK deformers when the skin is added. You'll be able to link them to the bone rotations to automate some basic muscle sliding and bulging.

Repeat this process for the other leg.

Add calf muscles to the backs of the shin in the same way.

Add biceps and triceps muscles in the same way.

You should now clean up your work, by moving everything to the necessary layers and organizing your Schematic view. Select everything in the IK hierarchy, which should now include all the rigid elements and all the muscles. Make the IK layer active with the drop box at the top of the MCP, and move all those items to that layer.

Select the entire control rig hierarchy and move it to the appropriate layer. Remember that if there is any contamination between the two hierarchies something is badly wrong. You should be able to select either hierarchy as a tree without selecting the other.

Save your work as HumanIK10.

Reset All Transforms	Ctrl + Shift + R		**Transform**
Reset Scaling			
Reset Rotation			0.2168 X s
Reset Translation			0.2168 y
Reset Active Transform	Shift + R		0.1416 z
Freeze All Transforms			2.6813 x r
Freeze Scaling			-88.2046 y
Freeze Rotation			-108.603 z
Freeze Translation			
Freeze Active Transform			-0.5835 X t
Match All Transforms			-0.271 y
Match Scaling			0.5107 z
Match Rotation			
Match Translation			Global Local View
			Par Ref Plane
Move Center to Vertices			COG Prop Sym
Align Objects			
✓ Show Axes of Active Transform			**Snap**
Ignore Transform Setups			ON ● ● ● ▦
Create Reference Plane	Ctrl + -		**Constrain**
Create Transient Plane			
Reference Planes		▶	Parent Cut
			Comp
Kinematics...			
Transform Options...			**Edit**

The Match commands are in the Transform Menu.

Now the leg has thigh, quad, and calf muscles.

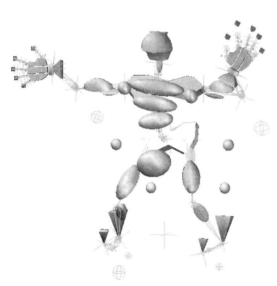

Now the rig has bones, solid shapes, and soft tissues to hold up the skin.

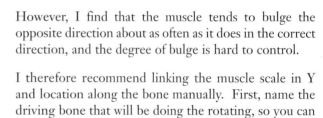

muscle contraction

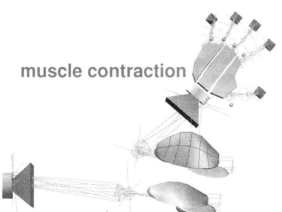

Now as the bone rotates, the muscle bunches and slides.

LINKING IN MUSCLE BEHAVIORS

What now remains for the rig is to just link the muscle behaviors to the joint rotations. Each muscle will be slightly different, but in general you want the muscle to get taller from the bone, shorter along the bone, and move slightly up the bone, as the joint below it bends.

There are two ways to accomplish this: the automatic Link with Orientation feature and the manual Link With feature. To use the Link with Orientation feature, simply select the muscle, activate the Scale in Y cell to mark it for the command, use the Link With Orientation command from the Animation Menu in the timeline, then pick on the IK bone that will be rotating to drive the muscle bulge. Sometimes the driving joint is the bone below, in the case of the thigh and quad, and sometimes the driving bone is the parent of the muscle, as in the case of the calve muscle. A series of Interpolator sliders will be generated on the Local Transforms PPG of the muscle to help you control the results.

However, I find that the muscle tends to bulge the opposite direction about as often as it does in the correct direction, and the degree of bulge is hard to control.

I therefore recommend linking the muscle scale in Y and location along the bone manually. First, name the driving bone that will be doing the rotating, so you can find it in the explorer list in just a moment.

Next, with that bone selected, pop a floating explorer and tap the F hotkey to frame the target bone. Look at the where it is in the hierarchy so you'll be able to find it for the Link With Command.

Next, select the muscle, and open the Local Transforms PPG. Lock the PPG open so you don't have to find it again. Right-click on the Scale Y divot and choose Link With. Expand the list to find the bone in question, and expand the bone when you find it to see the bone's kinematic local orientation Euler in Z. Click on the ori.euler.z property to link the Y scale of the muscle to the Z rotation of the bone.

Next, set reference keys to define how the bone will grow. Use the rig to fully extend the limb. At this point the muscle should be rather slender, so select it and scale it down in local Y. In the Kinematics Local PPG for the muscle, use the animation divot menu again, and choose Set Relative Values.

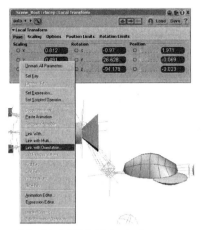

The Link With Orientation command links the marked property with a new expression and an interpolation curve.

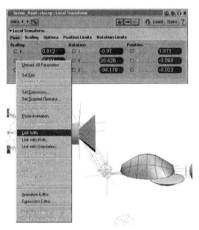

Link the scale in local Y of the muscle to the rotation in local Z of the bone.

You can now store actions comprising every element in the rig with one command.

Again use the rig to move the limb, this time to a position where the limb is quite bent. Again scale the muscle in Y, and use the Scale Y divot to set a relative value between the rotation of the lower bone and the scale of the muscle. You can set as many of these reference keys as you wish to define how the muscle ripples as the joint rotates. Repeat the process to link the local translation of the muscle to the rotation of the bone, so that the muscle moves up and down the bone as the joint rotates. Remember that the shape of the muscle object will not affect the envelope; only its scale, rotation, and translation.

Repeat this process for each of the muscles you built.

Save the results as HumanIK11.

USING HIGHER ASSIGNMENT DEPTH

A quick note is in order here to discuss again the envelope assignment depth. Previously, the IK chains were so simple that an assignment depth of 2, meaning that each skin vertex was weighted to two IK bones or other deformers, was sufficient. Now, however, consider the skin in the butt area of the character. In that one region there are the following deformers: lowest spine bone, top leg bone, belly deformer, quad deformer, thigh deformer, and gluteus deformer. That's six IK deformers underneath that one area of the skin. If you bound an envelope using the default assignment depth, most of those deformers would go unused. As a result, when you build IK systems with more complex skeletons and musculature, you need to increase the envelope assignment when you bind the skin.

SETTING KEYFRAMES AND SAVING ACTIONS

Congratulations! You just built a complex human control rig, and IK with rigid elements and dynamic muscle movements. You can use the same ideas and techniques to build any kind of creature at all, everything from worms to snow leopards. During your own work, keep in mind that the more limbs the creature has, the more work it is to set up.

Setting keys on this rig is simple. After you use the rig controllers to pose the character as needed on a given frame, you select the control elements that you have changed, and set a key on the translations. You can also set rotation keys on the wristControllers, and translation keys on the small spheres that help orient the resolution planes of the limbs.

Actions are also easy to use with this rig. You can pose the rig, and even without setting any keys use the Store➜Transformations – Current Values to make a clip that describes the location and rotation of each item in the rig.

You can also set keys on elements of the rig and use Store➜Fcurves – Animated Properties to collect all the animated transformations on the rig, along with any changes that might have been keyed on the custom controls.

CONCLUSION

Building a functional IK rig and all the skeletal supports, bones, muscles, and fatty tissues for a human character is a big setup job, but if you don't take the time to do it right in the beginning of the process, your character just won't be able to do the things you need him to do. If your IK system just doesn't hang together properly, you are going to have a horrible time actually animating with it. However, it must be said that building rigs like this is not for everyone. If your interest is more in line with using the IK rigs than with making them, you should hook up the closest technical director and cooperate with them. For many TDs, building the rig is a lot more fun than actually using it, so together, the both of you will make a great team.

Quiz

1. **Control rigs must only drive the root of the IK chains.**
    a. True
    b. False

2. **Control rigs must only drive the effector of the IK chains.**
    a. True
    b. False

3. **The local preferred axis of a 2D joint is:**
    a. X
    b. Y
    c. Z

4. **Which can control the resolution plane of IK chain?**
    a. Up Vector Constraint
    b. Preferred Axis Constraint
    c. Both Constraints

5. **If an object has both a parent and a position constraint, which one translates the object?**
    a. Parent
    b. Constraint
    c. Both Together

6. **The forearm rotates:**
    a. at the wrist
    b. at the elbow
    c. along the radius and ulna

7. **Can you re-use a rig for another character?**
    a. Yes
    b. No
    c. I don't know

8. **What kind of objects should you not use as parts of a control rig?**
    a. Nulls
    b. Implicit objects
    c. Effectors

9. **Can you use polygon objects as IK deformers?:**
    a. Yes
    b. No
    c. Depends

10. **How many bone segments are in each finger IK chain?**
    a. One
    b. Two
    c. Three

10

SAVING TIME WITH EXPRESSIONS

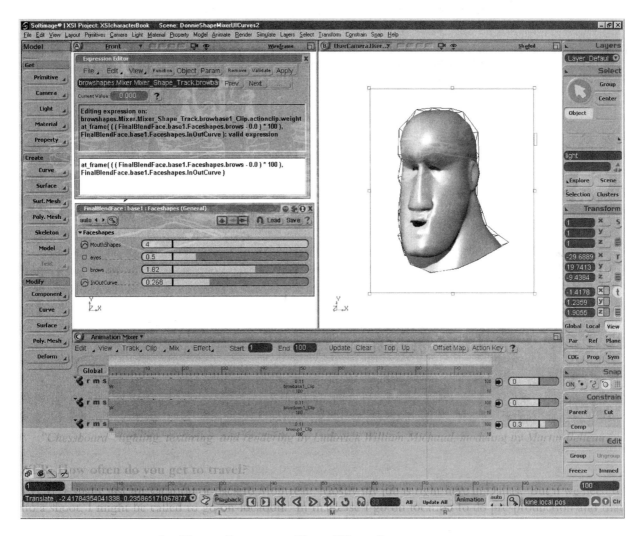

IN THIS CHAPTER YOU WILL LEARN ABOUT:

- How to automate simple tasks with expressions
- How to think creatively with math and formulas
- How to simply do special effects that are otherwise impossible
- How to control Mixers to blend shapes
- How to write exprssions using custom controls
- How to write expressions using custom Curves

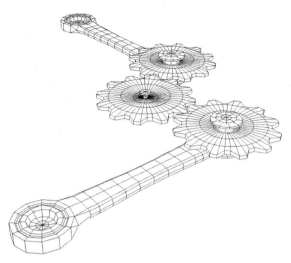

Only one gear needs to be animated; the others will respond perfectly.

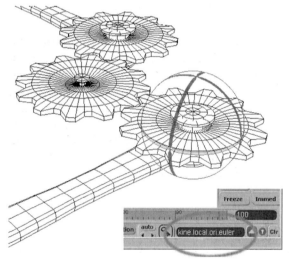

The feedback line is a good way to find out what a property name is.

INTRODUCTION

XSI was built from the ground up to be extensible. What's even more unusual is that XSI can be extended with standard scripting languages like VBScript and Jscript, as well as with a C or C++ development kit. Making a program open and extensible means that you'll always be able to do what you need to do, even if you have to write a bit of code to get it done. Fortunately, XSI has a continuum of extensibility, starting with the easy-to-use and simple expressions, followed by the still easy-to-use but slightly more complicated scripting functionality, and ending at the full-blown computer science of the SDK (Software Development Kit). This section addresses the first method, the easy one: expressions.

WHAT IS AN EXPRESSION?

An expression is a formula written to change the value of an animatable parameter (a property) in Softimage|XSI. For instance, a simple expression could be written to set the translation in X of an object in your scene to 5 units along the X-axis, or to set the color of a character to purple, or to make a strobe light flash quickly over and over.

A simple way to think about it is to imagine that an expression replaces an animation curve. For instance, you could write an expression to change the value of the X rotation of a propeller at each frame, causing the propeller to spin over time. Expressions, in fact, can only be applied to properties that are animatable, and an expression on a property supersedes an animation curve on the same property.

Expressions are evaluated, and changes made to the value of the property expressed, at every frame during an animation, and whenever you use the mouse to transform an object on screen (scale, translate, or rotate it).

WHY ARE THEY SO USEFUL?

Expressions are really good at repetitive functions, like spinning a gear a little bit each frame. Expressions are good at performing mathematical calculations, like rotating a small gear at twice the speed of a gear twice as big, in the opposite direction. Expressions are good at making careful changes on many objects, like the small changes in each joint of a lizard's tail as it swishes back and forth. And expressions are good at making decisions, like opening a door automatically when a character approaches.

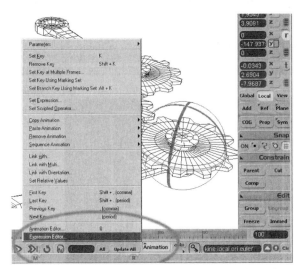

The expression editor in the Animation menu applies to the marked property.

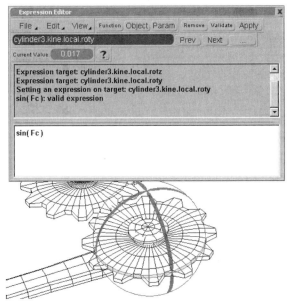

The Expression Editor

Expressions can also be used creatively to build characters that have very sophisticated, realistic motion but are easy to control and animate. In short, expressions solve problems. Fruitful use of expressions is all about creative problem solving. I say, "laziness is the mother of invention." This is certainly true in regards to expressions: they can be a tremendous time-saving tool.

WHAT KIND OF PEOPLE USE EXPRESSIONS?

Fundamentally, people who use expressions are inventors. Faced with a need or a problem, these people use critical thinking skills to imagine an easier way, and then they just try it out. Creating useful expressions can be a creative challenge as well, and ending up with a cool expression that makes something new possible is a rewarding experience.

In the animation business, these folks are often called Technical Directors, or TDs for short. Their job is to construct animatable puppets that are simple, intuitive and efficient to animate. Often this includes writing complex expressions on the character to ease the duties of the animators. Sometimes it means writing expressions (or scripts) that actually make new visual effects possible, like crowd software, or flocking software to control thousands of flying bats. Having a basic knowledge of expressions in your bag of tricks will come in handy. Just keep them in mind as you plan your work, and try to think of creative ways to use simple expressions to save time and wear and tear on your mouse arm.

PROPERTY NAMES

Throughout this material I'll need to refer to the animatable properties in XSI. The first step in understanding expressions and scripting is to understand how the properties are named, so you can check them and change them.

Valid property names look like this, where there are a series of words, separated by periods:

```
Sphere.kine.local.posy
```

The first word is always the name of the object in the scene. In the example above, the object is a ball named "Sphere". If the object belongs to a Model, the Model name comes first, like this:

```
Modelname.Sphere
```

The Validate button checks for errors, but the Apply button actually adds the expression.

Following the name comes a list of Property Editors, separated by periods, until the final word, which is the name of the actual property. The middle words in the name tell you where each particular property can be found. For instance:

```
Sphere.kine.local.posy
```

…means that the property position in Y can be found in the Local Property Editor, which is in the Kinematics Property Editor, which belongs to the object named Sphere.

As humans we don't care much about the path through the property editors, so we would just call it "sphere posy", leaving out the stuff in the middle.

ADDING EXPRESSIONS ONTO OBJECTS

Since expressions go on specific properties, the easiest way to add expressions is to call up the property editor that contains the property you want, and then use the animation divot (the small green button) right next to the property to call up the expression editor. When you right-click on the animation divot, a menu cascades out. Choose the Expression Editor option to see how this works.

The expression editor is a floating tool box with a set of menus across the top, a feedback line showing you the currently selected property, a history window in gray below that, and a white area at the bottom for you to type in the expressions.

If you brought up the expression editor from the animation divot on a property editor, it will already be set to the property you want to work with. Otherwise, there are two other ways of choosing a property to set an expression.

First, you may click on the Object button to browse a scene explorer, and select the object you want, then click the Param button to browse a list of available properties. Pick one, and then keep going back to the Param button to move down the hierarchy until you arrive at the final property you want.

Second, if you click on the Object button you can expand each object to see its properties, then expand those properties, and so on, until you find what you need, and click on it. This way often results in very long explorers to navigate, and sometimes the list closes unexpectedly, which is a hassle.

Lastly, you can also drag and drop properties into the expression editor, which is a lot easier since you don't have to build up the name or dig through a huge dialog.

Just select the object that has the property, open a PPG that contains the property, and then drag and drop the target property animation divot into the white area of the expression editor and let go.

SIMPLE EXPRESSIONS

Before we go any further, let's create a simple expression so you can begin to see what the possibilities are.

Step 1: Create an object to on which to apply the expression. Use the Get➔Primitive➔Surface➔Sphere menu cell to bring a sphere object into a new scene.

Step 2: Open the property editor for the sphere's translation in Y. (In the property explorer that would be the sphere's Kinematics→Local Transform.)

Step 3: In the property editor, right-click on the animation divot next to the Position Y text entry box, and choose the expression editor. Now at the top of the expression editor it should say "sphere.kine.local.posy".

Step 4: Write the expression! In the white space at the bottom type in exactly:

```
5 + 3
```

Then hit the Validate button. The Validate button checks your work for errors. If it finds any, it reports "Error found at this point" and repeats the line with the error.

If there is an error in the expression you wrote, you'll need to go through it and correct the mistake. Some common techniques useful for finding errors are to add a space between names and operators to make it easier to read, make sure that parentheses are in matching pairs: one like (and one like), and to check the spelling of your names.

If no errors are founds, Validate reports "Valid Expression:" and then repeats the expression again. This does not actually add the expression to the object property, however, it just checks it for errors.

To complete the expression, click the Apply button. Your sphere should now hop up in space 8 units high!

If you check the property editor for that parameter, it will have a small equals sign (=) on top of the animation divot to indicate that the property is controlled by an expression. Your expression will be evaluated at every frame for the sphere, but the result will always be the same (the value 8) so nothing much will change.

Try another expression in the expression editor. Delete the "5+3" and type in:

```
Sin( Fc * 5 ) * 5
```

...which means, "find the sine of the current frame times 5, then multiply that by five as well".

Validate the expression and apply it. Click the playback button in your timeslider to see the sphere move up and down. This example shows how expressions can return a different result at each frame.

THE PROCESS OF GRADUAL REFINEMENT

Using expressions requires a "try it out and see" kind of attitude. You don't have to write the correct expression in glorious completion the first time; you just have to get something down that validates OK, and see what the results are. Next, try making gradual changes to the formula to examine how the results are affected. Gradually build up a more complex formula until you meet your objectives, or until it just looks cool enough to keep. In the example above try changing the numbers 5 to be other numbers to make the ball oscillate faster or slower, or go higher or lower. You could enclose the entire expression in parentheses () and then add or subtract a number to move the whole motion up or down. You could make the ball bounce instead of oscillating by enclosing the whole expression in an absolute value equation, which would look like this:

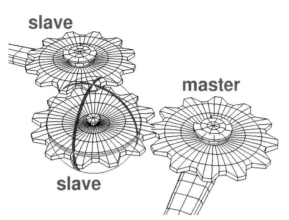

The expression goes on the slave object. Changes to the master object then activate the slave.

```
abs( sin( Fc * 5 )*5 )
```

The important thing is to view expressions as a creative method of exploration and problem solving. Don't be afraid to try things out.

EXPRESSION SYNTAX

The key to working easily with expressions is understanding the expression editor and the underlying syntax of the expressions themselves. In this section you'll find a more complete explanation of property names, expression syntax, and some useful functions.

OBJECTS, PROPERTIES, AND ANIMATION CURVES

Expressions are formulas that replace an animation curve, and are applied onto object properties. Each object in your scene may therefore have a maximum number of expressions on it equal to the number of properties or animation curves it has. For example, on a primitive object I can have one expression on the explicit translation in X, another completely different expression on explicit translation in Y, another on scale in Z, and so on, until I run out of properties.

When an object has an expression applied to an animation curve, no manual changes may be made to that property. For instance, when I apply an expression to a gear that controls the rotation in Z, I cannot manually rotate the gear in Z anymore; the expression has taken over control of the rotation in Z.

Expressions are most often applied to geometry objects in a scene, but you can also write expressions to control other objects, like lights, materials, textures, and the camera. For instance, if you wished to apply an expression to the diffuse color of a ball so that it changed color when it hit the floor, you can do that in the same way, by finding the property you want to change (in this case sphere.Material.Phong.diffuse.red and applying an equation to it in the expression editor. Note: Applying an expression on a material color is a little harder than other properties, because the color is really four properties: the red, green, blue, and alpha. You have to open a blank Expression editor first, then set the effected element manually instead of right-clicking on the Color divot in the material PPG.

The expression editor needs to know the exact name of the property to change, and properties can also be called by name within the expression itself. As a result, you need to know more about how property names are made up and where they can all be found.

WHERE IS POSITION IN X AND WHAT IS A EULER?

The properties are grouped into categories by general use, and you must use these category names when you write out a property name in an expression. Some of the categories (like visibility) make sense, but others are less clear.

The category group "kine", short for kinematics, contains the sub-categories local and global, and within them all the transformations. Kine also contains the sub-group constraints, many of which affect the transformations.

The sub-group local contains all the transformations that are stored local to a parent object or null.

The sub-group global contains all the transformations that are relative to the global center, at 0,0,0.

Unfortunately, the graphical interface uses different words for some of the properties than are used elsewhere in the application. In the Main Command Panel (MCP), the transformations are labeled s, r, and t for scale, rotation and translation. In property editors those same properties are called scaling, rotation, and position, while in expressions they are called scaling, orientation, and position. Confusing? Yes.

Sometimes one of the properties is also grouped under a major category name, like Euler. In this case, Euler is just a specific way of representing orientation in space (named for Leonhard Euler, a Swiss mathematician), and doesn't really mean much when you are writing expressions. You may ignore it, because it doesn't actually show up in the property name.

Here is a brief list of the most commonly used properties and their names:

objectname.kine.local.pos.posx – The position in X, relative to the parent, of "objectname"

objectname.kine.local.scl.sclx – The scale in X of "objectname"

objectname.kine.local.ori.euler.rotx – The rotation in X of "objectname"

You can abreviate these to:

```
objectname.kine.local.posx
```

```
objectname.kine.local.sclx
```

```
objectname.kine.local.rotx
```

You can replace the X above with Y or Z for the other axes.

You can find the exact name for any property in a few different ways. The clever way is to open the property editor for the parameter you want to know the name of. Click the animation divot to save a key. Look at the feedback line in the bottom-left corner to see the name of the property that got keyed. The slow way is to open the expression editor and use the Object button to select the object that has the parameter, then use the Param button (discussed in depth later) to browse the hierarchy of properties to build the full name.

Note: You can mark each property using the property marking menu (the small triangle in the bottom-right corner) but it won't always give you the full, accurate name of the property in the feedback line.

WHICH OBJECT DOES THE EXPRESSION GO ON?

The expression should be applied to the object in your scene that you want to change automatically. One way to think about this is to assign one object to be the slave object and another to be the master object. The expression goes on the slave object and commands it to change based on the behavior of the master.

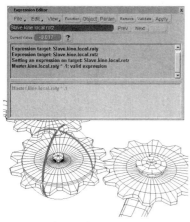

A simple math equation on the slave gear

NAMING CONVENTIONS

It is important to correctly name all the objects you will be using in your expressions, so you aren't confused with meaningless lists of items all named similarly, like cube1.rotz, cube1.roty, cube2.rotx, etc.

Note: Interestingly enough, if you use a name of an object in an expression, then later on change the name of that object, the expression you wrote will automatically update the reference with the new name.

Since each expression can reference other objects' animation curves, this naming convention is very important. For example, setting one gear to exactly follow the rotation of another gear would look like this:

```
slavegear.kine.local.rotz =
mastergear.kine.local.rotz
```

Where the first item, slavegear, would be the driven object, and the second item would be the entire formula entered in the white space in the expression editor.

MATHEMATICS, ORDER OF OPERATIONS, AND PARENTHESIS

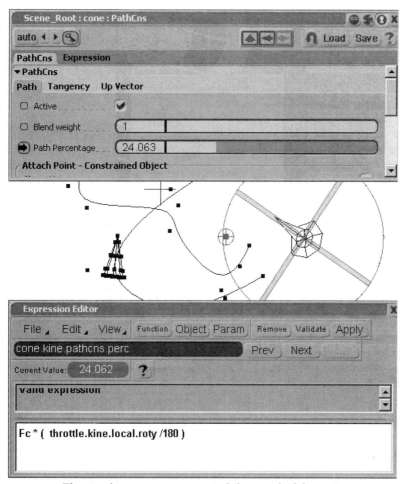

Expressions are formulas that describe equality between the property you put it on, and some other arbitrary expression that you will write. In the expressions dialog box you do not exactly write:

slavegear.kine.local.rotz = mastergear.kine.local.rotz

...because the dialog has specific text boxes for each part of the equation. The left side of the equation, describing the object and animation curve that will be changed by the expression, goes in the top (darker gray) edit box. The equality is provided automatically, and the right side of the equation is the business end, where you will do most of the work. That part goes in the large, white text at the bottom of the box.

The simple expression to control the speed of the train

You can write any mathematically valid formula for the right side of the equation in the expression editor box. A simple equation might just be:

```
slavegear.kine.local.rotz = 90
```

...where the entire expression is just the number 90. Or it can be an arithmetic formula, like:

```
slavegear.rotz = 12 + 34 + 23 * 45 / 10
```

...where the operators +, -, * , and / stand for addition, subtraction, multiplication and division. The order in which you place the operators does matter. Expressions follow standard order of operations, which means that the expression calculates multiplication and division first, then addition and subtraction. Therefore:

```
slavegear.kine.local.rotz = 2 + 4 + 6 * 5
```

...is not the same as:

```
slavegear.kine.local.rotz = 5 * 2 + 4 + 6
```

...because the multiplication gets evaluated first, then the additions. If you do not wish to understand how and why order of operations will affect your formulas, you may group operation in parentheses to force the expression to evaluate in the order you want. For instance:

```
slavegear.kine.local.rotz = (2 + 4 + 6) * 5
```

...will add 2, 4, and 6 first, then multiply the resulting number by 5. Very often, grouping parts of your formulas in parentheses is a big help in clarifying your own thoughts about what should be calculated first, second, etc. Since the XSI expression editor has as many lines as you need in the bottom expression entry area, feel free to break the lines up, and put one set of parentheses on a new line just to make it easier to read.

USING ANOTHER OBJECT IN THE EXPRESSION

Certainly, the most powerful feature of the expression syntax is the ability to use a value taken from another object in the scene in your expression formula. You've already seen this, in the form:

```
slavegear.kine.local.rotz = mastergear.kine.local.rotz
```

...where the value of the slave's rotation in Z is set to the value of the master's rotation in Z. You can extend this concept quite a bit further. First, the specifics: you must reference an object by name followed by a period, then a valid animation curve of that object. This pair, object.animation_curve, will return the value of the object's animation curve at the point in time when the expression is evaluated. In other words, the expression will be evaluated at each frame in your animation, and re-lookup the referenced object, check the animation curve at that point, and return the value given there.

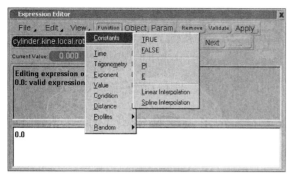

These constants are available in the expression editor.

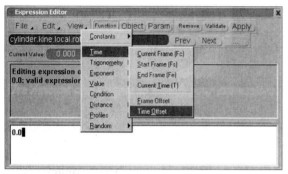

These variables are available in the expression editor.

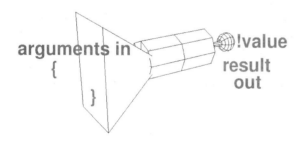

Functions take arguments as inputs, and return results as output.

Any number of objects can be referenced in an expression. For instance, the expression:

```
slave.kine.local.rotz =
(master.kine.local.rotz +
big.kine.local.rotz +
little.kine.local.roty) /
switch.kine.local.etrnx
```

...is perfectly valid.

As an example, imagine an electric train track, where the train goes faster or slower as you twist the throttle. That could be easily done in XSI. The train would be placed on a path (PathCns) and the Path Percentage property could have an expression on it that adds a little bit to it at each frame. The amount added could be the rotation in Y of the train throttle. You can try this yourself with the following simple instructions.

Step 1: Draw a spline in the top view for the track. Close it with Modify Curve→Open/Close

Step 2: Get a cone to be the train. Name it "train". Constrain it to the spline you just drew using a Path Constraint. Get a cylinder for the throttle, scale it to be flatter, and pull out one point from any side to make an indicator needle. Name the cylinder "throttle".

Step 3: Select the train cone, and view the PathCns property editor. Set an expression on it by right-clicking on its Path Percentage animation divot to call up the expression editor. Note the name of the affected property in the top edit line:

```
train.kine.pathcns.perc
```

This means that you'll be adding an expression that will take over control of the train's kinematic (movement) location along the path.

Step 4: In the bottom entry area, make the path percentage equal to the current frame (the function named Fc), multiplied by a small number based on how much the throttle is rotated in Y. An easy way to get a small number from the throttle would be to divide 180 degrees by the throttle's current rotation in Y. Try setting the expression on the PathCns Path Percentage to:

```
Fc * ( throttle.kine.local.roty / 180 )
```

Validate the expression, fix any syntax errors that crept in, apply the expression, and then turn on loop and hit the playback button. While the playback loops, change the speed of the train by rotating the throttle in Y.

FUNCTIONS, CONSTANTS AND VARIABLES

In addition to regular arithmetic operators and other scene objects, the expression syntax includes a number of useful functions and variables that you may use in your formulas. These are located in a drop menu under the Functions button at the top of the expression editor.

CONSTANTS

A constant is a mathematical certainty, like the number pi, useful in certain formulas. Pi and E are provided for your use, and are most often found in geometric calculations. True and False are also constants because their value never changes.

VARIABLES

Some variables are maintained by Softimage|XSI itself, like the current frame variable, which reports what frame the timeslider is currently on. (The current frame variable is represented as Fc for "Frame: current".) Other variables are the current time (T), the start frame (Fs) and end frame (Fe). These variables are all located under the Functions button in the Time sub-category.

There is no provision in the expression syntax for explicitly global custom variables, which seems like a serious omission, until you consider that absolutely every object in your scene is a global variable that can be tested and set.

If you have five objects that all need to communicate, you may create a dummy object in your scene, and use a property of that object, like scalx, as a global variable. Each of your five objects can read the state of the global variable, and expressions on the global variable itself can change its state based on the behavior of the five objects. Since the VBScript language also lacks global variables (in XSI) this is a valuable strategy in scripting as well as in expressions.

There are special self-referencing variables in XSI, used with the special keyword "this." Followed by the animation curve you want to access. If you replace the name of an object with "this", it tells the expression to refer back to that object, whichever object it was. Using "this", the expression can be made more generic, and can be copied to other objects without modification. This can make for some neat tricks, like locking the scale of an object in X to the scale in Y with the expression, entered on the scale X property:

```
this.kine.local.scly
```

FUNCTIONS

A function is an abbreviation for a bunch of code written by a programmer that takes in one or more pieces of information from you, and spits out some information in return. That information provided by the function can be used in a longer expression.

We say that a function "takes" one or more arguments and "returns" a value. The trick to each function is determining what the proper arguments are for that function. Functions start with the name of the function, followed by the arguments enclosed in parenthesis and separated by commas, like Function(arg1,arg2,arg3,arg4). Most functions take a set number of specific arguments, but some do not. For instance, the MAX function takes any number of arguments, and returns the biggest of them.

```
MAX(9, 11, 23, 4, 9, 15)
```

…would return the number 23 to you.

The available functions in XSI (under the Functions button) are grouped into categories by their common uses: Trigonometry, Exponent, Value, Conditional, Distance, Profiles, and Random.

You can use the function list to give yourself some hints about the arguments required for each function. Generally, when you insert a function into your expression, it will come in with either one parenthesis or a list of arguments. If it has only one parenthesis, it takes one value as an argument, and one more closed parenthesis. If it has a list of arguments enclosed in brackets like "<Argument>, <Argument>, <Argument>", you may replace each one with a value.

The values can be numbers (like 7, 2, 43.6, etc.), the values can be properties on the same or another object, or the values can be other functions or formulas.

For example, if you click on the Center Distance function, which finds out how far it is from one object to another, you see a line like this:

```
ctr_dist(<elem1>, <elem2>)
```

You then must give it the information it needs, which here is the name of the two elements it is measuring between.

Here are just a few functions, with their arguments explained in plain English.

TRIGONOMETRY: SIN(), COS()
Sine and cosine return a value that varies gradually from 0 to 1 and then back again, endlessly. The value returned would graph like a sine wave (hence the name). Sin() and Cos() are opposites – when one is increasing, the other decreases. They each take one argument, which should be a number that changes over time quite dramatically, like the current frame.

VALUE: ABS()
Absolute value takes any single value and returns the positive version of it. If the number is already positive, it returns the same number it took in. If the number is negative, it returns a positive version. This is useful for removing negative values.

VALUE: AV(), MIN() AND MAX()
Average, minimum, and maximum are unique in expression functions, in that they operate on sets on data. Each can take a comma-separated list of as many values as you want to give them, from 2 on up. av() finds the average value of all the values given, MIN finds the least, and MAX finds the greatest.

EXPONENT: SQRT()
Square root takes a single value, and calculates the square root of it. The square root is useful in solving many geometric calculations, like the Pythagorean theorem.

EXPONENT: POW(X,Y)
Power takes two values, and raises the first value to the power of the second.

TIME: AT_TIME() AND AT_FRAME()

It is also possible to reference another object at a point in time other than the current frame. You can reference time at a given frame, or you can reference time relative to the current frame. This is really useful for making one object seem to react to another. To reference the value of another object at a specified frame in time that never changes, use at_time(). at_time takes two arguments: the frame desired and the object.animation_curve pair that has the value you want.

```
at_time(50, littlehand.kine.local.rotz)
```

...would return the rotation of the little hand at frame 50.

You can also reference time relative to your current frame, so that the values change either before or after the target object. In other words, you could set one object to follow another but lag behind in time a few frames. To do that, use the at_frame command like this:

```
at_frame (Fc - 5,littlehand.kine.local.rotz)
```

Be careful: when inserting the at_frame command, it comes in with <Fc – 30> as the offset. If you wish to keep the Fc-30 you must remember to remove the <> brackets.

DISTANCE: CTR_DIST(), CTR_DIST_CAM(), CTR_DIST_CAM_INT()

Sometimes you want to find out how far apart two objects are, or how far an object is from the camera, or the camera interest. These functions return the distance in Softimage|XSI units between two objects, or between an object and the camera or camera interest. ctr_dist() takes two arguments, simply the names of the two objects to be measured. ctr_dist_cam and ctr_dist_cam_int() take just one argument, the name of the object that is to be measured from the camera or interest.

If you use the Center-To-Center function, be sure to give it the arguments formatted just as it wants them: the names of the objects followed by a period like this:

```
ctr_dist (master. , slave.)
```

Be sure to include those hanging periods.

RANDOM: NOISE()

Noise is a 3D fractal-type noise generator. It generates numbers that have a random distribution, but change gradually from one to another. Using the noise is a good way to add in some variability to a character without looking like the character has palsy, or is shaking with cold. Noise() takes three arguments, an X value, a Y value, and, you guessed it, a Z value. If you change any or all of these values over time, the value returned by noise() will also change, gradually and in a complex pattern. Applying this noise pattern to a field of small objects each with its own X, Y and Z locations given as the noise in conjunction with the current frame would result in a rippling, 3D wave pattern not unlike water. Because the formula below is self-referencing (it uses the word "this" to refer to itself), it can be automatically copied between hundreds or thousands of objects. Try this on a bunch of spheres, and imagine displacing a sheet of water like this:

Affected Property: sphere.kine.local.posy

```
noise(this.kine.local.posx,(Fc * .15), this.kine.local.posz)
```

RANDOMIZATION FOR JITTER

Very often the hardest thing to do in an animation package is to make things look natural. That's because animation software is so precise and measured, while nature has so much chaos and noise in it. You can add noise to your animation easily with the random functions. For instance, if you have a guttering candle, and you need to simulate the light coming off the candle by varying the end falloff of the point light, you could use a random function to automatically make that happen. There are two random functions in the expressions language: the randBool() and rand_0_1() function.

The difference between them is that the rand_0_1() function returns a decimal number between 0 and 1, while the randBool() function acts like an on/off switch, returning a 0 or a 1. Both random functions take a single argument, a seed value, explained below.

THE RANDOM SEED

It is awfully hard for a computer to be random, and these functions don't really calculate true random numbers; they just look up random numbers from a predefined random number table. So you might notice that the results are the same, time after time. You can vary the results by forcing the random functions to offset into the random number table a different amount, called the random seed. The random functions take as an argument a single integer number as the random seed.

To actually use the random function to jitter a parameter, first decide on the maximum and minimum values that you want to have. For the guttering candle example, you don't want the candle to ever be completely dark, but you don't want it too bright either. The maximum falloff for the candle could be 90 Softimage|XSI units, while the minimum could be 10. In this case, the amount of jitter you want is the max value minus the min value, multiplied by the random number. This would return random numbers between 0 and 80 Softimage|XSI units. Then you would add the minimum value back into the expression, ensuring that the candle never goes completely dark. Here is the expression, applied to the end falloff parameter (stop) of the candle point light. The number 23 is the random seed, but could be any number.

The expression is going on the End Falloff property, in the light property editor under the Light Attenuation section.

Note: You do have to have the Light Falloff property checked on for this to work, and the effect is more obvious with the light falloff mode set to Linear (although a candle would in reality definitely use the Use Light Exponent setting).

Affected Property = MyLight.light.soft_light.stop

```
(rand_0_1(23)  *  (50 - 10 ))  + 10
```

DECISIONS AND LOGIC

You will often want to make choices in your expressions. For example, if the light switch is in the up position, then you want all the lights to turn on. Or, if the foot of a character raises above the floor, you want the toes to curl. Or, if an object approaches a certain area, you want a trap door to open. These "if... then" decisions are called conditional statements, because the outcome is conditional on a logical decision. The logical decision must be a statement than can be evaluated as either true or false, for instance "1 = 2" evaluates as false, while "1 < 2" evaluates as true. You can use other objects' values and other functions in the conditional statement. For instance, "sin(slave.kine.local.roty) > cos(master.kine.local.roty)" is a valid conditional statement that asks whether the sine of the slave's rotation is greater than the cosine of the master's rotation.

After the conditional statement evaluates the logical decision, it returns a value specified by the user. You can specify one value to be returned for true statements, and one to be returned for false statements. That's the beauty of the conditional: you give it the two options for the way the final value is calculated, and XSI picks between them based on the circumstances at the time.

The syntax of the conditional statement works like this:

cond(logical_decision, outcome_if_true, outcome_if_false)

...where there are three arguments to the conditional function. The first is the logical decision, which must have a logical operator in it like =, <, or >; the second is the value you want returned if the decision is true, and the third is the value you want returned if the decision is false.

In addition to the standard arithmetic operators, the expression language also uses logical operators. Logical operators are those operators that evaluate out to either True or False. You may use these in the conditional function, generally to test more than one condition at a time and make more complex decisions.

The logical operators are:

== meaning "equal". If the left and right side are equal, then == returns True.

=| meaning "different" (not equal). If the left and right side are different, then =| returns True.

> meaning "greater than". If the left is greater than the right then > returns True.

< meaning "less than". If the left is less than the right then < returns True.

=> meaning "greater than or equal to"

=< meaning "less than or equal to"

&& meaning "and". If both sides of the equation evaluate True, then && returns True.

|| meaning "or". If either side evaluates as True then || returns True.

Below is an example of an expression that would turn on a light based on the rotation of a light dimmer knob. This expression would be applied to a light intensity parameter, and would increase the intensity to a maximum of 5 times regular brightness when the light switch turns past 45 degrees, and set it to 0 when the switch is not rotated enough to turn the light on. This more complex conditional simulates a sticky dimmer switch that comes on suddenly.

Affected Element: MyLight.light.soft_light.intensity

```
cond(  switch.kine.local.roty  >  45  ,  (.3  +  (3  *
(switch.kine.local.roty / 360))) , 0)
```

You might use several logical operators at once to test whether either or both of several statements are true. For instance, this statement is valid:

```
cond( 1<2 && 3<2, 10, 20 )
```

It forces the conditional to decide if both 1 is less than 2, and 3 is less than 2 at the same time. The answer is False in this case, so the value 20 would be returned by the expression.

SWISHING THE TAIL: AT A GLANCE

TOPICS COVERED

One neat trick that can be easily set up with expressions is the automatic swishing of tails, like lizard tails, dinosaur tails, fish tails, etc., using inverse kinematic chains. The goal is to create a totally organic-looking tail motion controllable by the animator, where the tail can whip back and forth, with each segment following its parent, delayed in time bit to create the perfect serpentine motion.

You'll learn how to:

- Use a separate object as a control in an expression
- Apply expressions on IK
- Offset the effects of an expression in time

MATERIALS REQUIRED

No external scenes or materials are required.

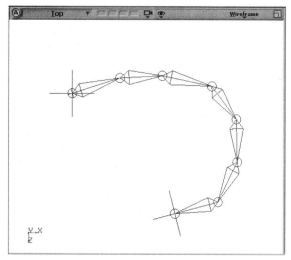

Draw a 2D chain in the top view.

TUTORIAL: SWISHING THE TAIL

The first segment of the tail will get an expression that makes it rotate based on the rotation of the tailcontrol cube. Then, each successive tail segment will get an expression that looks at the segment before it on the tail, and changes a little less than that prior segment. The last trick is that each successive segment will rotate, but that rotation will be delayed slightly in time.

STEP 1: MAKE THE TAILCONTROL

The trick is to create a tail control that will be animated to run the tail. This control will be a simple cube primitive, named "tailcontrol". Create your tailcontrol cube now.

The roty of the tailcontrol must be animated before you begin, so you can refer back in time to it. Set keyframes for it over at least 100 frames, changing a few times from -80 degrees or so to +70 degrees. This setup requires animation on the tailcontrol – it won't work without it.

Each segment will have an expression that takes a portion of the rotation from the tailcontrol, and applies that rotation to the rotz of the IK chain segment. The segments near the base of the tail will take more of the rotation, while those near the tail will take a smaller portion. In addition, each segment, starting from the base, and working to the tip, will delay itself a bit, causing the rippling, serpentine motion.

Each expression will be almost the same, changing only the variables for the amount of rotation to use and the amount of delay to use. This makes it possible for you to quickly assign all the expressions by writing just one, then copying that expression to each segment, and finally editing the variables for each segment.

STEP 2: SET UP THE FIRST SEGMENT EXPRESSION

Make a 2D IK chain with 7 bones in the Top view to be the tail. Select the first segment at the base of the tail and call up the local transform PPG, then right click on the Rot Z divot to call up the expression editor. Making sure that the top edit box reads "bone.kine.local.rotz".

The rotation in Z of an IK chain is always the preferred axis of rotation. You can use any axis you want if the Z-axis doesn't rotate the tail in the way you want.

In the expression below, A and B are temporary variables, which will be different for each segment.

```
at_frame( Fc - B, tailcontrol.kine.local.roty ) * A
```

For the first segment use the number 0.5 for A, which will be the multiplier for the rotation of the tailcontrol. In the B variable location, use the number 3, which will be the delay in frames for that segment. Make the expression:

```
at_frame( Fc - 3, tailcontrol.kine.local.roty ) * .5
```

Remember to use the correct name of your control handle instead of the name "tailcontrol" if you used a different name.

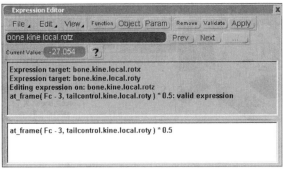

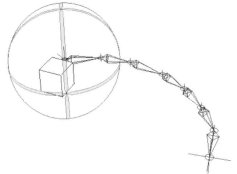

Each IK segment rotates independently.

Validate the expression, accept the changes, and play back your animation to see the first segment sway with the animation of the tail control.

STEP 3: COPY TO ALL SEGMENTS

Quickly copy the expression you wrote to each segment by selecting the expression you wrote in the expression editor, and either using CTRL-C or the menu command Edit→Copy. Select the next bone segment in the top of the expression editor, and paste the expression formula into the edit area for that bone with CTRL-V or Edit→Paste. Repeat for each segment, until they all have the same expression. Test your animation.

STEP 4: CHANGE THE VARIABLES ON EACH SEGMENT TO TWEAK THE TAIL

Starting at the base, each segment should rotate slightly less, and should delay in time a few frames. Select the second segment, and use Expression→Edit to call up the expressions dialog. Change the A variable to 0.45, which means that this segment will have 5% less rotation. Change the B variable to 5, which means that this segment will lag behind the tailcontrol by five frames. Close the expressions dialog.

Repeat with each segment, gradually decreasing the rotation, and gradually increasing the lag time. Examine the results in your animation, and change it to suit your tastes.

The default swishing of the tail control was just for show. You now need to change the rotation of the tail control to fit your specific needs. Due to the magic of expressions, simply animating the rotation of the tailcontrol now starts a chain reaction of tail segment rotation, with each segment changing in subtly different ways.

PULSING LASERS AND OTHER REPETITIVE STUFF: AT A GLANCE

TOPICS COVERED

In this tutorial you will learn how to use expressions to pulse, oscillate, and generally turn values up and down automatically.

You'll learn how to:

- Apply expressions to materials
- Think about expressions using Variables
- Use the absolute value and sine functions

MATERIALS REQUIRED

No outside materials are required.

TUTORIAL: PULSING LASERS AND OTHER REPETITIVE STUFF

Sometimes you will need repetitive motions on precise timing. For example, you may need a jackhammer bit to pound up and down rapidly, or a light to strobe, or a laser to pulse. A great way to schedule repetitive motions is to use the sine and cosine functions on the current frame variable. Both sine and cosine return values that oscillate between 0 and 1 based on the value of an argument. You can scale up the argument to increase the speed (the frequency) of the oscillation, making faster pulses, and you can scale up the whole formula to change the output value to the range you want.

This expression could be applied to any object property to change it rapidly.

STEP 1: SET UP THE MATERIAL

Let's make a cylindrical shaped object that you could later animate growing out rapidly to make a beam shooting forward. Get a primitive cylinder and call it MyRay.

To pulse the transparency of a cylinder, set the diffuse color to green with the color value set much higher than 1, like to 2, in order to make it glow. Make the material transparent. For extra realism during the render, apply the glow property to the cylinder, creating a passable laser effect.

STEP 2: SET UP THE EXPRESSION

In the Indirect Illumination tab of the Material property editor, set the incandescent color to something pretty and then right-click on the divot next to Intensity to call up the expression editor. Now the Affected Element line should read something like:

MyRay.Material.Phong.inc_inten

In the formula below, the A variable will be the frequency, or speed of the pulse:

```
abs( sin( Fc * A ) ) * (C - B)
```

Initially you'll use 10 for A. The B variable starting at 2 will be the minimum value returned for the intensity of the incandescence. Set C to 4.5, which will be the maximum value returned. Separating the min and max values like this will make it easy for you to apply this same expression to another object parameter, like rotation, and easily scale the results up to the larger values required for rotation, or for scale, or for whatever you want to do. The absolute value function, abs(), keeps the value of the oscillation positive at all times. Enter the expression:

```
abs( sin( Fc * 20) ) * ( 4.5 - 2 )
```

Which will oscillate between C and B according the value of the current frame and the speed variable A. Increase A to speed up the oscillation, making the material pulse faster.

STEP 3: TWEAK

So what if you need the laser to snap cleanly on and off, instead of gradually pulsing up and down? Well, you could use a conditional to evaluate the oscillation, and return either a 1 or a 0 depending on the value of the oscillation.

```
cond( ( abs( sin( Fc*10 ) ) * ( 1.5- .1 ) ) > 0.5 , 1 , 0)
```

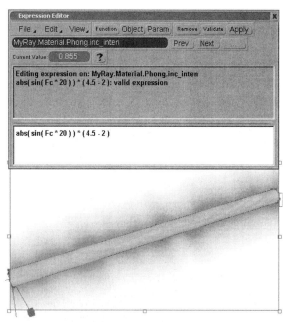

The finished laser, rendered with a glow property

This is a simple example of pulsing using an expression. You can also use the cosine command (cos) and the actual Oscillate command, which takes arguments directly for the frequency and the amplitude of the oscillation. It would be really sly to add in a random factor to jitter the effect, making it less regular and more believable.

HOT WHEELS: AT A GLANCE

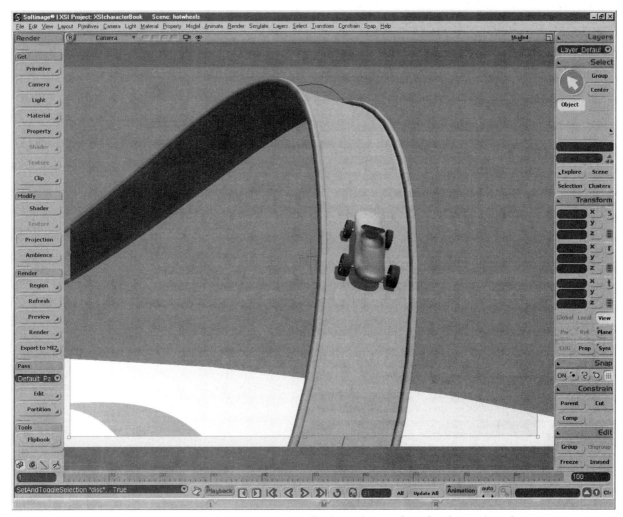

The wheels spin on the car automatically depending on how far the car travels.

TOPICS COVERED

In this quick example I'll provide a few ways of calculating rotations based on distance traveled.

You'll learn how to:

- Use Info Selection to find length of splines
- Use a constraint in an expression
- Writing expressions to control local rotation

MATERIALS REQUIRED

This tutorial requires the HotWheels scene from the courseware that accompanies this book.

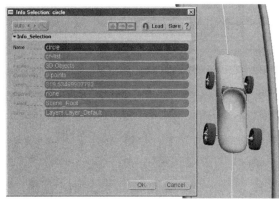

The Info dialog for the path shows the length.

How many times should the wheel rotate to travel all the way to the end of the path?

TUTORIAL: HOT WHEELS

In this quick example I'll provide a few ways of calculating rotations based on distance traveled. If you open the HotWheels scene you'll find a small matchbox racer on a path, traveling around a track.

The problem is that the wheels are not spinning. If you hand-animated the wheels, then the rotation would only match one speed for the car, and as you've seen, you might want to flexibly control the progress of the car around the track, and have the wheels spin accordingly.

You could express the rotation of the wheels in some way that is relative to the distance traveled. Fortunately for us, XSI gives a few bits of info that will help here.

STEP 1: MEASURE THE DISTANCE TRAVELLED

The track was made from an extrusion along a path. Selecting the path and using the Edit→Info Selection tool tells you that the path is 319 Softimage units long.

STEP 2: MEASURE THE WHEEL DIAMETER

By matching a circle to the wheel diameter of the front wheels on the car, you can find out what the circumference of the tire really is. To do this, I got a primitive curve circle, then used Transform→Match All Transforms, and picked one front wheel. The circle surrounds the wheel.

I scaled the circle down to just fit on the wheel, then froze the circle to remove the scale transformation, and checked Edit→Info Selection, which tells me that the circle is now 3.10 Softimage units in diameter.

STEP 3: CALCULATE THE WHEEL ROTATIONS REQUIRED

What follows next doesn't even require trigonometry. Unless the tires are spinning out, the tires must rotate one time for each 3.1 units that the car travels down the path.

Divide the length of the path (319) by the circumference of the tire (3.1) to get the number or revolutions needed for the front wheels. 319 / 3.1 = 102.9. So, to travel 100% of the way along the path, the wheels will need to turn 102.9 times. Since each rotation is 360 degrees, that means that to travel the whole path the wheels must turn 102.9 * 360 = 37044 degrees.

STEP 4: SET AN EXPRESSION USING PATH PERCENTAGE ON THE WHEEL

Since path percentage is expressed as a decimal percentage of the way along the path, you can just multiply that by the number of total degrees the wheel must turn to get the rotation of the wheel at any point.

Select a wheel, open the local transform PPG, and in the wheels local rotation in Z use the animation divot to call up the expression editor. Set the rot Z equal to:

```
Carbod.kine.pathcns.perc * 37044
```

STEP 5: REPEAT FOR REAR WHEELS

The inside front wheel has been done for you in the HotWheels scene.

The rear wheels are not the same diameter as the front wheels. In fact, they are 1.2 times as big. I leave it to you, this time, to figure out how many times they must revolve to match the position along the track.

When you have done, select the four wheels and go into local translate mode just to see the manipulators spin, and drag along the timeline to see the car roll and the tires rotate. The advantage of this method is that no matter what happens to the car, rolling backwards, forwards, speeding up, slowing down, the tires will always spin the correct amount.

Note: I note that, due to the lack of differential gearbox on the car, handling will be less than optimal in the chicane. Some wheel slide is therefore to be expected due to differences in the distance traveled by the inside and outside wheels.

EXPRESSIONS MIXING SHAPES: AT A GLANCE

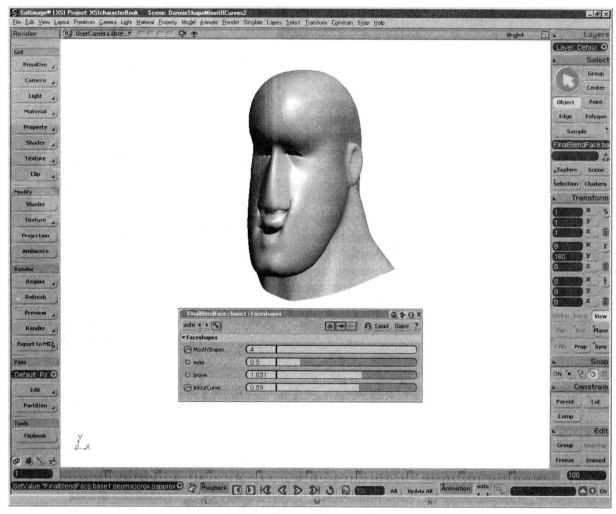

Mixing shapes with expressions

TOPICS COVERED

With expressions on the blend sliders in Mixers, you can build simple controls that aggregate complex mixer setups together. This makes life easier for animators, and speeds character animation.

You'll learn how to:

- Put expressions on Mixers
- Drive expressions with Custom Sliders
- Draw your own response curves
- Use response curves in expresions

MATERIALS REQUIRED

This tutorial uses the DonnieShapeMixerUI and DonnieShapeMixerCurves scenes.

TUTORIAL: EXPRESSIONS MIXING SHAPES

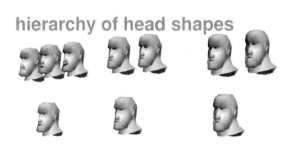

hierarchy of head shapes

the base head

This is a hierarchy of head shapes.

In the chapter on shape animation, you built a series of Mixers, each one controlling a part of the face. Then you mixed the Mixers into one main Mixer that brought together the effects of the eye Mixer, the brow Mixer, the mouth Mixer and so on.

One big problem with this approach is that since four Mixers are required for keyframing, there really isn't much screen space left over for actually looking at your models. Another is that remembering which Mixer is which is simply too complicated for animators to remember easily. You need a custom control for the character that will easily mix shapes.

You can do that. The general idea is to add a series of sliders to the CustomControl PPG you have built for your model to control theses many Mixers.

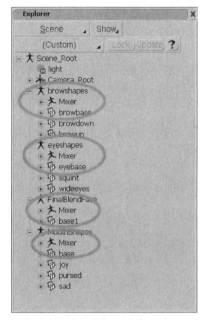

There is a Model, and therefore a Mixer, for each head.

STEP 1: UNDERSTAND THE MIXERS

Since you built each Mixer to control one area of the face, and since we decided early on that each Mixer would have a slack position in the middle, with a constricted pose on one side and a loose pose on the other, it seems like there could just be one slider to control each area of musculature in the face.

For instance, there could be one slider for the muscles under the brows, one slider for the muscles of the eyes, and one for the mouth muscles.

STEP 2: UNDERSTANDING TRANSITIONS BETWEEN SHAPES

Taking the brow Mixer sliders for instance, the new unified slider should blend between the three shapes: brow up, brow middle, and brow down. You never want it to be possible to blend the brow up position with the brow down position, because that would make no sense. The brow position needs to travel through the intermediate slack position on the way from the brow up to the brow down.

Therefore, imagine a slider that went from 0 to 2. When the slider is in the middle, at 1, the Mixer slider for the slack shape is all the way up at full weight (1). When the slider goes to the far end at 2, the slack shape Mixer returns to no blend weight, while the contracted shape Mixer blend weight goes up to 1, which is full weight.

So, only one Mixer track can be at full weight at one time. If the constricted pose is blended at 0.25 weight, then the slack pose must be at 0.75 blend weight.

In this way you enforce that the weight can never be greater than a total of 1, and that shapes transition cleanly from one to another.

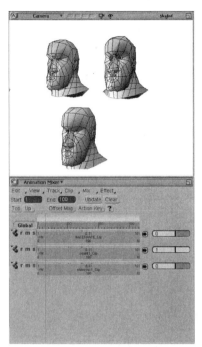

Now each Mixer has several blend sliders that are all independent.

In this case, you would put the expression on the Mixer blend weights themselves. You would need one expression that controlled each blend weight going up and then down from 0 to 1, based on the position of our custom slider. Each blend weight would use a different portion of the slider, and they would all overlap correctly.

STEP 3: GET STARTED

Open the DonnieShapeMixerUI scene.

There is a hierarchy of Mixers. Select the final head, at the base of the pyramid of heads, and open the FaceShapes custom control. Lock it open.

There are three sliders: one for the mouth, one for the eyes, and one for the brows. Slide the brows slider back and forth to see the action on the final head.

Now locate the Browshapes model, which has its own Mixer, and open the Mixer.

Slide the brows slider to see how the blend weight sliders change as the slider moves.

Since blend sliders belong to Mixers, and Mixers belong to models, the property you are controlling is on the model. For a model called "MyModel", the name of the blend slider looks like this:

MyModel.MixerName.MixerShapeTrack.ShapeClipName.actionclip.weight

STEP 4: SET AN EXPRESSION ON THE FIRST MIXER BLEND SLIDER

Right-click on the animation divot for the first blend slider in the first Mixer track, and pop up the expression editor. The expression is:

```
cond( cond( 1 - FinalBlendFace.base1.FaceShapes.brows == 0,
1, 1 - abs( 1 - FinalBlendFace.base1.FaceShapes.brows ) ) <
0 ,0 cond( 1 -FinalBlendFace.base1.FaceShapes.brows == 0, 1,
1 - abs( 1 -FinalBlendFace.base1.FaceShapes.brows ) ) )
```

This is a nested conditional statement.

Note that those sets of equal signs are two equal signs together, and means "equals", as in, "the left side equals the right side".

In this case you're using it to divide up the space of the slider into sections, and limit the blend slider in the Mixer so it can never go above one or below zero.

STEP 5: UNDERSTAND HOW TO MODIFY THE EXPRESSION FOR OTHER TRACKS

The business end of the expression is the last statement:

```
1 - abs( 1 - FinalBlendFace.base1.FaceShapes.brows )
```

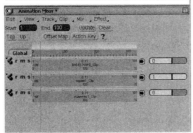

This Expression links the first blend slider in the Mixer with the "brows" custom slider.

...which is executed only when the brow slider is in the range for that brow base position, between 1 and 2. It sets the final blend shape to some number between 0 and 1.

At first glance, all the "1 - abs(1 -" business seems redundant, but that's actually how you tune the same expression to work on a different range of the slider for the next shape track.

For instance, the second shape track has the same formula, except:

```
1 - abs( 0 -
```

...which results in the blend weight working when the brow slider is operating in the first position, from 0 to 1.

Likewise:

```
1 - abs( 2 -
```

...would tune the expression to work in the third position of the slider, from 2 to 3.

STEP 6: DO IT OVER, THIS TIME THE EASY WAY

Thinking through this type of logical exercise works for some people, and not for others. I started by drawing curves on a whiteboard that represented the reaction I wanted, and then tried to develop formulas that made those curves. An easier way might be for you to actually draw the curve, as a function curve on a property you create just for that purpose.

For instance, if you created a property called "InOutCurve" in the Custom Properties, you could build a curve that goes from 0 at frame 1 to 1 at frame 50 and back to 0 at frame 100, by just setting some keyframes on that property, perhaps in the Animation Editor. Then you could reference that curve instead of trying to build complex formulas when you need a nice Gaussian distribution of something.

For instance, in the example above, if you wanted a curved response based on the brow slider using this method, you could put an expression on the Mixer blend weight that finds the value of the curve you drew at the frame given by the value of the brow slider.

If the curve was named InOutCurve, and the custom property page was named FaceShapes, that expression would look like this:

```
at_frame( ( FinalBlendFace.base1.Faceshapes.brows * 100 ),
FinalBlendFace.base1.FaceShapes.InOutCurve )
```

Since you want the brow slider to have a throw of 1 unit, and the curve extends over 100 frames, you multiply the brows slider by 100. That produces a curved response on that Mixer blend weight from 0 to 1.

If you want the blend weight to activate in a range of 0.5 to 1.5, so it overlaps the first range, you'd change the expression to:

```
at_frame( ( ( FinalBlendFace.base1.Faceshapes.brows - 0.5 )
* 100 ), FinalBlendFace.base1.FaceShapes.InOutCurve )
```

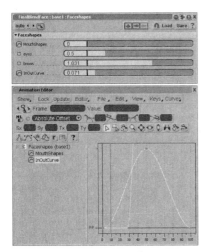

A new custom property has an animation curve drawn on it.

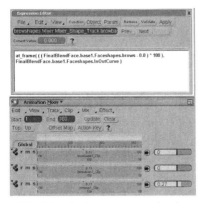

This (simpler) expression also has a response curve.

By subtracting 0.5 from the brows slider, you get a different response range out of the curve, delayed by 0.5 units of the brow slider.

The third Mixer slider would have the same expression, modified again to delay the response to a different part of the brow curve.

```
at_frame( ( (
FinalBlendFace.base1.Faceshapes.brows - 1.0 ) *
100 ), FinalBlendFace.base1.FaceShapes.InOutCurve )
```

Open the scene file DonnieShapeMixerUICurves2 to examine a scene with these elements added and working. Open the FaceShapes custom controls, and see how the Mixer weights in the BrowShapes Mixer. Look at the expressions on the Mixer blend weights, and examine the animation curve of the InOutCurve that has been added to the FaceShapes controls.

CONCLUSION

Expressions can be powerful allies for lazy animators, but using them takes the mind of an inventor, as well as a little math. Try to imagine what operations in your animation you will have to do over and over again. These are candidates for an expression. Expressions are also a good solution to problems that require more detail or accuracy than setting keyframes will provide.

QUIZ

1. WHERE DO EXPRESSIONS GO?
a. On Fcurves
b. On Properties
c. On Models

2. CAN YOU ADD AN EXPRESSION TO AN ANIMATION CURVE WITHOUT USING THE MIXER?
a. Yes
b. No
c. Sometimes

3. WHEN ARE EXPRESSIONS EVALUATED?
a. Every frame change
b. When you interactively scale, rotate or translate
c. Both A and B

4. WHICH DOES THE EXPRESSION GO ON?
a. The master object
b. The slave object

5. WHICH PROPERTIES CAN HAVE EXPRESSIONS ON THEM?
a. Transformations
b. Transforms and Materials
c. All of them

6. `Fc * (throttle.kine.local.roty / 180)`

a. This is valid expression syntax
b. This is not valid expression syntax
c. This is compiled expression syntax

7. THE KEYWORD FC (FOR CURRENT FRAME) IS A:
a. Function
b. Variable
c. Constant

8. MAX(9, 11, 23, 4, 9, 15)P
a. is a Function
b. is a Variable
c. is a Constant

9. GIVEN THE EXPRESSION...

`cond( the moon is bleu cheese, eat the moon, go home )`

...WHAT WOULD THE EXPRESSION RETURN IF THE MOON REALLY WAS MADE OF BLEU CHEESE?
a. Eat the moon
b. Go home
c. Neither

10. WHAT'S THE BEST WAY TO BUILD COMPLEX EXPRESSIONS?
a. Plan it all out ahead of time
b. Hire a programmer
c. Start simple and build up

LUDOVICK WILLIAM MICHAUD
3D TECHNICAL DIRECTOR
JANIMATION

Anthony Rossano: Tell us about your role, Ludovick!

Ludovick William Michaud: I work as a 3D technical director at Janimation in Dallas Texas. At Janimation, Technical Director means the guy who actually builds the workflow, the pipeline, does the character setup, gets into all the scripting around all the workarounds, the fixes, the plugins, the lighting, and then goes into rendering. Sometimes passing by texturing, UV editing, shader building, and taking care of all the passes. Finally he renders every single thing there is to render in the building with a big render farm that he has got now.

ATR: What's a normal day look like for you?

LWM: Usually a normal day consists of getting in at 8:30, have a staff meeting for half an hour. Then at my computer I look through my email for another half-hour. Then I start on whatever project I am working on at the time. Perhaps 75% of our work is commercials, and 25% is movies. Usually I'll be working on a commercial, so I will be debugging what we have to do, checking renders, building character setups, weighting characters, writing scripts, or developing plug-ins. If we don't have anything to do, I'll ask the animators (Greg, John, Lyn, or whatever freelance we have at the time) what they need and they will say, "What do you think about this tool, we don't have this tool in XSI," so maybe I'll build it. That's a normal day. A crazy day.

ATR: So you spend a lot of your time overcoming limitations of the software and workflow?

LWM: Exactly. I build a lot of Synoptic views for what we call the Power Schematic view. What we do is we have this custom setup for selecting controls in complex rigs, and easy hiding and unhiding of groups. These are things to help the animators who are already working fast work even faster.

Image courtesy of Janimation, 7-Eleven (c) 2002

"Chessboard" lighting, texturing, and rendering by Ludovick William Michaud, modeling by Martin Belleau

ATR: How often do you get to travel?

LWM: Usually just for vacation or back to Montreal. Mostly my job is right here in Dallas. But if we need to do a shoot, I might be called to go on-location. In that case I go on location to do pre-production and that kind of stuff, to get ready for the 3D work. Or, I might go to do post-production in LA for a week at a time. When I worked for Softimage I traveled to England, and to LA for three months. For the last year and a half at Softimage I traveled around as a trainer and support person.

ATR: Let's go back to making the technology work. Do you think that technology is getting ahead of people, or is it just catching up to people?

LWM: Working with 3D apps is getting way easier. Take any application right now. It's getting easier. When software gets too technical it scares people, and makes them think they aren't working. People are afraid of scripting and the technical part, so my job is to show them that scripting is, in fact, powerful, and that we can save a lot of time with it. I think the technology is not the part that is catching up. The technology is there, and has been there for ten years, and people are just too reluctant to build on new technology.

For instance, Sub-Ds (Subdivision surfaces) have existed for ten if not fifteen years. There were tests 10 years ago of perfect Sub-Ds. Only Lightwave coded it. Now finally everyone is preaching Sub-Ds. But at the time, no one would take care of it, so that technology got left back, and nothing happened to it. Fluid dynamics and stuff like that always existed mathematically, and it just didn't get written because people didn't think they needed it. That's another technology that's been there all along. Pretty much people are late right now, catching up to something that used to be there. Technology hasn't really advanced enough. When people understand what they can do and don't limit themselves to what people are requesting from them, yes, then they will be able to do more and create new stuff.

As far as 3D goes, I think the games platforms are finally at the point where the platform tools are faster than the art technology required to feed them. The limitations becomes the artists. I think technology is turning itself toward what the people need. People need entertainment, so it's going to give them games first.

ATR: Thanks, Ludovick!

Image courtesy of Janimation, K-Mart (c) 2002

7-Eleven "Slurpee/Fish Tank" :30 TV
Agency: The Richards Group

Kmart "Get Down Tonite" :30 TV
Agency: Don Coleman Advertising

Production company for all spots: Janimation

Chief Creative Director	Steve GaÁonnier
Animation Director	Greg Punchatz
FX Producer	Pete Herzog
Technical Director	Ludovick William Michaud
Visual FX Supervisor	Lyn Caudle
Animator	John McInnis
Designer/Compositor	Alex Neuman
Designer	Jennifer Hudgens

11 ADVANCED CHARACTER SETUP

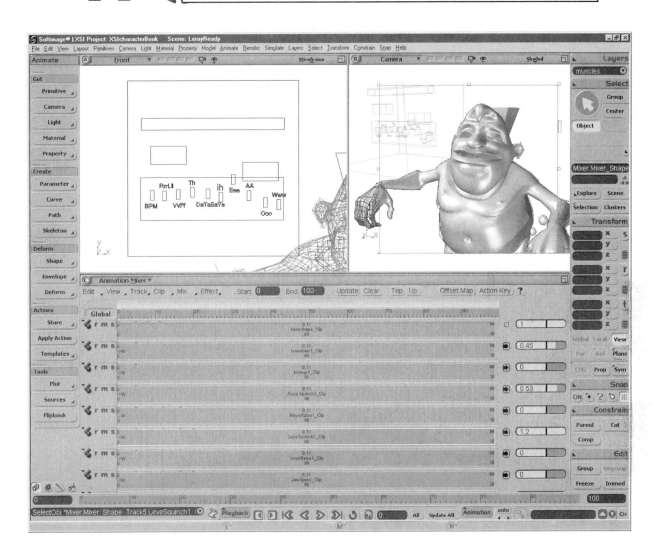

IN THIS CHAPTER YOU WILL LEARN ABOUT:

- What the role of the Technical Director is
- When to use 2D sliders and when to use 3D controls
- The difference between Amount and Degree
- How to build custom property pages
- How to build a custom Synoptic view
- How to set up 3D controls for the upper body and lower body
- How to build facial animation controls for emotion and lip sync
- How to connect shapes and controls with expressions
- Strategies for floor detection and collision detection
- How to build expressions for the hips
- How to build expressions for the collarbone
- How to control spinal roll with expressions

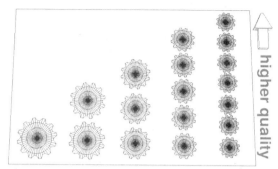

fast interaction, more iteration

Good work depends on fast interaction with good feedback, and lots of iterations to improve the work.

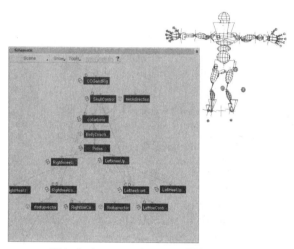

This is the control rig you'll be using.

INTRODUCTION

There are a lot of different roles involved in the production of computer graphics, and not all people will be involved in all tasks. In an organization large enough to have a few different digital artists working on each project, each artist will naturally gravitate to the tasks they are best at and find most enjoyable. In really large organizations with well-defined job titles, people will be hired for their specific abilities in certain job areas.

One important set of tasks revolves around setting up characters prior to actually animating them. This setup process might involve enveloping and weighting the skin to the IK hierarchies, building custom control rigs to drive those IK hierarchies, and possibly writing small expressions or scripts to automate parts of the animators' work.

Not every person needs to be excited by this part of the process. Not every person will want to be involved in the setup process. Many very fine animators wish to limit their attention to issues of animation pose and timing, and little time or enthusiasm for the setup process, desiring to keep their characters stick-figure simple instead.

On the other hand, some people do have the time, the background, and the inclination to invent new character setups, IK control rigs, and code snippets to automate tasks. These fine folks are generally called Technical Artists or Technical Directors, and this chapter is for them.

BECOMING A TECHNICAL DIRECTOR

The Technical Director's (or TD's) duties include setting up characters so that they are flexible, easy to use, and can be puppeted with a minimum of technical thought, and a maximum of artistic and creative control.

Often, after the TD sets up the IK for a character, he will build in expressions to automate many of the details that would otherwise be handled manually by the animator. The goal of the TD is to save the animator time, and make the character easy to manage. Good TD'ing can make a character much more realistic and believable, and save a lot of time that might otherwise be spent setting thousands of redundant keyframes.

In this chapter we'll explore setting up a human character with expressions to automatically keep the pelvis located between the feet, prevent the feet from going through the ground, properly transfer weight from side to side as feet leave the ground, properly rotate the body to follow the leading foot during turns, properly shift the pelvis and collarbone to ensure good contraposto posture during weight transfer between feet, and a lot more.

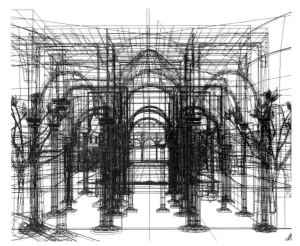

Where's the effector?

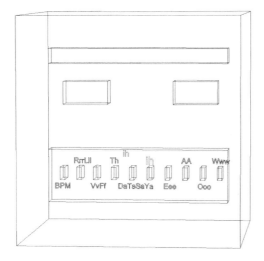

This is a simple, obvious, intuitive, and elegant interface.

A scrolling list of a thousand sliders is counterintuitive and slows down animation.

Throughout this chapter, I will be using the object names of the character I have created. You can name your objects to match mine, or build a character from scratch and modify the expressions to function as mine do.

Many of the expressions rely on the specific construction of the IK control rig, a diagram of which is provided here. In general, the rig is constructed so that the IK chains are not in any sort of hierarchy. Instead, they are constrained at the tops and bottoms to control elements that are themselves placed into a hierarchy.

In this chapter we'll also explore the use of several different kinds of custom user interfaces, including your own 3D elements, custom property pages, and the graphical synoptic view.

INNOVATIVE CONTROLS FOR ANIMATORS

If the TD doesn't create any special user interfaces or custom controls for the manipulation of the character, the job of the animator quickly goes from difficult to impossible. Imagine the simple difficulty of even locating and selecting IK effectors in a large scene every time the animator needs to set a keyframe on something. Creating the easy to select objects in the control rig was one example of a custom control that will make life easier and therefore faster for the animator. The TD can also create other geometry objects in the scene, that may or may not be actually a part of the control rig, for the animator to act on. In addition to visible geometry objects, XSI has a few other custom user interface tricks up its sleeve, including the heads-up display for custom PPGs, and the Synoptic property and Synoptic view, which is a completely customizable graphical button construction set similar to a web page.

The goal as TD is to make life easier for the animator without removing any possible control that the animator might later need. You want to automate only as long as you also make arrangements for that automation to be overridden by the animator.

The goal in creating custom controls is to make those custom controls obvious, intuitive, simple, and elegant.

If you make custom controls that are complex and arcane, the animators simply will not use them. If you make custom controls with too much detail, the animators will be bogged down searching through the controls. If you make controls that limit the range of the acting possible, you have limited the quality of the final animation.

These are all serious problems for the TD. For instance, if you build beautiful and elegant synoptic properties that are hidden way down in control rig on an element that the animators never touch, they might forget about the existence of the controls you built, and your effort would therefore be wasted.

You want to give control back to the animator, but you don't want to obscure the desired result with a mountain of useless details. For instance, I have seen custom property pages built to control movie characters where each and every finger joint, every facial muscle, each skin bulge, etc., was listed in a giant 2,000-line property page. This resulted in forcing the animators to scroll down page after page after page after page just to look for a slider to curl a little finger. Since text all looks pretty much the same to a 3D person when the PPG is scrolling, simply finding the right property to animate became a significant chore. The result was that the incredible detail and control built by the Technical Directors went unused, and the characters looked stiff and lifeless on the screen.

Remember, the goal of the TD is to manufacture simplicity out of complexity.

CUSTOM PPGS AND THE HEADS-UP DISPLAY: AT A GLANCE

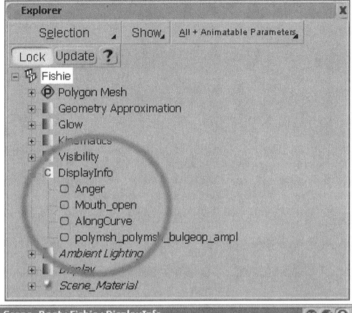

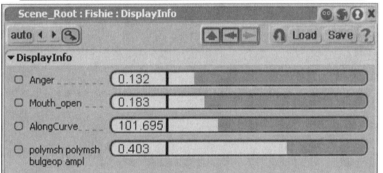

If the custom property page is not named DisplayInfo, this won't work.

TOPICS COVERED

In previous chapters you learned how to create a custom property page at the root of the control rig. What you need to do is create custom sliders within that PPG, and then write expressions to control the rig that include these sliders as inputs, or variables.

You'll learn how to:

- Create a Custom PPG
- Add custom properties to that PPG
- View and Edit thos Properties onscreen without a PPG

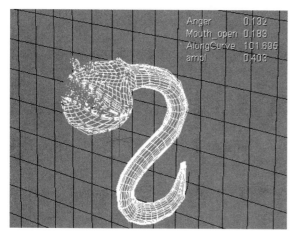

The Heads-Up Display is a way to add information without reducing the usable screen area.

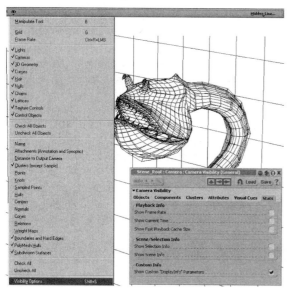

Toggling on the Show Custom "Displayinfo" will overlay that PPG in the view window.

TUTORIAL: CUSTOM PPGS AND THE HEADS-UP DISPLAY

There are some special rules for Custom PPGs you can take advantage of. If you create your Custom PPG on the root of the control rig, and name it exactly "DisplayInfo", then you can show the contents of that PPG on screen in a heads-up display fashion, superimposed over the 3D camera view.

The heads-up display then becomes a set of virtual sliders, so you can mark those properties, change the values, save keyframes, or store actions easily without calling up a PPG that lies over the 3D views and wastes screen real estate.

To see this in action before you use it for real, follow these steps.

Step 1: Get a sphere. Name it "Heads_Up".

Step 2: With the sphere selected, add a custom PPG with the Create→Parameter→New Custom Parameter Set command in the Animate module. Make certain that you name this PPG DisplayInfo. If the name is not correct, the heads-up display will not work.

Step 3: In an explorer window, select the new PPG you just made, and then open it up.

Step 4: Add a few custom properties to that new PPG with the Create→Parameter→New Custom Parameter command. They can be named anything you want, and the values should be integers or floats.

Step 5: Now you need to turn on the Heads-up display. In the camera view, go to the Show menu (the eyeball) and chose the very bottom item, Visibility Options. Click on the very last tab of the Camera Visibility PPG, called Stats. Toggle on the Show Custom "DisplayInfo" Parameters check box.

Step 6: If the sphere is still selected, you should now see the name of your custom property superimposed on the top-right corner of the camera view. All of the properties that you create in the custom property page named DisplayInfo will show up in this way.

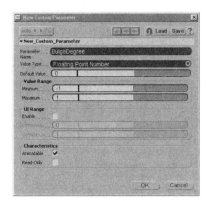

Degree is a multiplier for an expression, and should go from -1 to 1.

Amount is added on to modify the expression.

Step 7: You can change the value of the custom property by entering virtual slider mode. Click the F4 key, and your cursor will change to indicate that you are in virtual slider mode. See the different cursor icon. Release the F4 key, then click on a parameter on screen with the Left Mouse Button to mark that parameter, turning the parameter blue. Hold down the F4 key to enter virtual slider mode, then hold down the Middle Mouse Button and drag in the camera view to change the value up and down.

The heads-up display is just another way of seeing and changing values on an object while saving screen space.

THE AMOUNT SLIDER AND THE DEGREE SLIDER

You are going to use custom sliders (and other controls) as inputs to the expressions that will automate the control rig. These custom sliders will therefore be variables in the expressions. As the user changes the sliders, the variables will change in the expressions and the results of the expressions will change the control rig.

These variables will therefore be the way that the animators can control the results of the expressions, making them work more or less, or even overriding them if necessary.

You need each expression to have a manual component and an automatic component. You will build two variables for each aspect of the control rig you plan to control with expressions: Amount and Degree.

Amount is an absolute value that is added into an expression. When you drag an Amount slider to the value 1, you know that the output of the expression just got bigger by exactly 1.

Degree is a measurement of proportion. When the degree slider is at 0.5, the output of the expression will be exactly half of what it would be if the degree slider were at 1. When the degree slider is at 0, then the expression will have no effect at all.

In this way, the animator can adjust the sliders to add or subtract directly to the expression, and the animators can control how powerful the effects of the automatic expression will be.

By way of example, let us consider the sphere you just built to try out the heads-up display. You want the sphere to pulse over time, as if breathing, which you will accomplish by putting a Bulge op on the sphere. You want the sphere to bulge bigger and smaller on its own, but you want the animator to be able to control how much the automatic bulge happens, and also to be able to add in some manual bulge. Of course, you also want the animator to be able to animate these values over time.

When you make these custom sliders you need to choose the correct value type and range. You will want both to be floating point numbers, so you can have a fine degree of control. The Degree slider should have a value range of 0 to 1, with 0 meaning no automatic expression and 1 meaning full 100% automatic expression. The Amount slider will have a different range for each use. Generally you want the range to go from a negative value to a positive value, so the animator can take away from the effect of the expression, as well as add to it.

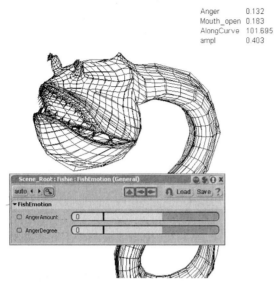

Anger   0.132
Mouth_open   0.183
AlongCurve   101.695
ampl   0.403

Use Amount and Degree to modify your expressions.

BulgeAmount   0.000
BulgeDegree   0.000

This sphere has a Bulge operator on it.

BulgeAmount   0.000
BulgeDegree   0.000
ampl   1.000

Drag and drop means left-click and hold, then drag and release.

Try these simple steps on the sphere above to see an example of this concept.

Step 1: Get your sphere, or open the Heads_Up scene from the courseware. Open the DisplayInfo custom PPG on the sphere. Lock it open.

Step 2: Add a Bulge deformer to the sphere. Open the BulgeOp ppg, and lock it open.

Step 3: Now you need to add the two sliders to the Custom PPG. Select the DisplayInfo PPG directly in an explorer view by clicking directly on the name of the custom PPG, to make sure that when you add the custom PPG it goes into the right PPG.

Use the Create→Parameter→New Custom Parameter command, and name this one "BulgeDegree". Make it a floating point number, with a min value of -1 and a max value of 1. This means that when you multiply BulgeDegree by whatever else you have in the expression editor, you can turn the results up or down, positive or negative.

Make another custom parameter, this time named "BulgeAmount", also a float, with a range from -1 to 1. This means that when you add BulgeAmount to the other stuff in the expression editor you can add or subtract a certain amount from the overall effect, separate from scaling the action up or down.

Step 4: Now it's time to hook up the expression on the Bulge Amplitude. In the Bulge PPG, right-click on the green animation divot belonging to Amplitude and choose Expression Editor from the context-sensitive menu that pops up. This will launch the expression editor, with the name of the bulge amplitude already entered in the affected element line at the top of the editor.

The fastest way to accurately build expressions using custom sliders is to drag and drop the custom slider into the expressions editor, avoiding possible spelling errors. Drag the green animation divot for the BulgeDegree custom slider into the white edit area of the Expression Editor and let go. You will see the name sphere.DisplayInfo.BulgeDegree appear.

Edit the expression to read:

```
sin( Fc * 10 ) *
sphere.DisplayInfo.BulgeDegree
```

You'll want to put parentheses around this part of the expression to show that this is a complete thought.

```
( sin( Fc * 10 ) *
sphere.DisplayInfo.BulgeDegree )
```

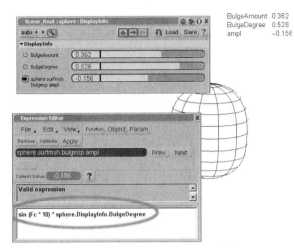

The bulge amplitude will be the sine of the current frame, multiplied by the BulgeDegree.

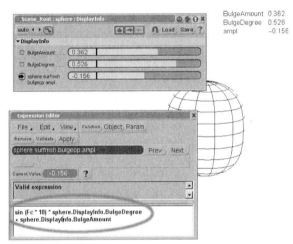

Now the BulgeAmount is added in as well.

Now drag and drop the BulgeAmount divot on the end of the equation, and add a plus sign (+) and another pair of parentheses, so the expression reads:

```
( sin( Fc * 10 ) *
sphere.DisplayInfo.BulgeDegree ) +
( sphere.DisplayInfo.BulgeAmount )
```

You now have two distinct things happening. The sin function is pulsing the bulge, and is amplified by the BulgeDegree. Then, through the magic of the plus sign (+), you've just added on the amount of the BulgeAmount slider.

Hit Validate, correct any errors you made, and then hit Apply and dismiss the expressions editor, and close the Bulge PPG.

Step 5: Test the results to understand Degree vs. Amount. You can use the heads-up display to change your Amount and Degree values. Enter virtual slider mode by holding F4. This only works with the XSI keyboard map; if you are using the SI3D key map, you'll have to change it in the File→Keyboard Mapping dialog. In virtual slider mode, mark a property with the Left Mouse Button by clicking the name on-screen, then change the values by dragging with the Middle Mouse Button held down.

Turn on looping playback, and set the BulgeDegree to 0. There will now be no automatic bulging at all. But when you drag on the BulgeAmount slider you can set the bulge manually, or animate it by setting keyframes.

Now increase the BulgeDegree to .25. You should see some small pulsing, added onto the value you set with the BulgeAmount.

As you adjust the Degree slider, you will see that the effect of the automatic part of the expression changes. If you want to add some bulge manually, you can do that too, with the Amount slider.

You'll need to add both aspects – Amount and Degree – to all the expressions, so that the animator can do whatever they want with the automated expression.

324   XSI ILLUMINATED: CHARACTER

3D CONTROLLERS VS. 2D SLIDERS

Sliders to control values are all the rage, but they have a few significant drawbacks. First, they are inherently linear and two-dimensional. You can only drag a slider to make the value greater, or lesser. Second, the slider is not visually connected to anything, so that while the slider certainly makes things happen on-screen, we as humans have a hard time feeling the connection between the two events. Third, because each slider changes only one value at a time, you end up needing many of them to control the characters. You could overcome these limitations with the use of 3D controllers in situations where you need more hand-eye coordination, fewer controls, and more complex actions.

For instance, if you simply created a cube, and then used the position of the cube in X as the input to an expression instead of the value of a slider as the input to that expression, you'd have solved the second problem, visual coordination.

If you then connected the Y translation of that cube to the input of another expression, and the Z translation to yet another input, then you'd be reducing the number of individual controls you need, grouping them together on-screen, and giving the animator better hand-to-eye coordination and visual feedback.

You could also then set keys on three input values at once, instead of needing to mark and key three separate properties.

If the controllers make some sense visually, and the inputs they drive are arranged to make sense to the animator, then there is an additional benefit.

BUILDING 3D BODY CONTROLLERS: AT A GLANCE

TOPICS COVERED

In this tutorial you will construct the 3D controllers that you will need to control the expressions that will drive the automatic parts of the character rig.

You'll learn how to:

- Organize and conceptualize 3D controllers

Moving the single poly cube can drive three different values.

TUTORIAL: BUILDING 3D BODY CONTROLLERS

In the case of the human IK system you constructed earlier, you will shortly be building expressions that control the position of the hips relative to the feet. When you do that you'll need to build custom controls for the amount and degree of lean, sway, and crouch. Lean is the position of the hips in front or back of the feet, as if the character was walking uphill or pushing a boulder. Sway is the side-to-side motion of the hips, as the hips move over each foot to transfer weight. Crouch is the height of the hips above the feet. There are three sets of values here, each one perpendicular to the others. That's a perfect match for the three axes in the 3D world, so let's use the Z-axis to control the lean, the X-axis to control the sway, and the Y-axis to control the crouch. You could then use the translation in each axis to drive the Amount, and the scale in each axis to control the Degree.

Note: I note that animators have a hard time remembering that the scale drives degree, so it is a perfectly good idea to use sliders in a Custom PPG for Degree, but a 3D control for Amount, if the TD wishes it so.

STEP 1: GET A 3D OBJECT

In a new scene, get a primitive cube. Name it "LowBody", and change the cube Length to 1 in the cube PPG so that the cube is rather small. Leave it at the global center for a moment.

STEP 2: BUILD A BOX FOR THE CONTROLLER

You want to use the local translation values of the cube in expressions, but you probably won't want the controller to be stuck at the global center, because that won't be very convenient. So, you need to build an outer box around the controller, as its parent, so that you can move the whole assembly to wherever it is most convenient to use.

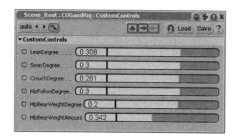

Get another cube, and name it "LowBodyController". Make it the parent of the smaller LowBody cube.

STEP 3: LABEL THE CONTROLLER

Use the Get→Text→Curves command to add some text curves to the scene. In the PPG for the Text operator, make the text read "Lower Body". Then, scale the text down to fit inside the larger cube, above the smaller cube. Freeze the text's operator stack and transformations. Make it a child of the larger cube as well.

STEP 4: TEST YOUR WORK AND SAVE

Now you can move this assembly in branch mode wherever you need it, and the local values of the inner cube will always be relative to the larger, outer cube, and the text label will make the controller obvious to the animator.

For now, save this assembly as a separate scene called, appropriately, "LowerBodyController".

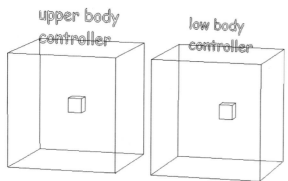

These simple cubes will drive the character rig, adding manual control for the animator.

STEP 5: MAKE THE UPPER BODY CONTROLLER

The upper body controller will be the piece that the animator manipulates to drive the shoulders of the character. The shoulders will move relative to the hips, in general, but on top of that they need to be able to lean (front to back), sway (side to side), drop (up and down), twist (rotate around the spine), front bend over (rotate front to back), and side bend (rotate side to side).

Once again, you could save a lot of single-action sliders with one multipurpose cube.

You'll use the local translations to drive the lean, sway and drop, and you'll use the rotations to drive the twist, front bend, and side bend.

Using the same steps as you did for the lower body controller, make an upper body controller, named appropriately, and with an appropriate text label. Save it to a separate file.

These two control boxes, though simple, will be very useful later on for controlling a whole bunch of complicated rig expressions.

FACIAL ANIMATION CONTROLLERS

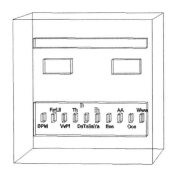

This simple controller replaces a huge stack of mixer tracks.

In the chapter on shape animation you learned how to build a complex set of shape mixers for facial animation. The remaining problem is that those mixers are awfully hard to use since they each occupy a section of screen space, and each have a series of those two-dimensional value sliders that you are trying so hard to do away with. Why don't you build a 3D controller that you can use to drive those mixers? Then you could have visual feedback, an on-screen organization that makes visual sense, better hand-to-eye coordination for the animator, a much simpler interface, and much better productivity.

FACIAL ANIMATION CONTROLLER: AT A GLANCE

TOPICS COVERED

The facial animation controller will be a hierarchy of 3D objects that drive shape mixers. The first step is to construct the control hierarchy. You'll do that in section one. Then the next step is to connect the controls to actual shape mixers. You'll take care of that in section two of this tutorial.

You'll learn how to:

> • Build a hierarchy of 3D control objects for facial animation

MATERIALS REQUIRED

For section one: no scene required. For section two: use the FaceControllerHookup scene from the course material.

TUTORIAL: FACIAL ANIMATION CONTROLLER

The facial animation controller will also be a bunch of cubes, but they will be scaled and positioned to look like a human face. This makes it easy and intuitive for the animator to select, translate, and keyframe the controllers.

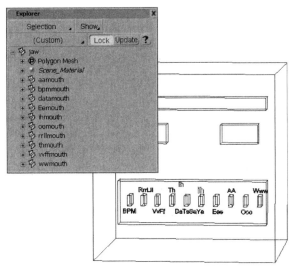

Each phoneme is driven by a cube.

SECTION 1: CONSTRUCT THE FACIAL ANIMATION CONTROL RIG

STEP 1: MAKE THE LARGE OUTER SHELL OF THE CONTROLLER

Get a primitive cube and name it "FaceController". Scale it somewhat larger, and freeze the transforms. If you build your face in something other than the Front view, then the axes that you use in the expressions will have to be different than mine, so it's a good idea to build your controller facing to the Front view, just as mine is.

STEP 2: MAKE THE EYEBROW CONTROLLERS

Get a cube and name it "LeftBrow". Scale it thinner, and move it to the top-left of the FaceController, looking in the Front view.

Take a look at the transform cells. It currently has a scale and a transformation on it, and you need it to be zeroed out in its current pose, so that the place where you put it becomes the default values for the left brow controller when used in an expression. Therefore, you must freeze all the transforms.

It's just a cube, named FaceController.

Make a duplicate, slide it over to the right side of the first brow, name it "RightBrow", and freeze that one to zero out the change in transforms. Make each brow the child of the larger FaceController.

STEP 3: MAKE THE EYE CONTROLLERS

Get two cubes. Place them each below a brow controller. Name them "LeftEye" and "RightEye". Make sure they are frozen so their transforms are removed. Make them children of the FaceController. These controllers will drive the blink shapes.

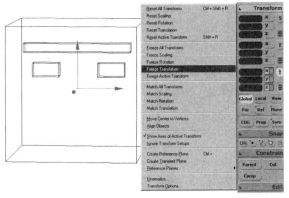

The brows and eyes must have their translations frozen after placement.

STEP 4: MAKE THE JAW CONTROLLER

Get one more cube, and scale it to extend across the FaceController. Name it "Jaw". It will drive the major opening and closing of the mouth and jaw. As usual, make it a child of the FaceController.

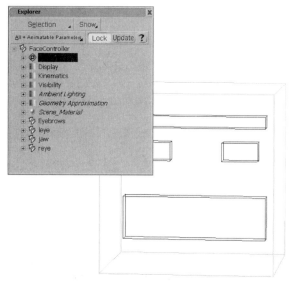

The jaw controller will house the phoneme controllers.

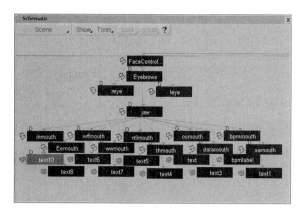

This is the organization of the FaceController hierarchy.

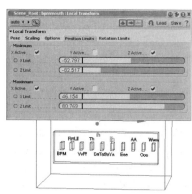

Now the cubes will only slide up and down.

STEP 5: MAKE THE PHONEME CONTROLS

You'll need at least nine phoneme controls, and what better place to put them than right there on the mouth? That way the animators will know where to find them, and will have a visual reference for the phonetic state of the model at all times. Make one thin cube for the first phoneme. Name it "BPM" because it will drive the shape of the mouth that matches the shape of your mouth when you make the Bb, Pp or Mm sounds. Move the cube to the middle of the left side of the Jaw cube.

Duplicate that cube eight more times, and distribute them evenly along the mouth.

Name each one, and for extra credit put the explanation in an Annotation property (Property→Annotation) for reference:

(BPM) – Lips lightly closed.

(RL) – Lips slightly open, tongue on roof of mouth.

(VF) – Lips open slightly, lower lip touching teeth.

(Th) – Lips open a third of the way, tongue on front teeth, corners of mouth contracted.

(DaTaSaJaYaCh) – Lips open half, lips loose, tongue in middle of mouth.

(Ih) – lips one third open, lips slightly curled down, tongue down.

(EeYeGee) Lips one third, lips pulled back to corners, no teeth, no tongue.

(Aa) Lips all the way open, no teeth, tongue on floor of mouth.

(Oo) – Mouth pursed to O shape, no teeth, no tongue.

(Whh) – Lips loosely together, pursed, no teeth.

When the animators are actually using the phoneme sliders, they will need visual feedback on each one to identify it when they need to select it. You can use the Show menu to toggle on the Name display for unselected objects, or just take the time to add text labels to each phoneme controller.

Now each one must have its transforms frozen, so that each starts with a local translation of zero (0) in X, Y and Z.

After freezing the transforms of the phoneme sliders, make them all children of the Jaw controller, so it looks like the character has teeth that move when you select the Jaw controller in branch mode and drag it up and down.

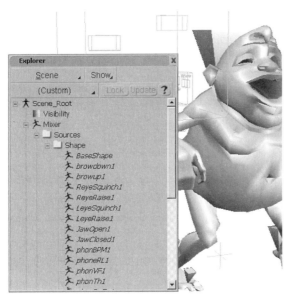

Stored shapes live in the Mixer, in the Shapes➔Sources folder.

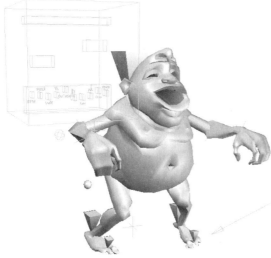

This controller will drive shapes on Leroy's head.

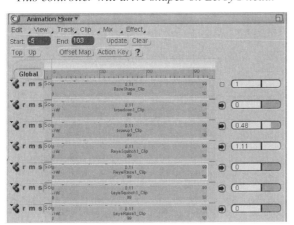

Each stored shape must be as long as the whole scene, filling the Mixer track.

These phonemes are themselves actually linear values – two-dimensional sliders, not 3D values – so you could limit the translation of these phoneme controllers so that they move only in the Y-axis. This step is not necessary, and will slow down the interaction significantly. If you do want to limit the motion of the controllers, select each one and open the Local Transform PPG. In the Position Limits tab, toggle on all the Minimum X, Y and Z limits, and the Maximum X, Y and Z limits. Set the min and Max X and Z values to 0. Set the Min Y to -1 and the Max Y to 1.1 to slightly overdrive the shape, exaggerating it a bit.

Now that you have completed the assembly of the FaceController, save it as a separate scene, or for extra credit, a separate external model. The good news is that you can reuse this controller for all your work.

The shape mixer on the character will be driven by this FaceController. That will make it easy to store actions on the FaceController to build up a library of reusable facial animations.

When you go about setting keyframes for facial animation using this method, you will actually be setting keys on the controller, not the character. You can even save these actions off to disk, with a small render region thumbnail, then use them to drive different characters with different facial shape animation, as long as it is linked to the same FaceController set up.

SECTION TWO: CONNECTING THE FACECONTROLLER TO THE SHAPE MIXER

You now have a great FaceController rig, but how will it actually drive the shape of the model? In this tutorial, let's hook it up.

Open the FaceControllerHookup scene, which has a sample face and the FaceController together in one scene.

The Leroy face already has shapes defined in the Mixer➔Shape➔Sources, as you learned to do in Chapter 4. The problem is that you have no good way to actually drive all these many shapes without having a giant complicated mixer that will inevitably confuse the animators and reduce the screen space they need to do their job.

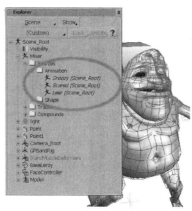

The animation action you stored can be found in the Mixer→Sources folder.

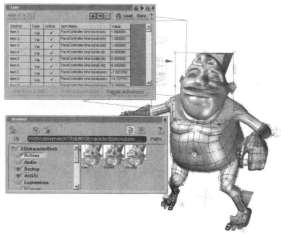

Saved animation actions can be shared with other characters, as long as they use the same controllers.

This expression drives the slider for the track that the BrowDown shape is in.

STEP 1: BUILD THE MIXER

Select Leroy's face, and show the Mixer. Remove the animation tracks, and add five new shape tracks. You'll eventually need one shape track for each shape you have stored. For instance, you have a default base shape, then you have a BrowUp shape, a BrowDown shape, shapes for the eyes, shapes for the mouth, and shapes for each phoneme. For this exercise you'll just hook up the brow shapes and two Phonemes. You will want to extrapolate from this exercise to add in all the shapes and hook up all the different parts of the controller.

In the first track, add in the BaseShape clip, and scale it longer to fill the Mixer completely. Use the weight slider to the right to increase the weight of the base shape to 1, which is 100%. You want all other shapes mixed against this one, so the face always returns to the default pose.

You can name the track to make it easier to read the expression by popping up a floating explorer with 8, then opening the Mixer→Tracks→Shape→ folder and right-clicking over the first track to use the rename command. Name this track BaseTrack.

In the next two tracks, add in the BrowDown and the BrowUp shapes, and name those tracks BrowDownTrack and BrowUpTrack so you can find them later. Eventually you'll want to add in all the other shape clips into their own tracks.

In the fourth track add in the PhonOo1 phoneme shape and in the fifth track add in the PhonAa1 phoneme shape. Make sure that the clips in each track extend all the way from the first frame you will need to the last frame you will need. Obviously, if you were working on a longer speaking part, you would want to set different start and end frames in the timeline and adjust the Mixer before you start.

Also be sure to change the Mixer from Average shape interpolation to Additive shape interpolation, by checking Normalize Off in the Mix→Shape Mixer Properties PPG. If you forget to do this, your animation will be mushy and not very dramatic.

STEP 2: ADD AN EXPRESSION ON THE BROWUP SHAPE WEIGHT SLIDER

The first track, the one with the BrowUp clip in it, needs to be mixed up gradually when the BrowController in the FaceController moves up above 0 in local Y (positive Y). You want to make sure that the value created by the expression never goes above 1 (or maybe 1.25) because that would overdrive the shape horribly. Similarly, you want to make sure that the blend weight never goes below 0 (or maybe -0.15) because that would under-drive the shape, causing weird results. You can right-click over the green animation divot next to the BrowUp weight slider to add an expression directly on it.

That expression would look like this:

```
cond( Eyebrows.kine.local.posy > 0, MIN( 1.2,
Eyebrows.kine.local.posy ), 0 )
```

This expression first checks whether the Eyebrows slider is above zero, and then if it is, sets the weight slider equal to either the value of the Eyebrows local translation in Y or 1.2, whichever is smaller. This makes sure that the animator can't move the slider too far up and make the shape blender freak out. In the expression above, 1.2 means 120% of full weight blend.

STEP 3: ADD AN EXPRESSION ON A THE BROWDOWN SHAPE WEIGHT SLIDER

The second shape, the BrowDown shape, should blend up when the BrowController moves down. It should start blending up when the brow controller drops below 0, and to stop at a blend of 100% (1 on the blend scale) if the brow controller drops below -1 in Y. In this way you build a stop or a limit on the controller, so that the animators can't drag the BrowController too far and create weird results. Also, since the BrowUp shape is driven when the BrowController goes up, and the BrowDown shape is driven when the BrowController goes down, you have one controller driving two separate shapes, simplifying the UI and making it more intuitive and easy to use.

The expression on the Brow down controller looks like this:

```
cond( Eyebrows.kine.local.posy < 0, -1 * MAX( -1.2,
Eyebrows.kine.local.posy ), 0 )
```

STEP 4: DO THE FIRST PHONEME

The phoneme sliders work slightly differently. Each phoneme controller drives only one shape Mixer track, not two, and they can only be blended from a value of 0 (no results from that phoneme) to a value of 1 (full phoneme).

Note: If you were extra-sly, you could pair off the phonemes into opposing pairs, so that as one blends up, the other blends down. That would be smart.

The expression on the PhonOo1 phoneme looks like this:

```
cond( oomouth.kine.local.posy > 0, MIN( 1.1 ,
oomouth.kine.local.posy ), 0 )
```

The expression on the Aaa phoneme looks like this:

```
cond( aamouth.kine.local.posy > 0, MIN( 1.1 ,
aamouth.kine.local.posy ), 0)
```

Click the Save button in the Action PPG to save a preset to disk.

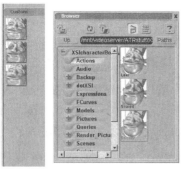

Drag and drop the saved presets from a browser to the custom menu stack.

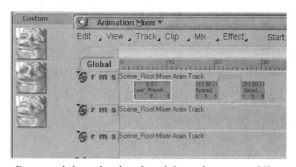

Drag and drop the thumbnail from the custom UI to any Mixer to use the action.

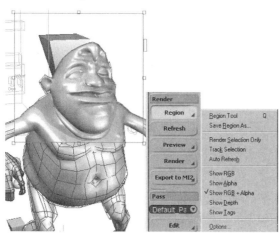

Draw a render region to create the thumbnail image for the saved action.

STEP 5: TEST

Grab the 3D object BrowController in the camera view, and slide it up and down. The brows on the character should wiggle up and down! Try the phoneme sliders on the FaceController for Oo and Aa to see the results of those sliders.

Now the animator can simply save keys on the translation of the 3D face controller, which in turn drives blend sliders in the Mixer, which in turn mixes the vertex positions of the saved shapes to create the resulting model shape.

This reduces the effort required from keying 20 or more sliders that are hard to distinguish to just a few 3D objects that make more intuitive sense to animators.

Go ahead and set up all the rest of the blend sliders, and save your work.

EXERCISE: SAVING A LIBRARY OF ACTIONS

To save an action to disk and then build a shape library in XSI, follow these steps:

Step 1: Set a pose on the FaceController, or set some keys on the FaceController.

Step 2: Store an action. Select the Entire FaceController hierarchy, from the big outer box on down. If you saved keyframes, use the Store→Animated Parameters – Fcurves command. If you set a pose without keys, use the Store→Transformations - Current Values command. Name the action appropriately so you can find it again.

Step 3: Pop up a floating explorer with the 8 button on your keyboard, locate the Mixer folder, and open up the Sources folder until you find the action you just saved. Double-click on it to open it up in a PPG.

Step 4: Make a render region. Frame your FaceController on screen, and draw a render region around it.

Step 5: Save to disk. In the top of the Action PPG, hit the Save button (officially called the Save Action Preset button), and save the action to your own database in the Actions folder.

Step 6: Make an action library. Change one of your views to a file browser, and navigate to where you just saved the action. Click the clapstick icon to view files with the thumbnail on it to see that your render region was used when you saved the action.

In the left-hand menu stack, click on the second small icon at the bottom to show the custom menu stack. There is an area labeled Custom, which is convenient to store actions in. Drag the thumbnail of your action from the browser to that custom control panel (note: drag and drop does not work on Irix or Linux) to load the action in.

Now no matter what scene you are in (as long as it has a FaceController in it), you can always drop this action into a Mixer track by dragging it from the custom menu.

CREATING AND USING THE SYNOPTIC VIEW

Imagine building little views like web pages that the animators can pop up, that show pictures of facial expressions, or character poses, or anything at all. The animator could click on the little images to make the character perform. That's the idea behind the Synoptic view. This is a similar idea to using a web page in the NetView to trigger scripts, but while the NetView only works on Windows-based computers, the Synoptic view is completely cross-platform and works properly on Irix- and Linux-based computers.

Just as saved actions are a way of remembering, storing, and applying poses and animation, the Synoptic view is a way or remembering storing and applying scripts. These scripts could be as simple as poses, or as complex as anything that you can write.

The advantage of a Synoptic view is that the TD can build a graphical user interface, using an image editing tool, to look like anything at all that you want. Then you can bind scripts to that interface so that they are executed when the user clicks the mouse over a certain area of the UI.

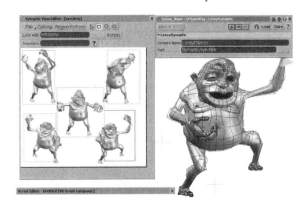

Speed up your work with a Synoptic view.

Synoptic views are properties, just like everything else in XSI, so the Synoptic property must be added to an object. However, there is no rule saying that the scripts that are executed by the Synoptic have to be related in any way to the object that the Synoptic property is on. So, you should choose to put the Synoptic property on the easiest-to-find, easiest-to-select object, and you should be consistent, so the animators know where to look to find it.

In general, the Synoptic should go on the top of the control rig hierarchy, just like the custom properties. In the case of the FaceController, it should go on the large box that surrounds all the control elements.

Once a Synoptic property has been added to an object, you have to go about the work of actually making a graphical user interface for it, and then writing the scripts that it will execute.

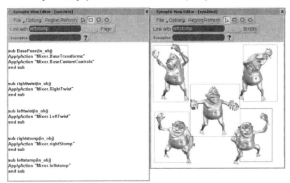

A Synoptic PPG is a clickable image map that runs scripts.

Finally, when the Synoptic property is hooked up to that UI and those scripts, the user can call it up by selecting the object with the Synoptic property and tapping the F3 button. Please note that the F3 button is mapped to show the Render module in the SI3D keyboard mapping, so if you want to use the Synoptic view, you will absolutely have to switch to the XSI keyboard map.

Let's make a simple Synoptic to explore the possibilities.

SIMPLE SYNOPTIC: AT A GLANCE

This is the jpeg file, cut and pasted together in an image editor.

TOPICS COVERED

In this tutorial you will build your own Synoptic view.

You'll learn how to:

- Add a Synoptic Property
- Define a Synoptic PPG
- Copy and Paste scripts from the Script Editor
- Pop up and use the Synoptic PPG to trigger scripts

MATERIALS REQUIRED

This tutorial uses the Synoptic scene and the image named synopticimage.jpg from the Pictures directory of the courseware.

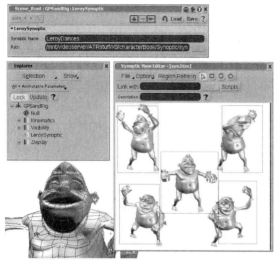

Connect the Synoptic property to the Synoptic definition.

TUTORIAL: SIMPLE SYNOPTIC

STEP 1: GET ORIENTED

Open the Synoptic scene, which is a completely constructed FaceController rig, driving Leroy's face.

I have already created an image to use in the synoptic, showing little renders of Leroy with different expressions on his face. I made it by rendering out lots of little render regions, saving them to disk, and then assembling them in Photoshop and adding titles to each. Examine that image, called synopticimage.jpg, in the Pictures folder.

STEP 2: ADD A SYNOPTIC PROPERTY

Select the top of the FaceController hierarchy, and use the Property→Synoptic command from the Animation module to add a blank Synoptic property to that object.

Use the Selection explorer to look at the property. It needs to be given a name, and it needs to be pointed at a synoptic description file that will describe the UI, the areas that are clickable, and the scripts that will be run. You haven't made that file yet, so just close the Synoptic PPG.

STEP 3: DEFINE THE SYNOPTIC PPG

Make the synoptic description file. Using the View→Views→Synoptic Editor menu command from the top of the UI, open up the Synoptic Editor. First, add in the image to be used as the UI. Use the File→Import Picture From File command from within the Synoptic editor, then navigate to the Pictures folder of the courseware and choose the synopticimage.jpg image.

Now that image will appear in the Synoptic editor.

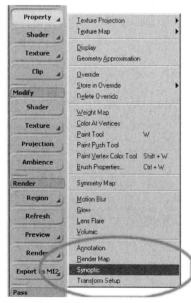

You can add a Synoptic property to any object.

Next, define a click region using one of the region tools. Start with the rectangle, and draw a rectangle around the first (top-left) Leroy face in the image. This region needs to be linked to a script that will be run when the user clicks anywhere within that area. Name the region by typing a name in the Link With edit box, replacing the chunk of text that says <no link>. This name will become the name of the subroutine that is run when the user clicks on the rectangle you drew.

STEP 4: COPY A SIMPLE SCRIPT TO TRIGGER

Pop up the script editor from the bottom-left of the screen in the timeline, and use the Edit→Clear History Log menu command to clear it out. The idea here is that you will use the FaceController to pose the different parts into an imitation of the face that Leroy was making in the current region of the UI image. The script editor will echo your changes, and then you can copy and paste these changes into the Synoptic editor to make the script that runs when a user clicks.

One by one, select each part of the FaceController and translate them to make the face that imitates the face you marked in the Synoptic editor.

You'll use these custom controls on the root of the control rig in the expressions you write.

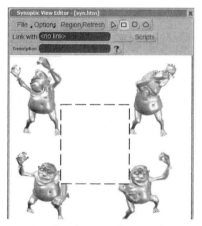

Use the shape tools to define regions for clicking.

The copied script commands go inside the subroutine named for the region.

When done, drag over all the commands that were logged in the script editor, and use the Edit→Copy command from the script editor to store them in the clipboard.

Back in the Synoptic editor, click the Scripts button. This associated the region you drew previously with a script. You can see that the beginning and ending of the script, the Sub and End Sub statements have been added for you. Whatever commands you add in between those two statements will be executed when the user clicks on the region.

Drop your edit cursor in between the two commands, and use the Edit→Paste command to put in all the commands that were logged from the script editor.

You can always toggle back and forth between the graphical picture view and the script view with the Scripts button, which turns into the Page button when you click on it.

Click the Page button to complete the work on that one region.

STEP 5: DO IT AGAIN

Click on the rectangle region tool in the Synoptic editor again, and draw a region around the second face in the UI image. Again open the script editor, clear it out, and then manually translate all the parts of the FaceControl into new positions for that facial expression. Again copy all the logged commands, and again name the region then click the Scripts button in the Synoptic editor, find the new subroutine that was defined for you, and paste the commands into the space between the Sub and End Sub commands.

STEP 6: COMPLETE THE SYNOPTIC PROPERTY

You now have two defined regions, which is enough to test the Synoptic. Save the new Synoptic definition with the File→Save As command in the Synoptic editor, calling it "MySynoptic" and placing it in the Synoptic folder of the courseware project. It's time to open the original Synoptic property and tell it where this Synoptic definition file ended up. Select the top of the FaceControl hierarchy, and use the Selection explorer to pop open the Synoptic property. In the Synoptic Name box, call it "MyFace", and in the Path edit box, browse to locate the "MySynoptic.htm" file that you saved and choose it. Close the Synoptic Property.

STEP 7: TEST

With the top of the FaceControl hierarchy still selected, tap the F3 button on the keyboard. A new edit box will pop up, showing you the UI image. Click over the first face to see the FaceController snap into that position. Click on the second face to instantly translate all the elements of the FaceControl into that position.

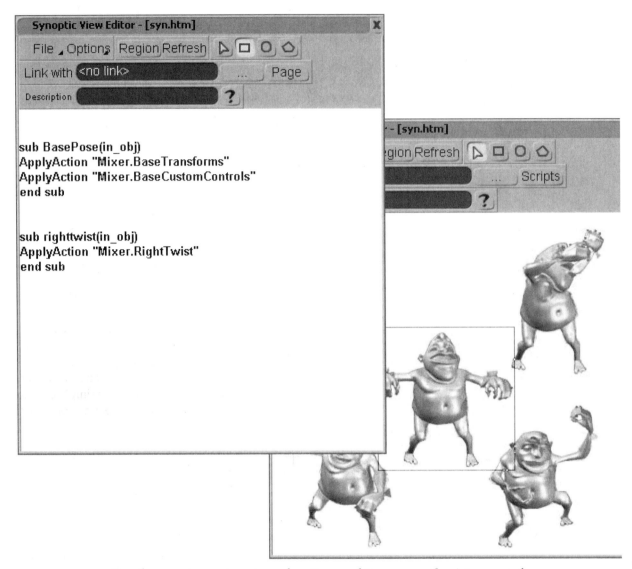

```
Synoptic View Editor - [syn.htm]                    X
 File ,Options  Region Refresh  ▷ □ ○ ◇
Link with <no link>                    ...   Page
Description                          ?


sub BasePose(in_obj)
ApplyAction "Mixer.BaseTransforms"
ApplyAction "Mixer.BaseCustomControls"
end sub


sub righttwist(in_obj)
ApplyAction "Mixer.RightTwist"
end sub
```

Now there are two regions, two subroutines, and two groups of script commands.

You could of course write more complex scripts that actually save keys, or even make decisions for the animators.

Synoptic property pages take a while to set up, but since they can execute any script, they can also save a lot of time in animation. Synoptic properties are most useful for complex rigs that would take many operations for the animator to set and key, and for making a consistent user interface so that many animators can all work on the same character and achieve consistent results.

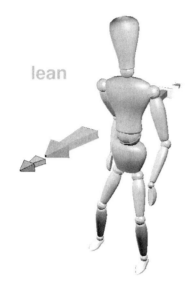

Lean means that the character will be able to lean forward or back over his feet.

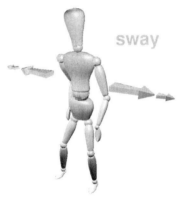

Sway means that the character can shift over one foot or the other.

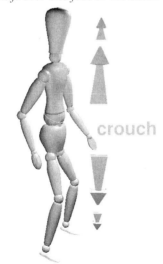

Crouch is the height of the hips above the feet.

EXPRESSIONS FOR HUMAN MOVEMENT

In this segment, we'll go over a number of expressions that will run different parts of the human skeleton and IK rig. The goal will be to automate a number of physical relationships between parts of the rig so that, for instance, the hips swing left and right to transfer weight as the feet come up, and the hips rotate in different ways to more accurately imitate how people actually move.

You'll use the custom properties you built to control the degree of automatic change, and you'll also use the custom controls you built for the upper and lower body to control the amount of manual change in each type of expression so that the animators can override the automatic effects and retain manual control.

AUTOMATIC HIP PLACEMENT BETWEEN FEET

The hips are the center of gravity for most human characters. The action of the body is driven from the hips in a real human, but the position of the hips is itself driven by the point where the character contacts the rest of the planet: usually the feet, and sometimes the hands. We'll assume in this section that the character is standing up, and therefore that the hips will be driven by the feet. When you are done, the animator will be able to control the motion of the character by simply animating the feet. The hips will move between the two feet automatically, swinging, leaning, and bouncing up and down.

These expressions will all go on the local translations of the hips control element in the control rig. Open the Expressions_Start scene to see an assembled IK skeleton, with upper and lower body controls, and custom properties on the top of the hierarchy.

PELVIS LEAN (HIPS.KINE.LOCAL.POSZ)

The hips should generally be located right between the feet, but if your character needs to lean forward over his toes, the hip would need to move forward. This would also happen if the character was headed uphill. When the feet move apart from each other in the forward direction (local Z) the hips need to slide in local Z as well, so the hips stay centered between the feet. The expression should find the average location in Z of the two feet, then add in the local Z of the lower body controller so that the animator can manually slide the hips, leaning them forward or backwards.

Therefore, the expression on the local Z of the hips is:

```
av( Leftheelcontrol.kine.local.posz,
Rightheelcontrol1.kine.local.posz ) +
( lbcontroller.kine.local.posz * 1.4 )
```

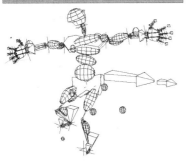

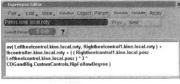

When one foot rises, the hips must shift rapidly to maintain balance.

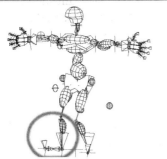

The hips should, in general, follow the feet.

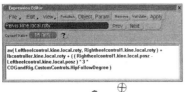

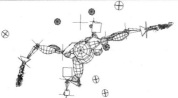

The hips should rotate to follow the forward foot a little bit.

PELVIS SWAY (HIPS.KINE.LOCAL.POSX)

The hips also need to remain centered between the feet from side to side, in the local X-axis. The animator must also be able to manually control the sway from side to side with the lower body controller.

This expression should find the average position in X of the two feet, then add in the local X of the lower body controller.

Therefore, the expression on the local X of the hips is:

```
av( Leftheelcontrol.kine.local.posx,
Rightheelcontrol1.kine.local.posx ) +
( lbcontroller.kine.local.posx * 1 )
```

PELVIS CROUCH (HIPS.KINE.LOCAL.POSY)

Now that the hips slide between the feet whenever the feet separate, you also need to address the height of the hips off the floor. As the feet get farther apart, the hips must drop to the ground, forming a triangle between the two feet and the hips. In a perfect setup, the character could do the splits when the feet are far apart and then be standing straight up when the feet are together.

So, as the feet get further apart the hip needs to drop closer to the ground. Don't bother to figure out the actual geometric solution, just use the Amount and Degree variables to adjust the formula to fit your needs.

You need to find the starting height (translation in local Y) of the hips, which will become the starting position for the formula. Then, find the distance between the feet in both X and Z, using the center distance function. Multiply that distance between the feet by the CrouchDegree slider you have already made in the custom PPG on the root of the control rig so you can control how much the hip dips as the feet separate. Finally, you need to add back in a manual component to make it so the animator can adjust hip height manually, using the local Y translation of the lower body controller.

That formula, on the Y translation of the hips, looks like this:

```
-1.44 + lbcontroller.kine.local.posy - ( ctr_dist(
Leftheelcontrol.kine.global.pos,
Rightheelcontrol1.kine.global.pos ) *
COGandRig.CustomControls.CrouchDegree )
```

WEIGHT TRANSFER FOR BALANCE (HIPS.KINE.LOCAL.POSX)

As you walk, you shift your weight from side to side. That's because as one foot comes off the ground, you need to rapidly shift the balance over the remaining foot that is planted on the ground, or you would fall over. Test this yourself by standing up, then trying to remain centered between your feet while you pick up your right foot.

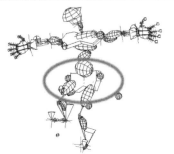

When one foot is bearing all the weight, the hips should dip in rotz.

You need the rig to exhibit a similar weight transfer as the feet come up, but you need a non-linear response to the rise of the feet, to be explained after you write the simple expression. Now, you already have an expression on the local translation in X of the hips, so you'll just add this part to that part, with a plus sign between the two parts.

To create the expression, you'll simply take the local Y position of one foot minus the local Y position of the other foot, then multiply that by the PelvisSwayDegree custom slider so you can adjust the results. If, when you test it, the hips shift the wrong direction, just reverse the order of the feet, so that if it was right minus left, now make it left minus right. That expression on the local X translation of the hips would look like this:

```
av( Leftheelcontrol.kine.local.posx,
Rightheelcontrol1.kine.local.posx ) +
( lbcontroller.kine.local.posx * 1 ) + ( (
Rightheelcontrol1.kine.local.posy -
Leftheelcontrol.kine.local.posy ) *
COGandRig.CustomControls.SwayDegree * 2 )
```

At the instant that a foot comes off the floor you need a very smooth but rapid shift in weight transfer, which falls off quickly as the foot rises more. If the expression controlling weight transfer was linear, as you raised the foot higher, the hip would shift further and further to one side, which is not what you want. You want the hips to shift over the down foot, but never go past it. That's called a limit. If you don't like to use a limit equation, you can also draw a custom animation curve on some object, and use that, as detailed in the previous chapter.

AUTOMATIC PELVIS ROTATION

Just as you want to control the shift in the location of the hips automatically as well as manually, you want to have some automatic hip rotation, to make the hips rotate to follow the feet, to bear the weight of the spine, and to point the pelvis up and down in case the character needs to do some Michael Jackson pelvis thrusts. It would also be good if it were easy to rotate the hips manually to make the character face in different directions, using both the direction of the feet and the lower body controller object you built for the animator.

HIPS ROTATE WITH FEET (HIPS.KINE.LOCAL.ROTY)

Currently you have no way of rotating the hips in local Y, except manually grabbing the hips and twisting them. This is a bad idea for a few reasons. First, the hips are hard to select. Second, the animator must remember to select the hips as a branch, or the up vectors will be left behind. It would be simpler if the hips just rotated automatically, like ours do, to face in the average direction of the feet. On the local rotation Y of the hips, add an expression that finds the average rotation of the two feet and adds in the rotation in Y of the lbcontroller so the animator can manually twist it and set keys. That expression would look like this:

```
av( Leftheelcontrol.kine.local.roty,
Rightheelcontrol1.kine.local.roty ) +
lbcontroller.kine.local.roty
```

FOLLOW FORWARD FOOT (HIPS.KINE.LOCAL.ROTY)

When one foot moves in front of the other, the hip naturally rotates somewhat around Y to make it easier to plant the forward foot while keeping the back foot on the ground. You can easily add this in to the character using the HipFollowDegree custom slider.

You need to find the difference in local Z between one foot and the other, then multiply that number by the HipFollowDegree slider, which will have a range of about 15 degrees positive and 15 degrees negative. Since there is already an expression on the hips local rotation in Y, you need to literally add this new part on to the end of the current expression, using an plus sign (+) in the expression editor. That expression looks like this:

```
av( Leftheelcontrol.kine.local.roty,
Rightheelcontrol1.kine.local.roty ) +
lbcontroller.kine.local.roty + ( (
Rightheelcontrol1.kine.local.posz -
Leftheelcontrol.kine.local.posz ) * 3 *
COGandRig.CustomControls.HipFollowDegree )
```

If, when you write your expression, the hips rotate in exactly the wrong direction, away from the forward foot, you have two choices. You can either switch the order of the feet in the expression, or just use a custom slider that has both a positive and negative range, then slide the slider to the negative side to invert the action of the expression.

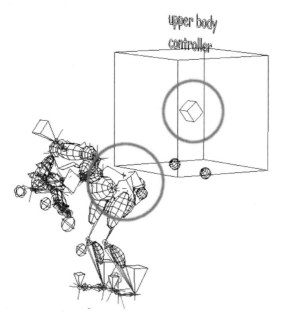

The hips rotate around X, driven by the lower body controller.

BEAR WEIGHT (HIPS.KINE.LOCAL.ROTZ)

If you take a look at Greek statuary, you may note that there are a significant number of statues of people lounging around. The Greeks carefully studied the posture of people, particularly young men, who were standing around naked. They pioneered the style of more realistically representing the way that human skeletons carry weight when at rest, called contraposto (counterpose). This posture is also known as the Praxitelean curve, where one leg bears most of the body's weight, while the other leg is bent at the knee. The hips rotate a bit, with the low side towards the bent knee, forcing a curve in the spine back in the other direction to keep balance over the hips. You can add this to the rig by finding the difference in local Y position between the feet, multiplying that by a Degree slider so you can control the results, and adding in the manual lower body controller. Later you'll pick up the collarbone expressions to finish off the effect. That formula would look like this:

```
( Rightheelcontrol1.kine.local.posy -
Leftheelcontrol.kine.local.posy ) * 10
* COGandRig.CustomControls.SwayDegree
```

BOWING AND BACKFLIPS (HIPS.LOCAL.KINE.ROTX)

At some point, the character may need to bow forward to the King and Queen, or perhaps do some backflips, or even tumbling high dives. To accomplish these maneuvers, the rig must be able to rotate the pelvis freely around the X-axis. Since the collarbone is a child of the pelvis, the entire upper body assembly will also automatically rotate along with the hips. The feet will not, so they would stay on the flow during a bow, and would need to be animated separately for a somersault.

The expression here is a simple link to the lower body controller's rotation in X:

```
Lbcontroller.kine.local.rotx
```

FOOT COLLISION DETECTION WITH THE FLOOR

When setting keyframes on a walking character, it's awfully nice to be able to slam the feet into the floor and have them stay there. Obviously, in a normal 3D animation setup, this doesn't happen, so the animator has to carefully edit the resulting keys to make sure that the feet don't go through the ground plane. You can set up an automatic ground plane to make sure this doesn't happen. One option is to write a conditional expression on the feet that checks to see if they go below a certain level. Another possibility is to use a bounding plane constraint to prevent the feet from going through the floor.

In the first case, add a new custom control to the rig called FloorLevel. With this slider you can set the ground plane height, or even animate it to achieve a ramp or stair-like effect. Make that property a floating point number with a range from –20 to 20.

There needs to be a conditional expression on each foot controller for the local Y translation to check whether the foot has been translated below the value of the slider, and if it has, set it back to the level of the slider. If the foot is not too low, leave it at the current value.

```
cond( this.kine.local.posy <
COGandRig.CustomControls.FloorLevel ,
COGandRig.CustomControls.FloorLevel ,
this.kine.local.posy )
```

In the other case, simply get a surface grid and scale it up to form a ground plane. Select each foot control, and use the Constrain➔Bounding Plane command to constrain each foot.

Check the results of your work by branch-selecting the feet and pushing them up and down to see if they stop at the ground level.

Note: This animator thinks the ground plane is neat, but it seems to slow down interactivity of the rig. You do not have to use the ground plane. It's an optional feature of the control rig.

COLLARBONE EXPRESSIONS

As the hips rotate in Z, the shoulders need to also rotate in the opposite direction slightly, and shift side-to-side to get back over the hips. The collarbone should also use the small 3D cube in the middle of the upper body controller, so that the animator can manually adjust the location of the shoulders easily.

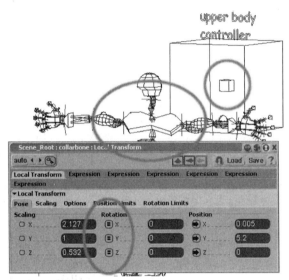

The upper body controller needs to be linked to the collarbone.

COLLARBONE LEAN

The local translation of the collarbone in Z helps show that the character is leaning forward and backward. The expression is a simple link between the upper body controller (ubcontroller) local Z translation and the collarbone local Z translation.

```
ubcontroller.kine.local.posz * 1.5
```

COLLARBONE SWAY

Similarly, the side-to-side motion of the collarbone should be linked to the ubcontroller, but it should also shift a bit when the hips dip. In other words, when the hips rotate around local Z to bear weight, the collarbone needs to shift a bit to the side of the down foot. Make this a small effect:

```
ubcontroller.kine.local.posx * 1.5 +
(Pelvis.kine.local.rotz * .05)
```

COLLARBONE DIP

Link the local Y translation of the collarbone to the local Y position of the ubcontroller so the animator can easily find, select, and key the Y position of the collarbone. The number below, 5.2, is just where the collarbone happens to start in this one case. Yours may be different.

```
5.2 + ubcontroller.kine.local.posy
```

COLLARBONE ROTATIONS

The rotation of the collarbone around the local axis should also be accessible to the animator. Although the animator could just select the collarbone rig element and manually rotate it, it might be better to use the rotation of the upper body controller cube. If you use the upper body controller rig instead, the animator has a visual reference of what to animate on, and the animator doesn't have to select the collarbone each time, which is hard to do with all that IK and skin stuff on top of it.

Just set an expression on each local rotation of the collarbone to make it equal to the local rotation of the upper body controller. Set the rotz of the collarbone to ubcontroller.kine.local.rotx, the local roty to: ubcontroller.kine.local.roty, and rotz to ubcontroller.kine.local.rotz.

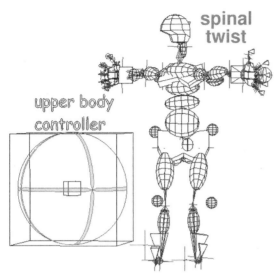

The spinal column needs to twist gradually and smoothly.

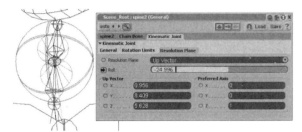

The Roll property in the Bone PPG controls twist, as needed in the spine.

SPINAL COLUMN EXPRESSIONS

When you stand up and twist your shoulders around as far as you can go, your spine twists gradually from your pelvis up to your shoulders. This natural, gradual twist is crucial to natural character movement. If your character cannot twist his spine smoothly, the result will be stiff and ugly animation.

Currently, the hips rotate sometimes, but you need to be able to rotate the collarbone as well. You also need to have up vectors controlling the orientation of the first joint in the spine (at the base, near the pelvis) and the first joint in the neck, at the point of the collarbone. Then, you need to select each IK bone in the chain and give it an up vector constraint to the first, bottom-most up vector. Check each bone's PPG and ensure that the Kinematic Joint→Resolution Plane is set to Up Vector so you know that the spine is correctly controlled. However, even this is not enough. You now need to control the roll of the spine bones in addition to the up vectors.

When a bone has an up vector to control the orientation, a new property becomes available in the Kinematic Joint→Resolution Plane PPG, called Roll. Roll allows you to manually rotate the bone around the axis that runs along the spine. Try this out manually, before you write an expression.

The expression you need will change for each bone. In the lowest bone, you want the roll to be mainly driven by the pelvis, but to be influenced a tiny bit by the rotation of the collarbone. Then, on the next bone up the spine, you want the pelvis to influence the roll a little bit less, and the collarbone to influence the roll a little bit more. In this way, each bone needs to be influenced by both the hips and the collarbone, in a gradual way so that the lower bones are most driven by the hips, and the top bones are most driven by the collarbone.

You can do this by adding some variables in the expression. On the lowest bone you leave the up vector alone to control the roll.

On the next bone up the spine (out of a five-bone chain) you write:

```
(0.3 * collarbone.kine.local.roty ) + ( 0.7 *
pelvis.kine.local.roty)
```

Then, the same formula on the next bone up the chain, but with more emphasis on the collarbone and less on the pelvis, like this:

```
(0.5 * collarbone.kine.local.roty ) + ( 0.5 *
pelvis.kine.local.roty)
```

And so on, increasing the weight of the rotation of the collarbone for those joints higher up the spine.

Now, when you rotate the collarbone in one direction and the hips in the other, the spine makes a smooth transition along the chest and back area of the character.

CONCLUSION

In this chapter you took the IK control rig, and created custom controls and 3D controls to add in functionality. Those controls were designed to be easy to find for the animator, and simple to operate. You looked at custom property pages, custom 3D controls, and custom Synoptic controls. You wrote expressions to link some hard-to-find parts of the rig, like the collarbone. You wrote more expression to automate different parts of the rig, like the movement of the hips, so that they stay centered between the feet. You also built innovative facial animation controls to drive shape Mixers, so that animators can use intuitive 3D controllers rather than the Animation Mixer.

This work of adding expressions to control the rig is difficult for many people, but it can significantly ease simple animation tasks, so that character animators can spend more time refining and improving the motion of the character.

QUIZ

1. **THE CUSTOM PPG MUST GO ON AN IK BONE.**
   a. True
   b. False

2. **WHICH CUSTOM USER INTERFACE USES CLICKS TO RUN SCRIPTS?**
   a. Custom PPG
   b. 3D Object Controller
   c. Synoptic View

3. **WHAT HAS MORE MANUAL CONTROL FOR THE ANIMATOR?**
   a. 3D Object Controllers
   b. Custom Sliders
   c. Synoptic View

4. **OF THE TWO VARIABLES, AMOUNT AND DEGREE, WHICH MODULATES THE AUTOMATIC EFFECTS OF THE EXPRESSION?**
   a. Amount
   b. Degree
   c. Both Amount and Degree

5. **FOR DEGREE VARIABLES, WHAT VALUE TYPE IS MOST USEFUL IN THE CUSTOM PPG?**
   a. Boolean
   b. Integer
   c. Floating Point

6. **HOW CAN YOU ADD TWO EXPRESSIONS TO ONE PROPERTY?**
   a. You cannot
   b. Create a proxy property
   c. use the plus sign

7. **HOW DO YOU SAVE ACTIONS TO DISK?**
   a. Drag from Mixer to Desktop
   b. Save button in PPG
   c. File→Save→Action

8. **WHAT S THE HOTKEY TO POP A SYNOPTIC PPG?**
   a. F2
   b. F3
   c. Shift-S

9. **IK BONE ROLL REQUIRES WHAT TO WORK?**
   a. Up vector or preferred axis
   b. Force IK
   c. Psuedo root

10. **WHAT CAN YOU USE TO DRIVE THE MIXER WEIGHT?**
    a. Custom Sliders, 3D Object Controllers
    b. Synoptic Views, Action Clips
    c. Both A and B

12 EMOTION AND FACIAL MUSCULATURE

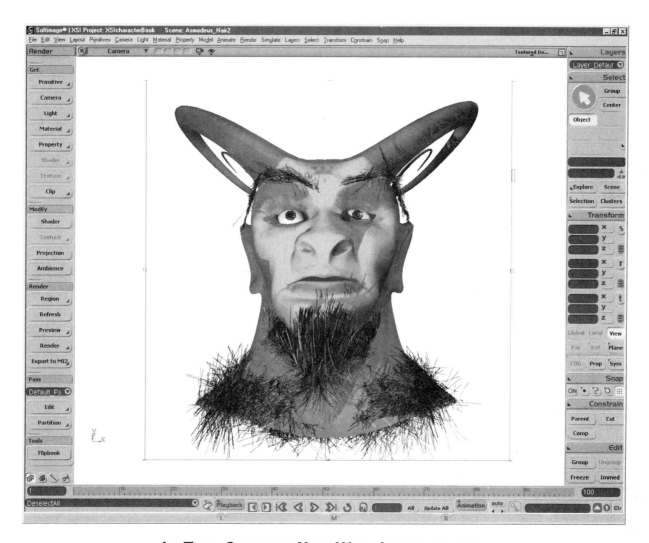

IN THIS CHAPTER YOU WILL LEARN ABOUT:

- A new approach to animating facial shapes
- How to break down and organize the muscles under the skin of the face
- Using envelope objects with Multipoint constraints
- Using Constraint to Cluster with Curve shapes
- Concepts of opposing Muscle Action
- How to drive shapes with control objects
- How to use a curve to add a limit to an expression

INTRODUCTION

In previous chapters you built a number of different shapes for lip sync and facial animation. In this type of shape blending system, all the shapes that are possible are created before animation begins, then linked in to sliders or a 3D UI, and the animator simply mixes between the shapes that are already possible. The advantages of this system are a high degree of consistency between the work of different animators, and good differentiation in the phases of the workflow, from concept art to modeling different shapes to finally mixing them. The disadvantages are that the character will be limited to what the original modeler built as possible shapes, the shapes are somewhat more difficult to integrate with full body IK, there are a higher number of elements to be animated, and it is possible for animators to mix shapes together that shouldn't be mixed together, resulting in weird animation.

In this chapter we'll investigate a different style, one that works very well for imitating that most difficult aspect of 3D animation: emotion communicated through facial expressions.

SETTING UP A FACE FOR EMOTION, NOT LIP SYNC

The shape mixing setup was great for lip sync, because you could precisely arrange the shape of the mouth ahead of time for each phoneme. In this chapter we'll assume that shape mixing is the right technique for lip sync, and devote our energy to finding a better (or at least different) method of building a facial rig to express emotion.

The goal is to create a facial rig that can react to the animator in real time, allowing the animator to manually and physically puppet the face, mixing any emotional state quickly and with good feedback.

Instead of building pre-defined shapes, you'll be building in the musculature that underlies the skin of the face. If you do a good job of simulating how the actual muscles in the face operate, you should be able to then hook those muscles up into a control rig and make them function. You'll build a simple basic set of muscles, but this idea can be carried forward to any arbitrary level of complexity. There is little or no reason why completely realistic human emotional communication could not be achieved with a little trial and error and a few days of revision, adding in smaller secondary muscle actions.

TRANSPORTABILITY

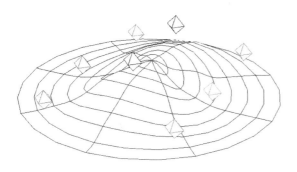

Another problem with using a hierarchy of shapes for facial animation is that it just isn't possible to reuse your shape work from one character to another. You saw that by abstracting the control rig from the shapes you could store and reuse animation, but for each character you would have to go through modeling each of the basic shapes used in the Mixer, and hooking them up to the controls. In this system you'll be constructing a generalizable facial control rig that can be used with any face, just by enveloping it to whatever skin you want to use.

The small octahedral studs are deforming the face

It is also possible to mix and match the two techniques, using the shape animation controller for the lip sync phonemes, and the emotion rig for the facial expressions.

To achieve the results you want, you'll be mixing together three things in XSI: multi-point constraints, envelope deformers, and shape animation.

USING ENVELOPE DEFORMERS AS MUSCLES

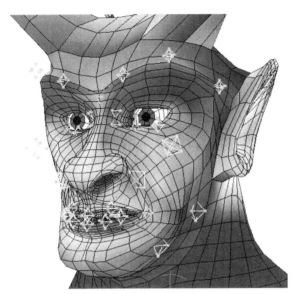

These studs imitate muscles under the cheek.

By now you should be quite familiar with using IK bones to deform a skin, and you have previously seen that you can also use geometry objects in an IK hierarchy to deform the skin around them. Such objects are called envelope deformers, because they work by moving points around them on the skin that is deformed with an envelope operator. You can use almost anything as an envelope deformer, including nulls, polygon meshes, and NURBS surfaces. In this case you'll be using small polygon objects. The shape of the object does not matter at all, so you'll be using little octahedrons, which are easy to see and to select.

Visualize the skin of the face, and how the skin of your cheeks is attached to the musculature underneath it. When the muscles underneath bunch up, the skin is pulled in one direction or the other as the muscle moves and gets bigger. Practice smiling with your hand on your cheekbone, under your right eye to see what I mean.

These small octahedrons will represent the muscles under the skin. Another helpful (though a bit gruesome) way to imagine what you'll be doing is to think of the octahedrons as small studs, pinned through the skin in some kind of weird urban piercing fashion. When you pull the studs, the skin around them will be stretched into a different shape.

You'll be creating quite a few of these studs, and then organizing them into a rig so that they move around in smooth, meaningful ways. Then, you'll envelope the whole lot of them to the skin of the face.

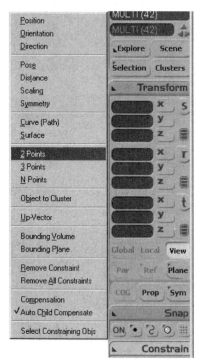

A 2-point constraint is a good way to suspend a stud between two other objects.

before

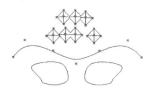

after

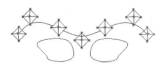

When the studs are attached to the curve, mixing the shape of the curve will move the studs.

MULTI-POINT CONSTRAINTS

You need the studs in the face to move around in a fluid manner. When one area of the skin moves, it naturally pulls on the neighboring regions, and affects them as well. This creates a stretching system, where almost every part of the face is influenced by every other part. The human face then acts like a rubber mask. If your character doesn't exhibit this behavior, the animation in the face will look too isolated, and the results will look dead, as if the mouth is moving but nothing else is connected. The goal is to build a system that is so interrelated that moving any one muscle has an effect on all the other muscles in the face. One good way to achieve this result is to use multi-point constraints to hang the studs around the skull. For instance, the cheek muscle might be constrained between the relatively solid nose bone, the moveable rear jawbone, and the corner of the mouth. When either the corner of the mouth or the back of the jaw moves, the cheek muscle will adjust to stretch the skin, anchoring the skin all the way to the nose bone. The more interrelated constraints you build, the more dynamic the face will become.

SHAPES AND CONSTRAIN TO CLUSTER

So, some of the studs will be floating in the face, blending the different muscle actions together. but how, exactly, are you going to organize the muscles and get the studs to move when the muscles themselves move? The answer is that you will build the muscles out of splines, animate them using shapes, and pin the studs to those curves so the studs move around as the muscles change shape. In the next section we'll concern ourselves with the actual organization of the muscles. Right now you just need to understand the concepts surrounding how the studs find themselves attached to the points along a closed curve.

If you had a simple CV NURBS line with four CV points on it, and four studs to attach to those points, you would create four clusters on the curve: one cluster for each point.

Then you could select the curve, pop up a floating explorer with 8, tap the E key to frame up the curve, expand the cluster folder to reveal the four clusters you just added, and lock the explorer so it doesn't go away.

You could then select one of the studs, choose the Constrain→Object to Cluster command, and then in the explorer pick the first cluster to complete the command. After repeating for each stud, you would have a row of polygon octahedrons stuck on to the control vertices of the line. If you move the vertices, you also move the octahedrons.

Now, it would be a hassle to manually move the vertices around on the line each time you want it to change shape. A much better idea would be to store some different shapes for that line, then use the Mixer to blend between the shapes of the line, which would in turn drive the studs into a different configuration. Later on, those studs would then deform the skin around them. In this way, changing the shape of a curve drives the deformation of the skin around the face.

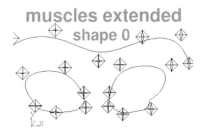

muscles extended
shape 0

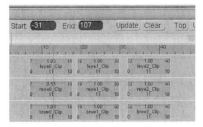

muscles relaxed
shape 1

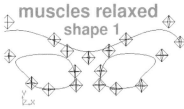

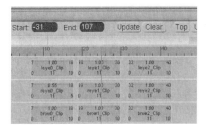

muscles contracted
shape 2

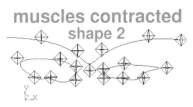

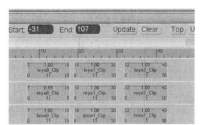

Each muscle has three positions: extended, relaxed, and contracted.

Note: There is a special deformer, called Deformation by Spine, that uses the vertices of a curve directly to deform a mesh. This works well on simple objects, but would present a variety of difficulties if you tried to use it here, blending it with IK. If you stick with the tried and true method of using geometry objects as envelope deformers, you can use higher levels of envelope assignment depth, you can use the skin weighting tools, and you can more easily integrate the results with the rest of the IK in the character.

THINKING ABOUT MUSCLES

If you put some thought into the construction of the muscles, building a common scheme and sticking with some basic naming conventions, the job will be a lot easier and more successful.

In general, muscles only do one thing: they contract. In the human musculature, muscles are often designed in opposing pairs, so that when one contracts, the other extends, and vice versa. If that were not the case, you would extend a limb and then it would be stuck there, until you reached over with the other hand and pulled it back again. This opposing muscle action solves the problem of being able to extend and retract the arms and legs. In the face another type of muscle organization is also used: muscle orbits. In the case of a muscle orbit, the muscle is designed like a ring, with no real beginning or end. When the muscle contracts, it squinches down into a tighter, smaller circle.

Regular, straight muscles are generally attached to the outside edges of these orbits in two or more locations. When the orbit needs to open up again, the orbit muscle relaxes and the outer, straight muscles pull on it from opposite sides, opening the ring up. Your eyes and mouth are both organized as orbits. Squinch up your eyes and mouth while feeling your face to get the idea. If you are in a public place right now, mumble a bit to complete the illusion for anyone who happens to be watching you.

Your eye orbit is anchored on one corner to your nose, and on the opposite side to the edge of your skull. At the top, the ocular orbit is anchored to the muscles in your forehead, which run under your brow. At the bottom, the ocular orbit is attached to the muscle running from the eye to the corner of the mouth.

The mouth orbit is therefore anchored to the eyes via the cheeks, to the bottom of the nose, and to the chin bone with another large, meaty, straight muscle.

In order to build a character whose face moves like a real human's, you need to build some muscles in the facial expression rig that work in the same way as the muscles in a real human face. You'll need orbits for each eye, an orbit for the mouth, a muscle for the forehead and brows, and muscles in the cheeks. So, you'll draw a curve for the left eye, a curve for the right eye, one for the mouth, and one for the brows. You'll use floating studs in between them all, for the muscles of the cheeks, the chin, and the jaw.

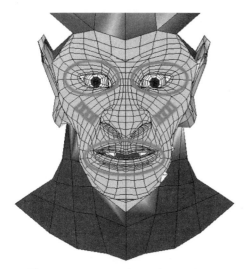

The organization of muscles in the face

OPPOSING ACTION WITH THREE SHAPES

Since the muscles work in pairs, opposing each other, you'll need three shapes for each muscle curve you draw. In the middle there will be the slack shape, the base shape for the way the curve was originally drawn. Then there will be a shape for that muscle in the contracted shape, and finally, a third shape for the extended muscle. Since these shapes oppose each other, you need to set up the rig so that you blend from the extended to the slack, and from the slack to the constricted.

Let's set up a naming convention to make life easier. Let's name the extended shape "muscle0", the slack shape "muscle1" and the constricted shape "muscle2". Now you are ready to actually build the rig!

FACIAL EXPRESSION RIG: AT A GLANCE

Asmo's face is very flexible.

TOPICS COVERED

The rest of this chapter will be presented in the form of a long, detailed tutorial.

You'll use a pre-existing polygonal mesh head model (named Asmodeus) and build for him a complete facial expression rig. Starting from scratch, you'll construct a novel facial expression rig to control the skin around the skull, the nose, the brows, the cheeks, the eyes, the mouth, and the jaw.

You'll define shapes for the muscle groups in the brows, around the eyes, around the mouth, and under the skin of the cheeks. You'll drop those shapes into the Mixer, then use expressions to hook the shape blend weights up to a control rig for the upper and lower face, to make it all much easier to use.

Finally, you'll envelope the face to the rig and test the results.

You'll learn how to:

- Build sub-dermal musculature from NURBS Curves
- Attach deformers to the curves with cluster constraints
- Add shapes to the curves, and drive with expressions
- Hook all the muscles to the same controls, for easy animation:

MATERIALS REQUIRED

The Asmodeus_Start scene from the courseware.

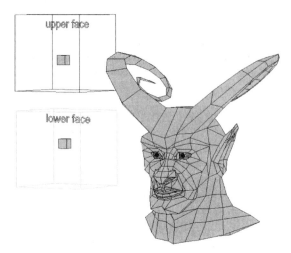

Examine the head and control rigs.

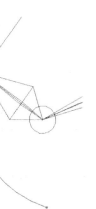

The effector will travel along this curve to open the jaw.

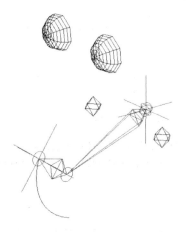

Add in a two-bone chain for the jaw.

TUTORIAL: FACIAL EXPRESSION RIG

STEP 1: INVESTIGATE THE HEAD YOU WILL BE USING

Open the Asmodeus_Start scene. This head model is a polygonal model, designed to be used as a subdivision surface. It has vertex colors and a render-mapped texture as well. We'll call him Asmo for short.

STEP 2: MAKE A JAWBONE FOR ASMO

Asmo's face will have exactly one IK chain in it, for his jaw hinge. The IK chain should have two segments: one long segment going from the middle of his head where the jaw should hinge to the middle of the chin, and another segment from there to the lip. This will allow Asmo to open his mouth and thrust his chin and lower lip forward in a nice organic manner.

However, you want to set joint rotation limits on the local Z-axis of the chain joints, so that Asmo never has to worry about his jaw being ripped free of his head by some sloppy animator. Select the first joint, pop open the bone property page, find the joint rotation limits, and set the first joint to have a good range of motion, a bit more than your own jaw.

Do the same for the second joint, giving it a very limited degree of rotation so that his lip can curl out only a little.

You know that this jaw will swing open only a certain amount. Draw a short curve describing the arc the effector can move along. About 4 points are enough.

Select the effector and use the Path→Set Path command to constrain the effector to the path. Make the path timing go from 1 to 10 frames. Don't check Linear, so that the jaw eases in and out at the ends of the path.

STEP 3: BUILD SKIN STUDS FOR THE JAW BONE

You need to have some skin studs to anchor to the jaw bone you just built, two in front by the chin, two in back by the hinge point. These studs will actually move the skin of the lower jaw. Create a primitive octahedron, and scale it down to an appropriate size. Name it "studTemplate". From now on, when you need a stud, just duplicate the template and use the duplicate.

Make four duplicates, and arrange them at the corners of the jawbone. Feel your own jaw to get an idea of where to put them.

Make all four studs the child of the first jawbone.

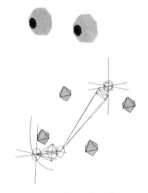

These studs anchor the skin at the corners of the jaw.

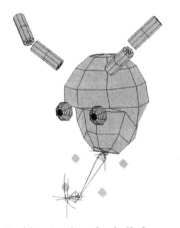

Build a simple poly skull shape.

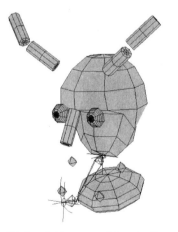

All the rigid parts of the skull are parented into one hierarchy.

STEP 4: BUILD STATIC PARTS: SKULL, NECK BASE, NOSE, HORNS

Asmo needs to have some solid structures to anchor his skin. His skull should anchor all the skin around the back of his head, and he'll need some hard parts attached to his skull to anchor his horns so they don't wiggle when parts of his face move around.

He'll also need a big anchor in the base of his neck, since this model has nothing below the jaw. If you don't anchor the neck, then the shoulders won't have anything to weight to, and they'll move around when the jaw opens.

The shape of the skull and other rigid objects is unimportant, but it might make the rig easier to understand if you modeled the skull sphere slightly to look like a skull. Remember to freeze the stack on the object before using it, to simplify the model and avoid problems later.

Asmo also needs a cylinder placed into his nasal cavity to anchor the top part of the nose.

Make the Neck anchor the parent of the skull, and the skull the parent of the nose bone, and the horn bones.

STEP 5: NOSE TIP

In the tip of the nose, the fleshy part, place a new stud, and make it a child of the hard nose bone. This will help Asmo flare his nostrils. You will also use this as one anchor point for some three-point constraints in the skin on either side of the nose.

STEP 6: STUDS BETWEEN NOSE TIP AND JAW

You need some studs under the cheek to help the skin slide when the jaw opens, or the eyes squinch up. Since you don't have the eyes in yet, you can't quite do that, so you'll just lay the groundwork. On each side of the face, you want two studs. One will be constrained to float between the nose tip and the front jaw stud. The other will float on a two-point constraint between the nose tip and the rear jaw stud. Later on you can remove these constraints and use three-point constraints, including the corner of the eye as well.

Remember that if you don't like the position of the stud after the constraint, you can use Compensate to offset it closer to the skin.

Make an identical pair of studs on both sides of the face.

These studs will also act as cheek muscles riding over the cheekbone, so later on you could scale these studs up to increase the size of the muscle under the skin over the cheekbone.

STEP 7: IMPROVISE

Feel free to add more floating studs. The more the merrier. However, you'll have more to work with after you add in the mouth and eye curves. Since you'll be hanging studs on these curves, you can use the curve-studs as part of the constraints, further blending the skin between, say, the nose and the eye and the jaw, all at the same time.

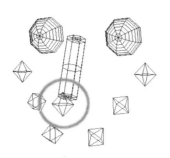

The nose stud will help Asmo flare his nostrils in a disturbing manner.

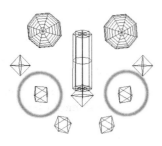

These studs will float between the top of the mouth and the nose.

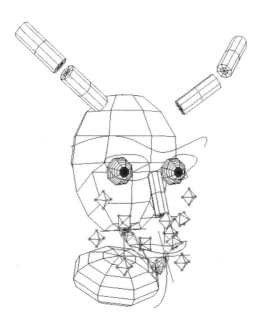

Add in your own floating studs, constrained to other floating studs.

STEP 8: DRAW CURVES FOR BROWS

The muscles of the brow are configured like curtains of muscle, anchored at the top to the skull, then wrapping over the brows, and connecting to the upper inside of the ocular orbits, anchoring both to the bone and the muscle there.

So, you want a curve that runs back and forth from top to bottom, like a flat muscle. You could easily use a grid here, but I want to stick with curves just for consistency.

You also want those curves to perfectly match the contours of the skin. An easy way to make this happen is to use the Snap to Point tool. Turn on Snap, click on the point option, and turn off the grid or other options that might be on. Now use the Curve➔Draw CV NURBS tool and click on Asmo's head to draw one brow curtain for the right side, and one for the left side. When done, make the curves children of the skull, so they don't come loose accidentally.

STEP 9: DRAW CURVES FOR THE EYES

You need one curve for the orbit of each eye socket. Use the same method of drawing a curve using point snapping to match the contours of the eye region. You want the curve to run around the outside of the eye socket, rather than the inside next to the eyeball. Poke your finger into your eye and flex the muscles there to feel where they go. Draw about 7 points for the curve, then close it with Modify➔Curve➔Open/Close.

Make each eye curve a child of the skull as well.

STEP 10: MAKE THE MOUTH CURVE

You need one more curve, this time for the mouth. Using the snap method, draw a curve around the outer edge of the lips, and close it as before. Make it a child of the skull, not the jaw. This way you can write expressions to move the mouth relative to both the jaw bone and the skull.

STEP 11: MAKE THE CLUSTERS

Now it's time to make all the clusters. Fortunately, the names of the clusters are unimportant, so this part is really fast. Start with the right brow curve. You need about six studs on it, arranged evenly top to bottom, so you'll need six clusters on the curve. Tag a point, hit the Cluster button at the bottom of the MCP, and repeat, counting off the clusters done.

Now repeat on the other side.

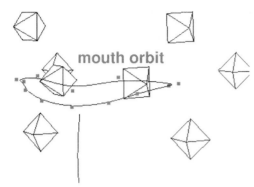

This curve will act as the muscle ringing Asmo's mouth.

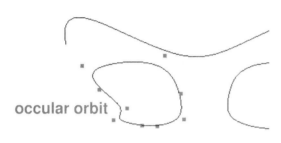

This curve is a ring, like the occular orbit.

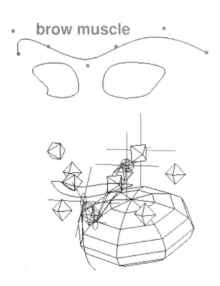

The brow muscle is a sheet connecting the forehead to the eye socket.

For each eye curve, add about six clusters. For the mouth curve, you need about nine clusters to really properly create accurate mouth shapes. You can use the explorer view, or the Cluster explorer in the MCP to check your work.

STEP 12: CLUSTER-CONSTRAIN THE STUDS TO THE CURVES

You now need to stick a whole bunch of little stud octa-hedra onto the clusters that are now saved on the curves. The workflow is as follows. First, make a whole bunch of studs, about 33 of them. Arrange them in a grid so they are easy to select one at a time.

Next, select the first curve, the right brow, to start with. Pop an explorer with 8, then use E to frame the curve in Selection scope. Open the Clusters folder, and lock open the explorer so the list of clusters will stay there even when you select a stud. Now, select the first stud. Use the Constrain➔Object to Cluster command, and pick on the first cluster in the explorer. The Stud will hop to the chosen cluster, and stay there forever. Select the next stud, and repeat the process until each cluster has a stud constrained to it.

Now, go on to the next brow curve, and repeat.

Do the same for each eye and the mouth.

When done, you should have studs pinned to each cluster around each curve. These studs will actually be doing the deformation on the head.

STEP 13: BIND THE STUDS, THE IK, AND THE RIGID BONES

When creating the shapes for the curves, it will be a big help if you can see the results of your work on Asmo's head. It makes sense to bind his polygon mesh to the deformers at this point. To make life easy, make a group for all the deformers by selecting all the studs, the jawbone, and the skull hierarchy from the neck on up, then clicking the Group button. Name the new Group "EnvelopeMe".

Select Asmo's head mesh, and use the Envelope➔Set Envelope command, then pick on the new group you just made in the explorer.

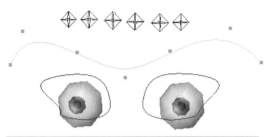

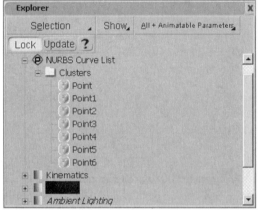

Each CV becomes its own cluster.

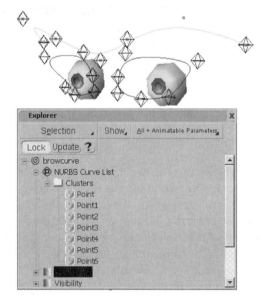

Cluster Constraints stick the studs to the curves.

Right-click to end the enveloping command, then increase the automatic envelope assignment depth (in the Clusters folder, under the EnvelopeWeightCls→Envelopes_Weights) to 4, so that each skin vertex considers the four nearest bones, studs, or other deformers, weighted by distance. You'll eventually need to do some manual weight painting, but this will be good enough to move forward.

STEP 14: STORE SHAPES FOR THE EYE CURVES

Now it's time to actually store shapes on the curves, using the naming conventions you invented, so that the shapes can be added to the Mixer, and then expressions can be written to drive the shape weights.

Remember the three shapes for each muscle group: shape0 is the wide open, extended state; shape1 is the middle, slack, relaxed base state; shape 2 is the contracted, tightened shape for that muscle group.

First, select the right eye curve and store a base shape for it, in the shape you drew it in, with Shape→Store Shape Key in the explorer, find that new shape in the sources folder, and carefully rename it to reye1 so you can find it later.

Next, with the right eye curve selected, use the M key to move points on the curve to a shape the eye would make if the muscles of the ocular orbit were slack, being pulled up by the brow and down by the cheeks. In other words, model the widest-open shape of the right eye, thinking about how the muscles would be pulling.

Store this shape, and rename it reye0.

Now restore the eye curve to its original slack shape before continuing to model the squinched position. The easiest way to accomplish this is to show the Mixer, add a shape track, and drag the reye1 shape into that track, then scrub the timeslider over it so it drives the shape of the right eye curve. Mute the track, and then sculpt the eye curve into the shape it would take if the ocular muscles were contracted, bunching up around the eyeball, closing the lip most of the way.

Store this shape, calling it reye2.

Repeat this for the left eye, making three shapes for it as well, using the same naming convention.

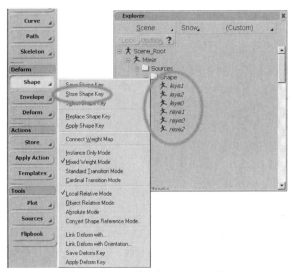

Three shapes for the eye muscles

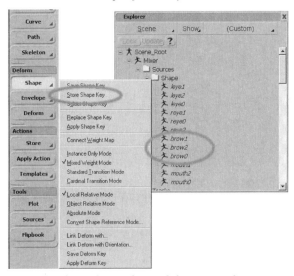

Three shapes for each brow muscle

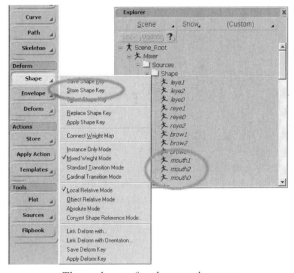

Three shapes for the mouth curve

STEP 15: MAKE SHAPES FOR THE BROWS AND THE MOUTH

Save three shapes for each brow muscle. The middle shape is the first one to save, in the shape the curve has as it was modeled. This middle shape is named brow1, since the number 1 is in between 0 and 2.

The brow0 shape should be the stretched-out pose of the brow muscle, as it is pulled when the eye constricts, furrowing the brow to be thicker and closer to the eye. As usual, feel your own face while wiggling your brow to get the idea. The brow2 shape should be the constricted pose of the brow, as it pulls together, furrowing the forehead, and lifting the eyebrow.

The mouth also needs three shapes. The mouth1 shape is the default shape as drawn. The mouth0 shape is the mouth pulled open, so that the muscles in the ring around the mouth are relaxed. The bottom of the mouth descends far below the upper. The mouth2 shape is the constricted pose of the mouth. Imagine the corners curling up a bit, and the mouth stretched in a rictus grin.

STEP 16: START SETTING UP THE CONTROL RIG

In the Asmodeus scene from the courseware, there are two simple control boxes, one labeled "upper face" and the other "lower face". The goal is to connect the shapes of the curves, the position of the jaw, and the location of the mouth curve all to those two simple boxes, so that sliding them around in space will activate all the muscles in the face, allowing for easy, fast, fun animation.

The first thing to do is to add a little bit of the lower face controller motion to the actual mouth curve itself, so that when you pull down the control cube the mouth curve drops a little bit. The mouth curve's translation should be frozen already, but if it isn't, freeze it so it is located at 0,0,0 relative to its parent, the skull. Now add these expressions to the mouth curve local translation.

On local.posx, put:

```
cond( lface.kine.local.posx > 0, MIN(
0.1 * lface.kine.local.posx, 0.4 ) ,
MAX( 0.1 * lface.kine.local.posx, -0.4
) )
```

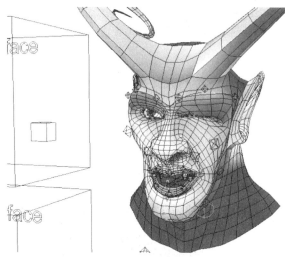

When Asmo is bound, you can see the results of changing the shape of the curves.

On local.posz, put:

```
cond( lface.kine.local.posz > 0, MIN(
0.1 * lface.kine.local.posz, 0.4 ) ,
MAX( 0.1 * lface.kine.local.posz, -0.4
) )
```

STEP 17: HOOK THE POSY OF THE LOWER FACE CONTROLLER

The jaw effector is on a short path describing the arc of the jaw opening. Right now that happens when you scrub in the timeline from 1 to 10. However, you want that action connected to the lower face controller, so that dragging it down opens the mouth. Here's the expression on the path percentage:

```
cond( lface.kine.local.posy < 0,
lface.kine.local.posy * -30 , 0 )
```

STEP 18: ADD ALL THE TRACKS TO THE MIXER

You now need all the shapes loaded into the Mixer. For each curve you have three shapes, so you need three tracks for each one. You want the shape0 first, then the shape1, then the shape2. Manually drag the weight slider for the shape1 track (the base pose for each curve) to a weight of 1, so the other shapes will blend against it. You'll be driving the other weights with expressions connected to the face controllers.

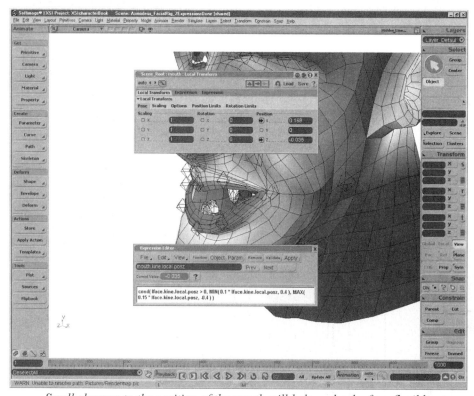

Small changes to the position of the mouth will help make the face flexible.

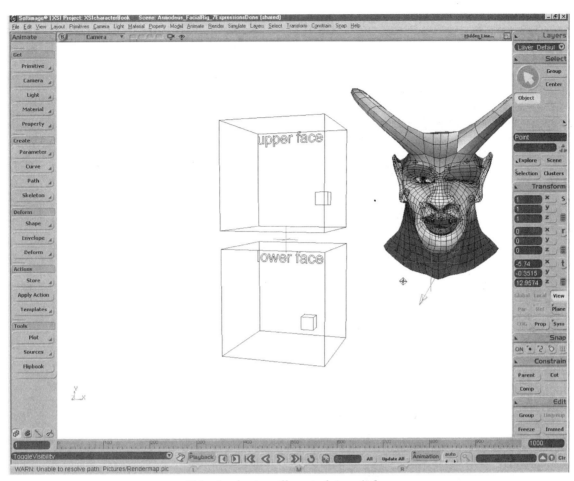

This simple rig will control Asmo's face.

Make sure to set the Mixer Shape Properties to non-normalized shape mixing, so you can get the full range of expression in the shapes you created. If normalize is on, you'll only get about 50% of the shape since each shape will be averaged against the base shape.

Be sure that you have shapes, each in their own track, for all three shapes of each curve: the right brow, the left brow, the right eye, the left eye, and the mouth. The shapes all need to extend as long in the Mixer as you want to set keyframes. If you slide the timeslider beyond the length of the shapes, the rig will stop working.

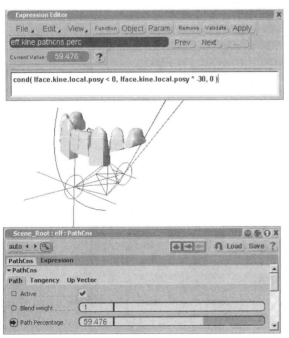

The expression uses the lower face controller to drive the path percentage.

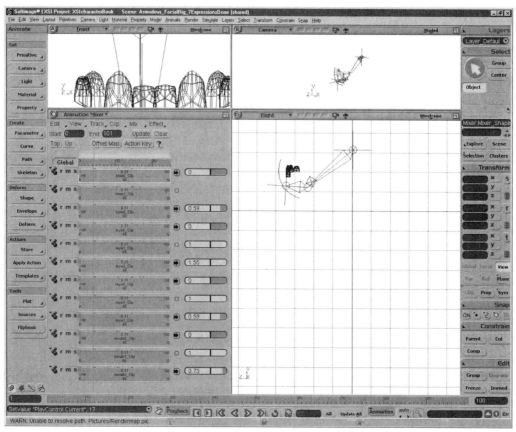

Load all the shapes into the Mixer, in an order that makes sense to you.

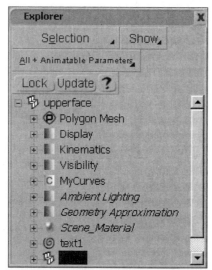

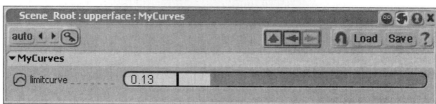

This custom PPG is on the upper face controller.

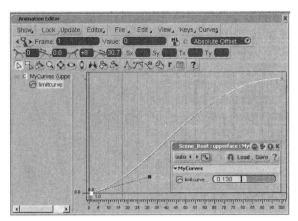

The limit curve clamps the min and max result, and makes a smooth response curve.

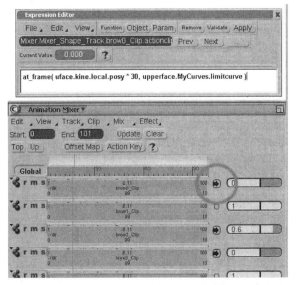

This expression mixes up the extended brow shape based on the upper face controller height in Y.

STEP 19: THE LIMIT CURVE

You now want to hook up some of the shapes to the simple controllers, but before you do, consider how you want them to move. You never want the value of the shape weight to drop below 0, you never want it to go above 1, and you want a non-linear response curve, to make it look more organic. In a human face, small muscle movements create highly readable expressions, then taper off to make broad, extreme expressions. You'll want a response curve that makes a lot of change to the shape weight when the slider is closest to zero, then tapers off the rate of change smoothly to come to a gradual stop, or limit, at 1. This can be done with a big complex expression, but it's sure easier – and a lot faster – both to write and to work with, if you just draw the curve and reference it in the expressions.

This curve can go anywhere, but you'll put it on a custom property page on the upper face controller. Look on the upper face controller for the custom property page called mycurves, and see the property in it called limitcurve. Right-click the animation divot for this property and look at the animation curve to get an idea of the shape of the response curve. That property is called upperface.mycurves.limitcurve, and you can get a value from that curve with the At_frame command. At frame 1 or less, the value of the curve is 0, and at frame 100 or greater, the value is 1. In between frame 1 and 100 the value smoothly varies.

If you want to make your own limit curve, make a custom property page on the upper face control and add a property called Limit Curve. Set two keys on it, at frame 1 = 0, at frame 100 = 1. Edit the shape in the animation editor.

STEP 20: HOOK THE BROWS TO UPPERFACE USING THE LIMIT CURVE

In the Mixer, find the weight slider for the right brow shape0, which is the extended pose. You want that to happen when the upper face controller comes down below zero. On the weight slider for that track, add this expression:

```
At_frame( -1 * uface.kine.local.posy * 30 ,
upperface.mycurves.limitcurve )
```

...which will return nothing at all if the controller rises above zero, but will blend the brow into the down position when the controller goes down.

On the weight blend slider for the right brow up (the shape2) you want the same expression, but inverted, so that it works when the face controller goes up but not when it goes down. That would be:

```
At_frame( uface.kine.local.posy * 30 ,
upperface.mycurves.limitcurve )
```

Asmo can now wiggle his brows to the right or left.

Repeat for the other brow shapes as well. For extra credit, add in some blend weight to the right brow when the upper face controller slides right (in local X) and to the other brow when the face controller goes left.

Test your results at this point to see where you are headed.

STEP 21: REPEAT FOR THE EYES

The game plan is the same for creating expressions to drive the shape Mixer on the tracks for the constricted eyes (shape2) and the relaxed eyes (shape0). Write an expression to connect the shape to the value of the limit curve, driven by the height of the upperface controller. That would look like this for the shape0 tracks:

```
At_frame( uface.kine.local.posy * 30 ,
upperface.mycurves.limitcurve )
```

...while the constricted tracks would be the opposite, using a -1 to flip the value around:

```
At_frame( -1 * uface.kine.local.posy * 30 , upper-
face.mycurves.limitcurve)
```

On the eye2 shape (the squinchy one's track) add in the pos in X of the upperface controller. That way the eyes can blink independently when the controller goes left to right, on top of whatever it's doing from the up and down.

```
At_frame( -1 * uface.kine.local.posy * 30 , upper-
face.mycurves.limitcurve) + At_frame
(uface.kine.local.posx * -30,
upperface.MyCurves.limitcurve)
```

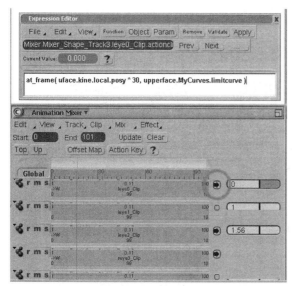

This expression drives the shape of the eye based on the Pos Y of the upper face controller.

STEP 22: NOW THE MOUTH

Mouth2 will be connected to the local position in Y of the lower face controller, so that when the controller drops below zero, the mouth blends in the open shape (the mouth0 shape) and when the lower face controller goes up, it blends up the constricted mouth2 shape. I'll let you derive your own expressions for the mouth sliders.

STEP 23: EXPLORE ON YOUR OWN

Now you have some basic expressions set up to do the following:

1) Swing the jaw open and closed as the lower face controller goes up and down.

2) Adjust the mouth position left/right, up/down, back/forth with the lower controller.

3) Blend between three shapes for each eye based on the position of the upper controller.

Asmo can open and close each eye separately or together.

4) Blend between three shapes for each brow muscle sheet, based on the upper controller.

5) Blend between three mouth shapes depending on the position of the lower controller.

The changes in the shapes of the curves then drive the location of many small skin studs. In turn, other small studs are constrained to float between the shape-driven studs and the rigid parts of the face, the nose, the jaw and the skull. These studs float around, smoothly interpolating the action of the muscles under the skin.

All these studs and the rigid deformers are then enveloped to the low-res envelope of the head.

You have completed the basic set up for the face. Now it's up to you to experiment, see what you like and don't like, then make changes. You could now rearrange the constraints that drive the floating studs, connecting them into the corners of the curves by using three-point constraints. You could re-weight the head, so the skull, neck, ears, and other parts stay rigid. You could smooth the weights further. You could see what it looks like when the model subdivision is stepped up.

You could set keyframes on the model (try rotoscoping over some video footage) by saving keys on the upper and lower controllers. Have fun!

One important benefit of this type of facial rig is that the same rig can be used across many different character faces, without much modification. If the same rig is used, that means that libraries of animation can also be saved to disk and shared between different characters. This facial rig is just one more way for an animation studio to scale up the volume of work that the studio pipeline can handle.

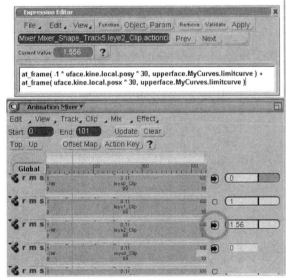

Now Asmo can blink either eye, using the Pos X of the upper face controller.

Asmo can make a lot of faces.

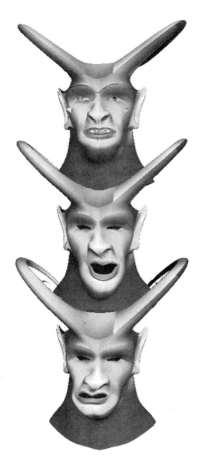

Asmo's mouth opens, closes, and wiggles around.

CONCLUSION

That's all for the last chapter. By now you should not only have a grasp of the tools in XSI, but you should also have an idea how they can be organized, and used together to create new ways of working that enable your specific tasks. Remember, XSI isn't just about features, it is about tools.

Many parts of the animation process are complex, so a large part of your energy should be dedicated to making those complicated parts of the puzzle simpler and easier to understand and use.

I would also like to say this: the ideas in this book are simply what I have come up with in my own head, and should not be taken as the limit of what is possible to achieve in XSI. Your task is now to go forward, invent new and interesting uses for the software, and share those with the community of 3D users. If you come up with something really novel and sly, please share it by shooting me an email, or posting to the XSI mailing list maintained by Softimage (you can subscribe on the Softimage web site, www.softimage.com).

Finally, remember that sometimes the simplest ideas work out the best.

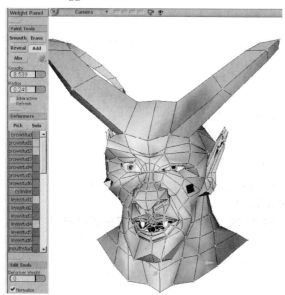

Asmo's head can now be re-bound and properly weighted to the IK, bones, and studs.

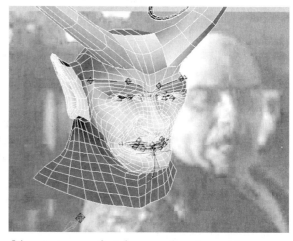

It's easy to copy facial expressions from video source material.

QUIZ

1. WHAT KIND OF OBJECTS CAN BE ENVELOPE DEFORMERS?
   a. IK bones
   b. NURBS and polygons
   c. Both A and B

2. WHICH CONSTRAINT IS MOST USEFUL FOR FACIAL MUSCULATURE?
   a. Cluster center
   b. Two points
   c. Surface

3. IN ORDER TO BUILD A FACE THAT WORKS LIKE A REAL PERSON S, YOU NEED TO:
   a. Make a lot of shapes
   b. Understand the muscles of the face
   c. Set a lot of keyframes

4. HOW MANY HORNS DOES ASMO HAVE?
   a. One
   b. Two
   c. Three

5. WHICH PART OF ASMO S FACE USES PATH ANIMATION?
   a. Eye sockets
   b. Mouth orbit
   c. Jawbone

6. HOW MANY SHAPES DO YOU NEED FOR EACH EYE MUSCLE (OCULAR ORBIT)?
   a. Two
   b. Three
   c. Four

7. CAN REGULAR GEOMETRY OBJECTS BE USED TO DRIVE THE SHAPE MIXER?
   a. Yes
   b. No

8. IF NORMALIZE IS TOGGLED ON IN THE ANIMATION MIXER PROPERTIES, OVERLAPPING SHAPES WILL BE:
   a. Averaged
   b. Added

9. HOW MANY SHAPES CAN YOU ADD TO THE MIXER?
   a. Less than 10
   b. Less than 99
   c. Unknown

10. WHY IS A 3D CONTROLLER BETTER THAN A PROPERTY PAGE SLIDER?
   a. Easier to find in the interface and simpler to use
   b. Each controller object can affect multiple variables independently
   c. Both A and B

ED HARRISS

3D ARTIST/TECHNICAL DIRECTOR

ALTERNATE ROUTE STUDIOS

Anthony Rossano: So Ed, how would you describe what you do?

EH: I am sort of a specialist in the area of rendering, lighting and texturing. I also do modeling, compositing, and the occasional animating, but not as much. At work they call me 3d artist and technical director rolled in to one.

I think you'll find that if you work in a place with only two or three people, everyone has to be pretty good at pretty much everything, while if you work at a place that is mid-sized (like where I work), people will do what they are best at. If you work at a really big facility there are going to be people who do the one thing they are best at. For example, there will be people that just do modeling, or even more specifically there will be people who only model characters and organic objects, while there are others that only model inorganic and inanimate objects.

ATR: How did you become prepared for your role?

EH: When I started doing CG, I tried to do it all. I did animating, modeling, texturing, lighting, compositing, and just about everything else. While doing this I learned what I was good at and what I liked. After a while I found out that I didn't enjoy modeling or animation as much as everything else, but I did like surfacing objects and I did like making sure everything looked good in the end. (When it was rendered and composited.) Because that was what I enjoyed doing, I ended up doing it more than anything else, and I ended up getting better at that particular area of CG.

ATR: At what point in your life did you find yourself having the opportunity to do 3D work?

EH: When I first started to get into computer animation I didn't know what I was getting into. I saw *Tron*, I saw *Last Starfighter*, and I thought to myself, "This is great! I like cartoons, and this is like a cartoon, but this is different. It interests me more. It doesn't have 'mistakes' and it has this look I really enjoy." So, I tried to find out what I needed to learn so that I can do that type of animation too.

When you're a kid you don't know which or your interests might turn into something you could do for a living. As time went by my parents got me machines that I could learn on (like the TRS 80, Commodore 64, and Apple II). It was on those primitive machines that I started to learn how to do computer graphics. Back then there was no point-and-click interface, it was either cryptic programs with lots of typing, or nothing. There was no way for a non-programmer to do easily do CG.

ATR: Where did your work on ancient computers intersect with the modern professional stuff?

EH: I went on to college and there they had Amiga computers. On these computers you could point and click to create 3D objects. I thought "I can do this, I don't have to be a Ph.D. in math to figure out how, I can just click to get it done."

I thought it was great, but people used to say to me, "That looks cool, but how are you going to make a living doing it?" I would tell people, "You watch, something is going to happen and people are going to start using this in real applications." Well just as I finished school, movies like *Terminator 2* and *Jurassic Park* were coming out. Suddenly you could make a living doing it, so I ended up going out and getting a normal job, doing computer animation.

ATR: How do you explain to people who aren't involved in CG what it is you do?

EH: You know, that used to be hard, but it's not a problem anymore because I've had to do it so many times. The easiest way for me to explain to someone who knows nothing about computer animation at all, is to tell them "You know, like *Toy Story*". They instantly get it. I don't have to explain it at all because they can see the difference between *Toy Story* and typical Saturday morning cartoons.

ATR: What is it about the 3D stuff that you think is so much more appealing than the 2D stuff?

EH: You can't get a look like that by drawing it. CG is exact: the next frame looks like the first but the objects are in a different position. To do that in cel animation your art would have to be either perfect or simple and flat, without rounded edges and shading. Because I always liked computers, I thought that computer animation was very interesting. I think another thing that drew me to it was the fact that I could make an animation relatively quickly, by myself. I didn't need a group of in-betweeners, and some key artists, and a bunch of cameras, and ink and paint artists, etc. I could actually get something out myself with no help at all. Me, myself, and my computer can produce full-color, full-screen, plays-back-on-TV, looks-perfect animation.

ATR: What's your exit strategy? How long do you plan to be an animator?

EH: Actually, I see this as something I do until I retire. I enjoy it so much that I don't see that there could be anything else that I would like as much. Even if I were to win the lottery tomorrow I would still do computer animation because I enjoy it. I might not come to work any more, but I would do it at home.

You can see more of Ed Harriss's work at http://www.EdHarriss.com
and learn more about Alternate Route Studios at http://www.AltRouteStudios.com

Copyright (c) 2001 Alternate Route Studios

Copyright (c) 2001 SouthPeak Interactive LLC

Copyright (c) 2000 SAS Institute Inc.

MESMER
Professional Training for
Digital Artists
Seattle, WA | San Francisco, CA
1.800.237.7311
www.mesmer.com

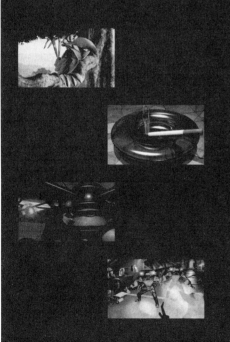